REFERENCE
and
INFORMATION
SERVICES
in the
21st CENTURY
an introduction

facet publishing

A companion web page keeps this text up to date!

www.neal-schuman.com/reference21st
or follow the link from *www.facetpublishing.co.uk*

This website features new readings for each chapter and information about changes in the reference tools described in these pages as well as important new ones.

Copyright © 2006 Neal-Schuman Publishers

Published by
Facet Publishing
7 Ridgmount Street
London WC1E 7AE

Facet Publishing is wholly owned by CILIP: the Chartered Institute of Library and Information Professionals.

First published in the USA by Neal-Schuman Publishers, Inc., 2006.
This simultaneous UK edition 2006.

British Library Cataloguing in Publication Data
A catalogue record for this book is available from the British Library.

ISBN-13: 978-1-85604-598-8
ISBN-10: 1-85604-598-6

Printed and bound in the United States of America.

Dedicated to you:
the intrepid librarian of the twenty-first century.

Contents

Preface / ix

Acknowledgments / xiii

Part I Fundamental Concepts / 1

1   Introducing Reference and Information Services / 3

2   Determining the Question: In-person, Telephone,
     and Virtual Reference Interviews / 15

3   Finding the Answer: Basic Search Techniques / 31

Part II Introduction to Major Reference Sources / 51

4   Answering Questions about Books, Magazines, Newspapers, Libraries,
     Publishers, and Bibliographic Networks—Bibliographic Resources / 53

5   Answering Questions about Anything and
     Everything—Encyclopedias / 69

6   Answering Questions that Require Handy Facts—Ready
     Reference Sources / 93

7   Answering Questions about Words—Dictionaries / 111

8   Answering Questions about Current Events and Issues—Indexes / 135

9   Answering Questions about Health, Law, and
     Business—Special Guidelines and Sources / 155

10   Answering Questions about Geography, Countries, and
     Travel—Atlases, Gazetteers, Maps, Geographic
     Information Systems, and Travel Guides / 183

11   Answering Questions about the Lives of People—Biographical
     Information Sources / 199

12   Answering Questions about Governments—Government
     Information Sources / 213

Part III Special Topics in Reference and Information Work / 231

13   When and How to Use the Internet as a Reference Tool / 233

14   Reader's Advisory Work / 253

15   Reference Work with Children and Young Adults / 265

16   User Instruction in the Reference Department / 273

Part IV Developing and Managing Reference Collections and Services / 287

17   Selecting and Evaluating Reference Materials / 289

18   Managing Reference Departments / 303

19   **Assessing and Improving Reference Services / 315**

20   **The Future of Information Service / 337**

      Subject Index / 347

      Index of Reference Resources Described / 361

      About the Authors / 379

Preface

The future of reference service is here. In the past few years we have seen digital and online resources take on new importance at the reference desk. We have been exposed to new models of communication and discovered new methods for selecting and evaluating authoritative resources. Tomorrow will bring additional advances and changes. Throughout all of this invention and transformation, we continue to field a myriad of questions with a commitment to serve and enlighten our users.

As perhaps the most popular and essential aspect of librarianship, reference service will be a primary focus for the future. Professionals must understand the fundamental concepts, essential sources, search techniques, special services, and basic managerial tasks of the reference desk. They must also learn to contend with a public that increasingly relies on the simplest and most generic source or the broadest aggregated reference gateway. Librarians provide unique skills—collection development, search construction, selection and evaluation of sources—which must be developed and utilized in order to provide users with authoritative answers to their questions rather than simple returns.

Purpose

The future of reference service is here; we have designed *Reference and Information Services in the 21st Century: An Introduction* as the most current reference text for a new generation of library and information professionals. We have sought to write an evolved text for an evolved profession. This approach acknowledges the impact of technology on our practice—you will find multiple formats referenced in our resource lists and considerations for new methods of communicating with users—even as it relies on the classic practices of the reference interview, reader's advisory services, and instruction.

Perhaps the most important section of this book is the part devoted to answering different types of questions. In our work as practitioners and educators we realize that the reference transaction works in an organic way—understanding a question, identifying resources, and providing the right answer. Traditional reference texts take the approach of dividing the formats of resources—bibliographies, dictionaries, almanacs, etc.—and explaining how they are used. *Reference and Information Services in the 21st*

Century: An Introduction correlates reference sources to the types of questions for which they are most likely to be used. As the natural progression of the reference transaction is question–search–answer, we felt it best to organize our content in such a way that it more accurately reflects your experience at the reference desk. You will find that this question-based approach also facilitates more advanced patron inquiries where multiple requests for information are being made within the same transaction. By understanding the various questions that are being posed, you may utilize various formats to answer each portion of the question. To better anchor this in the realm of practice, examples from public, academic, school, and special libraries are distributed throughout the text.

Reference and Information Services in the 21st Century: An Introduction is designed to meet three distinct goals:

1. To introduce the reader to the broad world of reference and information service: the reference interview; search strategies; evaluation, selection, and maintenance of reference sources and collections; the major reference tools; readers' advisory services; services to younger users; user instruction; management of the reference department; and future trends in reference work.
2. To serve as a ready resource for working reference librarians—a place for quickly identifying key reference sources for answering common types of queries.
3. To provide the profession with a current overview of what reference service encompasses in today's changing world.

Organization

Part I: Fundamentals Concepts

Chapter 1, "Introducing Reference and Information Services," provides readers with a brief history of reference service in libraries and overviews the breadth of services housed under the heading reference.

Chapter 2, "Determining the Question," outlines the first and perhaps most critical step in the reference process. Our work is, and always will be, predicated on contact and communication, even in times of change. That is why this chapter takes into account in-person, telephone, and virtual reference interviews.

Chapter 3, "Finding the Answer," is in many ways a conclusion to Part One and a prelude to Part Two. Having identified the question, the next step is to construct an answer. This chapter helps you organize thoughts, develop a strategy for the particular request, and find the solution.

Part II: Introduction to Major Reference Sources

This portion of *Reference and Information Services in the 21st Century: An Introduction* employs a unique approach. The chapters focus on where and how to answer types of questions rather than how to use types of resources. Included in this section are:

- Chapter 4 Answering Questions about Books, Magazines, Newspapers, Libraries, Publishers, and Bibliographic Networks—Bibliographic Resources
- Chapter 5 Answering Questions about Anything and Everything—Encyclopedias
- Chapter 6 Answering Questions that Require Handy Facts—Ready Reference Sources
- Chapter 7 Answering Questions about Words—Dictionaries
- Chapter 8 Answering Questions about Current Events and Issues—Indexes
- Chapter 9 Answering Questions about Health, Law, and Business—Special Guidelines and Sources
- Chapter 10 Answering Questions about Geography, Countries, and Travel—Atlases, Gazetteers, Maps, Geographic Information Systems, and Travel Guides
- Chapter 11 Answering Questions about the Lives of People—Biographical Information Sources
- Chapter 12 Answering Questions about Governments—Government Information Sources

Each of the above chapters begins with an overview of materials and how they are used to answer the particular type of question. We provide sample questions (and answers) for which those sources are best used and describe the major print, electronic, and Web-based materials available. Resources are explored holistically since most major reference works exist in both a print and electronic format. There is also guidance for collection development and maintenance practices; further considerations and special information particular to the topic; and a final list of the "top ten" reference sources in the subject area. As each chapter is uniformly structured, you will find it conducive to both advanced reading in preparation for service and as an effective reference source at the desk.

Part III: Special Topics in Reference and Information Work

Chapter 13, "When and How to Use the Internet as a Reference Tool," addresses one of the most challenging and ubiquitous reference resources to have emerged in our times. Outlining the strengths and weaknesses of the Internet as a reference source, this chapter also contains a five-step approach to using the Internet in reference transactions.

Chapter 14, "Reader's Advisory Work," brings together reference work and the other hallmark of librarianship—literacy. While readers' advisory (RA) is often housed in departments other than reference (Adult, Children's, or Young Adult Services), the librarian sitting at the reference desk should and often must be prepared to field all questions, including an RA question. This chapter, authored by Mary K. Chelton, describes the most common types of RA queries, offers advice for handling RA requests, and provides a list of resources for consultation.

Chapter 15, "Reference Work with Children and Young Adults," also authored by Mary K. Chelton, expands the reference conversation to a new and sometimes tricky user group. With unique perceptions and needs, children and young adults present opportunities and challenges to librarians—instruction, homework help, and concerned parents or guardians.

Reference work is more than simply answering questions—it can also be a learning experience for both the patron and the professional. Chapter 16, "User Instruction in the Reference Department," discusses the importance of information literacy in all types of libraries and offers suggestions for one-to-one and classroom instruction. In the right transaction, instruction can be a very appropriate and valued response to a query.

Part IV: Developing and Managing Reference Collections and Services

Essential to solid reference services is a solid reference collection. Chapter 17, "Selecting and Evaluating Reference Materials," provides sources for review and evaluation criteria. You will also find guidance for managing the materials budget, assessing collections, weeding titles, writing policy, and marketing the collection.

Chapter 18, "Managing Reference Departments," looks at staff, service, and department organization. This chapter provides options for managers and considerations for decision-making. While aimed at the manager, it is also a helpful glimpse for any professional into the form and function of today's reference departments.

Chapter 19, "Assessing and Improving Reference Services," moves from the day-to-day practice of reference work to the vision and development of future service. From why we should assess; what and how to assess; and what we should do with our findings, this chapter encourages a hands-on and proactive approach to improvement.

Finally, Chapter 20, "The Future of Information Service," looks ahead to the models, materials, and service, which will continue to evolve reference service.

Final Thoughts

Writing this book has been the pinnacle of our professional lives. We've talked with professors, students, and practioners; we've looked at publishers' catalogs and Web sites; we've become familiar with American, British, and Canadian information sources; we've looked at more reference syllabi than we thought could exist; we've held focus groups at ALA Conferences to see what both librarians and educators want from a new text; and we've written and revised chapters to reflect what we've learned. Working with the five members of our Advisory Board (listed on the verso of the title page) has been a professional privilege in its own right. They have commented on drafts, served as sounding boards, and, during our darkest hours, assured us that we were not lost. What you hold is the result. We hope you will find it as informative to read as we've found it inspirational to write.

Acknowledgments

This reference "knowledgebase" could not have accrued without the collective strengths provided by a number of people.
We thank:
Charles Harmon, who has been a continuing source of positive energy and ideas through the entire project. Thanks to Jacob Brogan for the fierce creativity and unity he brought to the book.
We thank:
The innovative members of the initial focus group: Marie Radford, Becki Whitaker, Carol Tobin, Elizabeth Thomsen, and Anna Perrault. Their animated input provided much of the impetus for deciding the structure of the book.
We thank:
The members of our Advisory Board, Marie Radford, Cheryl Knott Malone, Charlotte Ford, Carol Tobin, and Mary Kay Chelton. Their incisive observations were responsible for some of the most worthy revisions in the text.
We thank:
The members of various Listservs who generously responded to our requests with comments and real-life examples. Also Louise Sherby, who allowed us to use her Listserv.
We thank:
The reference librarians of the New York Public Library, the West Orange Public Library, and elsewhere who were willing to share their views and expertise.
We thank:
Our many friends for their understanding and support.
Kay thanks:
Marina I. Mercado for her support, patience, and love.
Norma Ross for her vision, leadership, and guidance.
The library schools students I have taught for helping me to shape my ideas about reference service.
Uma thanks:
Kay for her trust.
Bala for "being there" as always.

ACKNOWLEDGMENTS

Rajendra and Mohini for keeping the faith.

Ayesha the Inspirational, for her emblematic midnight battle with he-who-must-not-be-named.

Vani the Lifeforce, for her much-needed supply of chilled water and big hugs.

Part 1
Fundamental Concepts

1

Introducing Reference and Information Services

In libraries of all types and sizes reference and information services are a vital part of the function and mission of the institution. While the advent of electronic resources and digitized materials has changed the nature of reference, the essential service remains central. Indeed, far from minimizing the need for reference services, the rise of the Internet and other like innovations of the past few decades makes this element of the library all the more crucial. Whether at home on their computers or wandering through the stacks, many feel as though they are drowning in a sea of information. New media and technologies are like tributaries leading to this great new body of knowledge, and each stream makes the waters deeper and more perilous. Reference services are at once life raft, map, and compass to those who have been left adrift. In providing them with care, thoughtfulness, and enthusiasm, libraries reaffirm their centrality as twenty-first-century public institutions par excellence.

For all its contemporary relevance, the concept of reference service is over a century old. In 1876, Samuel Green, librarian of the Worcester Free Public Library in Massachusetts, formulated the idea of having librarians aid users in the selection of books to suit their needs. This served a dual function, increasing the use of his library's collections and thereby demonstrating the need for the library. Green thought the public library should be an inviting gateway to knowledge, arguing that users should be welcomed in by a pleasant and cultivated female staff (Genz 1998). Some forty years later, in 1915 at the thirty-seventh meeting of the American Library Association, a paper on reference work was delivered by W. W. Bishop, the superintendent of the Reading Room of the Library of Congress. Bishop defined reference work as "the service rendered by a librarian in aid of some sort of study," holding that it was "an organized effort on the part of libraries in aid of the most expeditious and fruitful use of their books" (Genz 1998). The project of reference service was further developed by Charles Williamson in his 1923 report, "Training for Library Service: A Report Prepared for the Carnegie Corporation of New York" which included a course description for reference work:

A study of the standard works of reference, general and special encyclopedias, dictionaries, annuals, indexes to periodicals, ready reference manuals of every kind, special bibliographies, and the more important newspapers and periodicals. Works of similar scope are compared, and the limitations of each pointed out. Lists of questions made up from practical experience are given, and the method of finding the answers discussed in the class. (Genz 1998)

Several including James I. Wyer, Margaret Hutchins, and William Katz wrote reference texts in which they continued to refine the role of the reference librarian over the subsequent decades.

Perhaps the most important thing to remember is that reference service seeks to fulfill the greater mission of the library by helping individual users. Despite the many transformations that have been wrought on reference work by both developments of our information society and paradigm shifts in the self-understandings of the library, much has remained the same. First and foremost, it is still a service in which the librarian interacts with a patron on a one-to-one basis. This level of personal service has become even more important in the twenty-first century in light of the alienating and depersonalizing effects of many information technologies. On the other hand, the way such service is provided has changed considerably—it now extends beyond face-to-face assistance thanks to the availability of the telephone, e-mail, and the technology for chat reference.

Kinds of Information Service

Information service, in the most general sense, is the process of helping library users to identify sources of information in response to a particular question, interest, assignment, or problem. Sometimes referred to as reference service, information service is not limited to helping users who approach the reference desk to ask a question. As suggested above, many libraries offer remote assistance via the telephone, e-mail, or Internet. Librarians are also creating Web sites, answer archives, and links to answers to "frequently asked questions," all designed to anticipate user questions and help people find information independently. Traditional reference desk service continues to be highly valued by library users in many settings, but the newer forms continue to grow in relevance. Consequently, it is all the more important that librarians understand the range of inquiries that can be expected, allowing them to provide a full and ready answer, regardless of the form in which the query arises.

Answering Reference Questions

In light of the immense diversity and range of possible questions, being approached by a patron with a reference need can seem like a daunting prospect. Indeed, much of the difficulty of information services arises from uncertainty about the kind of service or breadth of information called for by a given question. Categorizing reference questions by type is a useful way to make sense of such concerns. Three common types of information service are ready reference questions, research questions, and bibliographic verification.

Ready reference questions such as "Where was Abraham Lincoln born?" "Who won the 1992 World Series?" "What is the capital of Nicaragua?" or "Where can I find a copy of the U.S. Declaration of Independence?" can be readily answered using one or two general reference sources. The librarian may be tempted to tell the user the answer to simple ready reference questions. Yet, here, the old saying that giving a man a fish feeds him for a day while teaching him to fish feeds him for a lifetime is proven true. No matter how simple they initially seem, ready reference questions provide the possibility of teachable moments. Whenever possible, librarians should lead users through the process of looking up the information rather than simply providing the solution.

Libraries that assist users with ready reference inquiries on a regular basis sometimes choose to create a "ready reference" section of the most commonly used resources to answer quick questions. Typically, such sections include a general all-purpose encyclopedia, dictionaries, almanacs, and handbooks. Care must be taken to keep the sources up to date and to avoid depending so heavily on this subset of the collection that other sources are overlooked by library users and librarians. Librarians may find that ready reference questions have diminished due to the ease of answering basic questions through online information portals like Google. Nevertheless, ready reference remains a cornerstone of information services, and librarians should be primed to provide it at any time.

Research questions are more complex, may take much longer to answer, and typically require multiple sources of information. These are often the questions that require the user to consider a variety of sources and viewpoints and to subsequently draw conclusions from them. Sometimes questions that initially seem like ready reference questions are found to be far more complex as previously hidden facets of the user's inquiry are revealed. Here, the variety of possible sources increases with the complexity of users' questions. Librarians should, for example, guide the user in the use of bibliographic sources, citations, and back-of-the-book bibliographies. Likewise, users with complex questions may need to be taught how to find or request the full text of articles for which only citations are given in a search of the electronic databases, allowing them to move beyond cursory surveys of the literature.

Research questions, especially if the user is unable to fully articulate the nature of his or her query, require librarians to ask questions of their own, trying to get at the nature of the request before setting out to help the patron answer it. The librarian may, for example, have to determine how much information is needed, what level of information is needed, and what other sources have already been consulted. As will be discussed in Chapter 3, information services call for mutual engagement, especially with more complex questions. Reference librarians should never be passive participants, pointing the way to an answer. Instead, they should play the part of dynamic guides, joining users on their journeys to knowledge.

Naturally, the extent of such engagement may vary from one circumstance to another. Different libraries tend to have their own standards for how long librarians should spend with users on research questions. Many public libraries recommend that users be given five or ten minutes of personal assistance and then asked to return if more help is needed. A university library may have a similar standard, or depending on the institution, may be able to invite the user to make an appointment for more in-depth research assistance. Some libraries suggest that users call or e-mail ahead of their visit so the librarian can be prepared to offer the best possible assistance. Other libraries, including special libraries, may only be able to provide a basic level of help during the first visit. Libraries may refer users to other libraries with more specialized materials in the area of the user's research or may offer to call back if additional information is found.

Finally a library user may seek *bibliographic verification* when he or she has already obtained the information needed but must verify the sources. Sometimes this service is a matter of fact checking, while on other occasions patrons may have completed their research but lack full citation information. As users increasingly depend on electronic databases for information, compiling and formatting bibliographic citations becomes easier. Ironically, verifying and citing material found on Web pages is more difficult, since the information needed for the citation is not always easy to find.

Reader's Advisory Service

Reader's advisory service, sometimes considered a type of information service, is the quest to put the right book in the hands of the right reader. Librarians are increasingly expected to provide an answer to the dreaded question, "Can you help me find a good book?" Fortunately, as demand has increased, so too has the ease of providing this service. While there is no substitute for one's own knowledge or experience, many new technologies serve to make reader's advisory far easier than it was in the past. Many online databases, for example, have functions that automatically recommend other books for those who like a given title. Others have searchable lists of works by genre, helping readers match their favorite books to others like them. As always, however, remember that reader's advisory, like other reference work, is predicated on the interaction between librarian and library user. Asking directed questions, listening carefully to the users' responses, and tailoring assistance accordingly is the basis of excellent, truly helpful service.

Reader's advisory service is generally associated with public libraries and tends to be employed primarily by those looking for fiction. In academic libraries, it is far less common as users rarely come in searching for a mystery to read. Even so, reader's advisory may be needed to help lay researchers looking to deepen their knowledge of a particular field. A patron who has read and enjoyed Stephen Ambrose's *Undaunted Courage*, but is troubled by allegations about Ambrose's questionable accuracy and academic honesty, may want to know the titles of books about the Lewis and Clark expedition that are both reputable and engaging. Successful reader's advisory librarians are skilled at asking users questions that enable them to assess users' reading level, language, or educational background. They must also know a great deal about various genres of fiction and nonfiction and be intimately familiar with their library's collection. Significantly, it is also important that they be able to convey their expertise in a friendly and conversational manner. Truly mastering reader's advisory service requires a great deal of skill and practice, but the basics will be explored in more detail in Chapter 14.

User Instruction

User instruction, sometimes known as *information literacy*, may range from showing an individual how to use the library's online catalog and basic print reference sources to formal classroom sessions about conducting research in the library. The basic component of information literacy includes demonstrating how, when, and why to use various reference sources in an integrated way that will capture the user's attention at the teachable moment.

In today's educational settings, the ease of using electronic resources often results in a failure to teach more traditional research strategies. While finding superficial information has grown easier, in-depth information has become increasingly obscure for many students. In the library too, approaches to instruction may vary and librarians often question whether to simply answer questions posed by patrons or to teach users how to employ the available resources. This may be contingent on the mission or purpose of the library. Academic institutions may call on their librarians to help students understand how to engage effectively and independently in the research and information evaluation process. Public librarians, by contrast, may try to teach users about reference sources in a more informal manner as they lead users to the answers they seek. Thus, while instruction is always an important part of reference work, the degree to which they go about providing it is highly contingent on the circumstances.

In any case, all reference librarians must be skilled at helping users find information and answers quickly and be ready to teach users how to use the reference sources that are available. The best reference librarians develop an intuition for when to be information providers and when to be bibliographic instructors. In some libraries, only specific, designated librarians are charged with conducting library instruction courses. Nevertheless, an increasing number of librarians are required to participate in their libraries' bibliographic instruction program, and library school graduates are expected to be capable of teaching basic classes on the use of library resources. As should be clear, even those librarians not charged with providing formal instruction have the opportunity to teach those they serve. The various aspects of user instruction will be covered in greater depth in Chapter 16.

Selecting and Evaluating

Selecting and evaluating print and electronic information for the library's collection can be as professionally rewarding as providing expert information service. Reference librarians' involvement in evaluating and selecting titles for the collection helps them develop rich knowledge of the sources at their disposal, increasing their effectiveness.

The responsibility for selecting reference materials depends largely on the size and scope of the library. In large academic libraries, selecting reference materials may be assigned to subject bibliographers whose work may be limited to collection development responsibilities. On the other side of the continuum, the evaluation and purchase of resources in very small libraries may be the work of a single reference librarian or coordinator of reference. A range of shared evaluation and selection possibilities between these points include reference materials selection committees or group assignments.

The question, "What makes a book a reference book?" has long been debated in our profession. For the purpose of this discussion, reference books are those texts set aside to be consulted for specific information rather than to be read as a whole. In other words, reference books contain content meant to be "looked up." Typically, one turns to a reference source in search of something in particular rather than to the text as a whole. Another common characteristic of reference books is that they do not leave the library premises. This ensures that all of the works in the reference collection are always on hand, making for a consistently available body of knowledge. Note that labeling narrative or non-reference books as "reference" to deter theft or assure that a popular volume is always available may lead to bloated reference collections, and it is not generally recommended. Finally, with the addition of electronic reference sources that are increasingly available to remote library users from their homes, dorm rooms, offices, and so on, reference collections encompass much more than print books and serials and may be available twenty-four hours a day.

As the present trend toward shrinking budgets for reference collections, lean reference collections, and the elimination of duplication among print and electronic collections continues, the careful evaluation and selection of reference materials is essential. Libraries should determine the criteria that will be used in selecting sources for its reference collection. The following criteria may help determine whether an item is a worthy addition to a library's collection: scope, purpose, audience, format, arrangement, authority, currency, unique coverage, and cost. Criteria for selecting electronic products may vary, though all of the criteria used to evaluate print resources should be considered, especially in libraries that aim to avoid redundancy in their print and electronic reference collections.

Some libraries select reference materials by reading reviews in the library professional literature such as *Library Journal*, *Choice*, and *Booklist's* "Reference Books Bulletin." Other institutions insist on physically reviewing reference sources at trade shows or through special arrangements with publishers of reference materials. Most libraries employ a combination of these two. A more extensive discussion of selection and evaluation will take place in Chapter 17.

Creating Finding Tools and Web Sites

Another strategy employed by many reference departments is the creation of finding tools and pathfinders for library users. Here, librarians act as cartographers, mapping out the best routes through familiar territory and pointing out interesting sites along the way. Pathfinders are often prepared for commonly requested subjects such as high school and college assignments about capital punishment, drug abuse, and the history of Native American tribes. Similarly, public libraries may prepare pathfinders that address frequently asked questions of a more quotidian nature: documents describing how to search for job information, check the credentials of a health care provider, or research a family tree can all be of great use in a library. Depending on the topic, audience, and needs, the pathfinder may guide the user to a selection of appropriate reference books, relevant databases and search terms, a selection of current and authoritative Web sites, and tips for searching the library's Online Public Access Catalog (OPAC) for additional materials.

Librarians also create Web sites of carefully evaluated links organized by topic, sometimes known as "webliographies," that serve as finding tools. Who better than librarians to organize the World Wide Web of information, pointing the user to "the best" sources and helping them steer clear of the dubious? Web-based finding tools offer several advantages to print pathfinders. They are available to users 24/7, they can be updated as often as needed, and they can include direct links to Web sites and electronic reference tools.

Depending on the circumstance and the nature of a library's Web presence, such webliographies can be either general, providing direction to broadly targeted reference resources, or subject specific. General all-purpose lists of librarian-selected Web resources include *The Internet Public Library* (www.ipl.org) and the *Librarians' Internet Index* (lii.org). Examples of library subject specific webliographies include the New York Public Library's *Best of the Web* (www.nypl.org/links) and the University of Washington's *Information Gateway* (www.lib.washington.edu/subject). Larger libraries, whether academic or public, often produce indexes of both types. Smaller libraries may be better served by developing webliographies for specific areas in which they have subject specialists and linking to a general reference site like the *Internet Public Library* or the *Librarians' Index to the Internet*.

Evaluating Staff and Services

Libraries may seek to routinely evaluate their reference collections or reference service. In her book *Evaluating Reference Services: A Practical Guide* (2000), Jo Bell Whitlatch wisely emphasizes the importance of defining the purpose of the evaluation before setting a strategy. "The most important questions you must ask," according to Whitlatch, are "Why am I evaluating reference services?" and "What do I plan to do with the study results?"

The quality of the reference interaction, from either the user's or the librarian's perspective, may be assessed to help determine how effective the reference service is. Evaluating reference staff is one way to help determine how effective the reference service is, and is one way to help assure quality reference service. A librarian who knows the contents of the entire collection by heart but is abrasive and reluctant to answer questions will do little to serve the library. The American Library Association's Reference and User Services Association has developed "Guidelines for Behavioral Performance of Reference and Information Service Professionals," which are intended to be used in the training, development, or evaluation of library professionals and staff. The performance of reference librarians is typically evaluated on both the information conveyed to users and the satisfaction of the interaction on the library user.

The following factors are covered by the ALA Guidelines.

- Approachability: Are users able to identify that a reference librarian is available to help?
- Interest: Does the librarian demonstrate a high degree of interest in the reference transaction?
- Listening/Inquiring: Does the librarian identify the user's information need in a manner that puts the user at ease? Are good communication skills used throughout the transaction?
- Searching: Is the librarian skilled at creating search strategies that yield accurate and relevant results?
- Follow-up: Does the librarian determine whether the user is satisfied with the results of the search/interaction?

These performance guidelines may form the backbone of a library's staff evaluation instruments, whether the instrument is a simple self-evaluation checklist, a peer-evaluation tool, or a formal evaluation system influencing earning potential.

In addition to evaluating staff, the library may measure its productivity or efficiency with quantitative measures that include the number of questions answered and the frequency with which print or electronic sources are consulted. Smaller libraries may continuously count the number and type of in-person questions answered by the reference staff. In larger libraries, quarterly one-week periods are frequently used to estimate the number of questions answered over the course of a year. Depending on the available resources, data may be recorded using hand-held computers, by making marks on a form, or by any means in between.

A variety of other evaluation strategies are also available to libraries: Assessing the quality of the resources available may, for example, be another useful metric. Issues of resource allocation may also be incorporated into departmental evaluations, if one includes how the library's budget allocates for library staff, print and electronic resources, computers and networks, and buildings. Evaluation methods frequently used to gauge users' satisfaction with reference services and sources include questionnaires, surveys, focus groups, observation, and interviews.

It is crucial that library administrators determine what is to be measured and against what standards before choosing the preferred method of evaluation. There are many sources available for detailed information on designing evaluation instruments for libraries. Selecting the best method, developing and field-testing the instrument, administering the survey, questionnaire, or interview, planning the observation, avoiding interviewer bias, and scores of ethical issues should be carefully considered. Analyzing data and developing conclusions and recommendations may require advanced training, and in some cases evaluation experts are hired. These and other questions are considered in greater depth in Chapter 19.

Promotion and Marketing

Paying attention to promotion and marketing of libraries and reference service is becoming more important than ever. Without support from the community, the library will not stay viable. Promoting reference services among individual library users can go a long way toward achieving this goal, especially insofar as it demonstrates how the library can serve them. In large communities—urban public libraries, for example—promoting the library through individual users is not enough to attract new users and major marketing or publicity campaigns become important. In academic libraries, school libraries, and special libraries, promotion and marketing are equally essential. Use of print and online newsletters, Web sites, and opportunities to meet with faculty and staff can provide opportunities to promote the library's resources.

Ethics

Ethical awareness and engagement is a crucial aspect of all library services, and the ideals that have been established for the profession generally apply fully to those working in reference services. Just as a therapist would do his patients little good if he laughed at their problems, reference librarians must follow certain standards of behavior if the service they provide is to be effective. The American Library Association's current Code of Ethics, adopted in 1995, provides a perfect guide. This code, composed of eight broad statements, upholds a variety of the principles essential to the modern library.

The first proposition of the Code insists that librarians should provide for the "highest level of service to all library users" and service that is equitable for all with information provided that is "accurate, unbiased, and courteous." This statement is at the heart of good reference service that strives to provide good quality information and information that can be documented. Reference staff must understand what constitutes a good reference interaction and must strive to meet that standard with each user query (Bunge 1999).

The second statement calls for the protection of the "principles of intellectual freedom" and resistance to "all efforts to censor library resources." Library selection is reflected in this statement, as librarians attempt to provide information on a subject from many points of view. The third statement protects the user's right to privacy and confidentiality in requesting and using library resources. Reference librarians must be particularly cognizant of this professional obligation. They must respect the privacy of a user by keeping their reference interview and the resources used confidential.

According to the fourth claim, intellectual property rights should be recognized and respected. It is important that librarians keep current with changes in intellectual property laws, especially copyright, and keep their users aware of these laws. Librarians must know when copying is covered under the "fair use" provision of the law and when it violates copyright law. This is more than a good in itself; it also helps protect the institution, its employees, and its patrons from claims of copyright infringement and intellectual dishonesty.

Statements five through eight all treat the relationship between personal interests and professional responsibilities. The fifth encourages the respectful treatment of coworkers and colleagues and the safeguarding of the rights of all employees. This is a statement that encompasses the whole library and its staff. It is up to every staff member to see that others are treated fairly.

In the sixth statement, library employees are cautioned not to put private interests ahead of library interests. This means that employees should be circumspect in their dealings with vendors and others outside the library, such that their decisions are made on professional merit and are not influenced by personal interest.

The seventh cautions library employees not to put personal convictions or beliefs ahead of professional duties. This is also of special significance to reference librarians. Sometimes a librarian must help a user research an area that is personally against the librarian's beliefs or philosophy. But by putting professional duties first, the librarian can successfully assist the user and provide the information needed.

The eighth encourages all library staff to continue to grow in their knowledge and skills and to assist those entering the profession. We live in a time when change is constant, so all library staff must continue to learn and change.

Other professional library organizations have their own codes of ethics. These include the American Society for Information Science (ASIS), the Society of American Archivists, the Medical Library Association, and the American Association of Law Libraries.

The Changing Nature of Reference

As the form of the library has evolved in the years since Samuel Green's seminal pronouncements in 1876, so too has the nature of reference services. Today it stretches far beyond the walls of the library and strives to far loftier ends than welcoming users to the library with a "cultivated female staff." Users can ask questions 24/7 through virtual reference and expect an immediate response. Likewise, they can access electronic resources that the library provides through its Web site. Although virtual reference is growing slowly, the appeal of instant messaging and like services suggests the possibility of a generational paradigm shift ahead. Though some see them as depersonalizing, these online reference services have the advantage of being convenient and less threatening than coming to the library.

In numerous forms and fashions, technology continues to change reference service. Librarians must be ready to learn new technology and adapt to the needs of users unable to imagine a world without technology. Like few other professionals, librarians must be willing to ride the waves of such change, adapting to meet the needs of their users.

New models of reference are also developing to meet different user needs. Libraries are adding more points of service. For example, an information desk near the front of the library, reference desk(s) at strategic points throughout the stacks, and in-depth reference centers where a user can sit down with a librarian and work out a plan for researching a paper have all been instituted to positive effect at libraries around the world. In other situations, librarians rove the reference area to help users who do not approach the reference desk.

Technology is continuing to change reference service. Librarians must be ready to learn new technology and adapt to the needs of users being raised on technology. Whether it is the cell phone, the Palm Pilot, the MP3 player, or the iPod, users will want to receive and read their information on this new technology.

These and other novel strategies are changing the way information services are imagined and put into practice. As we look ahead, we must be aware that reference work will no doubt be based increasingly on electronic means of communication. It will at the same time continue to be a personal service although not necessarily face-to-face. There will be more emphasis on electronic materials while older materials will still need to be consulted in print format. Even so, many of the old forms of finding and conveying information are as fundamental today as they ever were. In the chapters ahead, we will explore the cutting edge of contemporary reference, demonstrating how to keep this crucial service central to the modern library.

Recommendations for Further Reading

Austin, Brice. 2004. "Should There Be 'Privilege' in the Relationship between Reference Librarian and Patron?" *The Reference Librarian* 87/88: 301–311. An exploration of whether privilege should be extended to the librarian-patron relationship.

Fritch, John W., and Scott B. Mandernack. 2001. "The Emerging Reference Paradigm: A Vision of Reference Services in a Complex Information Environment." *Library*

Trends 50, no. 2 (Fall): 286–306. A proposal of ways to respond to changes in reference service.

Jacoby, JoAnn, and Nancy P. O'Brien. 2005. "Assessing the Impact of Reference Service Provided to Undergraduate Students." *College and Research Libraries* 66, no. 4 (July): 324–340. Reports on how reference service can help students to learn to do research and to use the library.

Landesman, Margaret. 2005. "Getting It Right—The Evolution of Reference Collections." *The Reference Librarian* 91/92: 5–22. A history of the development of reference collections.

Puacz, Jeanne Holba. 2005. "Electronic vs. Print Reference Sources in Public Library Collections." *The Reference Librarian* 91/92: 39–51. A discussion of the impact of electronic resources on public library collections.

Samson, Sue, and Erling Oetz. 2005. "The Academic Library as a Full-Service Information Center." *Journal of Academic Librarianship* 31, no. 4 (July): 347–351. The development of an Information Center at the University of Montana–Missoula supports the changing nature of library service and combines one-stop service for library users.

Bibliography of Works Cited in this Chapter

Bopp, Richard E., and Linda C. Smith. 2001. *Reference and Information Services: An Introduction*. Englewood, CO: Libraries Unlimited.

Bunge, Charles. 1999. "Ethics and the Reference Librarian." *The Reference Librarian*, no. 66: 25–43.

Genz, Marcella D. 1998. "Working the Reference Desk." *Library Trends* 46, no. 3 (Winter): 505–525.

Gorman, Michael. 2003. *The Enduring Library: Technology, Tradition, and the Quest for Balance*. Chicago: American Library Association.

Katz, William A. 2001. *Introduction to Reference Work*. 2 vols. New York: McGraw-Hill.

Nolan, Christopher W. 1999. *Managing the Reference Collection*. Chicago: American Library Association.

Tyckoson, David A. 2001. "What is the Best Model of Reference Service?" *Library Trends* 50, no. 2 (Fall): 183–196.

Whitlatch, Jo Bell. 2000. *Evaluating Reference Services: A Practical Guide*. Chicago: American Library Association.

2

Determining the Question: In-person, Telephone, and Virtual Reference Interviews

The reference interview is more an art than a science, an ever-changing practice that requires responsiveness to context rather than the application of a predetermined set of skills. While librarians should learn the elements of a good reference interview, they must also recognize that these steps must be adapted to match each situation. Each reference interview will be different since each user and each question is different. The overall structure has three phases: "establishing contact with the user, finding out the user's need, and confirming that the answer provided is actually what was needed" (Ross, Nilsen, and Dewdney 2002, 5). Within this framework, librarians must learn to improvise like expert jazz musicians.

For librarians, answering the user's question correctly is the most important part of the reference interaction. Yet studies and experience show that users react to the manner in which the reference interview is conducted, paying special attention to both verbal and nonverbal cues. They are more likely to return to a librarian who has handled their request respectfully whether or not their information need has been completely fulfilled. Anyone who has ever studied under a professor so knowledgable about a subject that she could not express herself in conventional terms will understand this dilemma. Lessons learned from a friendly, approachable, and intelligible person almost always come more easily and last longer. Consequently, we must recognize that in reference situations conduct is as important as content.

Why Do the Reference Interview?

Sometimes the questions asked by users are very straightforward, prompting librarians to wonder why the reference interview is necessary at all. Upon looking into the matter, however, the librarian often discovers that the real question was not the first one asked. Users tend to believe they can ask a short question and get enough information to proceed on their own. In such circumstances, the ambiguity of their initial inquiry often leads to confusion. A user might, for example, ask for books about stars when, in fact, he wants to know the constellations one can see south of the equator or is seeking information about the home addresses of movie stars. On another occasion a user might ask for books on baking when he wants to find out about the chemistry involved in the rising of yeast rather than recipes for bread. In philosophy, errors prompted by the multiple meanings of words are known as "category mistakes," the grouping of dissimilar concepts under a single shared label. Errors of this kind may not have profound consequences in the library world, but they do waste the time of users and staff alike. By asking additional clarifying questions the librarian can avoid such problems, focusing on the meaningful meat of the user's request.

What We Know about the Reference Interview

A number of studies have been done about the reference interaction. Robert S. Taylor in his article "Question Negotiation and Information Seeking in Libraries" explored the reference interaction from the point of view of question negotiation. Taylor discussed "five filters through which a question passes and from which the librarian selects significant data to aid him in his research" (Taylor 1968, 183). Elaine Z. Jennerich and Edward J. Jennerich approached the reference interview as a "creative art" and a "performing art" (1997). Mary Jo Lynch studied the reference interview in public libraries and asked how reference librarians know when to interview a user, through what channels a librarian gathers information without asking questions, and what the characteristics are of an effective question sequence (Lynch 1978).

Brenda Dervin and Patricia Dewdney's article "Neutral Questioning: A New Approach to the Reference Interview" proposed the neutral questioning model—a user-oriented approach to answering reference questions (Dervin and Dewdney 1986). Patricia Dewdney and Catherine Sheldrick Ross continued the research in this area by looking at the reference interview from the user's point of view (Dewdney and Ross 1994). They asked Master of Library and Information Science students to visit libraries and ask questions of interest to them and to report on the results. Only 59.7 percent said that they would return to the same librarian (Dewdney and Ross 1994, 222).

Marie Radford in her 1998 article in *Library Trends* turned her attention to nonverbal communications. She identified five factors indicated by users that were critical in their decision as to whom to approach. They were initiation, availability, proximity, familiarity, and gender (Radford 1998). Mary Jane Swope and Jeffrey Katzer studied the question of why people do not ask for assistance and found that the reasons were dissatisfaction with their previous assistance, the belief that their query was too simple, and the disinclination to bother the librarian (Swope and Katzer 1972).

Intercultural communication has been studied by Terry Ann Mood and R. Errol Lam. Mood stated that foreign students learn best by hands-on experience. Lam emphasized more effective intercultural communication through the reference interview. Most recently, research has turned to the area of virtual reference and what are the differences and similarities to face-to-face reference with the work of Straw, Kem, Radford, and Nilsen.

Conducting the Reference Interview

The reference interview is composed of several parts, each of which will be discussed in turn over the following pages:

- Establishing rapport with the user
- Negotiating the question
- Developing a strategy for a successful search and communicating it to the user
- Locating the information and evaluating it
- Ensuring that the question is fully answered—the follow-up
- Closing the interview

Establishing Rapport with the User

When users arrive at the library or contact a librarian remotely (whether by phone, e-mail, chat, or instant messaging), they expect to find someone willing to help them. To make the initial approach easier, librarians must find ways to signal, whether verbally or nonverbally, that they are approachable. In Edward Kazlauskas's "An Exploratory Study: A Kinesic Analysis of Academic Library Public Service Points" he found that raising the eyebrow and lowering it when someone approaches, maintaining eye contact, nodding, and smiling all help make the initial encounter more positive and comfortable (Kazlauskas 1976). He also identified behaviors that make the librarian less approachable: lack of immediate acknowledgment of user, failing change in body stance as user comes closer, covering the eyes with the hand, reading, tapping one's finger, and twitching of the mouth (Kazlauskas 1976).

Marie L. Radford "observed reference interactions for thirty-seven hours, interviewing 155 users who approached thirty-four librarian volunteers." Her purpose was to discover behaviors that influenced which librarian the user approached. She identified five factors indicated by users that positively shaped user decisions:

- *Initiation.* The librarian begins the interaction by using one of the following non-verbal signals: eye contact, body orientation, movement toward the user, or verbal enforcement.
- *Availability.* The librarian indicates availability by turning around, moving toward the patron, using eye contact, or otherwise signaling attention to the user nonverbally.
- *Proximity.* Users decide who to approach based on their physical distance from the librarian.
- *Familiarity.* The user had previously met or been helped by a particular librarian.
- *Gender.* Users found it more comfortable to approach a female librarian. (1998, 708–710)

The librarian can also look approachable by roving through the reference area and helping users who may need assistance. Many users may not be comfortable initiating conversation a librarian when they need help, so roving gives users a less formal opportunity to get assistance. As they roam, librarians can simply ask users if they are finding what they need. They can approach users whom they have already assisted or perhaps users who have not approached the reference desk.

When serving users who telephone or send their requests by e-mail, the librarian can make the process easier by greeting the user in a friendly, upbeat manner—i.e., "Hello. How can I help you?"—and by responding to the information provided by the user. For example, the user may reveal that the reason he or she is using virtual reference is an illness or the inability to leave home. The librarian should respond to this comment by remarking on the situation in a friendly but neutral way—for example, by saying, "Hope you feel better soon."

Whatever the circumstances, the user must feel that the librarian is interested in his or her question. The librarian can accomplish this by "facing the patron when speaking and listening and by maintaining eye contact with the patron." The librarian signals his or her understanding of the user's question by responding verbally or by nodding. In a remote situation the librarian must stay in contact with the user by text messages and conveying in words his or her interest in the question. For example, he could say, "What an interesting question."

Negotiating the Question

Once the possibility of dialogue has been established, the next step is to establish the patron's query. Many approaches to negotiating the question have been suggested by researchers and practitioners. Brenda Dervin has suggested "sense-making" as a way of finding out exactly what the user wants (Dervin and Dewdney 1986). Sense-making is user oriented and approaches the reference interview in an organized way designed to ensure that the librarian understands what the user really needs. This method calls for an understanding of the user's situation, the gap that led to the question, and how the user plans to use the information. Dervin argues that it is important to understand that the "gaps individuals face (i.e., the questions they have) depend upon the way in which they see the situation and how they are stopped. The kind of answers they want is dependent on how they expect to use or be helped by the answers" (Dervin and Dewdney 1986, 507). Two questions, alike in form, may not, in the end, be at all similar if the users who ask them differ in their views of the situation. Dervin and Dewdney went on to develop a further approach to questioning called "neutral questioning," which grows out of "sense-making" (Dervin and Dewdney 1986). Neutral questioning involves asking open questions that will help the librarian discover the true nature of the question. Dervin and Dewdney state that the librarian through questions must assess the situation, assess the gaps, and assess the uses of the information (Dervin and Dewdney 1986, 509). They suggest that the most useful neutral questions are the following:

What kind of help would you like?
What have you done about this so far?
What would you like this book (information) to do for you? (Dervin and Dewdney 1986, 512)

An example of this questioning in action is the following:

"Do you want annual reports? What sort of details do you want? If you could tell me the kind of problem you're working on, I'll have a better idea of what would help you" (Dervin and Dewdney 1986, 510).

This form of questioning can be tailored to the needs of each individual by focusing on how the information will be used. Once learned, neutral questioning is not a long process since it is adapted to the needs of the individual. Neutral questioning can help librarians avoid the kind of category mistakes described above. It also helps facilitate other forms of disambiguation by ensuring that all possible information about the information desired by the user is made known. A person may ask where books on a certain subject are, thinking that they can browse when they get to the section and find what they are looking for. Another patron may need some specific information and think the library does not have it just because a particular book is not on the shelf—unaware that a librarian may be able to answer the question with another source.

In order for a positive reference interview to take place, the librarian must listen carefully to the user and ask clarifying questions as necessary. The librarian must begin with open-ended questions, giving the user a chance to express his reference needs. Often the first question asked by the user does not really describe what the user is seeking. The librarian must ask probing, open-ended questions such as "Please tell me more about your topic" or "What do you want to know about (the topic)?" "What additional information can you give me?" The librarian should continue with clarifying questions that may be open-ended or closed-ended questions once it is clear what the user wants. These clarifying questions might include the following:

Open-ended questions	Closed-ended questions
How much information do you need?	Do you need current or historical information?
What have you already found?	Do you need factual or analytical information?
What format for the information do you need?	Can you read languages other than English?

The librarian should rephrase the question to be sure that he or she really understands what is needed by the user. Of course, it goes without saying that the librarian should remain objective and not make judgments about the subject of the question. The same is true of a virtual reference question. The librarian must ask the same open-ended questions to give users a chance to type out their information.

Although the librarian should begin with open-ended questions that allow users to express more fully their questions, there is also a place for closed-ended questions. Once the librarian understands the question, he or she may want to narrow the search with some clarifying closed-ended questions. The important thing to remember about closed-ended questions is that the response from the user will be brief. For example, if the librarian asks the user, "Do you want books or just articles?" the user may respond with a one-word answer, such as, "books" or "articles." Sometimes a mix of open- and closed-ended questions works best. As the librarian listens to the user's question, he or she must not make assumptions about the user or the question. Assumptions may lead the librarian in the wrong direction, bringing the search up short. By working to avoid the always mistaken belief that the horizon of the user is the same as one's own, the librarian can extend the limits of his or her vision.

For this interchange to be truly effective, the librarian should include the user in the search. For example, the librarian may turn the monitor toward the user to show the user the information being located in the database. This will enable the librarian to continue to test whether they are proceeding in the right direction, and it will be less isolating for the user. As the exchange proceeds, including the user will give the librarian the opportunity to offer information about how to use the library that may be helpful to the user in the future.

In the course of assisting the user the librarian may need to help the user to reframe his or her question. The question may be too general or too specific, and the librarian must then work with the user to better formulate the question. For example, the user may ask for information on the Civil War but actually want information on the Battle of Gettysburg. The librarian should try to find out in carefully crafted phrases how the information will be used and what level of material is needed.

Finally, the librarian should paraphrase the question back to the user to be sure that the understanding is mutual. For example, "If I understand you correctly, you want information on the coral reefs in Key West, especially their geology, location, and water temperature." It is easy to misunderstand the user's question, so every effort should be made to make sure the user's needs are being communicated.

Developing a Strategy and Communicating It to the User

Once the subject is clear the librarian should construct a search, selecting search terms and identifying the most appropriate sources for the particular user. If the librarian has little knowledge of the subject, he or she should partner with the user in selecting the subject terms. No one, even a subject specialist, can ever expect to be an expert on that which might be of interest to library patrons, and the reference encounter is often as much a chance to learn as it is to teach. So long as one knows where to begin looking, the reference process can be exciting for both librarian and user. As the search is developed, the librarian should explain as much about the search as he or she thinks is of interest to the user. The librarian should also respect the user's time frame and work to assist the user to the fullest extent possible within that time frame.

Of the many kinds of information available on most subjects, the librarian must determine what information will fit the user's needs. Does the user want more general information or more technical information? This can only be judged by continuing to communicate with the user. The user may also have a preference as to the format of the information, the amount of information, and the level of the information. Ideally, much of this information should have been discovered in the earlier phase of determining the question. It is important that the librarian constantly keep in mind all that he or she knows about the user's needs and work to plan the search accordingly.

Locating the Information and Evaluating It

Whatever the extent of a reference query, the librarian should continually check in with the user to determine whether the material being discovered complies with the user's needs. This process should continue until the user has the information needed or has resources to examine.

Instruction in the use of the resources should be provided to the user if the user is unfamiliar with the source(s). Attention should also be paid to the quality of the information by evaluating that information to be certain that the sources selected are of high quality. This can be done by using the guidelines for the selection of reference materials.

Ensuring That the Question is Fully Answered—the Follow-up

The follow-up question is of great importance to the reference interview. It is necessary to check with users to see whether they have had their questions answered. The librarian may want to ask if the users found the information they sought or say, "Please come back if you don't find what you are looking for and we can look somewhere else." Or the librarian may be roving and check in with the user. Gers and Seward stated that the follow-up question "may be the single most important behavior because it has the potential for allowing one to remedy lapses in other desirable behaviors" (Gers and Seward 1985, 34). Dewdney and Ross found that librarians often fail to ask follow-up questions. This can result in a situation where the user lacks needed information but is unable to express the discrepancy (1994).

Closing the Interview

Like the closing moves of a chess game, the conclusion of a reference interview is a highly specialized art. Once it has been confirmed that the user has all of the information he or she desires, the consulting librarian should find a way to bring the conversation to a close without making the patron feel summarily dismissed. Christopher Nolan suggests that a reference department should develop goals for the interview, making it easier to know when the conversation should be brought to a close. He further states that "three factors are involved in the end of most interviews: knowledge or content of the interview, dynamics of the interpersonal interaction, and institutional or policy components" (Nolan 1992, 515). Keep in mind that, as is suggested elsewhere in this book, reference services are one of the primary means to spotlight the value of the library itself, so the interview should close on an open note. In particular, the librarian can make a follow-up comment that will encourage the user to return.

Problematic Strategies in the Reference Interview

The Imposed Query

Most librarians and researchers have based their evaluation of the reference interview on the assumption that the questions were self-generated. This is not always true. Melissa Gross defines and discusses the imposed query as "a process in which the imposer or end user passes the question to another who will act as the agent in the transaction of the query and then return to the imposer with the answer or resolution" (Gross 1998, 291). Although we do not know all the implications of the imposed query, it is logical to assume that the assumptions and stereotypes of both the person who asked the question and the person who transmits the query will affect the outcome. Gross points to the need for more research in this area. A good example of the imposed query is when a parent arrives in the library asking for information for his or her child's homework assignment. In this case the person who needs the information is not present and the parent may or may not be clear as to the actual information need. It is helpful to the librarian to identify this situation as the imposed query, since the librarian will realize that the person asking the question may not be able to clarify the question for the librarian, making it more complicated to help.

The Communications Trap

Sometimes the problem between the user and the librarian is one of communication. The article "Oranges and Peaches: Understanding Communication Accidents in the Reference Interview" points out this problem. This article begins by describing a scenario in which a student arrives at the library, claiming that he has been assigned a book to read entitled "Oranges and Peaches." The librarian is unable to find a book by this title and asks the student for the author. The librarian does not ask the student any open-ended questions or sense-making questions in order to get information on the context of the request. Finally the student does provide additional information, and the librarian realizes that the student is looking for Darwin's *On the Origin of Species* (Dewdney and Michell 1996, 520–521).

Sometimes the librarian misunderstands the question because the pronunciation of the key words is slightly different or the librarian hears the word and relates it to something familiar to him or her. In another example, Dewdney and Michell describe a user who arrives at the library asking for material on Socrates. But the librarian has just been weeding in the sports section and hears it as "soccer tees." There are, of course, many words that sound the same but have completely different meanings, such as China/china, Turkey/turkey and Wales/whales (Dewdney and Michell, 1996, 527–528). Other communication accidents happen when the user asks a question that he or she has heard from someone else. The solution to these miscommunications is first to restate the question, allowing the user the opportunity to restate himself or herself, and second to ask follow-up questions, helping to introduce context into the discussion.

Behaviors to Avoid

Librarians should take care not to fall into the many traps that can easily occur during the reference transaction.

Keep in contact with the user. It is tempting to just start typing on the computer once the user has asked a question. This is extremely confusing to the user, who knows neither what the librarian is doing nor whether the librarian really understood the question. Before beginning a search, be sure that the question is clear by restating it and explaining to the user what is being searched. If possible, let users see the screen so they can follow the search. If the librarian goes elsewhere to get the information for the user, he or she should try not to be out of sight of the user for any length of time, so that the user knows the librarian is still working on that question.

Avoid the negative closure—a dismissive behavior that falls short of providing full service. In a negative closure the librarian is more interested in getting rid of the user than in answering the question and sends the user away without the information needed. Here are some examples of this:

- The librarian provides an unmonitored referral. This is when the librarian sends the user somewhere else without any clear direction. For example, the librarian gives the user a call number and suggests looking in that area or points to a particular area and suggests browsing there. Similarly problematic would be a situation in which the librarian refers the user elsewhere in the library or to an agency without confirming that the user will actually find the required information there.
- The librarian suggests that the user should have done some work independently before asking for help.
- The librarian tries to get the user to accept information that is easily available rather than what the user needs.
- The librarian suggests that the information will not be found for one of a number of reasons, such as too hard, obscure, or elusive, or simply not available in the library and perhaps not in any library.
- The librarian tries to convince the user not to pursue his or her question.
- The librarian leaves the desk and does not return.
- The librarian, through a nonverbal action such as turning away from the user, indicates that the interview is over. (Ross and Dewdney 1998, 151–163)

Ross and Dewdney offer recommendations for positive behavior rather than the negative closure. They recommend that when the librarian refers the user to another part of the library or to another library or information source, the librarian should verify that the user will find useful information. The librarian should also encourage the user to return if the user does not find the information needed. Roving the reference section can help identify users who need more help or who need help but have not talked to a librarian. If the reference interaction is remote, the librarian might suggest a visit to the library for further information or encourage the user to contact the library again for more assistance.

Another behavior to avoid is simply not listening to the user. It is hard to listen intently to each user's question. But the librarian must do this in order to understand as completely as possible the user's question. To not listen closely and ask pertinent questions can lead to assumptions that will lead the librarian in the wrong direction. For example, the librarian might be asked about abortions and immediately go to the health section only to find out the person want to know about aborting space flights.

Finally, avoid making the user feel stupid. Sometimes the user does not know the library jargon. They may use "bibliography" instead of "biography" or they may use "reference book" when they mean a circulating nonfiction book. The librarian should correct the user in a nonjudgmental manner. It is the librarian who must learn to understand the patrons (Cramer 1998).

The Telephone Interview

The telephone interview is one step removed from the face-to-face interview. It does have the advantage of getting immediate feedback from the user. Although the librarian cannot see the user, the librarian can hear the tone and inflections in the user's voice and can ascertain how they are communicating.

The librarian should develop a pleasant speaking voice to aid in phone communication, aiming to sound approachable and attentive. As always, it is important to rephrase the user's questions to clarify their meaning and to ask open-ended questions to elaborate upon it. In this more ethereal context, it is doubly important that the user be kept informed as to how the search process is proceeding and that silent time be kept to a minimum. Once the answer has been found, follow-up questions should be asked in order to confirm that the question has been properly answered. Encourage the user to call again or visit the library (Ross 2002, 127–131).

Answering Questions Virtually

Centuries ago, those distant from a sizable library or knowledgable expert had to rely on slow moving letters to find the answers they sought, sometimes waiting weeks or months as letters traveled back and forth. Recently, the written word has again come into vogue as a means of soliciting and providing reference assistance. Answering questions by e-mail, chat, or instant messaging (IM) is not much different from answering questions face to face. The problem is that virtual reference lacks the advantage of the face-to-face reference interview where the user's tone of voice, facial expressions, and body language help the librarian to judge whether he or she is communicating well with the user. What is a handicap for some is, however, an advantage for others, who cannot leave home or do not communicate well verbally, making it a powerful means to support the mission of many libraries to make their resources available to all.

Librarians should approach the virtual reference question in the same way as a face-to-face one. In e-mail reference, the structure of the reference interview is still a well-designed form that captures essential information. This is the best way for the librarian to get information from the user. Chat and IM reference have considerable potential for the reference interview because it is done in real time.

When providing chat or IM reference, the librarian should not assume that the user does not have time for the reference interview. The fact that the user has not chosen to come to the library does not indicate that the user is impatient or in a hurry (Kem 2003). Librarians should greet users by name and acknowledge the receipt of the question. They should then proceed to do a reference interview, asking the user for the context of the query, followed by open-ended questions. He or she should explain that the questions are aimed at ensuring that the librarian understands the question, and should rephrase the question to that purpose. It is also important to tell the user what steps you are taking since the user cannot see what you are doing. The librarian should read carefully the user's reply for clues as to whether they are communicating well. Because the back-and-forth of e-mail, chat, and IM may become tiresome to the user, it is recommended that the librarian should "respond with a small amount of information plus a request for clarification" (Ross, Nilsen, and Dewdney 2002, 199). If the information needed is not available electronically, the librarian should arrange to get the print information to the user by fax or other convenient means (Ronan 2003, 158).

Virtual reference librarians should aim to be approachable in the way they word their responses to the user. Just as in the face-to-face interview, the librarian will want to strive to make the user comfortable with the process so that the user will return to the library. Follow-up should encourage the user to use the library virtually or in person. Recent research shows that the same mistakes happen in virtual reference as in face-to-face interviews, that is, the lack of the reference interview, unmonitored referrals, and failure to ask follow-up questions (Nilsen 2005). Straw comments that "a well-written response not only answers a question eloquently, but it also tells the user about the importance that the library places on the question" (Straw 2000, 379).

New RUSA Guidelines—a New, More Integrated Approach

The most recent guidelines for the reference interview, "Guidelines for Behavioral Performance of Reference and Information Service Providers," were approved by the Reference and User Services Association Board of Directors in June 2004. These guidelines cover approachability, interest, listening/inquiring, searching, and follow-up. Each of these five areas includes general guidelines, in-person guidelines, and guidelines for remote reference, that is, telephone, e-mail, and chat. For the first time, the guidelines have been tied to remote reference as well as in-person reference. This provides the librarian with a way to begin to blend the various ways of answering a reference question rather than treating remote reference separately as when it was first emerging. These guidelines stress the need for good communication skills, whether the question is asked in person or remotely, stating: "In all forms of reference services, the success of the transaction is measured not only by the information conveyed, but also by the positive or negative impact of the patron/staff interaction. The positive or negative behavior of the reference staff (as observed by the patron) becomes a significant factor in perceived success or failure."

About approachability it states: "Approachability behaviors, such as the initial verbal and non-verbal responses of the librarian, will set the tone for the entire communication process and will influence the depth and level of interaction between the staff and the patrons."

On the subject of interest it states: "A successful librarian must demonstrate a high degree of interest in the reference transaction. While not every query will contain stimulating intellectual challenges, the librarian should be interested in each patron's information need and should be committed to providing the most effective assistance."

About listening it states: "The reference interview is the heart of the reference transaction and is crucial to the success of the process. The librarian must be effective in identifying the patron's information needs and must do so in a manner that keeps patrons at ease."

On searching it states: "The search process is the portion of the transaction in which behavior and accuracy intersect. Without an effective search, not only is the desired information unlikely to be found but patrons may become discouraged as well."

And about follow-up it states: "The reference transaction does not end when the librarian leaves the patrons. The librarian is responsible for determining if the patrons are satisfied with the results of the search and is also responsible for referring the patrons to other sources, even when those sources are not available in the local library."

Cultural Differences

The librarian should try to understand and respect the cultural differences of the users. Some users may have trouble asking their questions. If patrons are difficult to understand, the librarian could ask them to write out their question. Librarians should avoid jargon and speak slowly and distinctly. When possible, give users struggling with English handouts that they can read. Other issues to be aware of involve differences in body language and personal space issues. In some cultures it is acceptable to stand very close to the librarian when talking to him or her. For others this can be uncomfortable. Etiquette also differs among cultures. In some countries it is important to greet someone formally before beginning the conversation and in others it is important to shake hands first. No matter what the cultural differences, it is important to treat all people with respect.

Improving Our Skills

Doing a good reference interview takes skills that only come with practice. The new librarian should continually evaluate his or her abilities and try to improve them.

- Practice looking approachable. This means being relaxed and open and not looking so busy that the person will hesitate to ask a question.
- Practice active listening skills. Listening to the nuances as well as the words of the user will help librarians to be sure that they understand the question.
- Develop knowledge of reference sources. Continuing to build knowledge of reference resources is essential in assisting the user.
- Practice posing questions. Think about how to craft and ask questions that will elicit more information from the user and help the librarian to better understand the question.
- Practice the follow-up questions and the closing of the interview. Both are essential in making sure the question is answered and making it comfortable for the user to return again.

A Look Ahead

As we look to a future that is a mix of face-to-face, telephone, or virtual reference assistance, the importance of the reference interview remains. It has been proven in all situations to be key to successfully answering the user's question. It is also important in having the user feel that the librarian has tried his or her best to answer the question. It is interesting that the user often values the behavior of the librarian more than the answer. Consequently, the development of good people skills is of great importance no matter the form of the reference interview. Kathleen Kem summed up the reference interview as follows: "we need to remember that the type and quality of the service we offer must depend on our philosophy of reference service and not on the mode of communication with the user" (Kem 2003, 49). As the ways we work to help library users continue to change, we would do well to keep these words in mind, remembering that it is an orientation toward excellent service that leads to satisfied users.

Recommendations for Further Reading

Bobrowsky, Tammy, Lynne Beck, and Malaika Grant. 2005. "The Chat Reference Interview: Practicalities and Advice." *The Reference Librarian*, no. 89/90: 179–191. This article offers practical information on how to conduct a chat reference interview.

Durrance, Joan. 1995. "Factors That Influence Reference Success." *The Reference Librarian* 49/50: 243–265. Based on the author's "Willingness to Return" study that identifies factors that are associated with successful reference interviews.

Dyson, Lillie Seward. 1992. "Improving Reference Services: A Maryland Training Program Brings Positive Results." *Public Libraries* 31, no. 5 (September/October): 284–289. Presents the Maryland Division of Library Development and Services survey and subsequent training program that identified verification and follow-up questions as the most important elements in the reference interview.

Fagan, Judy Condit, and Christina M. Desai. 2002/2003. "Communication Strategies for Instant Messaging and Chat Reference Services." *The Reference Librarian*, no. 79/80: 121–155. The author discusses effective ways to communicate using instant messaging and chat reference.

"Guidelines for Behavioral Performance of Reference and Information Service Providers." 2004. *Reference & User Services Quarterly* 44, no. 1 (Fall): 9–14. A discussion of these guidelines for providing digital reference service.

Owen, Tim Buckley. 2006. *Success at the Enquiry Desk: Successful Enquiry Answering—Every Time.* 5th edition. London: Facet. A helpful and up-to-date manual on the particulars of providing reference service.

Ronan, Jana. 2003. "The Reference Interview Online." *Reference and User Services Quarterly* 43, no. 1 (Fall): 43–47. The author discusses how chat communication norms for online communities can be applied to real-time chat reference service following the RUSA Behavioral Performance of Reference and Information Services Professionals guidelines.

Ross, Catherine Sheldrick, and Patricia Dewdney. 1994. "Best Practices: An Analysis of the Best (and Worst) in Fifty-two Public Library Reference Transactions." *Public Libraries* 33, no. 5 (September/October): 261–266. This survey confirmed that 55 percent of the users would return to the same librarian again. Unhelpful practices in the reference interview are listed.

Stover, Mark. 2004. "The Reference Librarian as Non-Expert: A Postmodern Approach to Expertise." *The Reference Librarian*, no. 87/88: 273–300. An exploration of the reference interview using the "postmodern psychotherapeutic view of the therapist as a non-expert."

Ward, David. 2004. "Measuring the Completeness of Reference Transactions in Online Chat." *Reference & User Services Quarterly* 44, no. 1 (Fall): 46–57. A study of the effectiveness of online chat reference and to see if the questions were answered completely.

Ward, David. 2005. "How Much is Enough? Managing Chat Length." *Internet Reference Services Quarterly* 10, no. 2: 89–93. A discussion of how to handle long chat sessions—both policies and suggested practices.

Ward, David. 2005. "Why Users Choose Chat: A Survey of Behavior and Motivations." *Internet Reference Services Quarterly* 10, no. 1: 29–46. A study of why people choose chat and their overall satisfaction.

White, Marilyn Domas. 1981. "The Dimensions of the Reference Interview." *RQ* 20, no. 4 (Summer): 373–381. Discusses the importance of explaining to the user what is happening during the reference interview.

White, Marilyn Domas. 1998. "Questions in Reference Interviews." *Journal of Documentation* 54, no. 4 (September): 443–465. A discussion of the types of questions asked in a presearch interview.

Bibliography of Works Cited in this Chapter

Cramer, Dina C. 1998. "How to Speak Patron." *Public Libraries* 37, no. 6 (November/December): 349.

Dervin, Brenda, and Patricia Dewdney. 1986. "Neutral Questioning: A New Approach to the Reference Interview." *RQ* 25 (Summer): 506–513.

Dewdney, Patricia, and Gillian Michell. 1996. "Oranges and Peaches: Understanding Communication Accidents in the Reference Interview." *RQ* 35, no. 4 (Summer): 520–536.

Dewdney, Patricia, and Catherine Sheldrick Ross. 1994. "Flying a Light Aircraft: Reference Service Evaluation from a User's Viewpoint." *RQ* 34, no. 2 (Winter): 217–230.

Gers, Ralph, and Lillie J. Seward. 1985. "Improving Reference Performance: Results of a Statewide Study." *Library Journal* 110 (November 1): 32–36.

Gross, Melissa. 1998. "The Imposed Query: Implications for Library Service Evaluations." *Reference and User Services Quarterly* 37, no. 3 (Spring): 290–299.

Guidelines for Behavioral Performance of Reference and Information Service Providers. www.ala.org/ala/rusa/rusaprotools/referenceguide/guidelines behavioral.htm.

Jennerich, Elaine Z., and Edward J. Jennerich. 1997. *The Reference Interview as a Creative Art.* Englewood, CO: Libraries Unlimited.

Kazlauskas, Edward. 1976. "An Exploratory Study: A Kinesic Analysis of Academic Library Public Service Points." *Journal of Academic Librarianship* 2, no. 3: 130–134.

Kem, Kathleen. 2003. "Communication, Patron Satisfaction, and the Reference Interview." *Reference and User Services Quarterly* (Fall): 47–49.

Lam, R. Errol. 1988. "The Reference Interview: Some Intercultural Considerations." *RQ* 27, no. 3 (Spring): 390–395.

Lynch, Mary Jo. 1978. "Reference Interviews in Public Libraries." *Library Quarterly* 48, no. 2 (April): 119–142.

Mood, Terry Ann. 1982. "Foreign Students and the Academic Library." *RQ* (Winter): 175–180.

Nilsen, Kirsti. 2005. "Virtual Versus Face to Face Reference: Comparing Users' Perceptions on Visits to Physical and Virtual Reference Desks in Public and Academic Libraries." Reference and Information Services Section, World Library and Information Congress, Oslo.

Nolan, Christopher W. 1992. "Closing the Reference Interview: Implications for Policy and Practice." *RQ* 31, no. 4 (Summer): 513–523.

Radford, Marie L. 1998. "Approach or Avoidance? The Role of Nonverbal Communication in the Academic Library User's Decision to Initiate a Reference Encounter." *Library Trends* 46, no. 4 (Spring): 699–717.

———. 1999. *The Reference Encounter.* Chicago: Association of College and Research Libraries.

Ronan, Jana Smith. 2003. *Chat Reference, A Guide to Live Virtual Reference Service.* Westport, CT: Libraries Unlimited.

Ross, Catherine Sheldrick, and Patricia Dewdney. 1999. "Negative Closure: Strategies and Counter-Strategies in the Reference Transaction." *Reference and User Services Quarterly* 38, no. 2 (Winter): 151–163.

Ross, Catherine Sheldrick, Kirsti Nilsen, and Patricia Dewdney. 2002. *Conducting the Reference Interview.* New York: Neal-Schuman.

Straw, Joseph E. 2000. "A Virtual Understanding: The Reference Interview and Question Negotiation in the Digital Age." *Reference and User Services Quarterly* 39, no. 1 (Summer): 376–379.

Swope, Mary Jane, and Jeffrey Katzer. 1972. "Why Don't They Ask Questions?" *RQ* 12, no. 2 (Winter): 161–166.

Taylor, Robert S. 1968. "Question Negotiation and Information Seeking in Libraries." *College & Research Libraries* (May): 178–194.

3

Finding the Answer: Basic Search Techniques

All the right questions have been asked in the reference interview. What next? In a perfect reference world as epitomized in a children's poem, the questions are asked, understood, and answered to the complete satisfaction of the user.

The Firefly

"How DO you make your bottom glow?

How DO you make your sitter light?"

The firefly cleared his throat and said,

"Bioluminescence is the oxidation of an enzyme

or protoplast called lucifern or luciferase."

I thanked him and went home to bed.

—Jack Kent

At a reference desk, however, the absence of that vocal, erudite firefly makes for a more challenging interaction. As described in the previous chapter, the reference interview is not merely conversation. It is skilled conversation with a definite purpose. It requires the use of preestablished procedures and practiced skills to be effective. The conscious use of tools such as keeping eye contact to be approachable; repeating the user's question to verify; and asking open-ended questions that can elicit further details are not a function of individual personality but requirements for which every reference librarian should be trained.

A less-studied aspect of the reference interview is the reference answer. It is assumed that once the user's question is understood to its fullest extent, reference librarians will, like the firefly, clear their throats and spill out a fully formed answer. As even the most experienced librarian can vouch, the clearing of one's throat is the closest one approaches to the above perfect scenario. The reference answer, much like the interview, benefits greatly from preconditioning, practice, and a conscious adoption of answering tools. With these tools, the reference answer is less vulnerable to the randomness of the librarian's knowledge coinciding with the user's idiosyncratic questions. A professional interaction is ensured regardless of the personalities involved.

Tools of the Answering Trade

Questions, queries, quests, and quizzes, the range of user needs is vast. It is both the most exhilarating and the most terrifying aspect of the reference librarian's job. Below is a list of requests received during a day at an academic library:

- *I need examples of funerary sculpture from the eighteenth century.*
- *Do you have articles about deforestation in the Dominican Republic in Spanish?*
- *I have to write about how the Internet has negatively affected American society.*
- *Do you have an outline map of Georgia?*
- *What is the date for the first Seder in 2006?*
- *I need to do a paper on the relation between monasteries and printing.*
- *Are there cookbooks in this library?*
- *Which New Jersey governor signed the Declaration of Independence?*
- *For my senior thesis, I have to research the life of Emily Brontë.*
- *How can I tell if a journal has been peer-reviewed?*

The act of leaping reflexively from one type of answering level to another can be done by everyone, much as hitting back at an approaching tennis ball is done. To effectively leap, however, requires much the same dedicated training as a professional tennis player who learns to hit balls with skill combined with instinct. Answering skills can be developed, just as questioning skills can be developed in a successful reference interview. As the reference interview proceeds, the librarian should simultaneously consider the following three steps to avoid a scattershot search:

- Categorizing the answer;
- Visualizing how the final answer will appear; and
- Testing the waters to check if the answer is proceeding in the right direction.

Step 1: Categorizing an Answer

Time-consuming or quick answer?

Slotting an answer into ready reference versus time-consuming is of immense help.

- It helps in avoiding panic and frustration on the part of both the librarian and the user by setting up a level of expectation.
- It also helps in organizing the flow of a reference desk. Alerting the user that finding the answer could take five minutes or fifteen minutes or one hour or more allows the user to vacate the desk and plan his or her time more effectively.

- It assigns a more professional stamp on the interaction. For telephone reference, if the answer does not fall in the realm of ready reference, the librarian can say "I will call you back with an answer within fifteen minutes." This way, the user is not left dangling in a seemingly endless abyss of waiting for the phone to ring.
- It alerts the librarian to possible complications. Approximating a time value to each answer can sometimes be miscalculated, but most questions in a school, public, and academic library are answerable within fifteen minutes of research. If not, the question may be based on incorrect assumptions, or must be upgraded to an in-depth research question rather than a quick reference question, or a referral may be in order. The question on the New Jersey governor who signed the Declaration of Independence, for example, was printed on a school assignment sheet and occupied two reference librarians. Almost one hour was squandered before it was finally deduced that such a governor simply did not exist. It was suggested that perhaps the assignment was alluding to the New Jersey governor who signed the Constitution rather than the Declaration.

Simple or Complex Answer?

Simplicity allows the librarian to think within the box and allot relatively little time to finding the answer.

- A question can be simple because it is pedestrian. An outline map of Georgia, for example, has no hidden complexities. It is a graphic. Moreover, it is an ordinary graphic that can be found in well-established sources such as the *Outline Maps* folder published by Facts on File, Inc. or printed via a simple *Google—images* search.
- A question can be simple because it falls within the purview of the librarian's own interests and therefore the resources are highly familiar. Locating, explaining, and presenting the best resources does not require fresh initiative or the rapid acquisition of "knowledge on the fly."
- A question can be deceptively simple such as the above request for cookbooks, which proceeded to develop into a search for obscure recipes for cocktails that could use cardamom as an ingredient. In such cases, when original searches balloon into quite another direction, time and simplicity estimates must be recalculated.

Current or Retrospective?

It can be useful to delineate questions that require current information from those that do not. Literary critiques, biographies, histories, word etymologies, and etiquette books are subject areas that require currency but do not put a premium on it. Stock reports, directories, almanacs, and statistical yearbooks do. Deciding on whether the question is retrospective helps to veer the search process to appropriate formats. A question on the life of Emily Brontë would most definitely benefit from an exhaustive print biography. Searches on a database for current articles on Brontë would be more likely to provide a single, scholarly perspective on some aspect of her work. The question on the first seder of 2006, on the other hand, would be most efficiently answered by an Internet search.

Specific or Cross-disciplinary?

Being alert to differences in questions aimed at facts versus analyses helps in structuring the search process. Factual information is usually to be found in one classification area, though not necessarily one source. Analyses requiring cross-disciplinary perspectives will have to be broken down into their component parts in order to select multiple classification areas. See, for example, the difference between the following two inquiries:

- What are the different kinds of illegal drugs?
- I need to do a five-page report on the impact and incidence of illegal drug abuse in the teenage population of the United States.

In the first question, the Dewey area of the 360s or the Library of Congress call numbers in the RC566–RC568 area would amply cover a listing of all the different kinds of illegal drugs. In the second assignment, however, additional research would have to cover the 306 or HV5825 area on drug culture; 613 or RA564.5 for impact of drugs on teen health; the 310 or KDZ32 area for criminal statistics; 909 or H35 for overviews such as those found in CQ Researcher; and databases for articles.

Single Source or Multisource?

Questions requiring no more than a single source are usually closed-ended questions. "I was born on 10 January, 1976; what day of the week was that?" The question requires one perpetual calendar. There is no need for further confirmation or evaluation. The World Almanac would suffice. A question on the "impact of ancient Roman architecture on the perceived power of Rome" on the other hand, would draw from multiple sources dealing, at minimum, with the history of Rome and the dynamics of architecture and architectural forms.

User Appropriate?

Academic librarians are faced with students attempting to pick up resources for absentee friends, just as public librarians are invariably approached by parents wanting resources for the "Civil War," "The Holocaust," or "a famous African American." A printed sheet in their hands, a slight disconnect in their enthusiasm for the subject, and a successful reference interview should establish their role as middlemen, rather than as end users of the information. For such "imposed queries" (Gross 2001), ascertaining the age, grade level, or purpose of the end users' needs is critical in choosing the appropriate answer source. Recognition of the reading level of the user is also required. A question on the workings of democracy in America could be answered with

Tocqueville's dense treatise or with Cliffs Notes' simple explanations in *American Government*.

Step 2: Visualizing an Answer

This book describes hundreds of important resources. While envisioning the exact resource to consult for each question is an unlikely scenario, it is both possible and advisable to triangulate onto the category of sources. Indexes, guides, directories, catalogs, dictionaries, journals, statistical yearbooks, government publications, almanacs, Web sites and databases: the strengths of each are established so that a move toward any one appropriate category or format is a logical first step.

Most reference librarians follow the visualizing search strategy without consciously practicing it. The librarian who spends time looking for the "oversize commercial atlas that was right here in the business section" has admittedly used a visualization tool, but has been stumped by the change in shape as the publication has morphed into two smaller-sized publications, as was the case with the 135th edition of the *Rand McNally Commercial Atlas and Marketing Guide*. Conscious practice improves the visualizing process. As Tim Owen (2003) suggests, "You can't see the fine detail, and you don't know yet whether there is a source . . . [but] . . . conjure up a picture in your mind's eyes of what the final answer will look like."

The focal points for successful visualization of answer resources are not color and size, but a rapid mental slide show of whether the answer would be in:

- Print/Internet/Database;
- Textual/Graphical/Statistical; or
- Reference/Circulating/Children.

While the first step of categorizing the answer is essential in visualizing the answer source, shuffling through rapid images of format, category, source type, and reading level appropriateness not only helps triangulating onto the right resources, but aids the process of continuing to ask the right follow-up questions. Here are three questions on Africa:

1. What were some of the causes and effects of imperialism in Africa?
2. What are current crime statistics for countries in the African continent?
3. Is the African setting necessary for character and plot development in the novels of J. M. Coetzee?

Given the breadth of information and the analytical requirements inherent to Question 1, a circulating print textual manuscript may be the first choice in resource visualization. For Question 2, current crime statistics for all countries might be most accessible through the Internet with globally vested sites such as the United Nations at www.uncjin.org/Statistics/WCTS/wcts.html. Unless there is a specific critical study of all aspects of Coetzee's works, a database of literary criticism might be the best bet for answering Question 3.

Step 3: Testing the Waters

In basketball, players are urged to use soft focus techniques and peripheral vision to be aware of the entire playing area. While providing answers, it is useful to use a similar technique to continually gauge whether the answer is proceeding in the right direction.

- Creative browsing:
  Float a trial balloon with introductory information and check user response. Calibrate accordingly. As studies have shown, individual research can be highly non-linear. Users are far more likely to recognize the information they need when they see it than know all the details of what they need before they start.

  For example, a somewhat taciturn user asked this question: "Where is your section on airplanes?" A reference interview of some length established that the user needed "pictures of planes flying together." Faced with an illustrated encyclopedia of aircraft, the user was interested but continued to want more material. At this point the ongoing verbal interview was not producing new insight, so a trial balloon was floated. The user was asked which type of illustration was closest to what he wanted. He pointed to a V-formation of military aircraft, but remembered that the V was disrupted at one point during the flight. This was the clue that it was the classic "missing man formation" aerial maneuver enacted at parades and funerals to honor the MIA. That further piece of information led the user to remember that he had seen it in a broadcast of President Reagan's funeral. That was the exact image he wanted and the librarian was able to get it for him.

  In short, the more inchoate the question and the more limited the ability to draw clues from a reference interview, the greater is the value of trial balloons in locating the right answer.
- Subcategorizing:
  Draw the user into various subcategories of the question to see if any strike the right chord. As the user shows interest in one category over another, focus on the chosen material and add to it.

  For example, a user was interested in sexually transmitted diseases (STDs). The topic, being of a somewhat sensitive nature, was treated to a less than exhaustive interview. Presented with monographs, statistical data material, a dictionary of diseases, an illustrated encyclopedia of diseases, and a quick sample of online sites, the user was most interested in graphic images of people afflicted with STDs. In this case the online option worked best as the user was a concerned mom who wanted gory pictures to scare her adolescent son into following the straight and narrow.
- Overviews:
  Provide a range of synopses of material and ask "do any of these appear to answer your question?" While ready reference questions require a single source, broader queries can be answered through different perspectives requiring different resources. However, as Joseph Janes has correctly pointed out, "users often want a response that is good enough—not perfect but optimal" (2003). The optimal response, though, must necessarily be decided by the user rather than the librarian. A way to navigate between the line separating the overzealous librarian flooding

the user with material and the Spartan librarian assuming the optimal choice, is to provide "bites." A quick look at the "About" icon in an online resource, or a scan of the preface, table of contents, or back page blurb in print resources is enough to provide a sweeping overview of the kinds of perspectives available to answer the question.

Whether the user is gently pushed into creatively browsing through the material to clarify the research and enable the librarian to select the right answer source; or the librarian organizes the range into subcategories from which the user can choose; or the user is provided with a quick and sweeping overview of the resources available, the end result is still the same. The librarian tests the waters to see if the initial response to a question is heading into the right answer field.

Types of Answers

Like all of human language and communication, the phrase "reference answer" conceals as much as it conveys. An "answer," far from being a uniform entity, can be of many different types, and more pertinently, provide various levels of utility for the user. Both during and after a reference interaction, it helps to be clear about what kind of answer was given to a user and whether another level of utility could have been possible.

Levels of Utility

Value-added answer   ←   Skilled answer   ←   Elementary answer

While all of the three broad answer gradations given above are helpful to the user, the highest level of utility can be assumed to derive from the value-added answer.

Value-added Answers

The value-added answer goes a step beyond merely providing the right resources. It organizes the material, prioritizes the resources, keeps an eye open for potential research needs being generated by the material, and presents the answer with élan.

- On paper, providing a cover letter annotating the various sources so that their relevance is made clear goes a long way to adding value to an answer. Corporate and law librarians are perhaps the best practitioners of value-added answers. Not only are the right resources to the question selected, but the relevance of each resource is made clear so that answers are presented as professional time-saving reports. Such reports, of course, are far from the fifteen-minute answers averaged by desk reference and can take up to weeks or months to prepare (Williams 2002).
- In-person answers can benefit greatly from professional tips and the librarian's perception as to why one source is more relevant or reliable than another. If six print resources have been presented to the user, for example, the librarian can point out that the top two resources are the ones to begin with as they

contain the most relevant information and are from highly reputable publishers. Alternatively, if different resource formats have been presented, the librarian can explain why a certain Web site would provide the most current updates; or how a database has a better chance of leading the user to a richer range of sources through hyperlinks.

- Answers provided via e-mail can employ simple cut-and-paste methods to consolidate the relevant facts from a variety of Web sites or database articles. With citations provided for each extract, the user has the option to do further research if necessary. If not, the user is provided with a high-utility answer that has saved both time and energy.
- In live or chat reference, thinking ahead and out of the box makes for a value-added answer. For example, a user had a question on the control of pests without the use of pesticides. The librarian was able to locate a perfect environmental Web site and a transcript of a radio interview on the subject. Most librarians would stop at this point, having provided a complete answer. This librarian picked up on the minor clue that the information was for a college paper and did a follow-up question on whether the user had access to a style guide to cite Web sites and transcripts. The user was most appreciative.
- Concerns, suggestions, and possible referrals can also be included in all formats, so that the user has the best possible overview of a topic before starting the research process.

Skilled Answers

Value-added answers, however desirable, can be quixotic in the working life of many librarians. Oftentimes, there is just not enough time or staff to provide the icing on the answer cake. At this point, the skilled answer adequately serves the purpose. To provide such an answer, the right resources are located, sifted, and judged so that only the best sources are selected for research consumption. As Kathleen Kluegel (2001) states: "Most of the decisions a searcher makes in the search strategy are made to achieve the appropriate balance between the two aims of information retrieval: precision and recall. 'Precision' refers to getting only relevant material. 'Recall' refers to getting all the relevant material."

Sifting through all the material available on a subject, especially in a large library with vast resources, is almost as daunting as having no information at all. While there is some truth and much humor in Roy Tennant's aphorism (2001) that librarians like to search and users like to find, a complete and calibrated answer includes both the challenge of a search and the satisfaction of a find. Fast and effective ways to vet multiple sources and create a hierarchy of utility for the user are to:

- Check the table of contents to get a quick overview of subjects included and pertinent keywords included.
- Locate keywords in the index to see if there is a long list of entries or pages on the subject.
- Skim through the preface to gauge the focus of the author.

- When available, review excerpts on book jackets may also provide a clue to the strengths of the resource.
- Past experience with certain publishers or series can be used to expound on resource choices. For example, a *Gale* encyclopedia can be expected to have glossaries, boxes highlighting interesting or important facts, enlivening illustrations, and extensive cross-references. A *DK* publication is guaranteed to have spectacular graphics. *CQ Researcher* can be relied upon to provide an unequivocal overview, chronology, statistics, and evaluative account of hard-to-find sociocultural issues.

In chat reference too, the skilled answer would require professional weighing of resources. For example, a question was asked about Turner's syndrome. The librarian was able to locate two authoritative Web sites. One was the acclaimed *Merck Manual* and the other was a special-interest national organization, the *Turner Syndrome Society*. The user wrote back to say that he or she was confused because the occurrence rates listed in the two sites were variant. Here was the librarian's assured answer: *"That's a tough call; they are both reputable sites. While the Merck is a reference book, the site for the Turner Syndrome Society may be more in touch with the actual statistics, because they deal exclusively with the condition"* (Gurzenda 2005).

Elementary Answers

There are occasions when you simply do not have the right resources or you do not have the time to provide a value-added or skilled answer.

Collaboration

- If the resources are not available, a strong system and ethic of referrals is both valid and highly useful for the user. As mentioned elsewhere in the book, keeping a list of the nearest medical, legal, and business libraries is essential to all library reference services. The areas are specialized and invariably require more in-depth research. Keeping a list of databases available in other open access libraries is also helpful. At the Harvard University Library Web site, links to catalogs far beyond the university are offered so that it is possible to check even the British Library Catalog and Germany's Karlsruhe Virtual Catalog.
- Encouraging the increasingly sophisticated system of electronic bookmarking and "blinklisting" can help when sufficient resources do not appear to be available. Traditionally, librarians have a list of "Favorites" bookmarked on reference desk computers. This tradition has carried over to roving librarians with laptop computers. However, with each computer having to be bookmarked individually, there is a pattern of irregularity in what gets bookmarked in one and forgotten in another. With innovations like "Blinklist" at www.blinklist.com, links can be stored online so that they can be accessed from any computer. A "tagging" system allows for a categorizing of the links. Yet another iteration currently gaining relevancy is "social bookmarking." Furl, Spurl, del.icio.us, and Frassle, to name a few, allow for a "finding, keeping, and sharing" of online information (Fichter 2004).

Strategizing

When there is not enough time, there are some methods that can stave off the inclination to simply not answer a user's question or to keep them waiting indefinitely.

- Ascertain whether the question can be "tabled" and answered at your convenience or whether it requires an immediate response.
- Hand over a handy introductory resource such as an encyclopedia to get the research started.
- Escort the user to the right area to browse and inform them you will be rejoining them in a certain number of minutes.

Common Pitfalls in Reference Answering

Wrong Information

The pressure to "just answer" can sometimes be overwhelming. An irate user on the telephone who wants the location and number for a gas station "right now" because she's running out of gas on some highway; the trusting teenager who asks a trivial question for which your mind draws a blank; the new coworker who is at the desk with you and looking to you for reference know-how—the world of human reference can be fraught with the pressure to "just answer." The thing to remember is "do not do it."

Anticipating the pressure and recognizing that it is part of every reference librarian's experience helps in developing a resistance to "just answering." Wrong information can range from being irksome to dangerous. Rather than just answering, compromises can always be negotiated. The highway driver can be asked to pull over to the shoulder so you can conduct a more reliable search. The teenager can be drawn into a minute of conversation as you Google the trivia. The new coworker can learn along with you as you consult with a colleague.

Inappropriate Information

A poor cousin to wrong information is inappropriate information. Heaping a researcher with resources on African American culture because of an inability to find a specific resource on Kwanzaa is counterproductive. It not only may not answer the question; it wastes the time of the researcher. In addition to librarian lassitude, a poor reference interview is usually at the root of inappropriate information. The school librarian who pulled out multiple biographies of Karl Marx even though the student had continued to expand on his need for a Marx biography as part of a book report for Black History Month could easily have established the confusion between Marx and Malcolm X. The futile medical information plied on the user who needed to research Wounded Knee is a painful product of poor reference interviews leading to inappropriate information.

Avoidance

Avoidance of difficult questions is highly unprofessional and unethical. It is usually an outcome of momentary panic in the face of a seemingly impenetrable question. A guard against falling prey to avoidance techniques is to remember a few helpful tips when faced with a panic attack.

- Develop handy referral systems both within and outside the reference area. Knowing staff special interests or aptitudes can help refer users to the right person in the event of a difficult reference question in that area.
- Keeping pathfinders, how-tos, "knowledgebases," and referral lists on intractable subjects are other tools to prevent avoidance tactics. An interesting online incarnation of this can be found in the infant blog created by Q&A NJ, the virtual reference answering service established in New Jersey. The blog, inaugurated in October 2005, aims to keep a set of handy FAQs (Frequently Asked Questions) with successful search strings for the use of librarians conducting live answering sessions.
- Establish a context for the question. Technical jargon, for example, can be intimidating on its own, but is considerably tamed when located within a subject context for which material is handy. The user looking for "Mott insulator transitions in Bose condensates" is really looking for a basic textbook on condensed matter physics.
- Attack questions from different angles. If all the books on the Reformation in sixteenth-century Europe are out, you can still help a user by providing biographies of Martin Luther.
- If a resource simply cannot be located for a query, allow yourself to play Sherlock Holmes for a moment and reasonably deduce what institution might have a vested interest in creating, organizing, or advertising such information. An overview of soybean production in Argentina, for example, would most likely be located in online sites for organizations such as the Ministry of Economy and Production for the government of Argentina or the Economic Research Service of the U.S. Department of Agriculture.
- Finally, do not allow yourself to feel that you have to know everything. If the topic is unfamiliar, get familiar with it. Ask the user for clarifying information. Or else consult a ready reference resource. Even wildly unfamiliar concepts and words can be decoded with a handy dictionary, encyclopedic entry, or a quick browse on the Internet. Having understood the word, the question no longer appears as unapproachable.

Disappearing into the stacks, as one study found (Ross and Dewdney 1998), is quite simply unthinkable.

Poor Knowledge of Resources

There is no getting away from the inevitable errors committed by not knowing the reference collection. While there is not a librarian alive who has, at some point in his or her career, forgotten a perfect resource available in their collection, it is an experience that must be avoided at all costs. The best way to minimize the margin of error is to consciously refresh familiarity with resources on an ongoing and unremitting basis. Studying a new acquisition as it is received provides a bedrock of knowledge that is both incremental and absorbed at an unhurried pace. Shelf reading, weeding, swapping stories of successful answering resources with colleagues, and testing alternate sources with hypothetical questions are all ways of getting intimate with the collection.

Lack of Follow-up

A less obvious but equally egregious error in answering reference questions is not following up after providing the resources. As mentioned in the chapter on the reference interview, user questions tend to grow roots as more research is done. It is good practice to return to the user to see if anything else is required. Even live reference usually has a preset message requiring the user to write back if "further information is required."

Inadequate Search Skills

The most powerful deterrent to the answering of complex questions, however, is an underlying sense of inadequacy in searching skills. This is easily remedied. All reference librarians can become proficient search strategists if they consciously practice the art of "searching," rather than fall into the habit of "browsing." Search skills can be practiced on three major tools of reference:

- The local library catalog;
- Electronic databases; and
- The Internet.

Given that Internet searching has sounded a dominant note in the past few decades, Chapter 13 has been devoted to the study of finding answers on the Internet. Here, it is the other two tools for which search strategies will be outlined.

The Library Catalog

As one reference veteran correctly remarked, the catalog is the "first-resort tool for identifying and locating reference works in the library and if the catalog records includes links, on the Web" (personal communication, 12/29/2005).

Catalogs in the majority of libraries use the Library of Congress Subject Headings (LCSH). A conscious recognition of the structure of authority headings goes a long way in honing the art of catalog searches. The LCSH, for example, can offer "magic searches" (Kornegay, Buchanan, and Morgan 2005) if one acknowledges the efficacy of its form subdivisions. Form subdivisions, of little value in pre-online cataloging times when author and title searches predominated, allow "librarians to combine the precision of the cataloger with the freewheeling style of a Googler" (ibid.). They do this by establishing what the material "is," rather than what it is "about." So, for example, if a user is searching for primary documents on the Revolutionary War, a search strategy that recognizes form subdivisions would look like this:

<Revolutionary War—Diaries>
OR
<Revolutionary War—Correspondence>
OR
<Revolutionary War—Sources>

By directing the search to what the material "is," namely primary documents such as diaries, correspondence, and sources, the search avoids the necessary irrelevancies associated with random topical keyword searches. It also obviates the necessity for having any prior knowledge of a controlled vocabulary, as would be required for a strict subject search where the search string would have to look like this to get the same results:

<United States—History—Revolutionary War, 1775–1783—Diaries>

While the list of form subheadings runs into the thousands, a study of actual usage found a highly skewed pattern with barely 100 subdivisions being used 90 percent of the time (O'Neill et al. 2001). It is therefore both a productive and feasible exercise for reference librarians to keep a handy list of some of the most-used form subdivisions. A selected list of twenty common LCSH form subdivisions is given below:

Common LCSH Form Subdivisions

Periodicals	Case studies
Biography	Dictionaries
Bibliography	Pictorial works
Directories	Guidebooks
Statistics	Indexes
Maps	Databases
Handbooks	Study guides
Poetry	Interviews
Fiction	Popular works
Scores	Tables

Similarly, in an effort to train new reference librarians, a list of "25 high-performance subdivisions" was created by the reference staff of the Hunter Library of Western Carolina University and reported in a study (Kornegay, Buchanan, and Morgan 2005). A lengthier list of selected subdivisions can be seen at Princeton University's reference cataloging at http://library.princeton.edu/departments/tsd/katmandu/reference/formssubdiv.html. Having a handy kit of subdivisions that anchor topical keywords to subject areas allows for a speedy and effective search of the online library catalog.

Database Searching

A bewildering array of interfaces prompts one to believe that databases are very different creatures. While the differences in databases must be acknowledged, there are some basic search patterns and strategies that prove effective, regardless of whether one is looking for images in Accunet/AP Multimedia Archive or global equity pricing in MergentOnline.

Step 1 involves identifying the research topic.

Writing out the topic either as a full sentence or as a list of concepts central to the topic is critical in establishing the framework for starting the search. Database searches can quickly derail with misleading or unnecessary keywords. Worksheets such as the one designed by the J. Paul Leonard Library at San Francisco State University and reproduced below (Figure 3-1) can be used to clarify the initial topic.

Step 2 requires identifying the appropriate database.

Database collections typically resemble a suburban mall. There are a few "big name" databases highlighted by the library, accompanied by a host of smaller or more subject-specific acquisitions. Each of these has an "About" or "Help" icon that lists the scope and focus of the collation. Combining a comprehensive "big name" database with a more specialized subject database can result in a well-balanced search. Randomly wandering through a mall of databases in search of specific information can conversely be an enervating, even fruitless, experience.

Step 3 encourages getting familiar with the search screen.

A number of major databases are subscribing to a somewhat similar form interface where the entry box for search terms is typically followed by a set of limiters. The limiters are of tremendous value and should be exploited to the fullest extent possible. Searches can be limited by date ranges, full-text availability, peer-reviewed entries, within-text searches, subject descriptors, and formats. Boolean operators such as AND/OR/NOT are also available to narrow, broaden, or eliminate unnecessary terms in a search string. Other standard search tools such as proximity operators, truncations, wildcards, and plurals are also part of the database search-polishing arsenal. A key describing what polishing tools can be found in any given database is always included. Sometimes the tools are nested within an "Advanced Search" button, and are invariably preferable to the "Basic Search" for all but the most trivial searches. Below is an example of the form interface for an innovative database of 351,029 open access e-prints (Figure 3-2).

Step 4 urges a search that goes beyond keywords.

If keyword searches using the advanced limiters do not produce the desired results, be prepared to step up to a higher level of search strategizing, as can be seen in the "Hints for More Fulfilling Searches" (p. 47). Refer to the controlled vocabulary inherent to each database. This can be done by consulting the thesaurus attached to most databases, or by retrieving the subject descriptors listed in every individual record. Most thesauri list terms with broader, narrower, and related terms as well. These can be methodically used to dredge up more accurate material. Alternately, the same results can be achieved by retrieving subject headings listed in an initial search entry. Many of these headings are linked and allow for a one-click entry to new descriptors.

Step 5 pulls together the search results into an organized whole.

Having conducted a successful search, it is important to remember that database results, unlike print material, disappear unless immediately organized. The results can

Database Search Strategy Worksheet

Name_____ Date_____ Reference Librarian_____

Please fill out this form to help the Reference Librarians assist you in determining the best databases and search strategy for your topic.

I. State your research topic (in complete sentence).
Example: How has the relationship between Blacks and Jews historically been portrayed in the popular media?

II. List any limitations such as language, period of time, periodical title, etc.

III. Concept terms you think might be useful in searching your topic.
Use another sheet of paper if your search has more than three concepts.
Note: Terms within the same columns are connected by the Boolean operator "OR" and are called a "set." Sets are connected by the operator "AND."
Sources for relevant terms:
  • natural language; that is, familiar words you know
  • database thesaurus (see if one is available for the specific database you are using)
  • subject headings & descriptors in relevant citations records you find
  • terms from encyclopedias, textbooks, coursework, etc.

Concept 1	Concept 2	Concept 3	
Example: Blacks African Americans Afro-Americans Negroes	Jews Jewish	Mass Media Radio Film Newspapers	Broadcasting Television Movies

                        AND   AND

Search statement example: (black* or African American*) and Jew* and (mass media or broadcast* or televis* or film*)

The asterisk (*) symbol in this statement is used to truncate. Truncation symbols vary among databases. Look in the database help sections to find which symbol is used.

San Francisco State University • J. Paul Leonard Library • www.library.sfsu.edu

Figure 3-1 Database Search Strategy Worksheet

CORNELL UNIVERSITY LIBRARY

Search for [＿＿＿＿] In [All papers ▼] [Go!]
(Help | Advanced search)

Search arXiv.org

No query specified

Author/title/abstract search

Select subject areas to search

☐ Computer Science ☐ Mathematics ☐ Nonlinear Sciences ☑ Physics

[archive: [All ▼]] ☐ Quantitative Biology

Select years to search (default is to search all years)

☐ Past year or the year [＿＿＿] or the years from [＿＿＿] to [＿＿＿]

Author(s): ▼	[＿＿＿＿＿＿＿＿＿]	AND ▼
Title: ▼	[＿＿＿＿＿＿＿＿＿]	AND ▼
Abstract: ▼		

Show [25 ▼] hits per page

[Do Search] or [Reset] selections to default values.

Hints for more fulfilling searches

Experimental full text search

Search for: [＿＿＿＿＿＿＿＿＿] in [Physics ▼] [Do Search]

The full text search facility is an experimental service which may be less up-to-date than the normal search. See full text search help for details (the query syntax is different from that described below for the normal search).

Figure 3-2 Database Search Strategy Worksheet (continued)

Hints for More Fulfilling Searches

Boolean Operators

"AND," "AND NOT," and "OR"

Metacharacters

The bad news: In general, punctuation and other non-alphanumeric characters are not indexed and cannot currently be searched for. Currently some interesting characters like (,), and = are not searchable. Regrettably, this means that one cannot search for SU(3) or c = 1 at this time (but searching for "c" AND "1" will give hits on "c = 1").
The good news: The characters ^, _, {, }, +, and – are indexed. For example, searching for K^+ or nu_e will work—be aware that authors are not always consistent in how superscripts and subscripts are presented.
Non-indexed characters are stripped out from the search query.

Stemming

Most fields stem words automatically (searching for superconductors will match superconducting).

Wildcard truncation

Wildcard "*" can be used anywhere but at the beginning of a term (but see author examples below).

Grouping

Grouping can be done with parentheses.
Binary Booleans are not associative—parentheses are mandatory if a field has multiple Booleans.
First two fields are grouped together in form before the third field is added in.

Exact phrases

Use double quotes (")—Warning: can be slow (try AND instead).

Hyphenated terms

Hyphens have been removed from most phrases (domain-wall becomes domain wall). This is because use of hyphens is often inconsistent.
Hyphens have not been removed from e-print archive names, nor have they been removed when it would result in a single letter being left over: c-theorem remains hyphenated and is searchable.
Try searching for domain AND wall or for "domain wall." The latter is more accurate, but can be much slower than the former.

Figure 3-2 (continued)

Example author searches

- T Bhattacharya
- T Bhattacharya AND NOT (S R Sharpe OR Rajan Gupta)
- "Bhatta*" is okay, but "T Bhatta*" will not work (initials and "*" cannot be used together).

Example journal references

"Phys Rev Lett"

Year searches

"Past Year" overrides individual years.

Subject Classes

Covers Subj-class, ACM-class, and MSC-class.

Figure 3-2 (continued)

be printed so that a hard copy is available. They can be saved on diskette, CD-ROM, or flash drives or exported directly into software such as EndNote or RefWorks. Students and staff at Yale University, for example, have open access to import citations into Ref-Works. Alternately, the results can be e-mailed, a welcome management addition for users who do not have the immediate means to print hard copies, and for research collaborators alerting members to pertinent research. The results can also be tagged as the search is being conducted. This is particularly useful when an introductory or overview of a research field is conducted and a large number of entries are being scanned for possible relevance.

However careful the original search strategy, it is vital to keep in mind that the strategy has to be constantly revisited and redefined as the research process continues. New subject descriptors suggest different tacks to the same topic. Indexed terms are certainly not graven in stone, and "related" terms can vary quite noticeably between databases. Searches may also have to be repeated over time since there can be significant time lags. As the University of Glasgow library Web site has noted, "MEDLINE gives priority to American titles and is notoriously slow to index non-U.S. specialty journals such as the British Journal of General Practice" (www.lib.gla.ac.uk/Docs/Guides/searching.html, accessed on 1/3/2006).

With the ongoing development of federated searching and open URL link resolvers that allow a single query interface to trawl across multiple databases, the future trend of database searching appears to be striving for increased search-friendliness. *Kids Search, Power Search, Metafind, Serials Solutions Article Linker, Muse Global Muse Search,* and *Innovative Interfaces Web Bridge* are just some of the innovations that "offer a bridge between the reluctant searcher and the wealth of information in library databases" (Curtis and Dorner 2005, 35).

Raison d'être

Finding answers is what we do as reference librarians. All of our skills in collection development, format management, and reference interviewing find their full flowering in the effective answering of user questions. It is quite simply our raison d'être.

Clarity in establishing the processes that go into the making of an answering strategy is a good thing. Deconstructing the process can appear as a slow-motion take that confirms and validates what the experienced reference librarian is doing almost instinctively. Or it can provide an instructive framework to condition and hone the librarian's techniques in answering queries of wildly different provenance. Either way, it aims to emphasize the pedagogical aspects of search strategies and the answering process.

Recommendations for Further Reading

Duckett, Bob, Peter Walker, and Christinea Donnelley. 2004. *Know It All, Find It Fast: An A-Z Source Guide for the Enquiry Desk.* 2nd edition. London: Facet. Cross-referenced and comprehensive, this book is a helpful guide for reference librarians confronted with unfamiliar enquiries.

Eurodesk. Available at www.eurodesk.org:8080/edesk/Supportcentre.do?go = 17, this Web site is an example of an answering process set up on *"How to answer European questions."* Designed for *Eurodesk*, an online support site for professionals working with young people in the European region, the site also gives examples of successfully answered questions that followed the process.

"The Exchange." A one-time regular column in *RQ/Reference and User Services Quarterly*, "The Exchange" is an interesting way to study the asking and answering of tricky reference questions, some of which were never answered. The compilation of questions and answers is available to RUSA (Reference and User Services Association) members at www.ala.org.

National Health Service (NHS). Sponsored by the NHS, a national British pharmacy service available online at www.ukmi.nhs.uk, aims to provide collaborative and evidence-based information on medicines and supplies an interactive template for "standard search patterns" such as one for drug interactions. Templates such as these can be useful for searches that are repeated often. In academic libraries, subject specific templates can be developed based on curricula. In public libraries, genealogy searches, relative car prices, personal finance resources, doctor information, and researching a house, are some general areas that one can find ready answers with prepared pathfinders.

Project Wombat. Since 1992, *Stumpers-L* was a popular reference listserv where librarians could post challenging questions that had "stumped" them. As of January 2006, Project Gutenberg hosted the new version of the listserv, known as *Project Wombat*, named after the mascot of the earlier listserv. Available at http://project-wombat.org, the list has various levels of subscription so that the user can choose between unmoderated and filtered lists.

Bibliography of Works Cited in this Chapter

Curtis, AnneMarie, and Daniel G. Dorner. 2005. "Why Federated Search?" *Knowledge Quest* 33, no. 3 (January/February): 35–37.

Fichter, Darlene. 2004. "Tools For Finding Things Again." *Online* 28, no. 5 (September/October): 52–56.

Fisher, Karen, Sanda Erdelez, and Lynne McKechnie, eds. *Theories of Information Behavior.* Medford, NJ: Information Today, Inc.

Gross, Melissa. 2001. "Imposed Information Seeking in Public Libraries and School Library Media Centers: A Common Behaviour?" *Information Research* 6, no. 2 (January).

Gurzenda, Mary-Jean. 2005. Q&A NJ live reference of April 26.

Hacker, Diana. 2006. *Research and Documentation in the Electronic Age.* Boston, MA: Bedford/St. Martins.

Janes, Joseph. 2003. *Introduction to Reference Work in the Digital Age.* New York: Neal-Schuman.

Kent, Jack. 2005. "The Firefly." *Cricket* 32, no. 11 (July): 4.

Kluegel, Kathleen M. 2001. "Electronic Resources for Reference." In *Reference and Information Services*, 3rd ed., edited by Richard E. Bopp and Linda C. Smith, 97–124. Englewood, CO: Libraries Unlimited.

Kornegay, Becky, Heidi Buchanan, and Hiddy Morgan. 2005. "Amazing, Magic Searches." *Library Journal* 130, no. 18 (November): 44–46.

O'Neill, Edward T. O., Lois Mai Chan, Eric Childress, Rebecca Dean, Lynn M. El-Hoshy, and Diane Vizine-Goetz. 2001. "Form Subdivisions: Their Identification and Use in LCSH." *Library Resources & Technical Services* 45, 4: 187–197.

Owen, Tim Buckley. 2003. *Success at the Enquiry Desk: Successful Enquiry Answering—Every Time.* London: Facet Publishing.

Ross, Catherine Sheldrick, and Patricia Dewdney. 1998. "Negative Closure: Strategies and Counter-Strategies in the Reference Transaction." *Reference and User Services Quarterly* 38, no. 42 (Winter): 151–163.

Saxton, Matthew L., and John Richardson. 2002. *Understanding Reference Transactions.* Boston, MA: Academic Press.

Tennant, Roy. 2001. "Avoiding Unintended Consequences." *Library Journal* 126, no. 1 (January 1): 38.

Williams, Sinead. 2002. "Teaming for Research Excellence." *Online* (November/December): 31–35.

Part 2
Introduction to Major Reference Sources

4

Answering Questions about Books, Magazines, Newspapers, Libraries, Publishers, and Bibliographic Networks—Bibliographic Resources

Overview

Bibliographic resources answer questions about books, magazines, newspapers, libraries, and publishing. With these resources in hand, the librarian can answer questions about everything from recently published novels to back issues of obscure academic journals. Many requests of this kind arise from the need of users to verify citation information for texts that they have previously consulted. Bibliographic resources can also assist in such tasks as finding a copy of a book published at the end of the eighteenth century or copies of a nineteenth-century magazine. Further, they can help users find libraries with special collections and publishers who publish books in a specific subject area. In this chapter the reader will be introduced to the questions that call for these resources and the ideal means of answering them.

Bibliographies are essentially lists of books or other materials that can be organized by author, title, or subject. They record pertinent information about each item listed, including its author, title, edition, place of publication, publisher, and date of publication. The particulars of a bibliography's organizational structure inform and delimit the ways it can be used. For example, the bibliographic information may differ depending on whether the information is meant to facilitate verification of the title, location of a specific copy, or purchase of an in-print book. Bibliographies may be comprehensive—attempting to include everything within the scope of the bibliography—or selective. Some bibliographies are current and are regularly updated. Others are no longer published and record the existence of materials at a particular time and place. These bibliographies are referred to as retrospective. In the future most bibliographies will be compiled in an electronic format, making them easier to produce, more flexible to search, and easier to keep current.

Bibliographies have a long and distinguished history. Even before the rise of print, records were kept of written materials. As early as the seventh century B.C. the Library of Sennacherib at Nineveh kept a list of clay tablets. (Harmon, 1989: 16) In the 14th century we find a catalog compiled by Franciscan monks, *Registrum librorum Angliciae*, that listed manuscripts in over 180 English monasteries (Harmon 1989, 17). One of the first bibliographies to be printed was a bibliography of ecclesiastical writers in chronological order compiled by Johann Triheim, abbot of Spanheim, and published in 1494 (Stokes 2003). Trade bibliographies began to be published with the invention of the printing press in the fifteenth century, as the need to make the public aware of new publications arose. In 1545 Conrad Gesner published *Bibliotheca Universalis*, a universal bibliography that listed 12,000 books arranged by the author's name, followed by an *Appendix* in 1555 with 3,000 additional works (Macles 1961). Libraries began to print catalogs of their collections in the eighteenth century, including Leyden (1710), Oxford (1738), and Bibliotheque Royale (1743) (Harmon 1989, 21). Scholars have compiled bibliographies either to record all books published in a single location or a single country, or a complete or selective list of books published on a certain topic, or a list of the works written by one author. These bibliographies have enabled librarians and scholars to know what books have been published and often where they can be found.

How Bibliographies Are Used

Bibliographies are used to:

- Identify or verify information;
- Locate materials;
- Select materials for the collection.

A bibliography can be used to identify or verify information about a book or other type of material. For example, there may be two books with the same title. The bibliographic record, which includes the author, title, publisher, date of publication, and other useful information, may help to distinguish one from the other; the date of publication or the place of publication may be a guide as to which book it is. A listing of books by date or by country can be used to verify the existence of a book. The *National Union Catalog* is an example of a bibliography used to both verify and locate books and other materials. In this case it lists materials held by the Library of Congress and by the many participating libraries. Bibliographies can also provide information for collection development by identifying new or retrospective titles on a certain subject. A library trying to build a new collection in a certain subject area may find bibliographies useful.

Questions Answered by Bibliographies

- Where can I find the author of the book *The Rise and Fall of the Great Powers*?
  If this book is still in print, the answer can be found in *Books in Print*. Otherwise, it could be found in a library catalog.
- Where is the periodical *Reference and User Services Quarterly* indexed?
  This information can be found in a directory of periodicals such as *Ulrich's International Periodicals Directory*.

- What publishers might be interested in publishing my book on child care?
  The directory *LMP* is one source of information on this topic.
- Are there any academic libraries in Portland, Maine?
  The *American Library Directory* is a good source for this information.

Major Bibliographies Used in Reference Work

There are several types of bibliographies:

- Enumerative;
- Analytical or critical;
- Descriptive; and
- Textual.

Type	Description	Example
Enumerative	Listing with bibliographic information	*Books in Print*
Analytical	Physical description of book	Harvard College Library. *Catalogue of Books and Manuscripts. Pt. I, French Sixteenth Century Books* and *Pt. II, Italian Sixteenth Century Books*
Descriptive	Full physical description of book	Greg, Walter. *A Bibliography of the English Printed Drama to the Restoration*
Textual	Relationship between printed text and text as conceived by the author	Pollard, A. W. *Shakespeare Folios and Quartos: a Study in the Bibliography of Shakespeare's Plays, 1594–1685*

Most bibliographies with which the librarian comes in contact are enumerative bibliographies. These are listings of books with their bibliographic information, that is, author, title, publisher, date of publication, number of pages, ISBN, etc. National bibliographies such as the *National Union Catalog* and trade bibliographies such as *Books in Print* are examples of enumerative bibliographies.

Analytical or critical bibliographies are bibliographies that provide a physical description of the book, including the details of the book's manufacture and its history (Stokes 2003). "Descriptive bibliographies are listings that provide full physical descriptions of the book or other materials they list, enabling us to tell one edition from another, and to identify significant variations within a single edition" (Harmon 1989, 82). Textual bibliographies are bibliographies that "study the relationship between the printed text and the text as conceived by the author. . . . In essence it deals with the study and comparison of texts and their transmissions through different printings and editions" (Harmon 1989, 4). It has a close relationship to literary studies (Stokes 1982).

Trade Bibliographies

Trade bibliographies are enumerative bibliographies usually produced commercially by the publishers and booksellers in a country to provide information on what is in print, what is out of print, and what will be published. The primary purpose of a trade bibliography is to provide information as to what materials are available for purchase. The materials listed are supplied by the publishers. For this reason, price, publisher, and ISBN are listed. The ISBN (International Standard Book Number) is a system that allows each book published to have a distinctive number. The number includes a country code, a publisher identifier, a title identifier, and a checkdigit. The materials listed have not been examined by the publisher compiling the information.

A trade bibliography can also answer questions such as: Is this book still in print? What books by a certain author are still in print? What books on a specific subject are still in print?

Books in Print is a comprehensive trade bibliography for books published or distributed in the United States including 1,868,000 active titles. It is available in print in an eight-volume work (five volumes by title, three volumes by author. An additional volume lists information about publishers). *Books in Print Supplement* is published in the middle of the year to update *Books in Print*. *Subject Books in Print* (a seven-volume set) is a companion work listing books in print by subject. *Forthcoming Books*, published three times a year, lists upcoming book releases. *Books in Print* is also available online through Bowker as well as through other online vendors. The online version combines in-print, out-of-print, and forthcoming titles, offering five million titles including audio and video titles, and features 140,000 tables of contents and 700,000 reviews of titles. *BookInPrint.com Professional*, the online version designed for librarians and booksellers, provides the option to check the availability of a title at selected distributors and to download bibliographic records. *PatronBooksInPrint.com* is the version designed for users. Special features for users include lists of bestsellers, book awards, and the ability to search by genre and character. *BooksOutofPrint.com* simply lists books not in print. *GlobalBooksinPrint.com* lists nine million English and Spanish language titles published in the U.S., UK, Canada, Australia, South Africa, and New Zealand. This is a useful tool in a library that needs to buy or locate materials outside the United States. *Whitaker's Books in Print* is the British equivalent of *Books in Print*, listing titles published in the UK as well as English language titles published in continental Europe. Authors, titles, and catchwords are listed in a single alphabetical sequence. *Canadian Books in Print* provides the same information for Canadian monographs.

Subject Bibliographies

Subject bibliographies are compiled to provide comprehensive or selective coverage of material on one subject. These bibliographies can be particularly useful in identifying retrospective material on a subject rather than beginning from scratch. Subject bibliographies can be current or retrospective, annotated or not annotated. They may be a book in themselves or printed in a magazine or journal.

Library Catalogs and Union Catalogs

Access to library catalogs online have made it easier to both identify and locate books, magazines, newspapers, manuscripts, maps, audio-visual materials, and other materials. In addition to its own catalog, the Library of Congress has an extensive list of online library catalogs on its Web site. The New York Public Library's online catalog CATNYP is available at www.nypl.org. This is another extensive database that includes U.S. and international titles.

When a catalog lists the records of several libraries, it becomes a union catalog. Many library consortia have union catalogs to make it easier for their members to identify and locate library materials.

National Catalogs and Bibliographies

National bibliographies provide listings of materials that are published in a particular country and often include materials received through the legal deposit. Each book or other material listed has been examined and cataloged, thus providing a high degree of accuracy. A national bibliography can answer the following questions: What books has a specific author written? What books are there on a particular subject? Who owns the following title?

The United States

Although there is no official national library in the United States, the Library of Congress serves many of the functions of a national library. There is no legal deposit requirement that all published materials must be deposited in a national institution (often the national library), and it is not needed for copyright protection. However, since 1976 copies of published works must be deposited at the Copyright Office at the Library of Congress, but "not all works deposited are selected for inclusion in the collections of the Library of Congress" (Balay 1996, 48). Because of this, all items published in the United States are not available in one location.

The National Union Catalog

The National Union Catalog (NUC) can be used to find a comprehensive listing of the writings of an author, to search by subject, to verify the existence of a particular work, to locate a book or other materials at the Library of Congress or one of the participating libraries, and to obtain cataloging information.

The National Union Catalog began as the card catalog of the Library of Congress in 1901. The first printed catalog was produced in 1942. In 1956 the NUC added the collections of other libraries to the NUC book catalog using Machine Readable Cataloging records. From 1968 to 1981 the pre-1956 card catalog was published as *The National Union Catalog: Pre-1956 Imprints*. This was published in both print and microfilm, called REMARC records. Today the NUC is available free through the Library of Congress at catalog.loc.gov (only books cataloged by the Library of Congress are included) and for a fee on the bibliographic networks, OCLC and RLIN. It includes books, maps, music, serials, and visual materials. The Library of Congress itself has a collection of 100 million items that includes 15 million books, 39 million manuscripts, 13 million photographs, 4 million maps, 3.5 million pieces of music, and 500,000 motion pictures.

The United Kingdom

In the United Kingdom the *British National Bibliography* has recorded new books and serial titles since 1950. "The BNB is the single most comprehensive listing of UK titles. UK and Irish publishers are obliged by law to send a copy of all new publications, including serial titles, to the Legal Deposit Office of the British Library. . . . The BNB is available as a weekly MARC Exchange File, a weekly printed publication and as a monthly CD-ROM" (www.bl.uk/services/bibliographic.htm). The *General Catalogue of Printed Books to 1975* and supplements to 1998 are available in print and are based on the country's legal deposit. This *Catalogue* is now part of the British Library Integrated Catalogue (http://catalogue.bl.uk).

Canada

In Canada the Library and Archives Canada (LAC) maintains AMICUS, an online catalog, and has published *Canadiana*, Canada's National Bibliography, since 1951. It "lists and describes a wide variety of publications produced in Canada, or published elsewhere but of special interest or significance to Canada" (www.collectionscanada.ca/canadiana/index-e.html). Among the publications included are books, periodicals, sound recordings, video recordings, government documents, and electronic documents. "*Canadiana* provides standard cataloguing information for each item listed . . . and lists information on forthcoming publications." *Canadiana* is available on CD-ROM and as an online service.

Periodicals and Newspapers

Libraries receive many questions about magazines and newspapers. For example, where is a magazine published? Where is this journal indexed? What is the subscription price of this magazine? When did the journal begin? How much does it cost to advertise in this magazine or newspaper?

One of the top sources for information about current domestic and international magazines, journals, and newspapers is *Ulrich's International Periodicals Directory*, which lists over 250,000 domestic and foreign serial publications including magazines, journals, newspapers, irregular serials, and online serials. *Ulrich's* provides bibliographic information about each title including address, subscriber information, a brief description of the serial, where the serial is indexed, whether the serial is available online, and the history of the serial as well as the ISSN. (The ISSN, like the ISBN, provides a way to distinguish similar titles from each other.) A listing of online databases is also included. The print version is a five-volume work arranged by subject. The online version, *Ulrichsweb.com*, includes open-access journals, *Magazines for Libraries*, and *Irregular Serials and Annuals*. *Magazines for Libraries*, 13th edition, is a source of recommendations for periodicals. Arranged by subject, it describes each magazine, evaluates it, and recommends what kind of libraries might want to purchase this magazine. There are more than 6,850 magazines and databases reviewed. Title and subject indexes are included.

Although *Ulrich's* is often the first choice of librarians for information on magazines and newspapers, there are several other directories that provide similar information or supplement it. The *Serials Directory*, published by EBSCO, a company that is also a periodicals subscription vendor, lists over 178,500 magazines and newspapers and is also available online. It is quite similar to *Ulrich's*, covering about the same number of titles and also arranged by subject. The *Standard Periodical Directory* is a smaller directory of periodicals listing 75,000 U.S. and Canadian newspapers and periodicals. It is published every two years and is known for listing many house organs and trade publications not listed elsewhere. The *International Directory of Little Magazines and Small Presses* is a source of information about little magazines and presses that may or may not get listed in the standard directories. Each magazine or press is described in nonevaluative terms. Subscription information is also provided.

As the number of electronic journals increases, users and librarians need to know what journals are available electronically, their subscription price, and whether they are available in full text as part of a database. The *Gale Directory of Databases*, a listing of databases, CD-ROMs, database producers, and online services, is available in print and online. This reference work pulls together current information on databases. For example, the librarian can find out what databases are available from the H. W. Wilson Company or from Ebsco. The librarian can also find out how to contact the publisher of the database. There are a number of other publications that help librarians and users to sort out the information on journals that are available electronically. *BooksandPeriodicals.com* lists publications that can be searched electronically through information providers such as Gale and Proquest. It has grown into four directories totaling five volumes covering law, business, and news; science and technology; medical and pharmaceutical; and humanities and religion. Searching of these directories can be by title, ISSN, subject, or keyword. "Each directory is arranged alphabetically by title and includes the publication title, the database(s) that index its articles, date of coverage and whether articles are offered in full text, abstract or bibliographic citation" (BooksandPeriodicals.com). *NewJour* (http://gort.ucsd.edu/newjour) is a free listing of all journals and newspapers available electronically. Users of the list are encouraged to send in new titles to add to the list. *Fulltext Sources Online*, edited by Mary B. Glose, Lara Fletcher, and Jennifer Fasolina, is "a biannual directory of periodicals accessible online in full text through over 28 aggregator producers" (2005). *Gale Directory of Publications and Broadcast Media* is both an online and print publication listing periodicals and newspapers as well as radio and television stations. This directory provides subscription rates, circulation, key staff, and advertising rates for both publications and media. It is organized geographically with subdivisions under a city for magazines, newspapers, radio, and TV, and also includes a subject index. Earlier compilations of serial titles and their locations were recorded in two volumes that serve as a way to verify and locate serial titles that have been in existence for a long period of time or were being published before 1999. They are *Union List of Serials in the U.S. and Canada before 1950*, which ends in 1949, and *New Serials Titles* that continued the *Union List of Serials* and ceased publication in 1999.

U.S. Retrospective Bibliography

A series of bibliographies make up U.S. retrospective bibliography. These bibliographies are useful for establishing the existence and sometimes the location of books published before the twentieth century. For many scholars doing research on the history of the United States and the work of early authors and scholars, these bibliographies are a necessary part of their work. Charles Evans, a librarian, compiled *American Bibliography: A Chronological Dictionary of All Books, Pamphlets and Periodical Publications Printed in the United States from the Genesis of Printing in 1639 Down to and Including the Year 1800.* "The most important general list of early American publications, . . . [it] includes books, pamphlets and periodicals, arranged chronologically by dates of publication. [It] gives for each book author's full name with dates of birth and death, full title, place, date, publisher or printer, paging, size and, whenever possible, location of copies in American libraries" (Balay 1996, 45). In each volume there are indexes by author, subject, and printers and publishers. An author-title index to the whole set was published in 1959. It is now available in a digitized format with full text of the materials listed as *Early American Imprints, Series I. Evans (1639–1800).*

Ralph R. Shaw and Richard H. Shoemaker continued the Evans bibliography with *American Bibliography: A Preliminary Checklist for 1801–1819.* This bibliography was intended to fill the gap between the end of Evans and the beginning of Roorbach in 1820. Shaw and Shoemaker also include library locations. It was followed by Richard H. Shoemaker's *A Checklist of American Imprints for 1820–1829* and *A Checklist of American Imprints for 1830–1846.* This is also available on microform and online.

Orville Roorbach, a bookseller, published *Bibliotheca Americana: 1820–1861.* This "trade catalog of American publications, including reprints" was intended for use by booksellers (Balay 1996, 46). The four volumes are arranged alphabetically by author and title providing the publisher and sometimes the date of publication. Though incomplete and sometimes inaccurate, it is all we have for this period. James Kelly compiled The *American Catalogue of Books . . . January 1861 to January 1871*, picking up where Roorbach ended. It is also a trade bibliography providing similar information to Roorback (Balay 1996, 46). It is arranged alphabetically by author and title.

Joseph Sabin's *A Dictionary of Books Relating to America from Its Discovery to the Present Time* lists books, pamphlets, and periodicals published in the Western Hemisphere and elsewhere with locations. It was published in 1936 having been finished by others. Arranged by author, each entry includes title, place, publisher, date, format, paging, and often information about the contents (Balay 1996, 45). John Edgar Molnar published an author-title index to Joseph Sabin's *Dictionary of Books Relating to America* in 1974. Sabin is now being digitized by Gale.

American Book Publishing Record Cumulative 1876–1949 and *1950–1977* are early Bowker publications arranged by Dewey number with author and title indexes, with separate volumes for fiction and juvenile fiction. They document books published during this period.

American Catalogue of Books 1876–1910 was both a national and trade bibliography. The first volume lists the books under author and title and the second volume by subject. It "aims to include, with certain exceptions, all books published in the U.S. which were for sale to the general public" (Balay 1996, 46).

U.S. Catalog is an in-print list published by H. W. Wilson from 1899–1928. This was followed by *Cumulative Book Index,* subtitled "A world list of books in the English language," which was published by H. W. Wilson from 1928–1999. Each volume is a listing of works published in English anywhere in the world during that time period. Authors, titles, and subjects are arranged in one alphabet.

Nonprint Materials

The nonprint equivalent to *Books in Print* simply does not exist. Librarians trying to identify, verify, and often order DVDs, CDs, videos, and audio tapes must search a series of sources in order to locate the information they need. *Video Source Book* provides information on a wide range of videos from children's features to documentaries to straight-to-video movies. The videos are arranged alphabetically by title and the list includes a detailed description. Six indexes are also available including subject, awards, and distributors. The *Internet Movie Database* (IMDb.com), now owned by Amazon.com, is a large online movie (feature film) database begun about 1990. For each movie the database provides the name of the director, the writing credits, the characters in the movie, the running time, and user comments. It also indicates the formats available (VHS, DVD) in the United States, the UK, Canada, and Germany. For educational, documentary, instructional and independent productions there is the *NICEM Film and Video FinderOnline,* which is available by subscription. This database covers over 640,000 items including films, videocassettes, CD-ROMs, and audiocassettes. *Bowker's Complete Video Directory* lists 250,000 videos in four volumes with basic information needed in order to locate the titles. In addition to VHS listings, it lists Beta, ¾", U-matic, 8mm, and laser disc formats. This reference work includes educational and special-interest videos as well as entertainment videos. *Books Out Loud: Bowker's Guide to Audiobooks* (formerly *Words on Cassette*) provides bibliographic information on spoken word audiobooks, both cassettes and CDs, including a content summary and an author/reader/performer index.

Bibliographies of Bibliographies

Theodore Besterman's *A World Bibliography of Bibliographies* is an international bibliography arranged by subject. It was concluded in 1963. Over 115,000 bibliographies in forty languages are listed. Alice F. Toomy produced a supplementary volume that spanned 1964–1974. For more recent works, the *Bibliographic Index Plus* is a subject index to bibliographies published in books, pamphlets, and periodicals. Two thousand and eight hundred periodicals are indexed with full-text bibliographies from 1,700 journals. It is available both online and in print.

Publishing and Libraries

Questions about publishing and libraries come from the public and from librarians themselves. The library users often want basic information about a publisher, its location, and what types of material it publishes. They are often looking for a publisher to publish a book they plan to write. *Publishers, Distributors and Wholesalers of the United States* is available online and in print. The list of publishers is extensive, including small press and audiovisual publishers. Updated annually, it provides information on publishing companies, distributors, and wholesalers in one alphabet. With 140,670 entries it can help the user find information on the fields of activity, trade imprints, and subsidiaries.

The *American Book Trade Directory* lists over 30,000 retail book dealers, wholesalers, and book trade associations in the United States and Canada in a geographical arrangement. Librarians can use this directory to locate subject specialists, distributors of hard-to-find books and other materials, retail stores for specialized materials including books in languages other than English, and library collection appraisers.

Bowker Annual Library and Book Trade Almanac is available in print. It provides reports on national and international library and book trade issues and news. The latest statistics ranging from the number of books published by subject to the average prices are included.

Literary Market Place: The Directory of the American Book Publishing Industry, an annual publication available in print and online, provides information on every aspect of the publishing business including publishers, what kinds of material they publish, and key personnel and related areas such as literary agents, translators, book fairs, printers, and manufacturers. This is a very useful reference work for authors and others working in the publishing industry.

American Library Directory, an annual publication available online and in print, is arranged by state and then by city and provides information and statistics about each library in that city, including special collections and key personnel.

World Guide to Libraries lists more than 450 institutions in 181 countries. This work is arranged by continent and country and then by type of library. All essential information about each library is listed including address, telephone, fax, e-mail, collections, and statistics.

Directory of Special Libraries and Information Centers covers thousands of special libraries and information centers. Volume 1 provides information on subject-specific resource collections maintained by business, education, and nonprofit organization, government, etc. There are international listings as well as North America. Volume 2 provides geographical and personnel indexes.

Bibliographic Control

Bibliographic control is the process of organizing pieces of information about books and other material so that they can be identified and located. Bibliographies perform this function of bibliographic control by organizing material by author, title, and subject so that it can be identified and then by identifying the location so that the material can be accessed. The best example of bibliographic control is the library catalog—either in card format or online. Cataloging each item in a library collection provides the means to retrieve each item in a variety of ways. Cataloging also provides consistency so that the same form of an author's name or a title is used each time and a standard set of subject headings is used.

The three elements that have made possible bibliographic control on an international level are Machine Readable Cataloging (MARC) records, the International Standard Bibliographic Description (ISBD) and Anglo American Cataloging Rules (AACR2) (Gorman 2001). MARC records were developed by the Library of Congress and have been used since 1968. "MARC is the way we encode the results of the cataloging process" (Gorman 2001, 3). The structure of the MARC record has made it possible to standardize the format of the data for each item cataloged. The ISBD "was seen . . . as a means of standardizing the presentation of descriptive data so that it could be machine-translated into MARC" (Gorman 2001, 2). Finally the AACR2 was an effort to "bring uniformity to cataloguing practice in the English-speaking world" (Gorman 2001, 2). The standardization has resulted in all permutations of a name being linked and a standard list of subject headings controlled by a thesaurus for consistency.

Verification and access are the results of bibliographic control. The more comprehensively an item is indexed the more accessible it will be since it can be searched from more access points.

In addition to individual library catalogs, there are also union catalogs that combine the catalogs of several libraries and make it possible to search for information and locations across several catalogs at one time. Bibliographic utilities also help the librarian to identify and locate books and other materials. The two most noteworthy of these bibliographic utilities are OCLC (Online Computer Library Center) and RLG (Research Library Group). OCLC is a nonprofit membership organization with over 50,000 member libraries from eighty-four countries. Libraries use OCLC to locate, acquire, catalog, and borrow library materials. WorldCat, its union catalog, provides access to "nearly 900 million pieces of information about who holds what and where" (www.oclc.org/membership). RLG is also a nonprofit organization with a membership of over 150 research libraries, archives, museums, and other institutions. RLG also provides an online union catalog, Eureka, listing the holdings of its member institutions (www.rlg.org). The presence of these bibliographic utilities has increased the standardization of cataloging and has greatly improved access to books and other materials.

Collection Development and Maintenance

Selection and Keeping Current

Librarians can turn to several sources to identify bibliographies. The primary source is Robert Balay's *Guide to Reference Books*. This is an excellent guide to mostly U.S. reference materials by subject. A new online edition is expected shortly. On a yearly basis *American Reference Books Annual* provides a comprehensive annotated list of reference books published in a specific year in the United States and Canada. It is available in print and online.

The British equivalent of Balay is *The New Walford Guide to Reference Resources*, a three-volume work that is constantly revised, and *Canadian Reference Source: An Annotated*

Bibliography, compiled by Mary Bond and Martine Caron, which covers reference, history, and the humanities but not social sciences or science and technology. These fields are covered by *Science and Technology in Canadian History: A Bibliographic Database* (http://acsweb2.ucis.dal.ca/slis/main.htm).

Evaluating Bibliographic Resources

The basic criteria for evaluating any type of materials also apply to bibliographies. They include accuracy, authority, scope, arrangement, methodology, bibliographical content, and currency.

- Accuracy is the most important criterion for bibliographies. Since bibliographies are used to verify information about a book or other type of material and often to locate it, the accuracy of the information is of the utmost importance. Each unit of the bibliographic record must be correct.
- The authority of the compiler and publisher helps the librarian or user to evaluate the credibility of the work.
- The scope can make a big difference, particularly in subject bibliographies. The librarian will want to know whether a subject bibliography covers the same ground as another bibliography or covers different dates or different types of material. The preface or introduction to the bibliography often describes the scope of the bibliography.
- The arrangement can make the bibliography easier or more difficult to use. How is the main body of the bibliography arranged—by author, title, subject, date, geography, etc.? And what indexes are provided to have alternative ways to access the material?
- The introduction of a bibliography usually describes both the scope and the methodology of the work. For example, it is important to know if the compiler examined each work listed in the bibliography. If not, the bibliography may not be very useful since listing items not examined usually produces some errors.
- Bibliographical content should be examined to see if the bibliographical entries include enough information to help the user to verify the titles and to proceed to locate them.
- A bibliography should be current within the boundaries of the work. The dates and material it covers should be inclusive unless otherwise stated.

Further Considerations

As one searches for bibliographic information for books, periodicals, or nonprint materials, there are certain basic considerations. First of all, it is important to know whether the title is current or older. Sometimes the user does not know, so the librarian must try all sources—those listing current materials and those listing older material. However, if the item is current, the librarian should start the search with bibliographic sources that list current material, such as trade bibliographies or library catalogs. If a price and publisher are needed to order the item, a current trade bibliography such as *Books in Print* is a good beginning source. If the user wants to find the book in the library, then either the library's own catalog or a union catalog such as OCLC's *WorldCat* can be a good starting place unless the item is too recent to be listed.

For periodicals the librarian can use a source such as *Ulrich's International Periodicals Directory* to find subscription information and to verify the title. Library catalogs usually list the periodicals the library owns and the holdings. For information about electronic serials, librarians can turn to *Fulltext Sources Online*.

If the librarian understands the user's needs, it will be easier to determine the appropriate bibliographic source. This is an area where there is often more than one appropriate source. Even in this electronic world, there is still a need to verify, identify, and locate materials. Bibliographies provide needed access to all formats of materials.

THE TOP 10 BIBLIOGRAPHIC RESOURCES

Title	Print	Online
American Library Directory. 1923– . Medford, NJ: Information Today.	Annual	Subscription http://books.infotoday.com
Balay, Robert. 1996. *Guide to Reference Books.* Chicago: American Library Association.	11th ed.	
Books in Print. 1905– . New Providence, NJ: R.R. Bowker Co.	Annual	Subscription www.bowker.com
Gale Database of Publications and Broadcast Media. 1969– . Farmington Hills, MI: Gale Group.	Annual	Subscription Ready Reference Shelf www.gale.com/pdf/facts/ grrs.pdf
Gale Directory of Databases. 1993– . Farmington Hills, MI: Gale Group.	Annual	Subscription Ready Reference Shelf www.gale.com/pdf/facts/ grrs.pdf
LMP (Literary Market Place). 1940– . Medford, NJ: Information Today.	Annual	Subscription http://books.infotoday.com
New Walford Guide to Reference Resources. 2005– . London: Facet Publishing.	3 vols.	

(*continued*)

THE TOP 10 BIBLIOGRAPHIC RESOURCES (*continued*)

Title	Print	Online
Publishers, Distributors and Wholesale of the U.S. 1978– . New Providence, NJ: R.R. Bowker.	Annual	Subscription www.bowker.com
Ulrich's International Periodicals Directory. 1932– . New Providence, NJ: R.R. Bowker.	Annual	Subscription www.bowker.com
WorldCat. 1971– . Dublin, OH: OCLC.		Subscription www.oclc.org/worldcat/

Reference Resources Discussed in this Chapter

American Book Publishing Record Cumulative 1876–1949. 1980. 15 vols. New York: Bowker.
American Book Publishing Record Cumulative 1950–1977. 1979. 15 vols. New York: Bowker.
American Book Trade Directory. 1915– . Medford, NJ: Information Today. Annual.
American Catalogue of Books 1876–1910. 1880–1911. 8 vol. in 13. New York: Publishers Weekly.
American Library Directory. 2005. 58th ed. Medford, NJ: Information Today. Also available online.
American Reference Books Annual. 1970– . Littleton, CO: Libraries Unlimited. Annual. Also available online.
Besterman, Theodore. 1965–1966. *A World Bibliography of Bibliographies.* 4th ed. 5 vols. Laussane: Societas Bibliographica.
Bibliographic Index Plus. 1982– . New York: H. W. Wilson. Available online.
Books in Print. 1948. New Providence, NJ: Bowker. Annual. Also available online.
Books Out Loud: Bowker's Guide to Audiobooks. 2005. 20th ed. New Providence, NJ: Bowker.
BooksandPeriodicals.com. Library Technology Alliance. Available online at http://booksandperiodicals.com.
Bowker Annual Library and Book Trade Almanac. 1957– . Medford, NJ: Information Today. Annual.
Bowker's Complete Video Directory. 2005. New Providence, NJ: Bowker.
British Library. *Catalogue.* Available at http://catalogue.bl.uk.
British National Bibliography. Available at www.bl.uk/services/bibliographic/natbib.htm.
Canadian Books in Print. 1967– . Toronto: University of Toronto Press. Annual.
Canadian Reference Sources: An Annotated Bibliography. 1996. Compiled by Mary Bond and Martine Caron. Vancouver: University of British Columbia Press/National Library of Canada.

Canadiana. Available at www.collectionscanada.ca/canadiana/index-e.html.

Cumulative Book Index. 1898–1999. New York: Wilson.

Directory of Special Libraries and Information Centers. 2005. 31st ed. Farmington Hills, MI: Gale.

Evans, Charles. 1903–1959. *American Bibliography: A Chronological Dictionary of All Books, Pamphlets, and Periodical Publications Printed in the United States from the Genesis of Printing in 1639 Down to and including the Year 1800.* 14 vols. Chicago: Self-published. Available online as *Early American Imprints. Series I. Evans (1629–1800)* Readex.

Fulltext Sources Online. Edited by Mary B. Glose, Lara Fletcher, and Suzanne Bromberg. Medford, NJ: Information Today. Biannual.

Gale Directory of Databases. 1993– . Farmington Hills, MI: Gale. Annual. Also available online in Gale's Ready Reference Shelf.

Gale Directory of Publications and Broadcast Media. 1990– . Farmington Hills, MI: Gale. Annual. Also available online in Gale's Ready Reference Shelf.

International Directory of Little Magazines and Small Presses. Paradise, CA: Dustbooks. Annual.

Internet Movie Database. www.IMDd.com.

Kelly, James. 1866–1871. *American Catalogue of Books . . . January 1861 to January 1871.* 2 vols. New York: Wiley.

Literary Market Place: the Directory of the American Book Publishing Industry. 1940– . Medford, NJ: Information Today. Annual. Also available online.

Magazines for Libraries. 13th ed. New Providence, NJ: Bowker. Available online as part of www.ulrichsweb.com.

National Union Catalog, Pre-1956 Imprints. A Cumulative Author List Representing Library of Congress Printed Cards and Titles Reported by Other American Libraries. 1968–1981. 754 vols. London: Mansell.

NewJour. Available at http://gort.ucsd.edu/newjour.

New Serial Titles. 1953–1999. Washington, DC: Library of Congress.

New Walford Guide to Reference Resources, ed. Ray Lester. 2005– . 3 vols. London: Facet Publishing. Distributed in the United States by Neal-Schuman.

New York Public Library. CATNYP. Available at www.nypl.org.

NICEM Film and Video Finder Online. Albuquerque, NM: Access Innovations. Available online.

Publishers, Distributors and Wholesalers of the United States. 1978– . New Providence, NJ: Bowker. Annual. Also available online.

Roorbach, Orville. 1852–1861. *Bibliotheca Americana: 1820–1861.* 4 vols. New York: Roorbach.

Sabin, Joseph. 1868–1936. *A Dictionary of Books Relating to America from Its Discovery to the Present Time.* 29 vols. New York: Sabin.

Science and Technology in Canadian History: A Bibliographic Database. Available at http://acsweb2.ucis.dal.ca/slis/main.htm.

Shaw, Ralph R., and Richard H. Shoemaker. 1958–1966. *American Bibliography: A Preliminary Checklist for 1801–1819.* 22 vols. New York: Scarecrow.

Shoemaker, Richard H. 1964–1971. *A Checklist of American Imprints for 1820–1829.* 10 vols. New York: Scarecrow.

————. 1972–1993. *A Checklist of American Imprints for 1830–1846*. Metuchen, NJ: Scarecrow.

The Standard Periodical Directory. 1989– . New York: Oxbridge. Annual. Also available online.

Ulrich's International Periodicals Directory. 1932– . New Providence, NJ: Bowker. Annual. Also available online.

Union List of Serials in the U.S. and Canada before 1950. 1965. New York: Wilson.

Video Source Book. Farmington Hills, MI: Gale.

Whitaker's Books in Print. 1874– . London: J. Whitaker. Annual. Also available online.

World Guide to Libraries. Munich: K. F. Sauer; distributed by Gale.

Recommendations for Further Readings

Beaudiquez, Marcelle. 2004. "The Perpetuation of National Bibliographies in the New Virtual Information Environment." *IFLA Journal* 30, no. 1: 24–30. Examines whether national bibliographies should be maintained and makes recommendations for what is needed to provide access in an Internet environment.

Kieft, Robert H. 2002. "When Reference Works Are Not Books: The New Edition of the Guide to Reference Books." *Reference & User Services Quarterly* 41, no. 4 (Summer): 330–334. A discussion of the development of the new edition of *Guide to Reference Books* that is being edited by Robert H. Kieft.

Morris, Susan, and Jane Mandelbaum. 2001. "Bibliographic Symposium: Control for the New Millennium." *Library of Congress Information Bulletin* 60, no. 1 (January): 16–18. A report on an LC symposium on bibliographic control. Lists recommendations from this conference.

Morrisey, Locke J. 2002. "Bibliometric and Bibliographic Analysis in an Era of Electronic Scholarly Communication." *Science & Technology Libraries* 22, no. 3/4: 149–160. Discusses some current issues in relation to the linkage of citations to publications.

Bibliography of Works Cited in this Chapter

Balay, Robert. 1996. *Guide to Reference Books*. Chicago: American Library Association.

Bell, Barbara L. 1998. *An Annotated Guide to Current National Bibliographies*. 2nd ed. Munich: K. G. Saur.

Gorman, Michael. 2001. "Bibliographic Control or Chaos: An Agenda for National Bibliographic Services in the 21st Century." *IFLA Journal* 27: 307–313.

Harmon, Robert B. 1989. *Elements of Bibliography: A Simplified Approach*. Rev. ed. Metuchen, NJ: Scarecrow Press.

Macles, Louise Noelle. 1961. *Bibliography*. Translated by T. C. Hines. New York: Scarecrow Press.

Stokes, Roy B. 2003. "Bibliography." In *Encyclopedia of Library and Information Science*, edited by Miriam A. Drake. New York: Marcel Dekker.

————. 1982. *The Function of Bibliography*. 2nd ed. Aldershit: Gower.

5

Answering Questions about Anything and Everything—Encyclopedias

Overview

The basic informational core of any library is the encyclopedia. The thinking mind's dream, the needy mind's crutch, and every librarian's staple, the encyclopedia is quite simply the closest approximation to a bookish God, omniscient and omnipresent. A librarian at the desk, in fact, is often confused for an encyclopedia. "Excuse me, just one quick question, in what years was the French and Indian war fought?" Professional dignity can be maintained only with a quick dive into the nearest encyclopedia.

Given its universal presence for the past two hundred years, the easy availability of an encyclopedia tends to obscure its breathtaking vision and purpose. To provide succinct, user-friendly information on *all* areas of cumulative human activity would be considered impossible, if it did not already exist in the form of the encyclopedia.

Structure of Encyclopedias

The etymology of the word *encyclopedia* is supposedly from "enkyklios paideia," Greek for a "well-rounded education." While the inspiration of an encyclopedia to foment a well-rounded education has not changed since the days of Aristotle, changes in the audience and choices in the format have resulted in a bewildering variety of encyclopedias.

The earliest scholars who compiled information primarily for their own use did not have user-friendliness in mind. The information collated was idiosyncratic in both content and arrangement. Yet the act of collating diverse information into a cohesive unit must have fed into a basic human need since variations of encyclopedic undertakings can be found in all parts of the world over many centuries.

By the eighteenth century, the first prototype of the modern encyclopedia was presented in the form of John Harris's *Lexicon Technicum*, a compilation of:

- alphabetically arranged articles
- written by multiple experts with
- a copious bibliography.

The three major structural elements of the modern encyclopedia slotted into place and have continued. Since then, the basic structure has been relatively unvarying, but encyclopedia choices have matured in response to different needs and innovations. Broadly, they are:

Age

There is a welcome recognition that knowledge is not the preserve of the adult scholar alone. Age-focused encyclopedias have overtaken the field so that today it is impossible to equate the encyclopedia with exclusive and sophisticated research needs, as was the case in past centuries. Encyclopedias for elementary school readers, middle school students, and young adults in high school are primary audience foci as are all levels of adult readers.

Focus

Given the vast demographics that are now the target audience, encyclopedias are now either general or specialized. Their breadth of coverage and ease of reading distinguish them from general titles. Specialized encyclopedias are known for intensity of focus on a single subject and in-depth accounting of all aspects related to that subject.

Scope

Encyclopedias come in all sizes to suit all needs and all pockets. There are the single-volume encyclopedias with brief entries or highly specialized topics. There are also the impressive multivolume series that can be breathtaking in their scope to cover anything and everything.

Format

In the past decade, the formats available to encyclopedias have grown from simple print to a dizzying array of choices. Cheap little diskettes, courtesy of CD-ROM technology, have been surpassed by online availability that is either free or available through subscriptions.

Since the purpose of the encyclopedia is to be all-encompassing, the potential to fall short is acute. It is imperative then that every reference librarian is completely clear about both acquiring and using the right encyclopedia for the right reasons. At a minimum cost of hundreds of dollars for a general, multivolume set, the financial premium for carefully evaluating and making the most productive choice is also relatively steep.

Questions Answered by Encyclopedias

Adult or child, layperson or professional, the act of reaching out to an encyclopedic source, be it multivolume or a single volume, print or electronic, is conditioned by certain basic expectations.

Ready Reference

Q—"*Is Agricola a drink?*"
A—"*According to* Encarta *"Agricola" was a Roman general who lived A.D. 40–93.*"

Encyclopedias provide quick and direct information on any topic. There are any number of sources that give statistical comparison charts of popular encyclopedias. Whether it be *Britannica's* 64,926 articles or the *Americana's* 40,000 entries, it is clear that a large number of questions can find an informational response within these pages. From straightforward biographies and country studies to more abstract conceptual ideas such as "values," the general encyclopedia is presumed to have it all.

Accessibility

Q—"*What are the workings of an electric motor?*"
A—"*The* World Book *has a clear three-page description with color graphics that is not technically abstruse and shows exactly how a motor works.*"

Entries in any encyclopedia are also geared toward high accessibility. From the simplicity of alphabetized entries to the text of the writing that eschews specialized jargon, encyclopedias are primed to be easily digested. Anyone who has turned to the *World Book* to define "ethics" will feel the immense sense of gratitude that a good encyclopedic account is able to engender. Complex intellectual constructs such as deontology and teleology are worded in simple explanations and couched within a clear context that makes the dense study of ethics seem approachable.

Scope

Q—"*I need to compare the economic, social, and political features of Japan with Germany.*"
A—Lands and Peoples *has specific sections on the land, people, economy, history, and government of both nations. The* Grolier Online *version can create a customized side-by-side comparison chart as well.*"

Accessibility is traditionally married to scope as well, so that users expect to get a fully outlined sketch of any topic. If it is a country that is researched, an encyclopedia is expected to briefly cover a description of the people, topography, government, economy, and history. If it is a biography, the important dates and achievements that merited an entry on the person are expected. The dimensions and definition of any topic are covered, however briefly, in an encyclopedia.

One-stop Source

Q—"*My sixth-grader needs to do a report on arch construction and give descriptive examples of such architecture; where can she start?*"
A—"*The* New Book of Knowledge *defines and describes arch structures. You can also check for examples in the related articles mentioned about the Arc de Triomphe, Romanesque architecture, and bridges.*"

The "mall mentality" so pervasive in the modern era also accrues to searches in an encyclopedia. It is frequently used as a one-stop source for multifaceted subjects so that if research on Picasso as a founder of the Cubist movement is required, entries for both the artist and Cubism are handily available.

Referrals

Q—"*Help! I know nothing about it and need to do a twenty-page report on the history and heritage of Korean Americans in my community.*"
A—"*The* Gale Encyclopedia of Multicultural America *will help and the* World Book's *entry on Asian Americans provides additional resources that you can check out for more in-depth research.*"

While breadth of topics covered is the prime expectation of any encyclopedia, depth of coverage is not. Instead, users have come to rely on bibliographies and cross-references to extend their research in any subject. The system of cross-references in an encyclopedia was introduced as early as 1410 so that it is, by now, firmly embedded in user expectations. Encyclopedias are frequently used as shortcuts to find out where specialized information is available by consulting the bibliographic "further resources" and "recommended reading" lists included in all encyclopedias.

Synopses

Q—"*I am writing a novel set in the late nineteenth century and need a brief overview of how much training and what kind of training was required to be a physician.*"
A—"*It took barely two years of 'deplorable' education to complete medical college in the United States. An interesting synopsis of 'Medical Education' provided in Great Britain, Germany, and America can be read in the 1911* Encyclopaedia Britannica.*"

The encyclopedia is also useful in defining the years in which it was produced. As a definitive account of human experience, the encyclopedia reports and testifies to the various differing stages of human thinking. The standard encyclopedic description of marriage in 2005 is "the legal agreement between a man and a woman." With same-sex marriages continuing to acquire social currency and legal legitimacy, it will be interesting to monitor changes in future descriptions. Much as changing definitions in dictionaries offer tantalizing glimpses into human sociology, encyclopedic entries expand on those glimpses to provide a fuller, synoptic picture of the era in which they are written.

Value Add-ons

Q—*"Where can I research Middle Eastern national anthems and get to hear them as well?"*
A—*"The* Encyclopedia of the Orient *at www.i-cias.com/e.o has a description of anthems as well as music clips you can hear."*

Depending on the encyclopedia, users have also come to expect "extras." Maps, photographs, illustrations, diagrams, statistical tables, primary text or excerpts from historic documents, multimedia attachments on electronic encyclopedias that run the gamut of audio and video configurations are all increasingly feeding into in-built user expectations. In all probability, the writers and compilers of thirteenth-century encyclopedias were the first to apprehend the human need for visual accompaniments as they delicately etched miniature illustrations and curlicue letterings into their laborious copying of encyclopedias. Those tiny, idiosyncratic additions to the script have certainly extended a long way to the multimedia encyclopedias that are continuing to develop since their recent inception in the 1990s.

The kinds of questions print encyclopedias are less suited to answer are:

Analytical Phrases

Analytically connected nouns such as *"the impact of Turkish immigrants in Germany"* are better suited to monographs than to an encyclopedia. Structured to explain "Turkey" and "immigration" and "Germany" as separate entities, print encyclopedias would not be the source to consult for a merged analysis of divergent topics. Electronic encyclopedias with the capacity for Boolean searching and hyperlinks may prove more productive, but the search could be random and require multiple links.

Current Issues

Print encyclopedias are also intrinsically unsuited to dynamic, quick-developing areas of information such as statistics. Demographic figures, economic transactions, or sports tallies are best accessed from other sources. Online encyclopedias, however, are constantly updated and can be accessed for this kind of information.

New Technology

Rapidly growing fields such as computer technology are prone to entry lags in both print and online encyclopedias. Even 2004 print editions of the major encyclopedias do not mention *MP3* technology or *blogs* or *zines*. Perhaps the encyclopedia's age-old need to provide a well-rounded perspective on any topic provides a built-in brake against rushing into describing ongoing technological advancements. The first editor of the venerable *Britannica* declined to edit the revised edition because the publishers wanted to include biographies of living persons. "How can we know if their lives merit an entry" (Kogan 1958) was his impassioned argument, elements of which account for a more restrained entry of dynamic developments. A. J. Jacobs, the editor of *Esquire,* who purportedly read all 33,000 pages of the *Britannica,* wryly wrote that Madonna was one of the few popular icons entered, though "you could tell the editors wrote the entry while wearing one of those sterile full-body suits people use when containing an Ebola outbreak" (Jacobs 2004).

Major Encyclopedic Resources Used in Reference Work

While there is an inchoate expectation that encyclopedias are expected to answer anything and everything, there are in reality two major types of encyclopedias:

- General: those that do answer everything.
- Specialized: those that answer anything to do with a specific subject.

TYPE	DESCRIPTION	EXAMPLES
General	Covers all areas of information	*Encyclopaedia Britannica* *Encyclopedia Americana* *World Book Encyclopedia*
Specialized	In-depth coverage of one area	*Encyclopedia of Homelessness* *Encyclopedia of Leadership* *Encyclopedia of Protestantism*

Both general and specialized encyclopedias can typically be acquired in multiple formats so that reference libraries have a choice between print, CD/DVD, and online versions. They can be single or multivolume print editions. Electronic versions provide multimedia options with audio and video in addition to text.

General Encyclopedias

William Smellie, the colorful, individualistic editor of the premier edition of the *Encyclopaedia Britannica* of 1768, was determined to expand the traditional audience for an encyclopedia from a limited, learned group to an unlimited democratic one. "Utility," he wrote, "ought to be the principal intention." He then went on to expand on his utilitarian strategy "to diffuse the knowledge of Science" so that "any man of ordinary parts, may, if he chuses, learn the principles of Agriculture, of Astronomy, of Botany, of Chemistry, etc." (Kogan 1958).

"Utility" and "the greater good of the greatest number" continue to underwrite the relative popularity of encyclopedias. The descriptions of current works have been crafted to establish both their structural framework and present analytical reviews on their "utility" to the public. The structural components will focus on the LURES of each encyclopedia.

LURES is a handy mnemonic to remind the busy reference librarian to check the:

- **L**evel of user
- **U**pdating policies
- **R**esearch aids
- **E**lectronic availability
- **S**pecial features

The analysis, deriving from the structure, will point out each encyclopedia's distinctive strengths, weaknesses, and overall utility.

The *World Book Encyclopedia*

Edition: 2005. Volumes: 22. Articles: 275,000. Illustrations: 27,500. Index entries: 150,000.

L The *World Book Encyclopedia* is a general encyclopedia that is aimed primarily at the reference needs of school-age students and secondarily as a general reference tool for families, educators, and the public.

U The print version is published annually with additions of new articles and selected revisions of existing articles and graphics. The additions derive from an ongoing "Classroom Research Project" that continually tests the actual use of the encyclopedia in selected North American classrooms.

R The *World Book* has an extensive system of cross-referencing that is additionally backed by a highly comprehensive index. "Related articles" point the user to other aspects of a topic. "Additional resources" provide a bibliography for further reading on more than 1500 articles.

E It is available as a CD-ROM. The *World Book Millennium* has two editions, the *Standard* and the *Deluxe*, both of which contain more articles than the print version, far fewer illustrations, and various electronic "perks" such as free updates for a year. A third CD-ROM product is the *World Book Macintosh Edition* that has all the articles in the print version as well as electronic add-ons such as a distance calculator and "virtual images." The *World Book* is also available online at www.worldbook.com through a paid subscription. The online version has more articles than the print version as well as hyperlinks and daily updates.

S The encyclopedia has certain unique features. It provides an instructional section in the final volume that aims to introduce the user to the basics of research and communication skills. It also adds on an annual *Year Book* supplement to cover major world events. A special graphics feature utilizes transparency in color overlays, to display dual aspects of a single subject, so that the picture comes alive.

Analysis

The *World Book*, while ostensibly designed for the school-age student, is unarguably one of the most popular general encyclopedic sources used by all ages today. It marks high on readability, with articles that are clear and frequently illustrated. Technical words are italicized and defined. Larger articles employ a graduated, simple-to-complex method that mirrors the process of human learning. Difficult entries are appended with an outline, so that the user can opt to get a bird's-eye view of the subject as well as develop a sense of the interrelationships within the subject. Questions are provided at the end of major articles to help focus the user on the most important aspects of a difficult field. In terms of Smellie's mission of "utility," the encyclopedia scores very high.

Overall Utility

Think salt. This is a source of basic information that is a staple for very different genres of libraries. It is both attractive and accessible. The only constituency for which it is inadequate is the one requiring in-depth information.

Encyclopedia Americana

Edition: 2006. Volumes: 30. Articles: Over 45,000. Illustrations: Over 23,000. Index entries: Approximately 353,000.

L   Like the *World Book*, it is advertised as a resource for "Grades 8 and up." The inclusion of articles on subjects like "ceratopsia," "seaborgium," and "marginocephalia," however, attest to its aim to be something more than a resource for school students.

U   The print version is published annually. Over 9,500 pages were either revised or added in the 2006 edition. A yearbook, the *Americana Annual*, is also published compiling the year's major developments.

R   It has a very detailed and singular index so that the ratio of articles to index entries averages four entries for each article. Information that has not been covered by a full-length article but is contained within a larger subject is also indexed. Major subjects have complete outlines included in the index. Cross-references are provided both within and at the end of each article. Bibliographies aimed at representing "divergent points of view" are provided.

E   The *Americana* is available as a no-frills CD-ROM that presents itself as just another version of the print format. An online version is also available by subscription. It has the same number of articles but is updated quarterly and has over 155,000 links. It also has the *Americana Journal*, a global news source that adds 200 news stories each week along with a Teacher's Guide. An Americans with Disabilities Act compliant version for users with disabilities allows for automated reading and keyboard shortcuts.

S   The editors pride themselves on several features such as the unusual coverage of era surveys. Articles on each of the centuries are provided as separate entries. "Almost book-length" articles have been written on issues such as the world wars. A glossary of unwieldy or technical terms is provided with the index, listing all the words in the glossaries.

Analysis

Touted as being "prominent among Abraham Lincoln's scanty store of books" (preface) the *Encyclopedia Americana* has been part of the reference landscape since 1829. Does the fact that it is the first encyclopedia to be published in the United States give it added cachet? Perhaps. The *Encyclopedia Americana* has been a familiar sight to generations of users and is therefore a trusted resource. Ostensibly a source for Americana, it is in reality not so limited and can be consulted for extensive general research. In fact, it has more than double the number of entries of the *World Book*, though far fewer illustrations. However, its greatest strength does lie in its fierce coverage of both the big and the small events of American history. Primary documents such as the Bill of Rights, the Declaration of Independence, and the Gettysburg Address can be found in the *Encyclopedia Americana*. A great many of the articles are signed, including short one-hundred-word articles such as the one on "twill" and the two-hundred-word article on "algorithm." The encyclopedia has been periodically criticized for being slow to include important current events in its print format.

Overall utility

In terms of acquisition, the greatest selling point of the *Americana* is contained in its title. Medium-sized libraries acquiring the *Britannica* and the *World Book* may have no pressing need for the *Americana*, but would feel vulnerable when faced with questions regarding such topics as Lochner v. New York, the U.S. Coast Guard, Alan Greenspan, the Carnegie Institution of Washington, or the Un-American Activities Committee without this resource handy. While being a solid general-purpose encyclopedia, the *Americana* is most trustworthy in its provision of domestic information.

Encyclopaedia Britannica

Edition: 2005. Volumes: 32. Articles: 64, 900. Illustrations: 24,000. Index entries: 215,000.

L   The *Encyclopaedia Britannica* is globally renowned as a general informational resource. Yet the style, presentation, structure, and content of the entries are unabashedly directed to a higher level of readership.

U   The print version has been revised multiple times, with the most recent edition published in 2005. The publishers claim a 35 percent revision of articles from the 2002 edition, as well as additions for recent topics such as SARS, PDE-5 inhibitors, John Kerry, and Yo-Yo Ma. *Book of the Year* is an annual supplement that covers major events throughout the world and is included at no additional charge to all subscribers.

R   "The Great EB," as it is popularly known, has developed an elaborate system of research aids that can be overwhelming. A full two volumes are devoted to the indexing of entries. Over 500,000 cross-references are also allied to the index entries. The one-volume *Propaedia*, aimed at aiding the user to clarify topics through intellectual structure rather than alphabetical convenience, tends instead toward mind-numbing erudition.

E   The *Britannica* is available in an increasing variety of nonprint formats: CD-ROM, DVD, and online. The software, which is available for less than fifty dollars, can be tailored to suit three age levels. The *Britannica Ultimate Reference Suite* has over 100,000 articles and 19,000 graphics, as well as entries from the encyclopedia's famous past authors such as Sigmund Freud, Marie Curie, and Orville Wright. A "research organizer" offers software glitz that allows for note taking, saving bookmarks, and formatting reports. The online reference is also available for both younger and experienced readers. Online biographies include popular cultural figures of a more recent vintage such as Catherine Zeta-Jones. Over 3,000 audio-video animations plus links to 166,000 Web sites and full-text articles from EBSCO combine to provide a formidable online presence.

S   To present what is "special" about the Great EB is to imply that there is something quotidian about it. There really isn't. Defined by a complex tripartite structure; an index that is analytical; non-standardized vocabulary; an authorship that reads like a Who's Who of global and historical personalities; and a hoary history, the encyclopedia is unique at all levels.

Analysis

The *Britannica* claims 235 years of experience in delivering the "world standard in reference." Marketing hyperbole aside, the *Britannica* can rightly claim preeminence in name recognition. With past contributors like Einstein and Trotsky, its credentials are stellar. The twelve-volume *Micropaedia* is the core resource for general reference, providing breadth of coverage in short, authoritative articles. The *Macropaedia* offers depth of coverage on selected topics. International coverage has always been of a high order so that even nonbiographical or nongeographical subjects such as AIDS receive a global perspective. The *Britannica* is harder to navigate than most current encyclopedias. The print is small and the *Micropaedia* is designed with three columns, separated by narrow margins that leave very little white space. Ease of readability is not a prime consideration as evident in the variant style of articles and the non-standardized vocabulary. There is no controlled vocabulary and a great many of the *Macropaedia* articles read more like academic treatises than as general reference resources.

Overall Utility

It is hard to imagine any library without the venerable and indomitable *Britannica*. It is the source that is reached for when something cannot be found in a more accessible, general reference encyclopedia. Ultimately, it remains the encyclopedia with the most gravitas.

Multimedia Encyclopedias

All the major print editions have been complemented or even eclipsed by digital or software versions. The formidable *Collier's Encyclopedia*, in publication since 1950, can now only be found in parts of the *Encarta* digital encyclopedia. However, despite fears that the print encyclopedia was destined for oblivion (*Boston Globe* 2002), publishers have found that educational institutions continue to have an interest in the purchase of print editions. If anything, online versions tend to support "the Web's counter-intuitive economic golden rule—give content away in order to sell more of it" (Reid 1999).

Wikipedia

"Beware lest your dreams come true." While all of the general encyclopedias in the preceding section are available in nonprint formats, the dream of early encyclopedists to cater to the masses and generate a utilitarian source of encyclopedic information has led, in the twenty-first century, to a surreal point where the masses are feeding information to the masses. *Wikipedia*, born on January 15, 2001, is an online encyclopedia that offers "free content," so that anybody is free to take the information, free to provide the information, and free to edit existing information. In the brave new world of burgeoning open-source software that feeds off voluntary authorship, *Wikipedia* hopes to be the ultimate people's encyclopedia. As of 2005, there were 3.7 million multilingual articles percolating in *Wikipedia*, reportedly being used by a record-breaking thirteen million people, marking it as the 37th most visited Web site on the Internet (Goodin 2005).

Use of Multimedia Encyclopedias

Multimedia encyclopedias have plenty to offer. The early CD-ROM versions that were simple transpositions of print to electronic format have gained both the confidence and the necessary technology to burgeon into spectacular multimedia extravaganzas. A quick search for "Antarctica," for example, can explode into a mesmerizing display of interactive pictures, sounds, streaming video, multiple hyperlinks, animation, atlases, and timelines. Of course, the option to consult merely the text always exists, but invariably, the lure of a click into multimedia proves irresistible and fascinating. The factor of visual seduction segues neatly into some of the major considerations to keep in mind when reviewing the acquisition and use of an electronic encyclopedia. Reviews and ratings for the top ten encyclopedia software packages for 2006 can be accessed at http://encyclopediareview.toptenreviews.com.

Options in Learning Styles

Electronic encyclopedias provide information in a variety of mediums—textual, auditory, and visual. If the education pundits are correct in believing that each person has the propensity to absorb information effectively through individualistic applications of all five senses, then the variety of choices inherent in an electronic format is certainly very appealing. The small print account of the Roman Empire as presented in the *Britannica* can blur before the eyes of a teenager who may respond more enthusiastically to the same subject when presented with voice-over narration and changing images as presented in *Grolier Online*.

Information Searching

Electronic encyclopedias can simplify and accelerate the process of information searching. Hyperlinks that leap from one aspect of an entry to a related one assist the careful user in covering vast ground in a short time. Keyword search capabilities can take researchers directly into multiple sources useful to their search.

Updates

Updating facts, figures, and statistical, biographical, and technological data is far easier to accomplish in an online resource. The researcher can thereby be relatively sure of the accuracy of current information. Quick editing also allows a majority of electronic encyclopedias to include popular culture, an area that most print encyclopedias are wary of covering.

Scope

Electronic articles are typically longer than print versions, since ultimate shelf space and production cost per page is not an issue as it is with print encyclopedias. In addition to longer articles, a greater number of articles are also the norm.

There is, of course, a flip side to the obvious charms of nonprint encyclopedias.

- The usage mechanism needs a more complex infrastructure in order to provide multiple services at the same time. Print encyclopedias need shelving space. Many users can consult different volumes at the same time. Electronic encyclopedias need hardware, software, computer know-how on the part of the user, computer accessibility, possible investments in multimedia apparatus such as headphones— in short, a far greater investment in infrastructure.

- The traditional allure of browsing through encyclopedias so that information on the Hebrides islands could just as well lead to a nonpertinent, yet exhilarating romp through the alphabetically proximate city of Hebron and the goddess Hecate is tamed in the electronic format. Browsing through hyperlinks is more suited to relevant related topics. The element of serendipitous knowledge, for which print encyclopedias are universally beloved, is dramatically muted in the more linearly conceived search technology of electronic encyclopedias.

- Through years of experience, librarians are a breed of professionals well suited to constant technological change. Yet the vulnerability never lessens. Electronic encyclopedias, in the past decade alone, have sprouted hydra-headed formats. CD-ROM technology led to a flurry of death announcements on the print encyclopedia in the 1980s. Paid subscriptions to online encyclopedias, with remote access to patrons, led to another flurry of epitaphs on CD-ROM technology. The advent of free online encyclopedias has left the publishing world, the librarians, and the users poised for future changes. Open-source encyclopedias further complicate the current scenario. While the ongoing sense of vulnerability to change is certainly a function of time, it is a vulnerability that has never been engendered by the stolid rows of print encyclopedias present in every library.

- Current user acceptance or use of online encyclopedias can also create a unique set of problems for the reference librarian. An alphabetical print resource requires little instruction and so the user has instant control. Electronic encyclopedias invariably require a set of instructions and, especially in public libraries, a process to sign up for the use of a computer. Troubleshooting can come in many forms. *Wikipedia*, for example, can be a framebuster that is hard to send directly—in order to send articles electronically one must instead employ a "copy and paste" method. Each unaware user needs to be informed individually. A sense of immediate control over the information resource is relatively lacking in the electronic format.

Specialized Subject Encyclopedias

Language has a peculiar impact on the way an object is perceived. Subject encyclopedias, so unconsciously allied with the more popularly known general encyclopedias are, in practice, acquisitions that cater to a very different constituency. The subject encyclopedia is "encyclopedic" only in that it is a comprehensive source of information arranged for easy access. The user of a specialized encyclopedia, however, is wholly different. Users are, for the most part, seeking relatively in-depth information on a highly specific topic—a topic that would merit perhaps a few pages in a general encyclopedia. Acquiring a subject encyclopedia, then, is really the equivalent of acquiring multiple books on a single topic, directed at a particular group of users. Acquiring a subject encyclopedia does not fulfill the traditional encyclopedia's "utilitarian" dictum of providing the "greatest good for the greatest number."

Being alert to this critical distinction can help the reference librarian choose among the thousands of subject encyclopedias that continue to flood the market at an ever-increasing pace. For the general encyclopedia, for which there is always a perceived need, the primary consideration is one of reliability. For the subject encyclopedia, the primary consideration would have to be demand or need. If there is an established constituency for the subject, only then can other considerations such as relative accuracy, reliability, and scope come into focus.

The word *subject* is also host to two important variations. Some subjects are really single topics such as the prize-winning three-volume *Encyclopedia of the World's Zoos*. Others are multiple topics within a field of knowledge, such as the well-established fifteen-volume *Encyclopedia of Religion*. Single topic encyclopedias require a crystal-clear demand for the topic, whereas some subjects encompassing a field of topics can be essential purchases for even the smallest libraries. For example, the valuable *Routledge Encyclopedia of Philosophy*, winner of an ALA Honorable Mention in 1999, is a handy compilation of philosophers, most of whom cannot be located in single-volume works. Similarly, the 2003 Dartmouth winner, the *Garland Encyclopedia of World Music*, is a comprehensive single purchase that covers vast areas of minor entries, not locatable in either the general encyclopedia or a topical manuscript. For example, the absolute relief felt by a librarian in locating an account of "Tumbuka healing," where African music is the equivalent of a prescription drug, is a feeling regularly engendered in reference librarians using subject encyclopedias. Multi-topic research fields such as Canada or broadcasting or Judaism are well served by indispensable subject encyclopedias such as *The Canadian Encyclopedia*, the *Encyclopedia of Television*, and *Encyclopaedia Judaica*. Equally noteworthy subject encyclopedias like the *Encyclopedia Sherlockiana* or *The Continuum Encyclopedia of Animal Symbolism in Art* are undeniably worthy acquisitions in and of themselves, but can be perceived as idiosyncratic luxury items unless the reference librarian has perceived a strong need in the constituency.

There are a handful of multidisciplinary titles that are of use to any and every library. The *McGraw-Hill Encyclopedia of Science and Technology* covers a wide range of scientific topics written in an authoritative yet understandable style. The thirty-four-volume *Dictionary of Art*, despite its deceptive title, is an encyclopedic compendium of Western and non-Western art, art themes and cultural influences, artists and their biographies, and art critics and art collectors, all supplemented with both color and black-and-white images. *Grzimek's Animal Life Encyclopedia* is the definitive compilation of information on insects, fishes, amphibians, reptiles, birds, mammals, and other orders. Each order is discussed and brought alive with representative examples of species within the order. Photographs, illustrations, and maps provide graphic enhancements. Anything that runs, flies, leaps, crawls, slithers, or swims can be located in this seventeen-volume work. Finally, the *Gale Encyclopedia of Multicultural America*, while not as generically relevant as science, art, and animals, is a useful addition to all libraries within the United States, land of immigrants. There are 152 original essays written on the individual minority, ethnic, and ethno-religious groups that make up the American mosaic. Historical background information, patterns of settlement, and cultural mores associated with each group are described along with useful contact information for organizations and research centers that are relevant for further research.

Some of the most copious publishers of subject encyclopedias are:

- *ABC-CLIO*: Publisher of the "Companion" series that focuses on popular American issues.
- *Berkshire Publishing Group*: Entered the world of independent publishing as recently as 2005, and yet have forged a strong profile with "Outstanding Reference" recognition from *Library Journal* and ALA among others.
- *Facts on File*: Publishes encyclopedias specifically for school and library consumption, with curriculum-based subject areas as the guiding framework.
- *Garland Publishing*: Though a member of the Taylor & Francis Group, it is an independent organization specializing in scholarly niche publications, many of which are focused on the physical sciences.
- *Greenwood Publishing Group*: The Group includes Greenwood Press, Praeger Publishers, Heinemann USA, GEM, and Libraries Unlimited, thereby constituting one of the more copious publishers of reference encyclopedias.
- *Oxford University Press*: The behemoth of American university presses and a global publisher of reference encyclopedias.
- *Scribners*: Despite its relatively smaller output, Scribners looms large in the world of subject encyclopedias as it has been awarded at least six of ALA's prestigious Dartmouth medals and Honorable Mentions in the past ten years. In 1999, Charles Scribner's Sons joined Thomson Gale.

- *Thomson Gale*: Publisher of some of the most user-friendly subject encyclopedias and distinguished by its composite style, Thomson Gale products are also expanded by imprint publications from the likes of U.X.L. and Macmillan Reference USA.

It is useful to contact publishers directly if interested in updates of existing editions, for feelers about forthcoming plans, or even with suggestions on what you may want to see published.

Reference librarians looking to fill a subject demand can check on a somewhat dated, yet wonderful resource: the two-volume *Subject Encyclopedias* by Allan W. Mirwis. The best picks from recent publishers can be culled from RUSA's annual *Outstanding Reference Sources* as well as the annual Dartmouth medal winners. Both lists are available at www.ala.org.

Encyclopedias for Children and Young Adults

Children's encyclopedias also cover vast swathes of information, but are usually short, heavily illustrated, and graphically simple with larger fonts and user aids.

- Aimed at grades three through eight, *The New Book of Knowledge* has 10,500 pages of information spread across 21 volumes. The 9,000 articles are supplemented with 23,000 illustrations and over 1,000 maps, making it a child-friendly reference resource. It claims the distinction of using the largest font size relative to other children's encyclopedias, and key words are highlighted in a bold font. The topics included, however, range from the simple (George Bush) to the complex (Oriental Exclusion Acts). A clear indication of the target audience is evident in the value add-ons such as project and experiment manuals, homework help columns, and "wonder questions" such as what makes a stomach growl or the stars twinkle. It is also available as a Grolier database with additional features such as a weekly current events update. The CD-ROM version, titled *Grolier Multimedia Encyclopedia Deluxe iMac Edition*, has multimedia enhancements and allows for free subscription to the online *New Book of Knowledge on the Web*.
- Updated every two years, Grolier's six-volume *Lands and Peoples* is aimed at grades six through twelve, but can be used by upper-elementary students as well. The countries of the world are not arranged alphabetically, but by geographic continent, with each volume covering a separate continent. For young users who are not clear in which continent the country of Nauru is placed, there is an alphabetical index repeated in each volume. Geography, history, economy, life styles, and beliefs are described for each entry with the idea of recreating a full social, cultural, and physical milieu of the various peoples. It is a useful encyclopedia for the annual reports required by school curricula.
- *Compton's by Britannica*, the 2005 incarnation of the more familiar *Compton's Encyclopedia*, has been an effective teaching tool since 1922 when it was first published. Designed specifically for middle and high school students, *Compton's* 37,000 articles are deliberately allied to National Curriculum Standards. Larger articles are introduced with a boxed preview that explains the internal structure of the article. Over 23,000 images, including charts, lists, and graphs both enhance the text and

summarize key data. Each of the twenty-six volumes includes a "Here and There" guide that provides an overview of subjects covered in the volume as well as a list of introductory questions that are aimed at stimulating reader interest. *Compton's* also prides itself on unique research aids such as the Fact Index, the final volume of almost 30,000 brief articles with an index.

- For upper-elementary students, *My First Britannica* is a pleasing new twelve-volume resource, hosted by the venerable Britannica publishing house. The distinction immediately apparent in this resource is the boldness in design, which comprises two-page articles with text on one page and illustrations on the facing page. Value add-ons include fun quizzes, factoids, and cross-references embedded in each entry. The font size is large and unfamiliar words are highlighted and defined in a comprehensive glossary. Like the previous resource, the entries are not alphabetical, but placed under subject headings for which consulting the separate index volume is a necessity.

- An alphabetic general encyclopedia aimed at the elementary student can be found in *The World Book Student Discovery Encyclopedia*. With 2,100 age-appropriate articles and over 3,300 color illustrations, the encyclopedia contains succinct, easy-to-read text and prepares the child for more mature research techniques such as cross and related references, pronunciation checks, and the relevance of guide words. The language is simple so that an earthquake, for example, is defined pithily as "the shaking of the ground."

Collection Development and Maintenance

Selection and Keeping Current

A number of established professional publications are also available to assist in finding the right encyclopedia. Among the most well-known sources are:

- *Kister's Best Encyclopedias*.
- An annual update of existing encyclopedias can be found in the September issue of *Booklist*.
- Word-of-mouth opinions expressed by veteran reference librarians should always be welcomed. Preferred usage recommendations are one of the best indications of a good encyclopedia.
- *Bowker's Best Reference Books*.
- *American Reference Books Annual*.
- *Kirkus Reviews*—special editions.
- Collated reviews of nonprint encyclopedias can be found in the software section of www.consumersearch.com/www/software/encyclopedias/reviews.html.

Evaluating Encyclopedic Resources

Around the year 1230, Bartholomew de Granville published one of the most popular early encyclopedias, the *De Proprietatibus Rerum* or The Properties of Things. A typical entry described:

Of A Maid: . . . a woman is more meeker than a man, she weepeth sooner. And is more envious, and more laughing, and loving; and the soul is more in a woman than in a man (Trevisa 1988).

Despite intense competition among encyclopedias in the thirteenth century, Bartholomew's descriptions of the properties of things such as the meek, weeping, envious, laughing, loving woman with more soul evidently struck the right chords. It was translated into multiple languages from its original Latin, and was a best seller for over three centuries. Fifty to sixty fatted calves had to be slaughtered to provide enough vellum for a single copy, and multiple scribes and illuminators had to be employed, so that the process of acquiring the right encyclopedia was a far bloodier and exorbitant acquisition than it is today. The owning of an encyclopedia was certainly a luxury reserved for the aristocracy.

With the technological breakthrough of the printing press and the sociopolitical establishment of democratic ideals, the notion of encyclopedias as Everyman's resource became more entrenched. Today we are inundated with scores of encyclopedias: general, age-specific, subject-specific, illustrated, and multi-formatted. Our energies are best spent in whittling down the choices to emerge with what best suits individual and institutional needs. In theory, this could prove to be a daunting task. In practice, the worth of an encyclopedia is relatively easy to gauge. Given the thousands of articles that continue to describe Bartholomew's ageless "properties of things," it is instructive to pick a few topics with which the reviewer is knowledgeable. A checklist composed of the following questions, *in order of preference*, can gird the reviewer with a sure sense of what is a work of quality and what deserves to be purchased.

Question 1: Is this encyclopedia reliable?

Above all else, reliability is essential. Given the thousands of articles penned by thousands of contributors, it is possible to gauge the reliability factor only through well-established indicators of authority. The list of contributors should be professionally qualified or known authorities on a subject. The publisher should be reputable. Both factors must be mirrored in articles that are accurate and current to the best of your knowledge. It is best to:

- Choose a topic with which you are highly familiar or have a specific question that needs to be answered.
- Establish a list of expectations, preferably in writing, prior to gauging the article. If, for example, your field of expertise is the U.S. Civil War, set up an a priori checklist:
  - When was the Civil War waged?
  - Where were the major battles fought?
  - Who were the primary personalities involved in the war?
  - What were some of the probable causes of the war?
  - How did the war come to an end?
  - Why is the war so important in the context of American history?
  - Are there other reliable sources listed for continued research?

- Large subject topics such as the Civil War would merit the entire gamut of the reference librarian's reviewing arsenal of who, what, where, why, when, and how probes. Others, like a biography, might merit a more specific list such as:
  - Who the person was.
  - Why the person was famous.
  - When the person was born and other significant dates.
  - Availability of additional resources.

Authoritative answers to an a priori set of questions that you are able to confirm is a simple and satisfying way of developing an educated preference for a much-used resource. In addition, you gain "added vision" while reading through professional critiques of encyclopedias, so that the ongoing evaluations offered by reference pundits has added resonance rather than the niggling uncertainty of a received truth.

Question 2: The source is reliable, but is it suitable for our constituency and the mission of our institution?

A clear perspective on the target audience can be mapped in terms of:

- Age/reading level: child, young adult, adult, or all age groups;
- Purpose: general knowledge, in-depth research;
- Institutional size: small, medium, large; and
- Institutional type: public, academic, special.

A child looking for general information on a subject in a small public library will both want and expect a very different encyclopedic source from an adult historian expecting to conduct research in a large special library.

Question 3: The source is both suitable and reliable, but can we afford to purchase it?

In increasingly financially strapped libraries, the relevance of cost cannot be underestimated. Given the variety of formats in which encyclopedias can now be found, the variation in cost adds to the flexibility of choice.

- If the *Britannica* is available online for free, and the CD-ROM version is a fraction of the price of print, what are the factors that would urge the buying of one format over another, or in addition to another?
- Are yearly updates necessary, or can the constituency live with a general encyclopedia set for five years, so that the average cost per year is less?

Question 4: Once the reference librarian has established that the encyclopedia is reliable, suitable, and affordable, it is time to ask the question: will it hold the user's interest?

Perfectly comprehensive sources of information are undervalued or underused because of poor readability factors. The layout, graphics, font size, paper, and binding quality all contribute toward a print source that is accessible. For online versions, quick loading, clean graphics, and updated Web links, are of the essence in holding user interest.

Secondary Questions

If the major questions have been answered, a second batch of questions can help fine-tune the acquisition process.

- What is the scope of the encyclopedia? The length, breadth, and intensity of coverage for all entries can be assessed.
- Is there any bias, either unconsciously evident or explicitly professed in any of the entries? Controversial topics such as abortion and stem-cell research are potentially fertile areas to check for bias.
- Is the encyclopedia necessary because it is unique and would constitute a niche publication? Niche publications appear infrequently and may need to be acquired when available rather than when actively needed.
- Is the encyclopedia a rich resource for pre-research queries? Does it have a high potential for providing a guide to further research through suggested readings and the availability of cross-references?

A unique, unbiased publication with great sources for further research is, however, of little value if the first four criteria have not been met. The bottom line in evaluation then is:

1. The encyclopedia must be reliable.
2. The encyclopedia must be suited to the needs of the institution.
3. The encyclopedia must be affordable.
4. The encyclopedia must be designed to hold user interest.

Further Considerations

Encyclopedias represent a significant and popular purchase. Even after careful evaluation of the product, an assessment of constituency needs and the reference department's mission plan are critical to making a choice. Visualizing some real-life scenarios can help prime the reference librarian in choosing the best possible options.

- You are head of reference in a medium-sized public library, serving a mixed-age constituency of 40,000 people. Your annual budget for reference acquisitions is $24,000 and you have ten public computers.
  Would you:

    - Budget for the thirty-two-volume *Encyclopaedia Britannica 2005* with a prepublication offer of $1,095?
    - Consider the 56,000,000 word *Encyclopaedia Britannica Online*® with its added access to the encyclopedia as well as the *Student, Elementary,* and *Concise* versions?
    - Purchase the inexpensive $35–$50 CD-ROM, DVD version of the *Encyclopaedia Britannica*?

On what factors would you base your decision?

- Computer literate constituency and the demand for online information?
- Option of remote access for online and a community that owns PCs?
- Computer availability—can library afford a dedicated computer?
- Shelf space for print?
- Combination purchase possibilities?

- You are the chair of a small academic library with a total student population of 7,295. Your annual budget for reference acquisitions is $38,000.
  Would you purchase the well-received twenty-volume *Encyclopedia of Applied Physics* for $5,950?
  On what factors would you base your decision?

- Large physics department?
- Competing needs of other departments?
- At $295 per volume, option to buy some volumes rather than the entire set?
- Existing collection of older *Encyclopedia of Modern Physics* adequate?

TOP TEN ENCYCLOPEDIAS

Title	Print	Online
Compton's by Britannica. Chicago, IL: Encyclopaedia Britannica, Inc.	26 vols.	Subscription (School edition) http://corporate. britannica.com/library/ online/bolse.html
Dictionary of Art. 1996. New York: Oxford University Press.	34 vols.	Subscription www.groveart.com
Encyclopedia Americana. 2006. Danbury, CT: Grolier.	30 vols.	Subscription http://auth.grolier.com/ cgi-bin/authV2?bffs–
Encyclopaedia Britannica. Chicago, IL: Encyclopaedia Britannica, Inc.	32 vols.	Free and subscription www.britannica.com
Encyclopedia of Religion. 2004. Farmington Hills, MI: Thomson Gale.	15 vols.	eBook subscription www.gale.com
Gale Encyclopedia of Multicultural America. 1999. Farmington Hills, MI: Thomson Gale.	3 vols.	eBook subscription www.gale.com

Grzimek's Animal Life Encyclopedia. 2003–2004. Farmington Hills, MI: Thomson Gale.	17 vols.	eBook subscription www.galegroup.com
The New Book of Knowledge. 2006. Danbury, CT: Grolier.	21 vols.	Subscription http://auth.grolier.com/ cgi-bin/authV2?bffs–
McGraw-Hill Encyclopedia of Science and Technology. 2002. New York: McGraw-Hill Professional.	20 vols.	Subscription www.AccessScience.com
The World Book Encyclopedia. 2006. Chicago, IL: World Book.	22 vols.	Subscription www.worldbookonline.com

Recommended Resources Discussed in this Chapter

Bunson, Matthew E. 1997. *Encyclopedia Sherlockiana*. New York: Hungry Minds.
The Canadian Encyclopedia. 2000. James H. Marsh, ed. Ontario: McClelland & Stewart. Most updated version available at www.canadianenyclopedia.ca.
Compton's by Britannica. 2005. Chicago: Encyclopaedia Britannica, Inc.
De Trevisa, John. 1988. *On the Properties of Things: De proprietatibus rerum*. Gloucestershire: Clarendon Press.
Dictionary of Art. 1996. Jane Turner, ed. New York: Oxford University Press.
Encarta. 2005. Available at encarta.msn.com. CD/DVD version *Microsoft Encarta 2006*. Washington, DC: Microsoft Software.
Encyclopedia Americana. 2006. Danbury, CT: Grolier.
Encyclopaedia Britannica. 2005. Chicago, IL: Encyclopaedia Britannica, Inc.
Encyclopedia of Applied Physics. 2004. George L.Trigg, ed. Hoboken, NJ: John Wiley and Sons.
Encyclopedia of Homelessness. 2005. David Levinson, ed. London: SAGE Publications.
Encyclopaedia Judaica. 2006. Cecil Roth and Geoffrey Wigoder, eds. Philadelphia: Coronet Books, Inc.
Encyclopedia of Leadership. 2004. George R. Goethals, Georgia J. Sorenson, and James MacGregor Burns, eds. London: SAGE Publications.
Encyclopedia of Modern Physics. 1990. Robert A. Meyers, ed. San Diego, CA: Academic Press.
The Encyclopaedia of the Orient. Available at www.i-cias.com/e.o. Accessed on 02.20.2006.
Encyclopedia of Protestantism. 2003. Hans Hillerbrand, ed. Oxford: Routledge.
Encyclopedia of Religion, 2nd ed. 2004. Farmington Hills, MI: Thomson Gale.
Encyclopedia Software Review. Available at *http://encyclopedia-review.toptenreviews.com*. Accessed on 01.07.2006.

Encyclopedia of Television. 2004. Horace Newcomb, ed. New York: Taylor & Francis.
Encyclopedia of the World's Zoos. 2001. Catherine E. Bell, ed. Chicago: Fitzroy Dearborn.
Gale Encyclopedia of Multicultural America. 1999. Farmington Hills, MI: Thomson Gale.
Garland Encyclopedia of World Music. 1999. Ruth M. Stone, James Porter, and Timothy Rice, eds. New York: Garland Publishing.
Grolier Online. Available at www.go.grolier.com. Accessed on 10.08.2005.
Grzimek's Animal Life Encyclopedia. 2003–2004. 2nd ed. Farmington Hills, MI: Thomson Gale.
Lands and Peoples. 2003. Danbury, CT: Grolier.
The McGraw-Hill Encyclopedia of Science and Technology. 2002. 9th ed. New York: McGraw-Hill Professional.
My First Britannica. 2004. Chicago: Encyclopaedia Britannica, Inc.
The New Book of Knowledge. 2006. Danbury, CT: Grolier.
The New Grolier Multimedia Encyclopedia. Danbury, CT: Scholastic Library Publishing.
Routledge Encyclopedia of Philosophy. 1998. Edward Craig, ed. New York: Taylor & Francis.
Werness, Hope B. 2003. *The Continuum Encyclopedia of Animal Symbolism in Art*. London: Continuum International Publishing Group.
Wikipedia. Available at www.wikipedia.org.
World Book Encyclopedia. 2006. Chicago: World Book.
The World Book Student Discovery Encyclopedia. 2003. Chicago: World Book.

Recommendations for Further Reading

"The 2005 Reference Review." 2005. *Kirkus Reviews* (November). An annual selection of significant reference publications, with a large percentage devoted to specialized encyclopedias. This edition has an interesting focus on the growing integration of print and digital sources.
American Reference Books Annual. 2005. Westport, CT: Libraries Unlimited. Also available at www.arbaonline.com. *ARBAonline* provides access to more than 12,000 reviews submitted within the decade. In addition, up to 200 new or updated reviews are entered at the start of each month. The print edition, organized by subject, has a section on "Dictionaries and Encyclopedias."
ARBA Guide to Subject Encyclopedias and Dictionaries, 2nd ed. 1997. Englewood, CO: Libraries Unlimited. Though dated, this selection of subject dictionaries and encyclopedias culled from ten years of *ARBA* reviews provides a broad overview of the breadth of material available. New reviews can be found in *ARBAonline*.
Goodin, Dan. 2005 "Science Journal: Wikipedia Pretty Accurate." *Associated Press*, (December 14). Available at: http://abcnews.go.com/Technology/wireStory?id=1407693. A thought-provoking report that argues for parity in accuracy levels between the *Encyclopaedia Britannica*, with its army of expert researchers; and *Wikipedia*, with its universe of anonymous volunteers.
Jacobs, A. J. 2004. *The Know-It-All: One Man's Humble Quest to Become the Smartest Person in the World*. New York: Simon & Schuster. A compelling and entertaining memoir that testifies to the age-old allure of encyclopedias, this book tells of Jacobs' attempt to read through all thirty-two volumes of the *Encyclopaedia Britannica*.

Janes, Joseph. 2005. "Pedias, Familiar and Otherwise." *American Libraries* 36, no. 9 (October): 76. A provocative, though brief, rumination on the world of wikis as opposed to traditionally developed encyclopedias.

Kister, Kenneth F. 1994. *Kister's Best Encyclopedias: A Comparative Guide to General and Specialized Encyclopedias.* 2nd ed. Phoenix, AZ: Oryx Press. This is a must-read resource for understanding the immensity and internal organization of encyclopedic resources. Though well over a decade old, chapters on choosing, evaluating, and assigning relative values to available resources continues to provide welcome structure to collection development policies on encyclopedias.

Kogan, Herman. 1958. *The Great EB: The Story of the Encyclopaedia Britannica.* Chicago: University of Chicago Press. This is an engrossing account of the making of the *Encylopaedia Britannica*, and the towering ambitions that were passed from one visionary to the next so that the *Britannica* became a reality. It reads like a novel.

Mirwis, Allan N. 1999. *Subject Encyclopedias.* Phoenix, AZ: Oryx Press. With almost 100 keyword-indexed titles, this two-volume resource provides competent and ranked overviews of 1,000 subject specific encyclopedias.

Pack, Thomas. 2004. "Specialized Encyclopedias for In-Depth Information." *Information Today* 21, no. 5: 29–30. This article argues the need for the dramatic upsurge in the production of specialized encyclopedias. Such encyclopedias, he claims, have far greater value and in-depth utility than general encyclopedias.

Pink, Daniel H. 2005. "The Book Stops Here." *Wired Magazine* 13.03 (March). Pink provides a quick tour of encyclopedia production principles from the One Smart Guy model (Aristotle), to the One Best Way model (Britannica) to the One For All model (Wikipedia).

"Print Encyclopedias Making Comeback." 2002. *Boston Globe* (December 30). Also available at: www.dclab.com/dclnews0501.asp. Based on the Outsell survey finding that "print is the preferred format for using content, but not the preferred format for finding it," the report argues for the continuing popularity of print encyclopedias.

Trevisa, De John. 1988. *On the Properties of Things: John Trevisa's Translation of Bartholomaeus Anglicus De Proprietatibus Rerum: A Critical Text.* Gloucestershire: Clarendon Press. A compelling glimpse into an early example of an encyclopedia, this text also testifies to the role of encyclopedias as synopses of an era, in this case the medieval age.

Bibliography of Works Cited in this Chapter

Awe, Susan, and Barbara Bibel. 2005. "Encyclopedia Update 2004." *Booklist* 101, no. 2 (September 15): 208–209.

Bailey, Annette. 1998. "The Good, the Bad, and the Dead! Using Encyclopedias." *School Library Media Activities Monthly* 15, no. 1 (September): 42–44.

Beede, Benjamin, R. 2001. "Editing a Specialized Encyclopedia." *Journal of Scholarly Publishing* 33, no. 1 (October): 1–10.

Cohen, Steven M. 2005. "Wiki While Your Work." *Public Libraries* 44, no. 4 (July/August): 208–209.

Hamilton, B. 2003. "Comparison of the Different Electronic Versions of the Encyclopaedia Britannica: A Usability Study." *The Electronic Library* 21, no. 6: 546–554.

Jacso, P. 2000. "How the Reference Market is Being Won." *Information Today* 17, no. 10 (November): 54–55.

Janes, Joseph. 2005. "What Does Google Know that We Don't?" *American Libraries* 36, no. 8 (September): 76.

McArthur, Tom. 1986. *Words of Reference: Lexicography, Learning, and Language from the Clay Tablet to the Computer*. Cambridge, NY: Cambridge University Press.

Reid, Calvin. 1999. "EB Transformed into Free Web Reference Portal." *Publishers Weekly* 246, no. 43 (October 25): 12.

Thompson, A. H. 2003. "The Ideal Electronic Multimedia Encyclopedia—Are We There Yet?" *Multimedia Information and Technology* 29, no. 4 (November): 111–113.

6

Answering Questions that Require Handy Facts—Ready Reference Sources

Overview

Moments of flamboyance in reference transactions are rare. When exhibited, they are invariably through the dramatic simplicity of a ready reference resource. Librarians seemingly pull out of a hat a string of dates, events, statistics, rankings, names, chronologies, and facts to ease the itch of patron queries that are short, factual, and non-analytical.

Ready reference work includes all the joys and tribulations of instant gratification. It is quick. It is immediate. It is fun. It contributes to the stereotype of the all-knowing reference librarian. It also requires the reference librarian to assemble a stable of ready reference sources that are handy and entirely familiar.

A significant number of library Web sites, in fact, have an icon directing the user to ready reference sources. It is variously termed as "quick reference" as at the Purdue University Library (www.lib.purdue.edu/eresources/readyref); "virtual ready reference desk" as at the Robarts Research Library (www.library.utoronto.ca/robarts/reference/resources.html) at the University of Toronto; or just plain "reference desk" as at the Library of Michigan (http://web.mel.org/viewtopic.jsp?id = 53). While online resources and the ability to "bookmark" and create "knowledgebases" has expanded the scope and range of ready reference resources, there continues to be a traditional substratum of established reference works to provide a footing for answering this genre of questions. This chapter lays out some of those handy reference resources specifically collated to cover the major who, what, which, where, when, and how questions faced by a reference librarian.

How Ready Reference is Used

The need for ready reference sources is felt when:

• Quick, rather than multistep, answers are required.
• Factual, rather than analytical, information is required.
• Relative facts need to be located in a single source.
• The information required is wide-ranging but not deep.
• Citations for primary research are required.

Ready reference is not necessarily "simple" reference. As Marydee Ojala writes, "it's the easy-sounding, fact-based questions that may be more difficult to answer" (Ojala 2001, 59). There is usually only one right answer. Selecting the right resource to find these right answers is the first step in ready reference work.

Questions Answered by Ready Reference

• What is the Earth's distance from the sun?
  91.4–94.5 million miles according to the *World Almanac*.
• Where are the Amtrak and Greyhound stations located in Mobile, Alabama?
  The address, telephone, and toll-free numbers are listed in *City Profiles USA*.
• How much would it cost to copyright a new computer software application?
  $30—the website at www.copyright.gov can provide more detailed information.
• Who publishes historical romances in Virginia?
  The *Literary Market Place* has a comprehensive list.
• Which character in the play version of *The Diary of Anne Frank* steals food?
  Mr. Van Daan, according to the *MagillOnLiterature Plus* database.
• How do I address a letter to the new Pope?
  Emily Post's Etiquette suggests "Your Holiness" or "Most Holy Father."
• In the United States, what is the difference in earnings between men and women with professional degrees?
  The *Statistical Abstract of the United States, 2006* (Table 217) reports the mean earnings for males to be $136,128 and for females to be $72,445.

Major Ready Reference Resources Used in Reference Work

Reference textbooks invariably discuss at length the minute differences between almanacs and yearbooks; annuals and compendiums; directories and indexes; and the many ready reference sources available to a librarian. Selecting from this range of ready reference resources, however, becomes easier if standard questions are visualized as falling into question categories: who, what, where, which, when, and how. The why questions typically require analysis and fall outside the purview of ready reference.

TYPE	GENERAL SOURCES	SPECIFIC SOURCE	EXAMPLE
WHO	Telephone books; government directories, almanacs	www.anywho.com	I need a telephone number for 5 Main Street, Anytown, USA.
WHAT	Consumer and citizen guides; college guides, grant books; occupation handbooks.	www.cem.va.gov	What are the eligibility requirements to be buried in a National U.S. Cemetery?
WHICH	Literary synopses; yearbooks	*Masterplots*	Which Russian character murdered a greedy old pawnbroker?
WHERE	Relocation directories, almanacs	*City Profiles USA*	Can I get the crime statistics, weather averages, and school rankings for Boise, Idaho?
WHEN	Timelines and events, chronologies, almanacs	*Chase's Calendar of Events*	What celebrities were born in the month of July?
HOW	Etiquette, statistics, manuals, almanacs.	*Robert's Rules of Order*	What is the minimum number of people required to form a quorum?

General Facts

The generalized query is best served with an encyclopedia, an almanac, or Web portals such as www.ipl.org, www.bartleby.com, www.xrefer.com, www.lii.org, and www.onelook.com.

Almanacs are the epitome of a ready reference resource. They are crammed with general information that is concise and factual. The earliest almanacs, dating back to the 1300s, were usually focused on the calendar and on weather. They gradually expanded to include a little bit of everything. Benjamin Franklin's beloved 1733 publication *Poor Richard's Almanac* even included lists of road names and a bit of poetry.

While poetry and road names have fallen by the wayside, the tradition of providing the widest common denominator of popularly requested facts continues to mark the successful almanac. The most respected and used almanac in America is the annual *World Almanac and Book of Facts.* Published since 1868, and an annual since 1886, the *World Almanac* is crammed with facts, features, rankings, directories, and information. The index is comprehensive and a critical key to opening up the riches of the *Almanac.* The print edition is 1008 pages and available in both paperback and hardcover editions. It is also available on CD-ROM and online via subscription through the *World Almanac Reference Database* at FACTS.com. A handheld edition can be purchased for smart phones and on PDA through PalmOS that allows for adjustable fonts, cross-references, and interactive quizzes. A free e-mail newsletter is available at www.worldalmanac.com/wa-newsletter.htm. It provides monthly updates to the month's events, holidays, birthdays, obituaries, news features, and chronologies.

Marketed as a dual-format resource, the annual *Time Almanac with Information Please*® is prominently linked to the free Web site www.infoplease.com. Rather than the traditional contents table and index bracketing the almanac, a detailed index prefaces the book. Graphical tabs listing the major sections replaces the table of contents, with "health and nutrition" given special focus and highlighted in red. Like the *World Almanac*, the *Time Almanac* has incorporated index marks on the edge of the book to facilitate quick delineation of different sections in the book. Free access to the Web site provides a distinct advantage to the almanac. Topics can be searched either by section or through an alphabetical index. If a user is unable to find an answer, the site provides the option of e-mailing a question. Given the publishing weight of *Time* and the name-recognition of *Information Please*, which started off as a popular radio show in 1938, the almanac has become a required acquisition for many libraries. There is a children's version of the almanac as well, the *2005 TIME for Kids Almanac*, with a free Web site at www.factmonster.com.

Canada and the United Kingdom

While a great many reference works are globally useful, regardless of the place of publication, the almanac gains in value when directed to a specific audience. Users looking up the *World Almanac* or the *Time Almanac* will find universal facts on statistics, measures, calendars, science, biographies, and news, but will also find a great deal of information on the U.S. government, political structure, and personalities. So also, a copy of the *Canadian Global Almanac* and the hoary *Whitaker's Almanack* would be a worthwhile investment to assure ready access to Canadian and British facts.

The 137th edition of *Whitaker's Almanack* continues a tradition that began in 1868, to register "the people, institutions and processes [that] keep the modern world's cogs turning." In addition to global cogs involving statistics and general information, Whitaker's is an invaluable fount of facts on the UK. Summaries of the year's newsworthy events are supplemented with distinctly local information such as the winner of the Irish Derby, the year's productions at the Royal Opera House in Covent Garden, and local government listings that allow the user to verify, for example, whether Exeter is a parliamentary constituency. The table of contents divides the information into six major categories and the all-important index is comprehensive. The almanac is not available online, though sample entries and Web links to useful sites can be found at www.whitakersalmanack.com.

Formerly known as the *Canadian World Almanac and Book of Facts*, the *Canadian Global Almanac* is divided into eleven sections, most of which focus on Canadian facts. The formula for representation in Canada's House of Commons, the average household expenditure in Québec, or the winners of the Genie Awards for film can all be located in the almanac. The sources are authoritative, with primary information derived from organizations such as Statistics Canada and Natural Resources Canada. The index is adequate. The almanac is not bilingual and is published only in English. There is no online version available.

Local Facts

An essential component of ready reference is accessible local information. The resources for this can be diverse and less than formal. The onus of collating a useful collection is squarely on the reference librarian, based on the demands of the users. Some resources that can help build this collection are:

- Town directory;
- Town map;
- List of elected officials and representatives;
- Local government, institutions, agencies, and associations;
- Visitor information;
- List of services such as nearest fax, notary public, passport services, post office;
- Transportation and directions to the library;
- Local datasheet.

A noteworthy sample of composite local information can be found in the online page created by Seattle's University of Washington Libraries at www.lib.washington.edu/ research/sea.html. Entering students, faculty, staff, and parents have access to consolidated information on everything from accommodations near the university to local weather, transportation, and community resources. The Parsippany-Troy Hills Public Library System in New Jersey has also taken the initiative in producing a pathfinder titled *New to Parsippany* that lists all services needed by a new resident. Given the high number of immigrants in the region, information about ESL (English as a Second Language), adult education, and the certification of foreign transcripts is provided along with the more traditional facts of local day care, employment, newspapers, and service agencies.

The "Who" Facts

The "who" questions are typically answered by the family of telephone directories or by biographical directories.

Letting your fingers do the walking with the ubiquitous telephone directory is good practice for the reference librarian. Given its commonality and public familiarity with usage, the *SuperPages* tend to be forgotten. They do, however, provide a slew of value add-ons in addition to business and name listings that can prove very handy to the busy librarian. Contact information for community agencies such as those for domestic violence, senior citizens, blood banks, and substance abuse can be found. Frequently needed numbers for local, county, state, and federal government offices are also listed in the Blue Pages. Verizon adds a Community Magazine to its directory, with area maps, graphics of airport and stadium layouts, local attractions, a recreation guide, and a calendar of events. Online telephone directories are highly effective resources as well; www.anywho.com, www.superpages.com, www.switchboard.com are all worthy sites to locate persons or businesses. Reverse look-ups are also possible in all three. The switchboard site also offers search capabilities for Web addresses, area codes, and zip codes.

Specialty directories can be a positive addition to the basic telephone directory. Publishers like Gale Group and Omnigraphics have produced a series of specialty directories, some of more value to ready reference than others. Omnigraphics specializes in rearranging or expanding upon telephone directories so that a more exact search is facilitated. The *Toll-Free Phone Book USA*, *FaxUSA*, and *Web Site Source Book* are annual directories with alphabetical listings of organizations. Entries can also be accessed through yellow-page-style subject classifications. In addition to their titular focus, the directories list complete mailing addresses and telephone numbers. An online source for toll-free numbers can be found at http://inter800.com, a bilingual Spanish and English Web site that was launched in 1995 to locate 800/888 numbers by listing either the product, service, or company name.

The Taft Group publishes directories that act like yellow pages with a particular focus. The *Corporate Giving Directory* and the *National Directory of Nonprofit Organizations* are two examples. The former profiles approximately one thousand funding sources in the United States. In addition to contact information, giving priorities and preferences are also analyzed. The latter lists names, addresses, telephone numbers, and annual revenues for over 180,000 nonprofit organizations. Both are updated annually.

Popularly known as a "crisscross directory," the print version of the *Hill-Donnelly Cross Reference Directory* provides succinct answers to questions posed by users who have an address but are in search of a name or telephone number. It is also used extensively by small business owners planning a marketing strategy as well as new homeowners scouting a particular area. The resource covers selected cities in forty-one states. Listings are most easily located either by the telephone number or by the address. Special sections include color-coded pages that provide location via census tracts, zip codes, and street names. Each listing is accompanied by a "relative affluence rating" based on census data as well as medians of home value and income. Published in print since 1948, the directory is now also available on CD-ROM under the title *Cross+Search Plus*. If a listing proves to be elusive, call 411, and a per-call charge service called *CNA (Customer Name and Address)* is offered by Verizon to do reverse searches.

With 43,000 post offices serving over 141 million homes, farms, and businesses through "snow, rain, heat and the gloom of night," the Postal Service publishes the detailed two-volume *National Five-Digit Zip Code and Post Office Directory*. The resource lists all the post offices in the country as well as the zip code for each named street. Arranged by state, each section is preceded by a map of the state, with three-digit zip code divisions outlined. A useful feature in Volume 2 is the listing of both new and discontinued zip codes as well as details of classes of mail and special services. The online version is freely available at www.usps.com. The "com" designation is based on the status of the Postal Service as an independent establishment of the Executive Branch, but users will be redirected even if they were to type in "gov." An online site for Canadian postal information is available at www.canadapost.ca/segment-e.asp. It provides information on postal (zip) codes and reverse searches, as well as a list of Canadian municipalities with defunct "old names" listed alongside.

Who's Who in America has been a familiar resource in America for over a century. First published in 1898, the current edition of *Who's Who* is a two-volume set that lists over 100,000 "high achievers." The value of this resource is that it covers living Americans about whom not much may be found otherwise. The mini-biographies are built around at least twenty set characteristics. Facts may be located for the glitterati, the literati, and the accomplished but relatively anonymous leaders of business, science, education, and the arts. There are two indexes to help the user find a name. One is by geographical location and the second is through an occupational category. *Who's Who in the World* is a valuable companion volume with the same format and coverage of over 50,000 global personalities. The publications are available online via subscription at www.marquiswhoswho.net. The online version is updated daily, and it is possible to search by name, gender, religion, and other access points. The online version also incorporates a total of twenty other *Who's Who* publications that focus on subject specialists. The subject coverage is useful for academic and special libraries but not necessary for the average public or school library.

A subject-special version of who is who can be found in the annual *Literary Market Place*, popularly known as the *LMP*. Given that the percentage of books published in the United States has risen at an exponential rate, the value of the *LMP* has risen in tandem. With sixty-five years of publishing history, the two-volume *LMP* has established itself as a reliable and exhaustive resource for the North American book publishing world. The 2006 edition includes contact information for publishers, literary agents, and editorial services in American and Canada. The entries are alphabetical, as well as by subject, geographic location, and type of publication. The confusing world of imprints, subsidiaries, and distributors is also listed. A calendar of book trade and promotional events is provided along with relevant awards and prizes. The information is updated throughout the year and revised annually in print. The online version, available at www.literarymarketplace.com, has both the *LMP* and the *International Literary Market Place* and is updated continuously. Users have the option of free access to limited information such as a list of small presses or of becoming paid subscribers with access to all the information contained in both publications.

The "What" Facts

The "what" questions typically cluster around consumerist concerns. In an age of dizzying choice, what to choose based on what criterion is a recurring responsibility. From the more trivial questions of what is the best restaurant, vacuum cleaner, MP3 player, or car to the more weighty ones of what occupation, college, or government aid is available, consumer guides have increasingly become a staple of reference libraries.

Monthly issues of *Consumer Reports* and the annual *Consumer Reports Buying Guide* are marketed as the consumer's most authoritative guides for "doing homework" on potential purchases. With ratings on home products that range from canned soups to minivans, the format is designed to aid the consumer in scoping the market, gauging trends, evaluating specific features, and scanning relative prices and advantages. The synoptic *Guide* is linked to the monthly *Reports*, which studies products in great detail. The *Guide* is handy in providing short overviews of popular items, but is more valuable as a comprehensive and cumulative index to the *Reports*. As a nonprofit organization,

Consumer Reports has staked much of its authority on the fact that it is independent of manufacturers' bias. It buys all the products it tests and accepts neither advertising nor free samples from commercial companies. An annual *Buying Guide Canadian* is also available. The online version has a four-year searchable archive and can locate items by keyword or through an alphabetical index, or by category. It is available for a fee at www.consumerreports.org.

A comprehensive source for pricing information on both new and used cars can be found in *New Cars and Trucks Buyers Guide* and *Used Cars and Trucks Buyers Guide*, commonly known as the Edmunds guides. Entries are alphabetized by the make of the car. For used cars, the model, year, body style, and mileage category are collated to suggest the market value for trade, private sale, and dealer sale. Photographs supplement each entry. For new cars, details of the car are also supplemented with a brief analysis, photograph, price range, and both consumer and editorial ratings. The online version, available at www.edmunds.com, is popularly requested as it was the first free auto Web site for car ratings. It continues to provide free access to ratings as well as value add-ons such as a monthly payment calculator and used vehicle listings by geographic location. The small, yellow *N.A.D.A. Appraisal Guides* are also a staple of ready reference and provide quick, continually updated prices on used vehicles of all types. *Kelley Blue Book*, available in print since 1926 and online at www.kbb.com, is another respected source for pricing on new and used cars.

A clear, well-organized synopsis of major occupational groups in the United States, the handy annual *Occupational Outlook Handbook 2006–2007* is the resource to consult when the user needs to know what qualifications are required to be a recreational therapist; or what is the exact nature of an account collector's job; or if there is any future in a job as a machine setter. A great many of the 822 occupations detailed by the federal government are presented in organized sections describing the nature of the job, working conditions, current employment statistics, future job outlook through the year 2012, required training, median earnings, related jobs, and sources for further information that include the union or association covering the job type. The structure of the descriptions for each occupation is unvarying, providing ideal material for quick reference. The information is also freely available online at www.bls.gov/oco.

There are homes that are sold for a single dollar to local governing bodies. There are special education grants for infants with handicaps. There are guaranteed loans for veterans in need of housing. The *Government Assistance Almanac* is a user-friendly and commercial version of the government behemoth, the *Catalog of Federal Domestic Assistance*, published annually. With a comprehensive listing of domestic financial aid available through government agencies, the almanac lists the purpose of the grant, eligibility, range, and scope of aid and assistance provided, as well as a referral to the grant agency's headquarters, telephone number, and Internet address. The Omnigraphics edition, with its detailed index, is far easier to use than the *Catalog* that contains more detailed information such as grant deadlines, renewal policy, and application procedures, but is far too unwieldy to be used effectively for ready reference. The freely available Web site is at http://12.46.245.173/cfda/cfda.html and updated on a biweekly schedule. An advantage provided by the Web site is the easy access to all formal grant applications, including the generic Form 424 used for most assistance grants. A plug-in of the Adobe Acrobat Reader is required to download the forms.

Over $27 Billion grants were awarded in 2004 by independent, company-sponsored, community, and grant-making operating foundations. 10,000 of the largest of such foundations can be researched in some detail in the substantial *Foundation Directory*. First published in 1960, the *Directory* is updated and revised annually based primarily on the tax returns of relevant foundations. It aims at both describing and providing contact information to all major grant-giving institutions. Entries are arranged by geographic state, though seven supplementary indexes, including a subject index, are provided to aid in searching. The *Directory* does not cover grants to individuals. At www.fdncenter.org, the *Foundation Directory Online* is available at four levels of coverage, the *Basic, Plus, Premium, and Platinum*. A CD-ROM version titled the *FC Search* is also available.

There was a time in the not-too-distant past when ready reference would include a messy collection of print catalogs and curricula from colleges and universities across the nation. While this collection is supplanted by the comprehensive online presence of individual educational institutions, wide-ranging information that can aid the college consumer still depends on collated guides. Peterson's six-volume *Annual Guide to Graduate Programs* is a definitive source for graduate and professional programs in accredited institutions, both in the nation and abroad. Profiles that cover the field of study, enrollment statistics, typical costs, computer and library facilities, housing, and contact information are provided for more than 1,800 institutions. Peterson's annual compilation of undergraduate institutions, *Two-Year Colleges* and *Four-Year Colleges*, also delivers rounded profiles of junior and community colleges. In addition to the information provided for graduate colleges, these volumes state whether the institution is state-supported, has an urban, suburban, or small-town campus, and the levels of difficulty in getting admission—from noncompetitive to most difficult. Barron's *Profiles of American Colleges*, College Board's *College Handbook*, and the *U.S. News and World Report's Ultimate College Directories* are all worthy publications to aid the college consumer.

In addition to mainstream colleges, a selection of specialized directories based on community interest are also of value to a collection. *The Handbook of Private Schools* lists selected, nonpublic educational institutions. *American Trade Schools Directory* is a loose-leaf publication that has an amendment service to continually update the listings of schools for classified occupations that run the gamut from acupuncturist and accountant to welder and x-ray technician. *The Guide to Cooking Schools* provides a hard-to-find listing of culinary schools and recreational cooking schools both in the nation and abroad. The Law School Admission Council, in cooperation with the American Bar Association, publishes the annual *Official Guide to ABA-Approved Law Schools*. Peterson's also has a whole series of subject-specific school directories such as the ones for *Visual and Performing Arts, Nursing Programs,* and *MBA Programs*.

The "Which" Facts

"Which" questions are interchangeable with "what" questions, but tend to home in on fewer or single options. Literary questions invariably fall under this category.

Masterplots is an ever-growing multivolume series that parses major bodies of literature such as fiction, drama, poetry, and short stories. Aimed at facilitating an understanding of all major literary works, this classical reference source has been around since 1949. In addition to a synopsis, some works are appended with critical evaluations, story segments, and review essays that have annotated bibliographies. The twelve-volume *Masterplots, Revised Second Edition* (1996) is a collection of all literary genres, whereas other series such as the eight-volume *Masterplots II, Short Story Series* and the four-volume *Masterplots II, Drama Series, Revised Edition* focus on one genre. The CD-ROM version, *MasterplotsComplete* (2000) is comprehensive. Covering over one hundred volumes, the CD-ROM provides short summaries and critical analyses of nearly 15,000 literary works. The index is searchable by title, author, subject, characters, locale, and genre with hypertext links between title, author, and character.

The "When" Facts

Published as a thirty-two-page booklet in 1957 by the Chase brothers, Chase's annual *Calendar of Events* is currently considered the most accessible and authoritative compilation of both famous and trivial events and holidays. The publication is arranged by each day of the calendar, so that all special events, celebrations, and birthdays of famous people on a particular day are clumped together. Presidential proclamations, religious observances, anniversaries of famous events, astronomical phenomena, and sponsored events provide the bulk of entries listed. A detailed index at the end of the book lists all events alphabetically so that a search is possible both by the name of the event or by the date on which it is celebrated. Obscure events also flood the pages of *Chase's*, as it is open to everyone to submit entries that will be added at the discretion of the editor. So, for example, Independence Day on July 4 is listed along with the World's Greatest Lizard Race in Lovington, New Mexico. National and state days of other countries around the world are also included. A free Web version of the publication is not available, though it can be downloaded as freeware from sites such as www.tucows.com or purchased on CD.

For quick facts on what happened on a certain day in history, the "Any Day" site at www.scopesys.com/anyday provides an ambitious, global list of births, deaths, holidays, religious observances, and trivial and nontrivial happenings around the world from ancient times. A perpetual calendar for the years from 1901 to 2100 can be found at www.vpcalendar.net. The site also provides handy information on the exact years that define centuries and millennia as well as the dates of seasons in both hemispheres and Australia.

The *American Decades* and *American Eras* series are comprehensive sources for chronologies, headlines, and facts required for a specific time period in U.S. history. The eras of pre-twentieth-century America and the decades of twentieth-century America are presented in composite capsules that cover the major events, laws, entertainment, business, government, and personalities of the age. The source is a unique addition to "when" references because it covers dates of more abstract entities than the more easily located births, deaths, anniversaries, and calendar events. Cultural, social, and economic trends are covered; so, for example, the date for Levittowns, the first prototypes of mass-produced suburban complexes, can be located through an exhaustive index. The *UXL American Decades* series is a children's version of this resource and is available in both print and as an e-book.

The "Where" Facts

The Statesman's Yearbook is an annual one-stop source for the social, political, geographic, and economic profiles of all the countries of the world. More general information such as time zones and ISO country codes can also be found in the first part of the book. Published since 1863, the information is concise, authoritative, annually updated, and supplemented with a foldout color world map with flags from all 192 countries. An interactive online version available at www.sybworld.com/views/home.html is updated on a monthly basis and has links to over 2000 other related sites. Similar information, updated frequently, can be found in The World Factbook at the Central Intelligence Agency Web site available at http://cia.gov/cia/publications/factbook/index.html. This site also contains one of the most current resources for checking on chiefs of state and cabinet ministers of nations and territories, as the information is updated on a weekly basis.

Omnigraphics publishes a host of descriptive directories aimed at users looking for pertinent information on U.S. cities. The Moving and Relocation Directory, 2005–2006, and City Profiles USA, 2005 are two examples. The Directory provides a list of over one hundred major cities that are deemed to be "popular relocation locations." Much of the information provided is from primary sources, collected by contacting individual offices and firms. Statistics such as the "quality of life indicator" are taken from government sources. While some of the features that have been included—such as time zone maps and area code tables—can be found in general almanacs, the directory is unique in its compiling of a comprehensive factual profile of the selected cities. Chambers of commerce, local moving companies, banks, television and radio stations, mass transit and telecommunications, employment agencies, and property appreciation rates are some of the included features listed for each of the 121 cities.

The "How" Facts

"How" questions are of two types: the "how many" variety that requires statistical resources and the "how to" sort that requires manuals.

How many

Published since 1878, the preeminent print resource for statistical queries is the annual Statistical Abstract of the United States, 2004–2005. It is an exhaustive compilation of the social, economic, and political profile of the United States, parsed into thirty sections and 1,385 tables. Each table is documented with a source that includes Web site information when applicable. An alphabetical index of all tables is provided at the end of the Abstract, along with a detailed guide to sources used. Given the torrent of statistical information contained in the book, the index is an invaluable lifeline to navigate through the numbers. Statistics as varied as the number of abortions in teens under fifteen years of age to the total production of wheat in the world can be found in the pages of the indomitable Abstract. It is available also on CD-ROM; this version has spreadsheets attached to each table so that there is more detail available. The Abstract also acts as a handy guide to the far more extensive and dense statistical information to be found in the online version at www.census.gov/statab/www. Links to both macro and micro data on counties, cities, states, and metropolitan areas are available at the site.

Use of the census Web site at www.census.gov can quickly transform a ready reference question into a lengthy reference session. The site is rich. Despite clear icons, detailed instructions, and fast-loading screens, it is well worth the time of any reference librarian to get familiar with the vast information and search strategies available for the site. Keeping in mind that the three factors of subject, time period, and location determine the data category and developing a search string for popularly asked questions goes a long way in making the best use of this seemingly infinite statistical resource. A suggested string for a demographic search, such as that created by reference librarian Lana Peker (2005), could be sketched as follows.

- Click on: American Fact Finder;
- Go to: Data Sets;
- Choose: SF3 and click on: Detailed Table;
- Choose: Place for Geographic Type;
- Choose: State;
- Select geographic area: Your Town;
- Click on: Add and Next;
- Choose a: Table (subject is easiest);
- Select: Ancestry and Search;
- Select a table and: Add; and
- Click on: Show Results.

With the above string, it would take the librarian or end-user a few scant minutes to answer a question like: *In Kalamazoo, Michigan, are there a larger number of inhabitants claiming Irish or German ancestry?* While the search strings evolve along with a changing Web and must be updated periodically, the habit of setting up a few search strings for dense but rewarding Web sites makes for effective ready reference.

A similarly well-endowed statistical site is www.fedstats.gov. It acts as a portal to over a hundred major federal agencies that expend more than $500,000 on any statistical activity. The information can be accessed either through the agency, by subject, alphabetically, or by keyword searches. The information is monitored and revised by each individual agency, so that the sites are not standardized and the librarian must be prepared to conduct different search strings for each search.

How to

A classic resource that has been around since 1922, *Emily Post's Etiquette* has been revised and rewritten by a great-granddaughter-in-law, Peggy Post. The new edition includes netiquette, online dating, and cell-phone etiquette in addition to the traditional issues of manners, table settings, ceremonies, and how to address correspondence. Changing social realities are also covered in the book so that a divorcee announcing her daughter's engagement is provided with clear guidelines as to how to phrase the invitation. A section on addressing Canadian government officials is also included.

The index is comprehensive and the structure of the book is readily evident in the nine area sections laid out in the contents page.

The reigning authority on parliamentary procedures, *Robert's Rules of Order Newly Revised* was first published in 1876. It is an invaluable resource for checking on the correct procedure for conducting an institutional meeting. The composition of a meeting, the call to order, the bringing and passing of a motion, the types of motions, rules of quorum and debates, voting procedures, disciplinary action, and the taking of minutes are laid out in formal detail. The index is both clear and comprehensive so that the locating of abstruse issues is convenient. A Web site at www.robertsrules.com offers twenty frequently asked questions and provides an open forum to ask and answer questions. However, the 4th edition published in 1915 is public domain and can be freely accessed at a number of sites such as www.rulesonline.com and www.bartleby.com/176.

Collection Development and Maintenance

Evaluation of Ready Reference Resources

Ready reference covers a wide range of materials. While authority, scope, cost, format availability, usability, reliability, and comprehensiveness are important in evaluating these materials, the prime directives are accuracy and currency. Ready reference has to provide up-to-date facts that are definitive. While keeping up on professional literature and reviews provides a bedrock of validating resources, it is the reference librarian who is responsible for

- Establishing which source serves which category of question.
- Gauging whether the source is consistently accurate and current.

Whether in print or online, the information provided needs to be constantly vetted for reliability. Most print sources have years of publishing experience and authority to back their use. Yet ready reference, with its compulsion for quick factual answers, draws heavily from online sources. Ninety percent of academic library Web sites have a ready reference section of selected sources that have presumably been selected by professionals. Public, school, and special libraries either provide an open access ready reference section or collate their own "Favorites" bookmarked for quick personal access. These sites can be monitored by:

- Checking for dead links;
- Checking the citation sources;
- Being alert to sites with commercial endorsements;
- Cross-checking answers to establish whether answers are consistently accurate; and
- Checking the updating timetable for each site.

Selection and Keeping Current

Having an accessible selection of multiple resources for each question category is a reasonable strategy as billions of facts are accommodated at different levels of coverage and currency by each resource. An efficient way to keep current with new Web sites is to subscribe to *New This Week*, a weekly newsletter provided by the hardworking team at the *Librarian's Internet Index*. Available at http://lii.org/search/file/mailinglist, the newsletter is free and keeps abreast with reliable information sites that are then categorized according to Library of Congress headings.

For print resources, subscribing to the *New York Times Updating* service is helpful. The service sends in a weekly update of ready reference facts. These must then be individually appended to standard reference tools such as the *World Almanac and Books of Facts, Statesman's Yearbook, Congressional Directory, Who's Who in America*, and others. The process is labor-intensive, but ensures that the currency of print sources is upheld on a weekly, rather than an annual, basis.

Further Considerations

The world of ready reference is as infinite as the minds of humans. Attempting to prefigure the range of queries is a paralyzing exercise. Almanacs, encyclopedias, dictionaries, and a selection of even five trusted resources for each category of the who, what, which, when, where, and how questions will arm the reference librarian with the tools to successfully answer 99 percent of ready reference questions. The stouthearted librarians of the New York Public Library have proven this time and again as they boldly venture into schools to play the game "Stump the Librarian." Students question the librarian, who must then find an answer within three minutes from a small traveling collection of ten to fifteen ready reference tools. The good news? The librarians have always won.

Below is a sampling of some of the questions they have fielded:

- This is my name in hieroglyphics: . What is it?
- What years constitute 10 B.C.?
- What does it mean to die a "natural death"?
- How long can a person lie on a bed of nails?
- What percent of the globe's land is arable?

TOP TEN READY REFERENCE SOURCES

Title	Print	Online
Chase's Calendar of Events. 1957– . New York: McGraw-Hill.	Annual	
Consumer Reports. 1936– . New York: Consumers Union of United States, Inc.	Monthly	Subscription www.consumerreports.org

Emily Post's Etiquette. 2004. New York: Harper Collins,	17th ed.	www.bartleby.com/95/ 1922 edition.
Librarians' Internet Index.	Weekly	www.lii.org
The local telephone directory. 2006.	Annual	www.superpages.com www.switchboard.com www.anywho.com
Occupational Outlook Handbook, 2006–2007. 1949– . Washington, DC: U.S. Department of Labor.	Biennial	www.bls.gov/oco
The Statesman's Yearbook. 1864– . New York: Palgrave Macmillan.	Annual	Subscription www.sybworld.com
Statistical Abstract of the United States. 1878– . Washington, DC: Government Printing Office.	Annual	www.census.gov/ statab/www
Time Almanac with Information Please. 2006. Upper Saddle River, NJ: Pearson Education.	Annual 1999– .	Subscription www.infoplease.com almanacs.html
World Almanac and Book of Facts. 1868–1876, 1886– . New York: World Almanac Books.	Annual	Subscription www.facts.com

Recommended Resources Discussed in this Chapter

American Decades. 1996–2001. Farmington Hills, MI: Thomson Gale.
American Eras. 1997–1998. Farmington Hills, MI: Thomson Gale.
American Trade Schools Directory. 1953– . New York: Croner Publications.
Annual Guide to Graduate Programs. 2005. Lawrenceville, NJ: Thomson Peterson's Guides.
Canadian Global Almanac. 2005. Hoboken, NJ: John Wiley & Sons.
Catalog of Federal Domestic Assistance. 2003. Baton Rouge, LA: Claitor's Law Books and Publishing Division. Updates available at www.cfda.gov.
Chase's Calendar of Events. 2005. New York: McGraw-Hill.
City Profiles USA. 2004. Detroit: Omnigraphics.
College Handbook. 2004. New York: College Board.
Congressional Directory. 2005. Washington, DC: Government Printing Office.
Consumer Reports. 1936– . New York: Consumer's Union of United States.
Consumer Reports Buying Guide 2006. 2005. New York: Consumers Union of United States.
Copyright. Available at: www.copyright.gov.

Corporate Giving Directory. 2004. Rockville, MD: Taft Group.
Dumouchel, Robert J. 2005. *Government Assistance Almanac.* Detroit: Omnigraphics.
Edmunds Guides. 2005. *New Cars & Trucks Buyers Guide* and *Old Cars &Trucks Buyers Guide.* Santa Monica, CA: Edmunds Publications. Available at www.edmunds.com.
FaxUSA. 2005. Detroit: Omnigraphics.
Foundation Directory. 2005. New York: Foundation Center.
The *Guide to Cooking Schools.* 2004. Coral Gables, FL: Shaw Guides.
The *Handbook of Private Schools.* 2005. Boston: Porter Sargent Publishers.
Hill-Donnelly Cross Reference Directory. 2005. Tampa, FL: Hill-Donnelly Corporation.
Kelley Blue Book. 2005. Irvine, CA: Kelley Blue Book Company.
Librarians' Internet Index. Available at www.lii.org.
Literary Market Place. 2005. New Providence, NJ: Information Today.
MagillOnLiterature Plus. 2006. Pasadena, CA: Salem Press.
Masterplots, 2nd ed. 1996. Magill, Frank N., ed. Pasadena, CA: Salem Press.
Masterplots Complete CD-ROM. 1999. Pasadena, CA: Salem Press.
Masterplots II Drama Series Revised Edition. 1990. Magill, Frank N., ed. Pasadena, CA: Salem Press.
Masterplots II, Short Story Series. 1986. Magill, Frank N., ed. Pasadena, CA: Salem Press.
The *Moving and Relocation Directory, 2005–2006.* 2005. Detroit: Omnigraphics.
N.A.D.A. Appraisal Guides. 2006. Costa Mesa, CA: National Appraisal Guides.
National Cemetery. Available at www.cem.va.gov.
National Directory of Nonprofit Organizations. 2004. Rockville, MD: Taft Group.
National Five-Digit Zip Code and Post Office Directory. 2005. Baton Rouge, LA: Claitor's Publishing Division.
Occupational Outlook Handbook 2006–2007. 2005. Washington, DC: U.S. Department of Labor. Available at www.bls.gov/oco.
Official Guide to ABA-Approved Law Schools 2006. 2005. Newtown, PA: Law School Admission Council and the American Bar Association.
Post, Peggy. 2004. *Emily Post's Etiquette.* 17th ed. New York: HarperCollins.
Profiles of American Colleges. 2004. New York: Barron's Educational Series.
Robert, Henry M. 2000. *Robert's Rules of Order Newly Revised.* New York: Perseus Book Group.
The *Statesman's Yearbook 2006.* 2005. New York: Palgrave Macmillan.
Statistical Abstract of the United States, 2006. 2005. Washington, DC: Government Printing Office.
Time Almanac with Information Please®. 2005. Borgna Brunner, ed. Upper Saddle River, NJ: Pearson Education.
TIME for Kids Almanac. 2005. New York: Time for Kids.
Toll-Free Phone Book USA. 2005. Detroit: Omnigraphics.
U.S. News & World Report Ultimate College Guide 2006. 2005. Naperville, IL: Sourcebooks.
UXL American Decades. 2003. Farmington Hills, MI: UXL (Thomson Gale).
Web Site Source Book. 2005. Detroit: Omnigraphics.

Whitaker's Almanack. 2005. London: A & C Black. Available at
www.whitakersalmanack.com.
Who's Who in America. 2005. New Providence, NJ: Marquis Who's Who, LLC.
Who's Who in the World. 2005. New Providence, NJ: Marquis Who's Who, LLC.
The World Almanac and Book of Facts 2006. 2005. New York: World Almanac Books.
The World Factbook. Available at http://cia.gov/cia/publications/factbook/index.html.

Recommendations for Further Reading

Fast Answers to Common Questions: A Gale Ready Reference Handbook. 1999. Carolyn A.
Fischer, ed. Farmington Hills, MI: Thomson Gale. As part of the Ready Reference
Handbook series comprising four volume specific guides and six industry
specific sourcebooks, this particular title presents common reference transactions
in a question and answer format with citations.

Frické, Martin, and Don Fallis. 2004. "Indicators of Accuracy for Answers to Ready
Reference Questions on the Internet." *Journal of the American Society for
Information Science and Technology* 55, no. 3, (February): 238–245. Just when you
think a Web site without advertisements is a sign of site-maturity, the authors
claim that such commonly held indicators may be fallible signposts of accuracy.
They go on to present Internet "link structures" as the more infallible way to
gauge accuracy on a ready reference site.

Mudrock, Theresa. 2002. "Revising Ready Reference Sites: Listening to Users
Through Server Statistics and Query Logs." *Reference & User Services Quarterly* 42,
no. 3 (Winter). This article is a strong reminder to reference librarians that ready
reference sites must constantly evolve according to the needs of users. Usability
heuristics, feedback, and usage statistics can be employed to structure the
evolution. Mudrock provides a practical example as applied to the University of
Washington libraries at Seattle.

Sowards, Steven W. 2005. "Structure and Choices for Ready Reference Web Sites." *The
Reference Librarian* 44, Issue 91/92: 117–138. After studying both academic and
public ready reference Web sites, the author finds commonality in the use of
subject categories and the selection and use of free Internet content, but a lack of
sophisticated search tools aimed at the end user.

Sowards, Steven, W. 2005. "Visibility as a Factor in Library Selection of Ready
Reference Web Resources." *Reference Services Review* 33, no. 2: 161–172. By
studying the ready reference Web sites of one hundred libraries, Sowards
deduces that reference librarians typically select sites that receive recognition
soon after the site is launched. It is also educative to check the sites that are
included in different kinds of libraries.

Wilson, Paula, A. 2004. *100 Ready-To-Use Pathfinders for the Web: A Guidebook and CD-
ROM*. New York: Neal-Schuman Publishers. This title features 100 convenient
and logically constructed pathfinders on topics applicable to different kinds of
libraries. The CD-ROM contains a blank template for creating pathfinders, as well
as a copy of all the pathfinders in XHTML so they can be tailored to individual
demands.

Bibliography of Works Cited in this Chapter

"Best Free Reference Web Sites: Seventh Annual List." 2005. *Reference and User Services Quarterly* 45, no. 1 (Fall): 39–44.

Bulson, Christine. 2003. "Just the Facts: A Look at Almanacs." *Booklist* 99, no. 18 (May 15): 1684.

Byerly, Greg, and Carolyn S. Brodie. 2002. "Get Ready for Reference: Featuring the Internet Public Library and Websites to Use for Fact Finding." *School Library Media Activities Monthly* 19, 4: 31–34.

DiBianco, Phyllis, and Linda Chapman. 2003. "Ready Reference 24/7." *Information Searcher* 14, 2: 5–14.

Goldsborough, Reid. 2002. "Double-checking Your Facts." *Information Today* 19, no. 10 (November): 51–52.

Ojala, Marydee. 2001. "Don't Sweat the Small Stuff: Business Ready Reference Decoded." *Online* 25, no. 1 (January): 59.

O'Leary, Mick. 2002. "xreferplus Heats Up Ready Reference Race." *Information Today* 19, no. 10 (November): 12–14.

Pack, Thomas. 2003. "Online Almanacs." *Information Today* 20, no. 5 (May): 41, 44.

Sims, Lee. 2004. "Academic Law Library Web Sites: A Source of Service to the Pro Se User." *Legal Reference Services Quarterly* 23, 4: 1–28.

7

Answering Questions about Words—Dictionaries

Overview

Humans may have started with a primordial grunt, but they sure have extended it. Fungible and pusillanimous; zephyr and logodedalian; mook and zax; every nuance and twitch in human existence morphs into a word that aspires toward universal and timeless communication.

Dictionaries make a valiant attempt to list all the words in a language along with meanings, usage, pronunciation, grammatical provenance, and syllabication. While there are many different types of dictionaries, they share two characteristics: they provide definitions and are, for the most part, structured alphabetically.

How Dictionaries Are Used

- A question requiring a definition should automatically prompt a reference librarian to consult a dictionary. The need for definitions ranges across many types of words—simple, archaic, slang, idiomatic, foreign, literary, and technical.
- In addition to simple meanings, the etymology and usage of a word can also be clarified by a quick dictionary search. Confusion over the spelling of words, even everyday ones that might "embarrass/embarass," are referred to a dictionary.
- Dictionaries act as invaluable pronunciation and syllabication guides as well. These are accomplished through phonetic symbols, supplemented with keys to the symbols used.
- The root history of words can be found in dictionaries so that users get to know etymologies such as *"algebra"* being the sum of the Arabic fractions *"al"* (the) and *"jabara"* (to reunite).
- Dictionaries list classes of words, so simpler grammatical quandaries can be directed to a dictionary. The principal forms of the word are also included.

- Even a general dictionary provides synonyms for many words. More in-depth needs can be met with a dictionary of synonyms.
- A visual or illustrated dictionary provides text as well as graphical representations to provide further clarity to a word.
- A dictionary of regionalisms provides specialized definitions of less universal usage. It can, for example, help the reference librarian direct a Maine user to the genealogy rather than the gardening section when asked about "seed folk."

Questions Answered by Dictionaries

- Definitions: *"What is an alb?"*
  According to the 11th edition of *Merriam-Webster's Collegiate Dictionary*, it is a full-length white linen ecclesiastical vestment with long sleeves.
- Orthography: *"Is the wit of Wilde 'mordint' or 'mordent'?"*
  Neither. To foul one spelling may be regarded as a misfortune; to foul two smacks of carelessness. Wilde's "mordant" wit can be checked in the *American Heritage Dictionary*.
- Pronunciation: *"When people say 'nuclear' with a 'nyook' sound, do I get a 'me-graine' or a 'my-graine'?"*
  You may want to indulge in a "my-graine," according to the *New Oxford American Dictionary*.
- Etymology: *"Is 'juggernaut' an English word?"*
  According to *The Oxford English Dictionary*, "juggernaut" is the English incarnation of the Hindu god Jagannath.
- Grammar: *"What is the transitive verb of 'sequence'?"*
  NTC's American English Learner's Dictionary sequences transitive verbs after the root noun, so that here it would be "sequenced."
- Synonyms: *"Is there a better word for 'nice'?"*
  Roget's New Millennium Thesaurus, available at http://thesaurus.reference.com lists eighty nicer synonyms for the word.
- Visual: What are the differences between a thumb knot, a reef knot, and a butterfly knot?
  Textual explanations are bound to tie one up in knots. Refer instead to the *Ultimate Visual Dictionary's* "Ropes and Knots" page for photographic representations.
- Regionalisms: *"I just moved to northern Illinois and my neighbors asked me to scramble. Should I be insulted?"*
  Accept your potluck invitation graciously, after checking the *Dictionary of American Regional English*.

Major Dictionaries Used in Reference Work

The use of dictionaries then, is ubiquitous, interesting, and widespread. Given such usage, the types of dictionaries that exist are many: general purpose, specialized, abridged, unabridged, rhyming, slang, polyglot, historical, illustrated, and etymological to name a few. Given such richness, the librarian has an important mandate to be aware of the choices, so that the reference collection has the right mix of dictionary selections to suit constituency needs.

General Dictionaries

"A definition is a snapshot of a word at rest" (McQuade 2003, 1688). General dictionaries strive to provide that perfect snapshot. Depending on the number of "words at rest" that are captured in a publication, a general dictionary can be unabridged with over 265,000 entries; abridged with over 139,000 entries; or pocket-sized with anywhere from 30,000 to 55,000 entries (Reitz 2004).

Unabridged Dictionaries

In unabridged dictionaries, depth and breadth of information is the prime directive rather than currency of words.

Webster's Third New International Dictionary, Unabridged is the direct descendant of Noah Webster's 1828 opus, *An American Dictionary of the English Language*. The cumulative weight of historical expectation is evident in the 470,000 descriptive entries that fill out the book. While the current edition dates to 1961, an addenda section has kept the dictionary somewhat updated to 2002. There is a CD-ROM version available as well with 476,000 entries, color illustrations, and thirteen search options. An online version is also available at https://member.m-w.com/subscribe.php for a monthly or annual fee.

The twenty-volume *Oxford English Dictionary (OED)* took forty-four years to complete. With over 500,000 entries that have multiple corollary word forms, extensive etymology, date of first recorded use of a word, and a "sense perspective" that includes the usage and status of the word, the *OED* is the accepted authority of international English. While an unrevised second edition was published in 1989, a completely revised and updated version is in the works. Available both online and on CD-ROM, the *OED* online is updated quarterly.

The *Random House Webster's Unabridged Dictionary* is available on CD-ROM as well as a 2,300-page hardcover book with a distinctive red cover. Both versions have 315,000 entries of which 1,000 are new words updated to 2001. In the print version, the updates are not integrated into the main text, but provide relative currency to the dictionary. It is the smallest of the three unabridged behemoths, and the most affordable. The entries are short and focus clearly on American English. There is no online version of this dictionary.

Abridged Dictionaries

The United States

With 90,000 words, over 4,000 color graphics, and a longstanding commitment to providing detailed usage information, the *American Heritage® Dictionary, Fourth Edition* is a respected standard in abridged dictionaries. The most recent edition is freely available online on sites such as www.bartleby.com. It is also a popular choice for "embedded lookups" in e-books so that a double-click on any word in a Stephen King title available through Glassbook provides a definition from the *American Heritage Dictionary*. The CD-ROM version has certain value-added features such as the ability to enlarge all thumbnail illustrations; supply audio pronunciation to words; and provide optional search limiters including the ability to block "vulgar" words.

Clarity, simplicity, and speed of access seem to be the motivation behind the relatively recent *New Oxford American Dictionary, Second Edition (NOAD)*. With 250,000 words, of which one word, "esquivalience," is a fake entry inserted to protect the copyright of the dictionary (Alford 2005), over 100,000 example sentences, and the publishing weight of the Oxford University Press to back it, the *NOAD* is establishing itself as a dictionary that goes to the heart of a definition. Rather than listing all the senses of a word in sequence, the "core" or most literal definition of a word is provided, along with related or less literal sub-meanings, all of which are derived from the ongoing North American Reading Program. The pronunciation guide is harder to navigate, since a guide is provided at the start of the book, rather than applied to each word. The 2005 edition has a portable version that can be downloaded to a PDA or a smart phone.

Merriam-Webster's Collegiate Dictionary, 11th Edition has over one hundred years of authority undergirding each edition. With 165,000 entries in the 11th edition, supported by 42,000 usage examples, it continues to be "runner-up to the Bible" as the "second-best-selling English hardcover book in history" (McQuade 2003, 1688). The new edition openly touts a belief in the "convergence" of formats to provide multi-accessibility, so that print, online, and CD-ROM versions are all provided as a single package. The online version is independently available at www.m-w.com and on AOL, with a huge clutch of value-added features such as a thesaurus, word stories, word of the day, kids' dictionary, and a message board to exchange word trivia. Some sections, such as "Signs and Symbols" available in print, are not included.

The United Kingdom

Unlike the venerable *OED*, which maintains a commanding global profile despite its British roots, the abridged dictionaries published in the UK are uniquely British.

"It's nice, rich, handy, modern. Obtain it!" is an anagram of the inimitable *Chambers Dictionary Ninth Edition* (www.worldwidewords.org/reviews/re-fou1.htm).

Over one hundred years old, the *Chambers* continues to pepper the collection with fey definitions such as "channel surf—switching rapidly between different television channels in a forlorn attempt to find anything of interest." These, of course, are not the norm and the more than 300,000 words making up the 2003 edition have clear definitions and include terms from dialects and historical forms.

The *Bloomsbury English Dictionary*, by contrast, is a new dictionary, the British edition of *Encarta Webster's Dictionary of the English Language*. It eschews the British tradition of using the IPA (International Phonetic Alphabet) and has its own phonetic system. It is also distinguished by user-friendly additions such as cross-references to almost a thousand of the most common misspelled words and labeling of words considered obscene.

The *Oxford Dictionary of English 2003* has a total of 355,000 terms that have been updated based on the massive "Oxford English Corpus" database. Since its first edition in 1998, popular usage words such as "muggle," "data smog," and "SARS" have been included. In the Oxford tradition, words have also been supplemented with brief etymologies.

The *Collins English Dictionary* is the most populist British dictionary in that its 2004 edition has, for better or worse, included highly "young" words—slang, dialect, and chat-group abbreviations that complement the collation of words derived from the 524-million-word "Bank of English" database. Uniquely British terms like "stealth tax" (indirect tax); abbreviations like SOHF (sense of human failure); and dialect such as "thraiping" (thrashing) distinguish the *Collins*, just as much as the pointed beheading of monarchical terms distinguishes it within British circles. As an outraged citizen pointed out, "Tudor" has simply been defined as a style of architecture in the *Collins*.

An online British dictionary has been posted by the Cambridge University Press based on the *Cambridge Advanced Learner's Dictionary, 2003*. It contains 150,000 terms and is available at www.freesearch.co.uk/dictionary.

Canada

Recognizing the subtle and not-so-subtle differences in English pronunciation, usage, and spelling fostered by different cultures in different countries, the Oxford University Press has created a uniquely *Canadian Oxford Dictionary*. Compiled by Canadians, examining Canadian sources and perspectives, the 2004 edition has 130,000 terms and various appendixes. Words such as "scraper," for example, include the Canadian usage of removing not only ice, but mud and paint as well. Canadian acronyms like "BQ" for Bloc Québécois; expressions like "jam buster" and spellings like "traveller" and "humour" make this a strong Canadian dictionary resource. The *Nelson Canadian Dictionary of the English Language* (till recently known as the *ITP Nelson*), has over 150,000 terms. It includes extensive Canadian biographies, history, government and folklore and uses Canadian spelling. In a country where a governmental ruling stated a preference for the "-our" spelling to the "-or," Gage Publications, while slow in adopting the usage, have currently updated the familiar *Gage Canadian Dictionary*. Distinctive Canadian words like "snowbird—a Canadian who goes south for the winter" also make the *Gage* a useful Canadian resource. An informative online presence focusing on Canadian spelling can be found at www.luther.ca/~dave7cnv/cdnspelling/cdnspelling.html.

Specialized Word Sources

Learners Dictionaries

With English, as spoken in McDonalds rather than by the Queen, becoming the dominant lingua franca of the world, there appears to be a rising market for dictionaries for learners. How is this different from a regular or even an abridged dictionary? For one thing, "less is more" (Dahlin 1999, 33), and the prime directives are not comprehensiveness and depth of meaning, but simplicity, ease of use, and frequency of words in daily American communication. This is largely calculated from computational analyses of electronic word corpora that cover popular media reports. So, for example, a learner's dictionary is far more likely to include an MTV word like "dude" than an obscure one like "ophiophagus" (serpent eating). All the major publishers of dictionaries such as

NTC, Cambridge, Merriam-Webster, Random House, and Macmillan have published recent editions of learner's dictionaries.

The *Macmillan English Dictionary*, for example, bases its dictionary on the enlightening fact that 90 percent of all text consists of only 7,500 words. These are the words that are highlighted along with 80,000 examples of usage. *NTC's American English Learner's Dictionary* selects 22,000 basic words that are defined and used in context, but eschew other traditional dictionary additions like etymology and synonyms of a word. *The American Heritage Dictionary for Learners of English* has over 40,000 words, with attention paid to the more confusing aspects of English such as homonyms, idioms, and synonyms. A reference section with basic grammar and American factoids is included.

Visual Dictionaries

In a visual dictionary, the words presented are not alphabetical, but grouped under subjects. The focus is on providing a pictorial of the word. Since terms are illustrated, selection is limited to the noun family. *The Firefly Visual Dictionary* has 35,000 terms organized into seventeen chapters. Insects, geology, sports, and architecture all find pictographic representation in full color. DK, known for its splendid graphics, publishes the *Ultimate Visual Dictionary* with fancier artwork, incorporating cutaways and exploded views that display internal structures. *The Firefly Five Language Visual Dictionary* covers 35,000 words in English, Spanish, French, German, and Italian, illustrated with over 6,000 color images. The role of the visual dictionary comes into sharp focus when, for example, a muskrat and a vole are both described as blunt-nosed and short-eared, but the homeowner needs to identify which one is destroying his summer garden. Visual dictionaries are also handy for those perennial school assignments that require labeling parts of the anatomy or the layers of the earth or the structure of an insect.

"Gated" Word Dictionaries

The user in search of words "gated" to a particular community, class, age group, region, or profession is best directed to dictionaries of slang, jargon, argot, regionalisms, or idioms.

Dictionaries of slang usually collate colloquialisms recurring within groups. Slang, by definition, is particularly vulnerable to passing fads so that what was "groovy" earlier and "sweet" today will, in all probability, be entirely different a few years from now. Publications such as *Dewdroppers, Waldos, and Slackers* (Ostler 2003) present slang over the decades from 1900 to 1999. The multivolume *Random House Historical Dictionary of American Slang* (Lighter 1997–) has over 300,000 slang words that date back to Colonial America, more of which will be added once the final third volume is published. For current slang, online options are a wise choice. Everything from hip-hop, to London, to street drugs and sex slang is available, for which a handy directory can be accessed through www.peevish.co.uk/slang. Particularly useful for virtual reference that caters to a high percentage of young adult users is www.urbandictionary.com. With both "exact" and "inexact" search options, the site provides meanings for urban slang as well as chat argot like g2g (got to go) and emoticons like :) which is a happy face, but not as happy as :O.

The preeminent dictionary for American regionalisms is the multivolume, exhaustive, and ambitious *Dictionary of American Regional English (DARE)*. Launched in 1960, it has yet to be completed. It alphabetically documents regional words unlikely to be found in standard dictionaries. The meaning of a word, spelling, pronunciation, area of usage, and actual recorded use is provided along with some maps that display the geographical distribution of the word. With entries completed from A to Sk, with the last volume scheduled for publication in 2009, *DARE* is both a dictionary of unfamiliar terms like "Irish confetti" (bricks and stones used while fighting), as well as an engrossing historical record of American culture. *DARE* has an explanatory Web site available at http://polyglot.lss.wisc.edu/dare/dare.html.

AAD

AAD? The need for *Acronyms and Abbreviations Dictionaries* in every reference library has never been felt more keenly. A string of letters that abbreviate a word (Mr.); initial a term (www); or synopsize a proper noun (UN) is a growing trend in human communication. Electronic communication, with its natural affinity for short forms, has added to the global legitimacy and relevance of truncations.

The most distinguished source for decoding these truncations is the Gale Group's multivolume *Acronyms, Initialisms, and Abbreviations Dictionary*. Arranged alphabetically in the contracted form as well as a reverse expanded version, users can consult the dictionary both to decode an acronym and to discover the accepted truncation for a given term. In the 2004 edition, 15,000 new terms have been added, primarily from areas dealing with computers, science, the armed services, crime, emergency management, and security. Contractions for bus and railroad stations, navigation systems, and stock exchange symbols have also been included. The Gale Group publishes three more specialized dictionaries, the *Subject Guide Series* focusing on computers, telecommunications, and business, the *International* series for global contractions, and one for *Periodical Titles*.

Available since the 1950s, a single-volume source can be found in the 267,000 entries of the *Abbreviations Dictionary*. The entries not only include abbreviations, initialisms, and acronyms, but symbols such as emoticons, signs such as $ (listed under "D"), and eponyms or "designations derived from names" such as "Legionnaire's disease." The entries are in alphabetical order, with signs listed under the first letter of the term it signifies. A person who does not know what "μ" stands for will therefore find it hard to locate it under "m," but is aided by the different subject areas that are also listed. Abbreviations for U.S. states, Canadian provinces, territories, and capitals, and both British and Irish counties are included.

An extensive online dictionary with over 409,000 entries can be found at www.acronymfinder.com. Search strategies allow for both exact searches and inexact ones that can use wildcard truncations, "begins with," and reverse lookups.

For the reference librarian who refers a user to any of these word sources, it is critical to establish the context usage of a contracted term. Acronyms invariably stand for multiple terms, so that "AA," for example, could stand for Alcoholics Anonymous as well as American Airlines or Aerolineas Argentinas. It may even represent a bond rating, a bra size, or the width of a shoe.

Rhyming Dictionaries

Rhyming dictionaries were created to help poets, song makers, and verse creators. They list phonetic endings in alphabetical form so that if users need words to rhyme with "blue," they would look up the phonetic suffix of "oo." *Words To Rhyme With* (Espy 2001) has a separate section on "eccentric" words that are difficult to partner with a rhyme, such as "aardvark." *The Oxford Rhyming Dictionary* (Upton 2004) has over 85,000 words in forty sound groups, but uses British pronunciation; www.rhymezone.com organizes rhymes by syllable or letter sound. Derived from Carnegie Mellon University's "Pronouncing Dictionary," a machine-readable collection of over 125,000 words, the online rhyming source has been freely available for almost ten years.

Metadictionaries

The online medium seamlessly lends itself to consolidating diverse resources while scavenging for individual requests. Why restrict oneself to a single dictionary resource when a simple click can trawl through so many more is the motivation behind the metadictionary.

For example, www.onelook.com is host to 6,257,269 words (as of 11/17/2005) culled from 993 dictionaries that include everything from the well-known *Compact OED*, and *Merriam-Webster's Collegiate, 10th Edition*, to lesser known sources such as *Dan's Poker* and *Orthodontic Terms*. The dictionary also provides for a reverse feature that allows users to describe a concept in order to find a word.

Another popular metadictionary, www.dictionary.com, is free and user-friendly. A simple search box at the top of the page in which the word or an approximation of the word can be typed is all that is presented. Over 900 online sources such as *The American Heritage® Dictionary* and the *CIA World Factbook* provide an answer with the source for each entry listed below the answer. Metadictionaries, then, act as hosts rather than producers of dictionaries. The spottiness of sources that contribute to an answer makes them a less than fully reliable reference resource, but certainly constitutes a handy site to add to the "Favorites" of a busy reference desk.

Thesauri

Thesauri play a different role from dictionaries. Whereas dictionaries are primarily responsible for defining a word, a thesaurus helps the wordsmith to find the right word. Each word is partnered with strings of synonyms and antonyms. This provides users with both variety and the tools to choose the right shading in meaning. Thesauri are arranged either alphabetically or by categories.

Introduced over 150 years ago by Dr. Peter Roget, the term thesaurus is usually synonymous with Roget and hence used by a number of publishers. *Roget's International Thesaurus* is a strong resource. The 6th edition has 330,000 words and phrases organized into over one thousand categories arranged according to meanings. *The Oxford American Writer's Thesaurus* (2004) is innovative in that it has introduced short articles attached to certain word usages. It has 25,000 words, supported by 300,000 synonyms and 10,000 antonyms. An online resource is www.thesaurus.com based on *Roget's New Millennium™ Thesaurus* and produced by the creators of www.dictionary.com.

Quotations

Dictionaries often provide quotations to establish the usage of a word. Quotation books exploit that need and provide thousands of memorable quotes that highlight words and concepts. The arrangement of quotation books is varied. The 17th edition of the venerable *Bartlett's Familiar Quotations*, for example, is laid chronologically, though supported by an in-depth index of keywords and authors. It contains 25,000 quotations, most of which continue from John Bartlett's original picks of 1855, updated with new quotes from modern personalities like Bill Clinton, Mother Theresa, and Jerry Seinfeld. *Bartlett's* quotes as listed in the 10th edition can be freely accessed at www.bartleby.com/100. It is searchable by keyword as well as through a chronological or alphabetic index of authors and a concordance index.

The *Random House Webster's Quotationary* (Frank 2001), on the other hand, has 20,000 quotations arranged by subject. Chronology plays no part in the arrangement, though cross-references by author are provided. The second edition of the *Oxford Dictionary of Modern Quotations* and the *Oxford Dictionary of Phrase Sayings and Quotation* are both published by the Oxford University Press, with the former arranged chronologically and the latter by subject.

The role of quotation books in providing dramatic or elegant expression to a certain word or concept is straightforward. A few comprehensive quotation books should suffice for that role. Most reference collections, however, tend to stock a variety of books because of the possibility that a user needs to know a specific quote, in which case the chances of finding it increase by varying the range to cover general, humorous, Biblical, political, gender focus, and other specialized quote sources.

Concordances

A variation of the quotation book, concordances are an alphabetical enumeration of major words in a book or a collection of books by an author, along with the immediate context of the word. Essential additions to any reference collection are concordances on Shakespeare and the Bible.

Much as Roget's, Bartlett's, and Webster's are public domain and used by multiple publishers to sell thesauri, quotation books, and dictionaries, Strong's, derivative of nineteenth-century theologian James Strong, is connected with Biblical concordances. *Abingdon's Strong's Exhaustive Concordance of the Bible* is a reliable concordance of the King James Bible. Concise dictionaries of words in the Hebrew Old Testament and the Greek New Testament are given in addition to the Authorized and Revised English Versions. The prefaced goals of "completeness, simplicity, and accuracy" are evident while using this concordance.

The nine-volume compilation *A Complete and Systematic Concordance to the Works of Shakespeare* or its single-volume version *The Harvard Concordance to Shakespeare* are both respected choices. The *Harvard* edition focuses on Volumes 4–6 of the nine-volume edition, covering the plays and poems of Shakespeare. The specific play, act, scene, line number, and line row in which the word appears is provided using the modern spelling laid out in *The Riverside Shakespeare*. The *Complete* version has elaborate concordances for characters and individual plays, as well as statistics, stage directions, etc. A well-reviewed online Shakespearean concordance has been developed by James Farrow at the University of Sydney Information Technologies Web site at www.it.usyd.edu.au/~matty/Shakespeare/test.html.

Style and Usage of Words

Much as a picture is enhanced by the perfect frame, words can come alive with the right grammar and punctuation. The bullet-spraying panda that eats, shoots, and leaves because of an extra comma struck a punctuation chord in both the United Kingdom and the United States (Truss 2004). Usage styles have become more elaborate with the explosion of formats, both print and electronic, that need to be cited. The printed book, pamphlet, thesis, article is compounded by the nonprint CD-ROM, video, CD, cassette; the oral interview, quote, broadcast, discussion, personal communication; and the flourishing Web site, database, Listserv, chat group, et al. Reference librarians must be prepared for two types of questions in the field:

* Grammar and punctuation
* Style and citation guidance.

The *Chicago Manual of Style* is the top choice for the user interested in publication. Originating in the 1890s as a single proofreader's sheet, the 956 pages of the 15th edition continues to be a crucial tool for countless writers and editors. Preparing a manuscript by dotting the right i's and crossing the right t's, conforming with editorial styles, checking on grammar pitfalls, outlining copyright restrictions, guiding one through the maze of citation differences, providing mathematical copy templates, and designing, producing, and marketing a printed or electronic publication, are all covered in the *Chicago Manual*. It is the source to consult when publication is the goal of the user.

For the scholar, the *MLA* (Modern Language Association) *Handbook for Writers of Research Papers* is the primary source. Every reference collection needs to stock the *MLA* simply because most users will specifically ask for it by title. Traditionally listed as the bibliographic guide for students, the *MLA* is strong on citation guidance.

For the professional, specifically the social scientist, the *APA* (Publication Manual of the American Psychological Association) is the most suitable resource. The print manual is aimed at the writing of reports, presentations, and papers. Guides on presenting statistical data, graphics, and metrication are provided in addition to grammar and citation styles. Notes on avoiding plagiarism are also included. Twenty-four of its "most popular" tips, such as when to use a hyphen in compound words or how to cite an e-mail, are freely available online at www.apastyle.org/previoustips.html. For a price, the *APA Style Helper 5.0* is available as both a CD-ROM and download at https://secure.apa.org/stylehelper/index.cfm?fuseaction+order.download.

Technological breakthroughs in style management software is resulting in a new generation of management software that can manipulate citations into more than six hundred styles including the above *APA, MLA,* and *Chicago* style. Products such as "Reference Manager," "Endnote," "RefWorks," and "ProCite" have the capability to "search Internet databases, organize references, and format bibliographies" (Poehlmann 2005). Academic libraries have been the first to offer bibliographic management software to students and faculty, such as the free subscription to RefWorks provided to all affiliates of the Johns Hopkins University.

Given the different departments in academic institutions, a collection of subject-specific style manuals must also be part of the reference collection. The field of political science, for example, requires the *Style Manual for Political Science*; chemistry would refer to *The ACS Style Guide*; government documents follow *The Complete Guide to Citing Government Information Resources*; journalism favors the *Associated Press Stylebook*; the medical field is guided by the *American Medical Association Manual of Style*. The list is long and style manual acquisition, as always, would have to draw from a clear consideration of local demand.

For those who are stuck wondering whether to use "that" or "which," split an infinitive, or dangle a participle, the inimitable *New Fowler's Modern English Usage* has been consulted for over seven decades. The most recent edition published has departed in controversial ways from the original. It has updated the pronunciation guidelines to cohere with the IPA; provided samples of English usage that are global rather than purely British; and updated "vogue words" and modern usage contexts. For those who are not amused by Burchfield's revised edition, the 1908 version is freely available online at www.bartelby.com/people/Fowler-H.html.

An admittedly descriptive, rather than prescriptive, usage book has recently been published in the UK by Cambridge University Press. The *Cambridge Guide to English Usage* is aimed at the "global and local communicators" of the twenty-first century. Two electronic databases, the British National Corpus and the Cambridge International Corpus, as well as hundreds of questionnaires, have been used to establish patterns that are presented in more than 4,000 alphabetical points of English usage and style.

Children's Dictionaries

The reference world of word sources for children focuses on all-purpose dictionaries. The market for children's dictionaries is geared toward three types of institutions: the school library, the public library, and the family library. For the family, hundreds of desk-sized print dictionaries are available with 12,000 to 15,000 words and a grab bag of bonus information aimed at the student. *A Student's Dictionary,* for example, adds on political factoids about the United States, weights and measures, and global trivia such as the seven continents and the nine planets. These publications are handy but not geared for purchase by reference collections. The definitions are spare, the binding fragile, and the entry is usually without synonyms or etymology or context usage. Reliable publishers of children's dictionaries for reference collections are Macmillan, American Heritage, World Book, and Merriam-Webster's.

It is a pleasure to use the *Macmillan Dictionary for Children*. The physical construction includes sturdy binding, large fonts, colorful guide words, and captioned color illustrations and photographs. The 35,000 entries have clear definitions, parts of speech, abbreviations, synonyms, etymology, pronunciation, and context usage. Homonyms are also included for many words, as are geographical and biographical entries. A critical addition is the spelling hints provided at the start of each letter. Children looking for "pneumonia" or "knighthood" under the phonetic "n" are directed to "pn" and "kn" spellings. Obscure words that nonetheless have relevance in student life, such as "multiplicand" (the number that is to be multiplied), are included. The dictionary is available on CD-ROM and appears as a text edition under the title *McGraw Hill School Dictionary*.

The educational psychologist Edward Lee Thorndike and the lexicographer Charles Lewis Barnhart aimed at producing dictionaries that were not "dumbed-down" versions of an adult dictionary. With more than six decades of publishing experience, Thorndike-Barnhart has expanded its publications to a cluster of children's dictionaries, the *Thorndike-Barnhart Children's Dictionary*, the *Junior Dictionary*, the *Advanced Dictionary* and the *Student Dictionary*. While the *Children's* and the *Junior* are for very young children, there does not appear to be a significant difference between the *Student* and the *Advanced*. The *Student Dictionary* intends to help students both define words "in simpler language than the main word being defined," as well as develop a sense for vocabulary by mastering word sources and word family clues. Forty-three word sources that trace back to a common language source and seventy word families that trace back to a common root are included. Synonyms, etymology, pronunciations, a style manual for writing, and illustrations in black and white as well as color complete the *Student Dictionary*. The currency of words is maintained by the "Scott Foresman citation files," which monitor changes in word usage of the 100,000 entries listed in the book. However, there have been no updates since 1998.

On the other hand, *The World Book Dictionary*, also derived from Thorndike-Barnhart files, has been published since 1963 and continually updated. The most recent edition has more than 248,000 entries, making it one of the largest dictionaries accessible to children. Clarity in definition is the key directive. Illustrations, grammar notes, and a 128-page "guide to communication" are included. Biographical and geographical entries are excluded and instead referred to the *World Book Encyclopedia*. Available in print, CD-ROM, and as part of an online *Reference Center* package, the *World Book Dictionary* is also one of the first to be available in handheld editions of pocket PCs and smart phones.

Bilingual Dictionaries

With porous national boundaries and an increasingly intimate world, the relevance of bilingual dictionaries appears heightened. The large "foreign language" tomes that traditionally graced academic libraries have multiplied into a dizzying variety of unabridged, dual, pocket-sized, and desk dictionaries suitable for academic, public, corporate, and personal libraries.

Cassell, NTC, Oxford, HarperCollins, and Random House are familiar names of brands and publishers that offer a range of bilingual dictionaries. While classic and European languages dominated the industry a century ago, today's landscape offers an extravagant choice of languages. Bilingual dictionaries are conveniently arranged so that the word can be looked up both by its English translation and in the original language.

The Cassell series has had more than 120 years of experience in publishing. *Cassell's Latin Dictionary*, first published in 1854, continues to be a classic addition for the serious researcher. *Cassell's Italian Dictionary* is typical of the later publications that are geared for both the beginner and the advanced speaker. Given that the many dialects of Italian would require multiple synonyms, the dictionary has "translate[d] rather than define[d]" words. In the Italian-English section, pronunciation is eschewed given the phonetic nature of Italian spelling, but included in the English-Italian section.

The Oxford University Press publishes a variety of world language dictionary series. *The Oxford Starter* series, the *Oxford-Duden Pictorial* dictionaries, the *Oxford-Hachette* and *Oxford-Paravia* dictionaries, and the *Compact, Pocket, Concise, Basic* series are all geared at varying levels of readership. Over forty different languages are published with most current projects in the area of pocket and desk editions. A complete list of editions more suited for library reference collections can be accessed at www.askoxford.com/shoponline/bilingual.

McGraw Hill's *Vox/NTC* series has also established itself as an aggressive publisher of world language sources, especially known for its Spanish language series. *Larousse* is the traditional choice for French dictionaries. In the area of world language dictionaries, sometimes even the smallest of publishers become urgent sources of reference acquisition. For example, after the conflict in Kosovo and the sudden influx of Albanians into the United States in the late 1990s, the frantic scramble for stocking libraries and other places with Albanian dictionaries heightened the role of Hippocrene, a small New York press that was able to offer the only *Albanian-English/English-Albanian Practical Dictionary* in print.

Given the nexus between politics and the demand for world language dictionaries, the reference librarian is well advised to acquire the major language dictionaries, as well as keep alert to changing local demographics or global events that can create a sudden demand for lesser-known language groups.

Special Constituency

Two major special constituencies for whom authoritative dictionaries are available are the visual and the hearing impaired. While usage of special constituency dictionaries is sporadic, an absence of these dictionaries when needed can be felt very acutely. The need can appear in academic, public, corporate, specialized, and school libraries.

Large print dictionaries typically tend to have shorter definitions, but wider margins and large, clear font sizes. The *Oxford Large Print Dictionary* was first published in 1989 and is derived from the same database as the *New Oxford American Dictionary*. Definitions are clear and supplemented with usage contexts, notes on confusing or variant spellings, and updated biographical and geographical entries. Abbreviations are used sparingly. The physical design of the book has received input from the Royal National Institute for the Blind so that page quality allows for clarity in type, a maximum of white space brought about by generous margins and line spacing, and accessible font size.

Webster's New Explorer Large Print Dictionary defines over 40,000 words with pronunciation. A special section on abbreviations is also included. Approved by the

National Association for Visually Handicapped, the guide words are in eighteen-point font with the entries in fourteen-point. *Random House Webster's Dictionary Large Print Edition*, published in both the UK and the United States, is another resource that has received a Seal of Approval from the National Association.

Sign language dictionaries are often confused with sign language manuals. While there is much overlap between the two, the dictionaries typically provide pronunciation guides, cross-references, and usage context in addition to sign entries with illustrations. *The American Sign Language Dictionary Unabridged* has more than 7,000 sign entries accompanied by 12,000 illustrations that are arranged alphabetically. It has been updated to include new signs since it was first published in 1981.

The American Sign Language Handshape Dictionary published by the Gallaudet University Press does not, on the other hand, follow alphabetical order, but is organized by a unique system of forty basic "handshapes." The more than 1,600 signs defined in the dictionary derive from these basic handshapes. Illustrations complement the entries and context usage is also provided. An alphabetical Index of English Glossaries at the end of the dictionary provides an alternative way of looking up the right word and sign.

Subject Dictionaries

A burgeoning use of the word "dictionary" has been in the area of subject dictionaries. These dictionaries also define words, but triangulate over an isolated subject area and focus with laser-sharp intensity on any and every word connected with that area. Be it medical, legal, business, scientific, technical, computer, mathematical, electronic, religion, or gardening, every subject appears to be inspiring its own dictionary.

While it is entirely probable that a word presented in a subject dictionary could also be found in an unabridged dictionary, subject dictionaries tend to:

- Provide more depth in definition. Some definitions are quasi-encyclopedic in coverage. For example, in the *Harvard Dictionary of Music*, the definition of "electro-acoustic music" runs over a page.
- Be informed by subject specialists and rate high on reliability. *Black's Law Dictionary* or Stedman's *Medical Dictionary* are authoritative additions to most reference collections.
- Provide quicker access to updated words. The most dramatic example can be found in the aftermath of the digital revolution, when even pocket-sized computer dictionaries were acquired by reference libraries in an effort to keep up with the torrent of new vocabulary flooding everyday global communication. In 1998, no general dictionary listed terms like "hypertext markup language," and a "mouse" was still just a rodent. The need for a subject dictionary on computer terms was dramatically demonstrated.

In most cases, however, the need is undramatic and subject dictionaries like *The Dictionary of Aquarium Terms* are acquired only when appropriate to the aims of the institution and the needs of its constituency.

Collection Development and Maintenance

Selection and Keeping Current

There are a number of ways to keep abreast of developments and updates of dictionaries.

- Reading professional reviews is the most standard way.

  - *Reference Books Bulletin,* though sectioned into *Booklist,* has its own editorial board and reviews all dictionaries, not just those recommended for purchase.
  - An annual *Supplement* to the *Library Journal* published in November each year lists recent and forthcoming reference titles with a separate subject listing for dictionaries.
  - Updates of prominent dictionaries are reviewed in multiple professional publications such as *Publishers Weekly, Booklist, Library Journal, Choice,* and *School Library Journal.*
  - *College & Research Libraries* publish a semiannual selection of recent reference books that includes reviews of general reference works such as dictionaries.
  - Reviews of online and CD-ROM dictionaries are frequently found in *Database.*

- Referring to regularly updated reference works is another way to keep informed. The ALA's *Guide to Reference Books* and *ARBA* are authoritative sources of information.
- A subject-specific monograph such as the 1998 *Guide to World Language Dictionaries* by British librarian Andrew Dalby covers dictionaries for 275 languages in alphabetical order. *Kister's Best Dictionaries for Adults and Young People* reviews 300 English-language dictionaries along with comparative assessments and charts. While dated, it is still a valid resource for insights into the structure of gauging dictionaries and getting a sense of the breadth of material available.
- For an in-depth look at dictionary sources, subscribing to the Dictionary Society of North America is a fertile possibility. Available at http://polyglot.lss.wisc.edu/dsna/ the society is probably the most well-known professional organization of lexicographers. The newsletters and annual journal provide steady insight into the inner dialogues preceding the updating or launching of a dictionary. For a European perspective, membership in EURALEX is possible at www.ims.uni-stuttgart.de/euralex.
- Individual dictionary updates are also possible. The *Oxford English Dictionary,* for example, provides a quarterly newsletter, the *OED News,* which reports research projects and new development initiatives planned for the dictionary. Regular reports on *OED* revisions and new features are guaranteed by signing up for an e-mail listing at www.oed.com/news/email.html.

Evaluating Word Sources

Authority and understandability are the prime criteria for evaluating a word source. If the definition of a word is presented in abstract or misleading ways, all other criteria become moot. Since constant and widespread usage of words decides on whether a word enters or is dropped from a dictionary, authority is as important as accuracy. In fact, there are times when the accuracy of a definition is decided by the authority of the lexicographer or lexical institution. For example, is "nigger" a noun or a racial slur, or both? The authority of Merriam-Webster and the Oxford University Press as responsible lexical giants has upheld the secondary definition of a noun despite charges of inaccuracy from the NAACP (National Association for the Advancement of Colored People). Similarly, the second sense of the term "anti-Semitism" as "opposition to Zionism" as defined in *Merriam-Webster's Third New International Dictionary* was criticized by the American-Arab Anti-Discrimination Committee but has yet to be revised.

Other criteria for evaluating word sources are currency, cost, format, scope, comprehensiveness, and, of rapidly increasing importance, value-added features. Given the ubiquity of spell-checking software, availability and added access to embedded and machine-readable dictionaries is forging ahead as a criterion for evaluation. Online dictionaries have the unique ability to provide clusters of value-added features such as audio availability so the pronunciation can be heard, variant spellings available through wildcard searches, and hyperlinks to related material such as thesauri, similies, usage examples, and word games. Most large dictionary publishers are adding online availability to the print editions so that it has become an increasingly important component of purchase evaluation.

That said, reference evaluators must keep in mind that dictionaries attempt to be definitive about words, and words by definition are both ephemeral and mutative. As Dr. Johnson laments in his preface to *Cassell's Italian Dictionary*, "Every other author may aspire to praise, the lexicographer can only hope to escape reproach" (1977, v).

Further Considerations

Having sampled just a few of the hundreds of dictionaries available, the reference librarian will need to apply the knowledge to the twin tasks of:

- Acquisition of word sources
- Information referral

Acquisition

To paraphrase Ranganathan: to every library its own collection of word sources. While general dictionaries, both abridged and unabridged, are staples of every collection, specialized word sources can play out in various permutations depending on the type, size, and in-built expectations of a particular library. A few caveats to keep in mind while acquiring word sources:

- Not all books titled "dictionaries" are really dictionaries. They are merely alluding to the alphabetical arrangement of a book. For example, *A New Dictionary of Irish History from 1800* lends little to the world of words, but a great deal to the world of history instead. Conversely, titles without the word "dictionary" may be just that. Clues can sometimes be found in publications that have "ABC" in the title, such as the classic subject dictionary, *ABC for Book Collectors* where a specialized term like "japon vellum" finds definition.

- Word sources can be highly derivative, even incestuous, in their capture of existing words and defining mores. For example, no dictionary listed obscene or "gutter" words until the *American Heritage* decided it was a necessary component of existing communication. Today, it is primarily the children's dictionaries that do not include such words. It is therefore not necessary to compulsively acquire every new title that comes up for purchase.

Referral

To paraphrase Ranganathan yet again: to every question its own word source. While reference librarians develop a "muscle" to efficiently field a wide variety of questions based on their knowledge of existing word resources, it is helpful to broadly deconstruct just what that "muscle" is.

- Visualizing: As the question is asked, fast-forwarding to the final answer helps establish the area for possible resources. If the question is *"What is a chassis?"* the final answer would read *"A chassis is____."* A simple dictionary would suffice. If the question is *"What's another word for assessment?"* the final answer would read *"Another word is____."* A simple thesaurus would suffice.
- Complexity: Is the question multi-tiered? Does it require analysis or oblique thinking? *"Was Thomas Edison aware that the use of mercury at his labs could adversely affect the health of his employees?"* With no recorded evidence of whether he did or did not, tracing the definition of "mercury" as it appeared in dictionaries at the turn of the century allowed one researcher to hazard a guess. For the librarian, the area of complexity lay in making the link between the question and the resource to be used.
- Depth: How much information does the question suggest? Instead of *"what is angst?"* if the question posed was *"Is angst an English word and can I use it to describe my teen years?"* more depth is required of the answer than a simple definition. A check into the etymology of the word as well as usage would provide a complete answer.
- Context: Given the mutability and infiniteness of words, placing words within a larger framework can sometimes ease the reference process. If a word is wholly unfamiliar, the context must be probed. For example, a graduate student wanted to know the meaning of "bovate," a word that could not be found in a general dictionary. The probe helped: *"Do you have the sentence in which this word appears?"* *"Did you hear this in a particular class at college?"* In this instance, the user had heard the word in the context of Elizabethan history. The possibility that it was an archaic word led the reference librarian to the *OED* where it was defined as a unit of land measure.
- Format: In the goal for conducting the most efficient search for the most efficacious answer, print or online resources are very often the personal choice of the librarian, but not always. In the world of word sources, for example, some words

are more ephemeral than others and better served by online searches. A virtual reference question that was phrased as *"Are there any statistics available on zero-heros?"* had the librarian frantically looking through *Merriam-Webster's Collegiate*, before tracking the definition online to slang for "designated drivers." Current slang and outrageously marginalized words such as those found in one-letter or all-vowel dictionaries usually suffer premature deaths and are best served by the Internet.

Below is a list of real questions asked at a library that can help exercise the reference "muscle" for answers deriving from word sources.

- I did a phone interview with the Mayor for my term paper. How do I cite his comments in my bibliography?
- Is the word "parsimony" ever mentioned in the Bible?
- I was reading the novel *Kite Runner*, and the word "Baba" was used. Is that generic for "father" in Afghanistan?
- How do you spell the word that was the title of the poem by British poet William Henley and Timothy McVeigh's last words before he was executed?
- What is the most relevant definition of the word "browser"?

TOP TEN DICTIONARY SOURCES		
Title	**Print**	**Online**
The American Heritage Dictionary. 2000. Boston, MA: Houghton Mifflin.	4th ed.	www.bartleby.com/61/ www.yourdictionary.com
Bartlett's Familiar Quotations. 2002. Boston, MA: Little Brown.	17th ed.	www.bartleby.com/100/ 1919 edition.
Dictionary of American Regional English. 2002– . Cambridge, MA: Harvard University Press.	4 vols.	100 entries available at: http://polyglot.lss. wisc.edu/dare/
Macmillan Dictionary for Children. 2001. New York: Simon & Schuster Children's Publishing.		
Merriam-Webster's Collegiate Dictionary. 2003. Springfield, MA: Merriam-Webster, Inc.	11th ed.	www.m-w.com
MLA Handbook for Writers of Research Papers. 2003. New York: Modern Language Association of America.	6th ed.	

New Oxford American Dictionary 2005. New York: Oxford University Press.	2nd ed.	Subscription to "Premium" www.oxfordreference.com/ pages/Subjects_and_ titles_t183
The Oxford English Dictionary. 1989. New York: Oxford University Press.	20 vols.	Subscription www.oed.com
Roget's International Thesaurus. 2001. New York: HarperResource.	6th ed.	www.bartleby.com/110 1922 edition.
Webster's Third New International Dictionary of the English Language, Unabridged. 2002. Springfield, MA: Merriam-Webster, Inc.		Subscription http://corporate. britannica.com/ library/online/index.html

Recommended Resources Discussed in this Chapter

Abingdon's Strong's Exhaustive Concordance of the Bible. 1980. Nashville, TN: Abingdon Press.

Acronyms. Available at www.acronymfinder.com.

Acronyms, Initialisms & Abbreviations Dictionary. 2005. Farmington Hills, MI: Thomson Gale.

The ACS Style Guide: A Manual for Authors and Editors. 1997. 2nd ed. Janet S. Dodd, ed. Washington, DC: American Chemical Society.

Albania-English/English-Albanian Practical Dictionary. 1996. New York: Hippocrene Books.

The American Heritage® Dictionary of the English Language, Fourth Edition. 2000. Boston: Houghton Mifflin.

The American Heritage Dictionary for Learners of English. 2002. Boston: Houghton Mifflin.

American Medical Association Manual of Style: A Guide for Authors and Editors. 1997. 9th ed. Hagerstown, MD: Lippincott Williams & Wilkins.

The American Sign Language Handshape Dictionary. 1998. Washington, DC: Gallaudet University Press.

APA (*Publication Manual of the American Psychological Association*). 2001. 5th ed. Washington, DC: American Psychological Association.

The Associated Press Stylebook. 2004. New York: The Associated Press.

Bartlett, John. 2002. *Bartlett's Familiar Quotations.* 17th ed. Boston: Little, Brown.

Black's Law Dictionary. 2004. 8th ed. Bryan A. Garner, ed. Eagan, MN: West Publishing Company.

The *Bloomsbury English Dictionary.* 2004. London: Bloomsbury.

British dictionary. Available at www.freesearch.co.uk/dictionary.

Burchfield, R. W. 2004. *New Fowler's Modern English Usage.* Revised 3rd ed. Oxford: Oxford University Press.

Cambridge Advanced Learner's Dictionary. 2003. Cambridge, UK: Cambridge University Press.

The Cambridge Guide to English Usage. 2004. Cambridge, UK: Cambridge University Press.

Canadian Oxford Dictionary. 2004. 2nd ed. Katherine Barber, ed. Oxford: Oxford University Press.

Canadian spelling. Available at www.luther.ca/~dave7cnv/cdnspelling/cdnspelling .html.

Carter, John, and Nicolas Barker. 2004. *ABC for Book Collectors*. 4th edition. New Castle, DE: Oak Knoll Press.

Cassell's Italian Dictionary. 1977. New York: Macmillan.

Cassell's Latin Dictionary. 1977. London: Cassell.

Chambers Dictionary Ninth Edition. 2003. Ian Brookes, ed. Edinburgh: Chambers Harrap.

Cheney, Debora. 2002. *The Complete Guide to Citing Government Information Resources*. 3rd ed. Bethesda, MD: Congressional Information Service.

The Chicago Manual of Style. 2003. Chicago: University of Chicago Press.

Collins English Dictionary. 2004. 6th ed. New York: HarperCollins.

A Complete and Systematic Concordance to the Works of Shakespeare. 1968. Marvin Spevack, compiler. New York: G. Olms.

Concordance—Shakespeare. Available at www.it.usvd.edu.au/~matty/Shakespeare/ test.html.

Corbeil, Jean-Claude, and Arianne Archambault. 2005. *The Firefly Five Language Visual Dictionary: English, Spanish, French, German, Italian*. New York: Firefly.

———. 2002. *The Firefly Visual Dictionary*. New York: Firefly.

Dictionary. Available at www.dictionary.com.

Dictionary of American Regional English. 2002. Vol. IV. Joan Houston Hall, chief ed. Cambridge, MA: Harvard University Press.

Encarta Webster's Dictionary of the English Language. 2004. 2nd ed. New York: Bloomsbury.

Espy, Willard R. 2001. *Words To Rhyme With*. 2nd ed. New York: Facts on File.

Frank, Leonard Roy. 2001. *The Random House Webster's Quotationary*. New York: Random House Reference.

Gage Canadian Dictionary. 2000. Scarborough, Ontario: Thomson Nelson.

Gibaldi, Joseph. 2003. *MLA Handbook for Writers of Research Papers*. 6th ed. New York: Modern Language Association of America.

Harvard Concordance to Shakespeare. 1973. Marvin Spevack, compiler. Cambridge, MA: Belknap Press.

The Harvard Dictionary of Music. 2003. 4th ed. Don Michael Randel, ed. Cambridge, MA: Belknap Press.

Hickey, D. J., and J. E. Doherty. 2003. *A New Dictionary of Irish History from 1800*. Dublin, Ireland: Gill & Macmillan.

Lighter, Jonathan E. 1997. *Random House Historical Dictionary of American Slang*. Vol. II. New York: Random House Reference.

Macmillan Dictionary for Children. 2001. New York: Simon & Schuster.

The Macmillan English Dictionary. 2002. New York: Macmillan.

McGraw-Hill's Dictionary of American Idioms. 2004. New York: McGraw-Hill.

Merriam-Webster's Collegiate Dictionary. 2003. 11th ed. Springfield, MA: Merriam-Webster.

Metadictionary. Available at www.onelook.com.

Nelson Canadian Dictionary of the English Language. 1997. Scarborough, Ontario: ITP Nelson.

New Oxford American Dictionary. 2005. 2nd ed. New York: Oxford University Press.

NTC's American English Learner's Dictionary. 1998. Richard A. Spears, ed. New York: McGraw-Hill.

Ostler, Rosemarie. 2003. Dewdroppers, Waldos, and Slackers: A Decade-by-Decade Guide to the Vanishing Vocabulary of the 20th Century. New York: Oxford University Press.

The Oxford American Writer's Thesaurus. 2004. Christine A. Lindbergh, ed. New York: Oxford University Press.

Oxford Dictionary of English. 2005. Catherine Soanes and Angus Stevenson, eds. Oxford: Oxford University Press.

Oxford Dictionary of Modern Quotations. 2003. Elizabeth Knowles, ed. 2nd ed. New York: Oxford University Press.

Oxford Dictionary of Phrase Sayings and Quotation. 2003. New York: Oxford University Press.

Oxford English Dictionary. 1989. 2nd ed. John Simpson and Edward Weiner, eds. New York: Oxford University Press.

Oxford Large Print Dictionary. 2002. New York: Oxford University Press.

The Oxford Starter Bilingual Dictionary Series. New York: Oxford University Press. Copyright varies.

Random House Webster's Dictionary Large Print Edition. 1997. New York: Random House.

The Random House Webster's Unabridged Dictionary. 1997. New York: Random House Reference.

Rhyming dictionary. Available at www.rhymezone.com.

Roget's International Thesaurus. 2001. Barbara Ann Kipferer ed. New York: HarperResource.

Shakespeare concordance. Available at www.it.usyd.edu.au/~matty/Shakespeare/test.html.

Slang dictionary. Available at www.urbandictionary.com.

Stahl, Dean, and Karen Kerchelich. 2001. Abbreviations Dictionary. 10th ed. Boca Raton, FL: CRC Press.

Stedman's Medical Dictionary. 2005. 28th ed. Philadelphia, PA: Lippincott Williams & Wilkins.

Sternberg, Martin L. A. 1998. The American Sign Language Dictionary Unabridged. New York: HarperCollins Publishers.

A Student's Dictionary. 2004. Charleston, SC: The Dictionary Project.

The Style Manual for Political Science. 2001. Washington, DC: American Political Science Association.

Thesaurus. Available at www.thesaurus.com and http://thesaurus.reference.com.

Thorndike-Barnhart Children's Dictionary. 1998. Tuscon, AZ: Good Year Books.

Tullock, John H. The Dictionary of Aquarium Terms. 2000. New York: Barron's.

Ultimate Visual Dictionary. 2002. London: DK Publishing.

Upton, Clive, and Eben Upton. 2004. *The Oxford Rhyming Dictionary*. New York: Oxford University Press.

Webster's New Explorer Large Print Dictionary. 2000. Darien, CT: Federal Street Press.

Webster's Third New International Dictionary, Unabridged. 2002. Springfield, MA: Merriam-Webster.

World Book Dictionary. 2005. Chicago: World Book.

Recommendations for Further Reading

Dalby, Andrew. 1998. *A Guide to World Language Dictionaries*. London: Library Association. This evaluative single-volume collation of dictionaries covering 275 languages from around the world, provides the most updated information in the area of language dictionaries. The listings are both annotated and listed alphabetically, so it is not necessary to have additional knowledge of language groups.

Kabdebo, Thomas and Neil Armstrong. 1997. *Dictionary of Dictionaries and Eminent Encyclopedias*. New Providence, NJ: Bowker-Saur. This edition provides a comprehensive and evaluative bibliography of 24,000 subject, online, historical, and language dictionaries and encyclopedias. While an updated edition would be welcome, the resource continues to be useful in providing an overview of the breadth of dictionaries available.

Kister, Kenneth. 1992. *Kister's Best Dictionaries for Adults and Young People: A Comparative Guide*. Phoenix, AZ: Oryx Press. Kister has written the definitive study of dictionaries. While the facts describing each dictionary are obsolete, the essays on the history, typology, and comparative evaluation of dictionaries continue to be powerful.

Reitz, Joan M. 2004. "ODLIS: Online Dictionary for Library and Information Science." Available at http://lu.com/odlis/. Also available in print as the *Dictionary for Library and Information Science*. Westport, CT: Libraries Unlimited. First popularized as an online resource, the author has now published this wonderful resource in a print version as well. Definitions for all kinds of dictionaries are provided in a clear style with helpful "compare with" suggestions for relevant entries.

Romero, Joseph M. 2004. "Life Among the Lexicographers." *Humanities* 25, Issue 2 (March/April): 20. This is both a well-researched and elegant article on the creation of a unique dictionary, the *Dictionary of American Regional English*.

Sweetland, James H. 2001. *Fundamental Reference Sources, 3rd ed*. Chicago: American Library Association. The author, who was president of the Reference and User Services Association in 1990–1991 and is currently professor at the School of Information Studies, University of Washington-Milwaukee, is highly qualified to write this "reference on reference" that configures a workable method to both determine and pick out the most useful print and non-print reference resources.

Wallraff, Barbara. 2004. "Dictionaries." *The New York Times Magazine* (October 5): 18. Written by the author of *Your Own Words*, this article alerts users to the fallibility of dictionaries in terms of differing and idiosyncratic entries and styles.

World Wide Words. Available at www.worldwidewords.org/reviews/re-fou1.htm. Michael Quinion, an established British lexicographer, author, and contributor to the *Oxford English Dictionary*, is the creator of this delightful online newsletter on the English language and reviews of new books dealing with language.

Bibliography of Works Cited in this Chapter

Alford, Henry. 2005. "Not A Word." *The New Yorker* (August 29): 62.

Dahlin, Robert. 1999. "You're as Good as Your Word." *Publishers Weekly* 246, no. 46 (November 15): 33.

"Dictionary Resists Pressure to Clean Up Language." 1998. *Newsletter on Intellectual Freedom* 47, no. 4 (July).

Douglas, Matthews. 2005. "The Devil's Dictionary." *The Indexer* 24, no. 3 (April): 161–162.

Levett, John. 2003. "The Death of the Dictionary?" *Australian Library Journal* 52, no. 4 (November): 309–310.

McKean, Erin. 2004. "Lexicographer." *The New York Times Magazine* (November 14): 46.

McQuade, Molly. 2003. "Defining a Dictionary." *Booklist* (May 15): 1688.

Nunberg, Geoffrey. 2004. "What the Good Books Says: Anti-Semitism, Loosely Defined." *The New York Times*, Section 4 (April 11): 7.

Poehlmann, Christian. 2005. "Software Reviews." *Technology and Libraries* 21, no. 1 (November 16). Accessed at www.lita.org/ala/lita/litapublications/ital/2101 software.htm on 1/5/2006.

Quinn, Mary Ellen. 2005. "Atlas and Dictionary Update, 2005." *Booklist* 101, no. 18 (May 15): 1684.

8

Answering Questions about Current Events and Issues—Indexes

Overview

Many user questions require the kind of information found in journals, periodicals and newspapers. Articles from recent periodicals and newspapers have the advantage of having more current information than can be found in books. Their content also tends to be expressed more concisely, making it ideal for those not looking for an extensive amount of information. Research in many disciplines relies on periodical and journal articles reporting on recent studies, discoveries and so on.

Librarians usually answer questions about current events and issues through the use of indexes and full text databases. "The primary objective of the database [index] is to help the reader find entire documents, typically journal articles, on specific topics within some large document collection" (Diakoff 2004, 85). Indexes dissect what is inside a periodical or newspaper so that the user has access to the individual articles. This enables the user to more easily find material on a specific subject or a specific article.

Indexes of this kind first came into being in the nineteenth century. The first index ever published was *Poole's Index to Periodical Literature*. It organized articles from 479 American and English periodicals by subject only. For many decades printed indexes provided access to periodicals and newspapers. Today we continue to have a few paper indexes, but even before the more recent shift to digital media across the LIS field, new ways of presenting indexes began to take shape in the 1960s. Dialog, beginning in 1966, and Bibliographic Retrieval Service, beginning in 1976, provided libraries an interface that allowed them to search a large number of indexes by computer. Mead Data Central released the online databases LexisNexis in 1973 and 1980 respectively. By 1982 Dialog and BRS introduced flat rate simplified versions for home use. In 1985, Infotrac, a videodisc product that enabled the user to search databases in one alphabet, was produced by IAC (Information Access Company). CD-ROMs provided an even better and more economical way to store large amounts of data in a small space. Libraries were able to network CD-ROMs to serve their public. Libraries began to lease database indexes, often loading the information on their own in-house servers so users could access the information through the Online Public Access Catalogs (Machovec 1995, 42–26). The advent of the World Wide Web made it possible for libraries to lease databases that the user could view over the Web and to provide full text for many or all articles. This has revolutionized indexes, making it possible to give users access to massive amounts of regularly updated information while guaranteeing flexible, open access.

How Indexes Are Used

Indexes are used to find articles in periodicals and newspapers. They are most often employed to research topics of current interest. In some cases they can also be used to help develop one's understanding of a contemporary debate, as a variety of material can be found on any controversial topic from many different points of view. It is also helpful to use periodical and newspaper indexes to research a subject not yet written about in books.

For example, new medical treatments are usually discussed in journals, newspapers and magazines long before receiving treatment in longer print media, thanks to the quick turnaround of periodical publishing. Many indexes are now full text databases that allow users to access the article along with the bibliographic citation. Also advantageous with today's indexes is their easy searchability, a feature that sometimes makes them an expedient supplement to printed reference resources. Along these lines, note that in addition to material published in periodicals and newspapers, indexes sometimes allow quick access to the contents of books, further streamlining the searching process.

As always, it is important to understand the kind and quality of information desired by the user before starting an index search. If the user just wants general, non-scholarly articles on a subject, then general, multidisciplinary periodical and newspaper indexes are probably the proper place to begin. Should the user's interests be more specialized, however, it is important that a more appropriate subject-based index be chosen.

Libraries have spent a great deal of time designing their electronic resources pages to lead users to specialized indexes. Simply pointing out resources is, of course, not enough, so bibliographic instruction is also important in this regard. Librarians can design tutorials or courses that introduce the users to specialized indexes in their field of study and demonstrate how to use them. New aggregators such as Webfeat, Muse Global, and Ex Libris can also help users search appropriate databases in a subject area by allowing the user to search across several subject indexes at the same time. The area of index databases is a rich one and invaluable to the librarian and users.

Questions Answered by Indexes

- Where can I find statistics on Hispanic immigrants to the United States?

  The answer can be found in a general full-text periodical index such as EBSCO's *MasterFILE Premier* or in a more specialized index such as *PAIS International*.

- Where can I find articles on companies that provide day care for working mothers?

  A general full-text periodical index such as *ProQuest Research Library* will have articles on this subject. Newspaper indexes such as *InfoTrac Custom Newspapers* would be good sources as well.

- How can I locate empirical studies about the effect of the Internet on American society?

  Try *Sociological Abstracts*. You can put in Internet as a subject term and look for empirical and society as free text terms. You might also want to try Google Scholar.

- I need five pieces of criticism for the Faulkner short story "A Rose for Emily." Where can I find them?

  Use a general index like EBSCO *Academic Search* or *Infotrac Expanded Academic* that will have full text for many articles. If you need to find more in-depth material and/or older material, use the *MLA International Bibliography* or *ABELL (Annual Bibliography of English Language and Literature)*. In most libraries there will be links to the full text from these databases.

- What is the status of the U.S. economy and what is predicted for the coming year?

  A general full-text periodical index such as Wilson's *Reader's Guide to Periodical Literature* will have articles on this, or a full-text newspaper database such as *Newsbank* will also have articles.

- Where can I find articles about deforestation in Mexico that are written in Spanish?

  PAIS International, which covers a variety of issues related to politics, legislation and economics, and indexes some Spanish language publications, might be a place to start. You could also use a more specific source like *HAPI (Hispanic American Periodicals Index) Online* or *Environmental Sciences* and *Pollution Management* or *Geobase*, all of which let you limit by language.

- What is the best place to look for research about the psychological effects of adoption on children?

  PsycInfo is the best place to start for psychological topics. Be sure to look at the thesaurus to pick the best terms for your search. You can link out to full text articles from the database if your library has the links set up.

- Where can I find information about which digital cameras are the best?

  General full-text periodical indexes such as *InfoTracOneFile* index include consumer magazines or computer magazines and are a good source of information.

Major Indexes Used in Reference Work

Indexes can be general multidisciplinary periodical or newspaper indexes or specialized subject indexes covering a particular subject area. General periodical indexes provide a way to do research on a wide range of topics. They index general publications that are widely available, usually providing the full text. General newspaper indexes do the same for newspapers. Some index a single newspaper while other index several newspapers. The subject indexes can be as specific as *Library Literature* or can be broadbased, such as *Educational Resources Information Center* or the *PAIS International* index.

General Periodical Indexes

Several publishers, especially EBSCO, ProQuest, Thomson Gale, and Wilson, dominate the index field. Each has its strengths and weakness, but overall the librarian will find any of them quite satisfactory. The choice a library makes as to which should be purchased must be predicated on the criteria important to their specific situation.

EBSCO has been in the periodical index business since 1985. This company began as and continues to be an important player in the periodical subscription business. It offers several multidisciplinary indexes to fit the needs of different types and sizes of libraries. *Academic Search Elite* is designed for smaller academic libraries but would also be useful in community college libraries and public libraries. Scholarly periodicals in the social sciences, humanities, ethnic studies, language and literature, engineering and computer sciences, natural and medical sciences, and education are indexed. Over 3,300 titles are indexed and abstracted, and most periodicals are available in full text. Coverage dates from 1985. EBSCO databases have good search facility. One can search by keyword in the article title, subject descriptors, author, and abstract fields. For libraries wanting a richer collection of resources there is *Academic Search Premier*, which indexes almost 8,000 titles. EBSCO also has three different indexes especially designed for public libraries. *MasterFILE Premier* is the largest of the indexes with more than 2,000 full-text periodicals. *MasterFILE Elite* and *MasterFILE Select* index fewer periodicals.

ProQuest was originally produced by Bell and Howell, a company in the microfilm business. This company has made full-text newspapers one of its specialties. *ProQuest Research Library* indexes journals, magazines and newspapers and is of use to all types of libraries providing information on a wide range of subjects including business, humanities, education, social sciences, and sciences. It indexes almost 3,750 titles of which around 2,550 are full text. The titles indexed begin in 1989. Its search methods are the usual—Boolean operators, advanced search and natural language—with complete subject indexing and a controlled vocabulary. *ProQuest 5000*, which indexes 10,000 periodical titles of which 5,400 are full text, is a larger index designed for academic libraries that begins its coverage in 1971.

Thomson Gale's general full text index database is *InfoTrac OneFile*. It indexes over 8,000 periodical titles as well as newspapers (including the New York Times and USA Today) and wire services. 6,000 of the 10,200 titles are full text, and backfile full-text coverage begins in 1980. Another of Thomson Gale's full text databases is *Expanded Academic ASAP* which includes material for the undergraduate but is also useful for high schools and public libraries. *Expanded Academic ASAP* indexes over 3,700 titles, of which 2,000 are full text. It also indexes the *New York Times*. Both Thomson Gale indexes have good searching capability and the ability to limit searches by full text, refereed publications, by date, and by journal title.

The H. W. Wilson Company has the longest record in the index business beginning at the end of the nineteenth century. It is known for the quality of its indexing and its name and subject authority files. Most of the Wilson indexes are now available electronically. The *Readers' Guide to Periodical Literature*, which began publication in 1890, is a general index that is useful in high schools, public libraries, and four-year colleges. Indexing over 400 periodicals, the *Readers' Guide* now publishes *Readers' Guide Full Text* with the full text of 200 publications back to 1994 with indexing and abstracts dating back to 1983. Wilson also publishes *Readers' Guide Abstracts*, which indexes and abstracts over 300 periodicals. In addition, Wilson now offers *Readers' Guide Retrospective 1890–1982* to provide the earlier indexes in electronic format. *Wilson OmniFile Full Text* combines full text, abstracts, and indexing from six Wilson indexes, *Education Full Text, General Science Full Text, Humanities Full Text, Readers' Guide Full Text, Social Sciences Full Text*, and *Wilson Business Full Text*, back to 1982. It also includes full text of titles indexed in five of Wilson's other subject indexes. This index includes the full text of articles from over 2,000 publications and abstracts and indexing from over 3,800 publications. The broad coverage makes it useful as a general multidisciplinary index. Wilson continues to make back files of their many indexes available electronically, although many of these electronic indexes do not have full text.

LexisNexis has several general reference indexes aimed at academic institutions, public libraries, and high schools, all providing a variety of full-text information on current events, legal issues, and issues in the news that can be searched by keyword as well as by subject headings. The extensive searching capability of the LexisNexis products makes this database extremely useful. The range of publications indexed in the LexisNexis database goes far beyond the usual magazines and newspapers and includes reports, official documents, briefing papers, conference proceedings, and organizational newsletters. The LexisNexis products include *LexisNexis Academic* that provides current events information as well as legal information, information on companies including financial information, and medical and science information from a wide range of publications, documents, and media sources. In addition to *LexisNexis Academic*, there is a *LexisNexis Current Issues, LexisNexis Statistical, LexisNexis Company Analysis, LexisNexis Country Analysis*, and *LexisNexis Government Periodicals*.

First Search from Online Computer Library Center includes over seventy subject databases, e.g., Wilson indexes, *PAIS International, ABI/INFORM* and the *MLA International Bibliography*. One of these databases, *Electronic Collections Online*, provides access to 1,700 full-text journals in practically every subject area with coverage since 1994. Users also have access to *WorldCat*, where they can identify locations of books and other information, and *Article First*, where they can identify the journal for each article and locations for the journal title. Basic, advanced, and expert search is available. This is a good way to provide access to many full-text journals with one subscription.

Dialog (Thomson), one of the earliest companies in the field, is still a player providing over 900 databases from many different publishers covering such subjects as science and technology, business, energy and environment, food and agriculture, medicine, social sciences, and reference. Dialog has more than one product and more than one pricing model. *DialogClassic* is its most comprehensive database, offering excellent search capabilities.

Access: The Supplementary Index to Periodicals (1975–present) indexes popular periodicals including city and regional magazines not indexed elsewhere. It often provides the first indexing for a new periodical. It is available in print and electronically.

Alternative Press Index, founded in 1969, is a subject index to over 250 alternative, radical, and left-wing periodicals, newspapers, and magazines often not found in other indexes. It is international and interdisciplinary in scope, covering such topics as labor, indigenous peoples, feminism, ecology, gays and lesbians, and socialism.

Newspaper Indexes and Databases

Newspaper databases are exceptionally useful to libraries and library users. These databases provide access to current and retrospective articles in many newspapers—often many more than the library might subscribe to. Many provide the full text of newspapers from smaller towns and cities. *Newspaper Source* (EBSCO) provides full text for the *Christian Science Monitor, USA Today,* and the *Washington Post,* twenty-six international newspapers and 224 regional U.S. newspapers, as well as twenty-three newswires and TV and radio news transcripts. There are also abstracts for articles from the *New York Times* and the *Wall Street Journal*—Eastern Edition. Beginning dates vary with the *Christian Science Monitor* coverage beginning in January 1995.

The *National Newspaper Index* (Thomson Gale) provides access to five important newspapers, the *New York Times,* the *Washington Post,* the *Christian Science Monitor,* the *Los Angeles Times,* and the *Wall Street Journal.* The coverage varies but the indexing begins between 1972 and 1982. The *National Newspaper Index* is, as its name suggests, simply an index. For full text it is necessary to subscribe to *InfoTrac Custom Newspapers* (Thomson Gale). This full-text database includes more than 120 U.S. national, regional, and local newspapers as well as international newspapers plus selected articles from another 280 sources. Newspapers in this package include the *Atlanta Journal-Constitution, San Francisco Chronicle, St. Louis Post Dispatch,* the *Financial Times* (London), *The Times* (London), and the *International Herald Tribune* (Paris), plus a rolling 365 days of the *New York Times.*

ProQuest Newstand offers as its core the *New York Times,* the *Wall Street Journal,* the *Christian Science Monitor,* and the *Washington Post.* Libraries can develop a customized database of full-text newspapers from the over 350 daily national and international newspapers offered. Indexing and abstracts are provided for another 150 newspapers. Overall coverage begins in 1986 but most of the coverage begins in 1995. ProQuest also offers its Historical Newspapers. This collection is continuing to grow. To date ProQuest offers the full text of these major newspapers: the *New York Times* from 1851 to 2001, the *Wall Street Journal* from 1889 to 1987, the *Washington Post* from 1877 to 1988, the *Christian Science Monitor* from 1908 to 1991, and the *Los Angeles Times* from 1881 to 1984. A total of eight newspapers are presently available, and the full text of more newspapers is planned.

Newsbank provides articles from more than 1,500 U.S. and international sources including periodicals, newspapers, government documents, and newswires. There are many different packages available tailored to the needs of specific types of libraries, such as *NewsBank Public Library Collection,* with articles from 1992 forward and *America's Newspapers,* with full text of over 1,000 newspapers. Packages for high schools, middle schools, and elementary schools are also available.

Subject-Based Indexes

Although many users will want to use the general database indexes, they should be introduced to the subject-based indexes, since many journals are not indexed in the general database indexes. Subject-based indexes index more specialized journals, newspapers, and documents. If someone is researching a subject in depth, they need to use subject-based indexes in order to find more detailed material. Indexes in major subject areas are described in the following paragraphs.

Science Indexes

Two indexes that have for many years been the only science indexes for the layperson are the *General Science Index* and the *Applied Science and Technology Index*. Wilson's *General Science Full Text* is designed for the student and nonspecialist. It includes the full text of over eighty periodicals from 1995 to date as well as abstracts and indexing for 280 periodicals from 1984 to date. The subjects covered include astronomy, biology, food and nutrition, mathematics, and the earth sciences. Wilson's *Applied Science & Technology Full Text* provides full text of articles from over 170 journals from 1997 to date as well as abstracts and indexing of 750 periodicals from 1983 to the present. The subjects covered include automotive engineering, transportation, petroleum and gas, plastics, robotics, textiles, the food industry, construction, etc. There is also *Applied Science and Technology Retrospective 1913–1983*. *Science Full Text Select* is a new database that includes the full text from three databases—*General Science Full Text, Applied Science & Technology Full Text* and *Biological & Agricultural Index Plus*—packaged together and is aimed at the high school and community colleges. This new product covers 325 journals.

Science Resource Center (Thomson Gale) includes articles from over 250 full-text journals and the text of Thomson Gale's science reference titles as well as links to Web sites. Aimed at a wide user base from high school students to the general public, it focuses on earth science, life science, the history of science, physical science, space science, and science and society. *Biology Digest* (CSA) covers all aspects of the life sciences from 1989 to the present. Intended for high school and undergraduate students, it provides abstracts of journal articles ranging from botany and ecology to biochemistry, physiology, and zoology.

For more academic audiences there are many in-depth subject indexes to meet specific needs. Among these, *SciFinder Scholar*, is the online version of *Chemical Abstracts* and includes the CAplus database, the CAS (Chemical Abstract Service) registry file and Medline as well as information on chemical substances and reactions. This database includes citations and abstracts from journals, conference proceedings, patents, and dissertions from 1907 to the present. *Biosis Previews* includes citations and abstracts from both *Biological Abstracts* and *Biological Abstracts/Reports, Reviews and Meetings* from 1976 to date. Both books and journals are included as well as reports. A recent addition to the science databases is *Scopus* (Elsevier). This is an indexing and abstracting service covering over 14,000 STM (science, technology, and medical) sources from 4,000 publishers back to 1966.

Education Indexes

Education is represented by two excellent indexes. *Education Full Text* is Wilson's *Education Index* with the full text of articles from 300 journals from 1996 to the present and abstracts and indexing for 700. The *Index* itself indexes over 525 journals back to 1983. *Education Full Text* indexes journals not indexed in ERIC. Its subject coverage ranges from Comparative Education and Educational Technology to Parent-Teacher Relations and Teacher Evaluation. *Education Index Retrospective: 1929–1983* provides electronic access to the back files of this index.

ERIC (www.eric.ed.gov) is a database funded by the U.S. Department of Education since 1966. It has been online since 1996. ERIC provides broad subject coverage in the field of education and extends into some related fields such as library science. It includes citations and abstracts from over 600 educational and education-related journals and other relevant documents with some full text available. The *Current Index to Journals in Education*, once a separate publication, is now part of ERIC online.

Social Science Indexes

The social sciences are a rich area for indexes due to the changing nature of information in this field. H. W. Wilson's *Social Sciences Full Text* includes the full text of over 200 publications from 1995 to the present. Its content covers social science journals published in the United States and elsewhere and include such diverse subjects as environmental studies, ethics, political science, and urban studies. The *Social Sciences Index* indexes over 600 publications from 1983 to the present. Wilson has also recently made available *Social Sciences Index Retrospective 1907–1982*, which provides electronic access to the retrospective indexing of social science journals.

Sociological Abstracts is a resource for literature in the social and behavioral sciences. With backfiles to 1952 it provides abstract of articles in over 1,800 journals as well as books, conference papers, and dissertations. The subjects covered include community development, family and social welfare, political sociology, and social psychology.

PAIS International, published since 1914, covers such subjects as government, legislation, public policy, economics, sociology, and political science. The online version begins in 1972. Now owned by CSA, it indexes more than 1,200 journals as well as 8,000 books, government documents, gray literature, research reports, and conference reports. As its title suggests, it is international in scope and indexes material in English, French, German, Italian, Portuguese, and Spanish. While this is an index only, not a full-text source, it is a very good one, indexing material not found elsewhere.

PAIS Archive 1915–1976 is also now available, providing an historical perspective on many social and public policy issues.

SIRS Researcher (ProQuest) is a reprint service providing full-text material from over 1,500 magazines, newspapers, journals, and government publications with a focus on social sciences, economics, political science, and current events worldwide. This database index is designed for high schools and colleges. It does not include full text of complete journals or newspapers, but rather selectively indexed articles.

America: History and Life (ABC-CLIO) provides citations and abstracts to articles on U.S. and Canadian history and related fields from prehistory to the present in over 1,700 journals. As with *Historical Abstracts, America: History and Life* is interdisciplinary and can be used to research many different disciplines including cultural studies, gender studies and literary studies. There are links to over 215,000 articles.

Historical Abstracts (ABC-CLIO) is a historical bibliography of world history from 1450 to the present (excluding the United States and Canada). It includes English language abstracts from journals of history and the social sciences articles from academic historical journals since 1955 in more than forty languages. Although for the most part it provides only citations and abstracts, it does provide links to over 130,000 articles through open URL compliance. It is multidisciplinary in approach and can be used for researching sociology, psychology, women's studies/gender studies, religion, anthropology, political science, multicultural studies, etc. Citations for books and dissertations are also included.

History Resource Center: U.S. (Thomson Gale) is a collection of primary source documents, reference documents, more than 2,000 photographs, maps, and illustrations, and full-text coverage of over 100 history-related scholarly journals. Person, time period, and subject can be searched.

History Resource Center: World (Thomson Gale) provides primary and secondary sources for the study of world history for all countries and all parts of the world.

Humanities Indexes

Humanities has been the last area to develop electronic resources, probably due to the nature of the scholarship which has relied more heavily on book material. The humanities is dominated by two indexes that have been in existence for a long time. H. W. Wilson's *Humanities Full Text* includes the full text of 200 journals from 1995 to date and indexes over 550 periodicals back to 1984. The subjects covered include classical studies, history, literature, performing arts, and religion as well as original works of fiction, drama, and poetry, book reviews, and reviews of ballets, theater, film, etc. Wilson has also made available through the *Humanities and Social Science Index Retrospective: 1907–1983* electronic access to the indexing of humanities periodicals (includes the *International Index*, the *Humanities Index*, and the *Social Science Index*).

The Modern Language Association (MLA) produces the *MLA International Bibliography*. It is a subject index for literature and linguistics with more than 4,400 periodicals indexed as well as books. The *Bibliography* began in 1922, but the online version dates from 1963. It is international in scope and includes bibliographic records in French, Spanish, German, Russian, Portuguese, Norwegian and Swedish. The *MLA International Bibliography* also has its own thesaurus. It is an excellent index for researching literary criticism or any other aspect of literature even though it does not have full text. It is available through several database vendors.

Francis is an international, multilingual database with citations and abstracts in English and French to more than 4,000 journals, books and other documents. The coverage includes the humanities, social sciences, and economics with an emphasis on European publications. The *ATLA Religion Database*, published by the American Theological Library Association, indexes journals representing all major religions and denominations. Its wide coverage extends to archeology and social issues. Over 1,400 journals with backfiles to 1949 are indexed.

Art Indexes

Art has three strong indexes that actually complement each other. Used together they provide wide coverage in art. H. W. Wilson's *Art Full Text* includes the full text of articles from over 125 journals from 1997 to the present, as well as article abstracts and indexing of 450 publications from 1984 to the present. It is international in scope, including material in languages other than English and a wide variety of subjects including antiques, architecture, art history, costume, and crafts. An *Art Index Retrospective: 1929–1984* is also available, providing indexing to over 600 publications.

ARTbibliographies Modern (CSA) provides indexing and abstracts for journal articles, books, exhibition catalogs, PhD dissertations, and exhibition reviews on all aspects of modern and contemporary art including crafts, photography, theatre arts, and fashion, as well as painting and sculpture from the nineteenth century forward. The coverage dates from 1974. Both English-language and material in other languages are included. This index has a well-developed thesaurus.

The *Bibliography of the History of Art* is said to be the "most comprehensive art bibliography available worldwide" (CSA catalog). All aspects of art are covered from paintings and sculpture to crafts and folk art. The citations include abstracts in English and French. This bibliography is the successor to *Repertoire d'Art et d'Archeologie* from 1973–1989 and the *International Repertory of the Literature of Art* from 1975–1989.

Library Science Indexes

There are two library science indexes—one with some full text and the other with abstracts. *Library Literature & Information Science Full Text*, published by H. W. Wilson, includes periodical articles, conference proceedings, pamphlets, books, and theses on library science. It began publication in 1936 and is available online from 1984 on. *Library Literature* indexes 400 periodicals dating back to 1984 with full text of articles from 150 periodicals back to 1997. It is international in scope and can be searched by keywords, subject headings, personal names, title words, publication, year, and type of article.

Library, Information Science and Technology Abstracts, now owned by CSA, is an international index with abstracts whose coverage began in 1969. It includes abstracts of over 450 periodicals from more than sixty-eight countries in more than twenty languages. It covers all aspects of library science and information science. *LISTA* has its own online thesaurus.

Psychology Indexes

PsycINFO, published by the American Psychological Association since 1967, has long been a major index in the field of psychology. It is arranged into twenty-two major categories including psychological, social, and behavioral sciences and related fields such as psychiatry, neuroscience, medicine, and social work. The scholarly, peer-reviewed online bibliographic index provides comprehensive coverage of over 1,000 journal titles relevant to psychology and covers over 1900 titles including books, dissertations, and reports. The publications included come from over fifty countries in twenty-eight languages. Each listing includes the bibliographic citation and abstract. There is a separate thesaurus to guide users through the subject headings. A separate database, *PsyArticles*, has been developed to provide full-text access to the articles from over fifty-four journals from 1988 to the present. *PsycINFO* is available from several of the major database vendors.

Psychology journals can also be searched through EBSCO's Psychology and Behavioral Science Collection, a comprehensive database with about 480 full-text titles covering topics such as emotional and behavioral characteristics, psychiatry and psychology, mental processes, anthropology, and observational and experimental methods. EBSCO's Academic Search Premier, ProQuest's Research Library, and Thomson Gale's Health Reference Center are also sources of information on psychology.

Ethnic Indexes

The *International Index to Black Periodicals Full Text*, an index to scholarly and popular material in Black Studies, began in 1902. There are citations for retrospective records from 1902 to 1991. From 1998 forward there are citations and abstracts for 150 journals, newspapers, and newsletters published in the United States, Africa, and the Caribbean, as well as full-text coverage of forty core Black Studies titles. This index provides bibliographic and full-text resources for a wide range of related issues including economics, history, religion, sociology, and political science. It is both international and interdisciplinary in scope.

EthnicNewsWatch is a full-text online database that began in 1991. It covers a wide variety of newspapers, magazines, and journals from the ethnic, minority, and native presses. A total of 240 titles are now indexed in subject areas ranging from history and politics to the humanities and social sciences. It is searchable in both English and Spanish with titles in both languages. This unique database provides the researcher with alternate points of view on subjects of current interest.

Hispanic American Periodicals Index Online (1970) indexes and abstracts books, articles, reviews, bibliographies, and literary works appearing in scholarly journals published in Latin America, the Caribbean, and the United States. It is available online.

Business and Medical Indexes

Among the excellent business indexes are EBSCO's *Business Source Elite*, ProQuest's *ABI/INFORM Global*, Thomson Gale's *General Business File*, and *Factiva*. These business indexes offer the librarian and user a good deal of choice. These indexes will be discussed in more depth in the chapter on Business, Medical, and Legal Resources, as will the following medical and consumer health indexes: *Medline, PubMed, Health Source Plus* (EBSCO) and *Health Reference Center* (Thomson Gale).

Citation Indexes

Citation indexes are very useful to researchers, since a researcher can follow an idea from the original writer to others who have cited the original writer in their work. A researcher can also determine which writers have influenced others or how a basic concept is now being used. Originally there were three citation indexes: the *Science Citation Index* (1900–present), the *Social Sciences Citation Index* (1956–present) and the *Arts and Humanities Citation Index* (1975–present) These three citation indexes plus *Index Chemicus* (1993) and *Current Chemical Reactions* (1986) are now part of *Web of Science* (Thomson), an international citation index with coverage of 8,700 authoritative journals with links to the full text of articles cited. Librarians should introduce their users to the *Web of Science* if they are writing substantial papers.

Indexes to Special Types of Material

ProQuest Dissertations and Theses is a database in which U.S., Canadian, British, and European dissertations and theses from 1861 to the present are listed. Abstracts exist for dissertations since 1980 and thesis abstracts began in 1988. There is some full text. This is a valuable source for researchers.

Essay and General Literature Index (H. W. Wilson) indexes books, about 320 single and multiauthor collections and twenty selected annuals and serials annually. The coverage includes the humanities and social sciences including literary works, drama, and film. The online coverage begins in 1985. Users can search by keyword, subject, title, author, and date of publication. Works of literary criticism can be searched by names of fictional characters and titles of literary works. This database has no full text but can be linked to the library's catalog. *Essay and General Literature Index* is a unique source of essays found in book collections that include literary criticism and essays on a wide variety of subjects.

Short Story Index (H. W. Wilson) indexes short stories by author, title, subject, genre, and technique. The online version goes back to 1984. This work indexes both collections of short stories and stories from 155 periodicals indexed by the *Readers' Guide* and *Humanities Index*. Most of this index simply provides bibliographic information, but there is full text for 1,622 stories. This index helps the user to locate short stories that are in multiauthor collections or in periodicals.

The *Play Index* (H. W. Wilson) is now available electronically from 1949 to date. This valuable resource indexes over 44,000 plays published individually or in collections. Full-length plays, radio and television plays, and one-act plays are indexed. Users can search by author, title, subject, style, genre, and cast type. This resource provides the librarian with a way to find individual plays in collections.

LitFinder (Thomson Gale) is yet another source for finding the full text of poems, short stories, essays, speeches, and plays. This easy-to-use database allows searching by title, subject, author nationality, gender, and date. International in scope, it covers all time periods. Users can locate the text of thousands of works of literature.

Book Review Digest has been published by H. W. Wilson since 1905. In addition to the bibliographic citation, each entry includes a summary of the book and excerpts from reviews. In order to be listed, a book must have two reviews if nonfiction and three reviews if fiction. *Book Review Digest Plus* is the electronic version covering 1983 to date and expanding the number of periodicals covered by adding entries from other Wilson indexes. Some full-text reviews are included in this version. This index is useful for readers' advisory work and collection development as well as finding reviews of books. *Book Review Digest Retrospective 1905–1982* provides the earlier years of *Book Review Digest*.

Book Review Index Online (Thomson Gale) includes the entire back file of the print index from 1965 to the present. More than five million review citations on more than two million titles are listed. Although there are only 73,000 full text entries, it does cover more titles than *Book Review Digest*.

The *Columbia Granger's Index to Poetry in Collected and Selected Works*, 2nd edition (2004) provides access to more than 65,000 poems by 266 poets. The poems are indexed by subject, first line, author, and title. The online version, *World of Poetry Online*, includes 45,000 full-text poems, biographies of poets, and links to poetry Web sites.

Indexes for Children and Young Adults

Librarians can choose from several indexes for young people. *Primary Search Plus* (EB-SCO), designed for elementary schools and children's rooms, is aimed at grades four through six. It provides full text of over fifty of the most popular K-12 magazines. There are abstracts and indexing for nearly eighty titles. It indexes such titles as *Highlights for Children, National Geographic Kids, National Geographic World, Ranger Rick, Cricket*, and *Science World*. *Middle Search Plus* (EBSCO), designed for middle and junior high school students, is aimed at grades seven through nine. It provides full text of over 120 popular K-12 magazine and abstracts nearly 150 titles. It indexes both kids' magazines and easy-to-read adult magazines such as *Time, National Geographic, Sports Illustrated, Popular Science, and Popular Mechanics.*

JuniorQuest, a ProQuest product geared to a middle and junior high school audience, offers full-text articles from about 100 magazines and newspapers, concentrating on general interest areas including social science, general science, humanities, and business. The coverage for this database index begins in 1988. *InfoTrac Junior Edition* (Thomson Gale) is aimed at junior high and middle school students. This full-text online database indexes over 215 general interest magazines, of which 196 are full text. Newspaper articles are also included as are several reference sources, including the *Columbia Encyclopedia, Merriam-Webster's Biographical Dictionary*, and *Merriam-Webster's Collegiate Dictionary* (10th ed.). *InfoTrac Student Edition* (Thomson Gale) designed for secondary school students, indexes 554 magazines of which 477 are full text. It also includes newspaper articles, reference books, and maps on a wide spectrum of topics, along with some of the same reference works as *InfoTrac Junior Edition*. Wilson's *Readers' Guide to Periodical Literature*, discussed elsewhere in this chapter, is suitable for high school students.

Collection Development and Maintenance

Selection and Keeping Current

Indexes are expensive, so libraries must take care in selecting them. In many cases, there is now more than one index in a particular subject area so that libraries have a choice and can make decisions based on the selection of materials indexed, the price, and other criteria that are important to a particular library.

Indexes continue to change rapidly as publishers try to expand their coverage and better fit their products to the market. Most index publishers have several products, usually for different types of libraries, and often different size packages so libraries can choose what package they need and can afford. The publishers continue to develop new products as well as acquire smaller companies or form partnerships with other companies. Major publishers are also developing linking agreements in order to offer more full-text services to their users. For example, *History Resource Center* (Thomson Gale) links to ABC-CLIO's *History Abstracts* and *America: History and Life*. This fast-changing field makes it hard to keep current. Many periodicals such as *Library Journal, Computers for Libraries, Online,* and *Searcher* report on new index and database products. These same periodicals also include full-length articles from time to time, summarizing the state of the field or a particular part of the field. The publishers themselves are active in contacting libraries as they develop new products or upgrade existing products.

Evaluating Indexes

Due to the number of indexes now available, the evaluation of indexes requires a careful examination of a number of factors:

* Authority of publisher;
* Scope/subjects covered;
* Number and quality of periodicals/newspapers indexed;
* Number of titles with full-text coverage;
* Currency and frequency of updating;
* Accuracy of citations;
* Subject headings/controlled vocabulary and access points;
* Statistics and training for staff; and
* Cost.

The publisher of the index is of prime importance since the track record of a publisher will usually tell a great deal about what the librarian can expect in terms of quality. Librarians also want to be assured that the publisher will stay in business. This is particularly important with indexes since they are a major purchase and the library needs assurance that the index will continue.

The librarian should consider the scope of the index, that is, the subjects covered and the beginning date of coverage. There is often more than one choice in a subject area, so librarians should strive to get the best fit of the subject coverage and the dates included for their particular library. The number of periodicals or newspapers indexed and their quality should be examined. This is not just a numbers game. Any publisher can state that they have more periodicals and newspapers indexed than another. But this can be a hollow statistic if the periodicals and newspapers indexed are not of good quality. In fact, indexing articles of lesser quality only serves to make it more difficult to find the better-quality material. To determine where particular periodicals are indexed, *Ulrich's* or *Magazines for Libraries* can be checked. Since many indexes offer a great deal of full text, it is important to find out whether full text is offered for the periodicals most needed. The librarian can check *Fulltext Sources Online, Books and Periodicals .com,* or *jake* (jake.openly.com). Sometimes none of the indexes offer the full text of a particular periodical because the publisher of the periodical has not agreed to it. But sometimes only one index has the rights to a certain periodical that is in high demand.

Another issue surrounding full text is whether the whole periodical has been included in the full text. Sometimes only the main articles in a periodical are provided while smaller articles, columns, letters to the editor, and even book reviews are omitted.

The currency of the index is of utmost importance, as is the frequency of the updating. Unfortunately one cannot assume that just because an index is available electronically that it is up to date. Pick a current subject in the news and check it out in several indexes to determine how fast they are updating their indexes. One should also note the accuracy of the indexing, especially the bibliographic citations. Frequent errors indicate that the quality control of the index is below acceptable standards.

Examine the consistency and the depth of the subject headings used. Many indexes use the Library of Congress Subject Headings or the Sears List of Subject Headings. Other subject-based indexes such as the *MLA International Bibliography* and *PsychINFO* develop a thesaurus to provide more specificity in the range of subject headings offered. The use of controlled vocabulary in order to have consistency is important to an index, so using an authoritative list of subject headings is absolutely necessary.

Compare the searching power of various indexes. Are some of them more user friendly than others? Do they use Boolean searching? Note whether it is easy to find what you want.

Some services are not seen by the public but are important to the librarian. First, there is the library's need to have statistics on the use of each index. The company producing the index must be able to supply these statistics on a regular basis to enable the library to determine how much each index is being used. Secondly, there is the issue of training staff. Since each index is slightly different from the other, staff needs training on each new index. Many companies are prepared to send a trainer to introduce the index to the staff. This is an important benefit.

Finally there is the cost. Costs vary tremendously, and most publishers negotiate individually with a library or group of libraries. Publishers usually have more than one way of determining the cost, so it is wise to be familiar with the various possibilities. Many now offer flat fees for their databases. Often publishers' fees are based on the size of a user group. For example, in a university, it might be based on the number of students and faculty. Sometimes companies offer "pay per view" plans to attract infrequent users. Publishers may also be willing to charge based on simultaneous uses. In this case the library pays for a certain number of simultaneous uses depending on how much they judge the database will be used. In any case, costs can be steep, and for this reason libraries often join consortia so that the price for the database can be spread over several libraries and thus lower the cost.

Further Considerations

What to Do When There Is No Full Text

Users have become accustomed to having full text in indexes. But not all indexes have full text. For example, the Wilson indexes have some full text but not for all citations. Also the *MLA International Bibliography*, an essential index for those researching literature, has no full text. So what is a librarian or a user to do? First of all, the software programs

Serials Solutions or EBSCO A-Z can be used to find out whether the full text of an article is available in another database owned by the library. New software, link resolvers, can be used to direct the user to full text of an article in another database owned by the library. If the library does not own the full text online, the librarian should turn to the library's print collection to see if the periodical is owned by the library and is available in bound volumes or in microform. If this is also unsuccessful, the library must either order the article through interlibrary loan or turn to a document delivery service such as Ingenta Document Delivery (www.ingenta.com), ISI Document Solution (www.isinet .com/prodserv/ids/idsfm.html) or the British Library Document Supply Center (www.bl.uk/docsupply) and purchase the needed article.

Searching

One of the most difficult parts of this rich array of general and subject databases is that the searching protocols differ from company to company and from database to database. Librarians must get familiar with the databases owned by their library. Often librarians in an institution work together to become knowledgeable about databases. Each studies different databases and then shares the information with the others. It is important to look at the similarities between databases and the differences. It is important to get to know the basics of doing a search in each database and some of the useful additional features. Many vendors will provide training on their databases, and libraries should take advantage of this.

Final thoughts

Index databases are one of the most useful and most popular reference tools available in a library. The advent of so much full text has made it much easier for the user to find the full text of articles. Each new software innovation makes it even more seamless to the user, who is always in a hurry. As more index databases develop, librarians can make more careful choices. Just as with reference books, duplication in databases is not always necessary. Libraries need to develop plans and annually reevaluate their holdings.

THE TOP 10 INDEXES

Title	Print	Online
Academic Search Elite. Ipswich, MA: EBSCO.		Subscription www.epnet.com
Alternative Press Index. 1969– . Baltimore, MD: Alternative Press Center.	Quarterly	Subscription www.altpress.org
Dialog Classic. Cary, NC: Thomson.		Subscription www.dialog.com/ products/dialogclassic/

Expanded Academic Text ASAP. Farmington Hills, MI: Gale.	Subscription www.gale.com/Expanded Academic/
First Search. Dublin, OH: OCLC.	Subscription www.oclc.org/firstsearch/
LexisNexis Academic. Bethesda, MD: LexisNexis Academic & Library Solutions.	Subscription www.lexisnexis.com/ academic/universe/ academic
Proquest Newstand. Ann Arbor, MI: Proquest.	Subscription www.proquest.com
Proquest Research Library. Ann Arbor, MI: Proquest.	Subscription www.proquest.com
SIRS Researcher. Ann Arbor, MI: Proquest.	Subscription www.proquest.com
Wilson Omnifile Full Text. 1982– . Bronx, NY: H. W. Wilson.	Subscription www.hwwilson.com/ databases/omnifile.htm

Recommended Resources Discussed in this Chapter

Academic Search Elite. Ipswich, MA: EBSCO. Available online.

Access: The Supplementary Index to Periodicals. 1975– . Evanston, IL: John Gordon Burke Publisher.

Alternative Press Index. 1969– . Baltimore, MD: Alternative Press Center. Also available online.

America: History and Life. 1964– . Santa Barbara, CA: ABC-CLIO. Available online.

America's Newspapers. Naples, FL: Newsbank. Available online.

Applied Science & Technology Full Text. 1997– . New York: H. W. Wilson. Available online.

Applied Science & Technology Retrospective 1913–1983. New York: H. W. Wilson. Available in print and online.

ARTbibliographies Modern. 1974– . Bethesda, MD: CSA. Available online.

Art Full Text. 1983– . New York: H. W. Wilson. Available online.

Art Index Retrospective. 1929–1984. New York: H. W. Wilson. Available in print and online.

Article First. Dublin, OH: OCLC. Available online.

Arts and Humanities Citation Index. 1975– . Philadelphia, PA: Thomson. Available online via *Web of Science*.

ATLA Religion Database. 1949– . Bethesda, MD: CSA. Available online.

The Bibliography of the History of Art. 1973– . Bethesda, MD: CSA. Available online.

Biosis Previews. 1976– . Philadelphia, PA: Thomson Scientific. Available online.

Biology Digest. 1989– . Bethesda, MD: CSA. Available online.

Book Review Digest. 1905– . New York: H. W. Wilson.

Book Review Digest Plus. 1983– . New York: H. W. Wilson. Available online.

Book Review Digest Retrospective 1905–1982. New York: H. W. Wilson. Available in print and online.

Book Review Index Online. 1965– . Farmington Hills, MI: Thomson Gale. Also available online.

Columbia Granger's Index to Poetry in Collected and Selected Works. 2004. 2nd ed. New York: Columbia University Press.

DialogClassic. Cary, NC: Thomson. Available online.

Dissertation Abstracts Online and ProQuest Digital Dissertations. Ann Arbor, MI: ProQuest. Available online.

Education Full Text. 1983– . New York: H. W. Wilson. Available online.

Education Index Retrospective: 1929–1983. New York: H. W. Wilson. Available in print and online.

Electronic Collections Online. Dublin, OH: OCLC. Available online.

ERIC. 1966– . Washington, DC: U.S. Department of Education. Available online.

Essay and General Literature Index. 1985– . New York: H. W. Wilson. Available online.

Ethnic NewsWatch. 1991– . Ann Arbor, MI: ProQuest. Available online.

Expanded Academic Text ASAP. Farmington Hills, MI: Thomson Gale. Available online.

First Search. Dublin, OH: OCLC. Available online.

Francis. 1984– . Bethesda, MD: CSA. Available online.

General Science Full Text. 1984– . New York: H. W. Wilson. Available online.

Hispanic American Periodicals Index Online. 1970– . Los Angeles: UCLA Latin American Center Publications. Available online.

Historical Abstracts. 1955– . Santa Barbara, CA: ABC-CLIO. Available online.

History Resource Center: U.S. Farmington Hills, MI: Thomson Gale. Available online.

Humanities Full Text. 1984– . New York: H. W. Wilson. Available online.

Humanities & Social Science Index Retrospective: 1907–1983. New York: H. W. Wilson. Available in print and online.

InfoTrac Custom Newspapers. Farmington Hills, MI: Thomson Gale. Available online.

InfoTrac Junior Edition. Farmington Hills, MI: Thomson Gale. Available online.

InfoTrac OneFile. 1980– . Farmington Hills, MI: Thomson Gale. Available online.

InfoTrac Student Edition. Farmington Hills, MI: Thomson Gale. Available online.

International Index to Black Periodicals Full Text. Ann Arbor, MI: ProQuest. Available online.

JuniorQuest. 1988– . Ann Arbor, MI: ProQuest. Available online.

LexisNexis Academic. Bethesda, MD: LexisNexis Academic & Library Solutions. Available online.

Library Literature & Information Science Full Text. 1984– . New York: H. W. Wilson. Available online.

LISTA: Library, Information Science and Technology Abstracts. 1969– . Bethesda, MD: CSA. Available online.

LitFinder. Farmington Hill, MI: Thomson Gale. Available online.

MasterFILE Premier. Ipswich, MA: EBSCO. Available online.

MasterFile Select. Ipswich, MA: EBSCO. Available online.

Middle Search Plus. Ipswich, MA: EBSCO. Available online.

MLA International Bibliography. 1922– . New York: Modern Language Association. Available online.

National Newspaper Index. Farmington Hills, MI: Thomson Gale. Available online.

Newspaper Source. Ipswich, MA: EBSCO. Available online.

Omnifile Full Text. 1982– . New York: H. W. Wilson. Available online.

PAIS Archive 1915–1976. Bethesda, MD: CSA. Available online.

PAIS International. 1972– . Bethesda, MD: CSA. Available online.

The Play Index. 1949– . New York: H. W. Wilson. Available online.

Poole's Index to Periodical Literature. Boston: Houghton Mifflin, 1802–1906.

Primary Search Plus. Ipswich, MA: EBSCO. Available online.

ProQuest 500. 1971– . Ann Arbor, MI: ProQuest. Available online.

ProQuest Newstand. Ann Arbor, MI: ProQuest. Available online.

ProQuest Research Library. 1989– . Ann Arbor, MI: ProQuest. Available online.

PsyArticles. 1988– . Washington, DC: American Psychological Association. Available online.

Psychology and Behavioral Science Collection. Ipswich, MA: EBSCO. Available online.

PsycINFO. 1967– . Washington, DC: American Psychological Association. Available online.

Public Library Collection. Naples, FL: Newsbank. Available online.

Reader's Guide Abstracts. New York: H. W. Wilson. Available online.

Reader's Guide Full Text. 1994– . New York: H. W. Wilson. Available online.

Reader's Guide Retrospective 1890–1982. New York: H. W. Wilson. Available in print and online.

Reader's Guide to Periodical Literature. 1890– . New York: H. W. Wilson.

Science Citation Index. 1900– . Philadelphia, PA: Thomson. Available online via *Web of Science.*

Science Full Text Select. New York: H. W. Wilson. Available online.

Science Resource Center. Farmington Hills, MI: Thomson Gale. Available online.

SciFinder Scholar. 1907– . Columbus, OH: American Chemical Society. Available online.

Scopus. New York: Reed Elsevier. Available online.

Short Story Index. 1984– . New York: H. W. Wilson. Available online.

SIRS Researcher. 1988– . Ann Arbor, MI: ProQuest. Available online.

Social Science Citation Index. 1956– . Philadelphia, PA: Thomson. Available online via *Web of Science.*

Social Sciences Full Text. 1995– . New York: H. W. Wilson. Available online.

Sociological Abstracts. 1952– . Bethesda, MD: CSA. Available online.

Web of Science. Philadelphia, PA: Thomson. Available online. Combines *Science Citation Index, Social Science Citation Index,* and *Arts and Humanities Citation Index.*

World of Poetry Online. New York: Columbia University Press. Available online.

Recommendations for Further Reading

Bucknall, Tim. 2005. "Getting More from Your Electronic Collections Through Studies of User Behavior." *Against the Grain* 17, no. 5 (November): 1, 18–20. Discussion of ways libraries can increase use of electronic resources by using such technologies as link resolvers.

Chen, Xiaotian. 2005. "Figures and Tables Omitted from Online Periodical Articles: A Comparison of Vendors and Information Missing from Full-Text Databases." *Internet Reference Services Quarterly* 10, 2: 75–88. A comparison of vendors of - full-text databases and how they deal with charts, diagrams, figures, and tables that were part of the original periodical articles. Focus of article is on databases from EBSCO, Factiva, First Search, Gale, LexisNexis, ProQuest, and Wilson.

Mi, Jia, and Frederick Nesta. "The Missing Link: Context Loss in Online Databases." *The Journal of Academic Librarianship* 31, no. 6 (November 2005): 578–585. A study of online databases and how the context of an article is sometimes lost with suggestions as ways publishers could index articles to maintain the context.

Persson, Dorothy, and Carlette Washington-Hoagland. 2004. "PsycINFO Tutorial: A Viable Instructional Alternative." *Reference & User Services Quarterly* 44, no. 1 (Fall): 46–56. An evaluation of the effectiveness of a tutorial developed to increase students' understanding of PsycInfo.

Tenopir, Carol, and Donald W. King. 2002. "Reading Behaviour and Electronic Journals." *Learned Publishing* (October): 259–265. A study of the use of scholarly journals by scientists. The authors found that scientists are reading traditional journals both in print and electronic format as well as other electronic sources of information.

Tyler, David C., Signe O. Boudreau, and Susan M. Leach. 2005. "The Communications Studies Researcher and the Communications Studies Indexes." *Behavioral & Social Sciences Literature* 23, 2: 19–46. A comparison of the online specialty indexes and the large, multisubject databases showing that the multisubject databases perform better.

Bibliography of Works Cited in this Chapter

Diakoff, Harry. 2004. "Database Indexing: Yesterday and Today." *The Indexer* (October): 85–88.

Golderman, Gail, and Bruce Connolly. 2003. "One-Stop Shopping." *NetConnect* (Summer): 30–35.

Machovec, George. 1995. "Identifying Emerging Technologies." In *The Impact of Emerging Technologies on Reference Services and Bibliographic Instruction,* edited by Gary M. Pitkin. Westport, CT: Greenwood Press.

Answering Questions about Health, Law, and Business—Special Guidelines and Sources

Overview

Medical, legal, and business questions constitute one of the most specialized, sensitive, and expensive areas of reference. The eternal realities of birth, death, and taxes that color all human existence feed inexorably into an urgent and steady stream of questions on health, legalities, personal finance, and business.

I have taken only one abortion pill, but wish to stop. Will that affect my pregnancy?
Hmm . . .

If I donate my house to charity, will I fall below the poverty line so I could apply for Medicaid?
Well . . .

What was the value of $300 in 1829 America relative to the current dollar in terms of the Consumer Price Index and the GDP per capita?
Er . . .

Like most medical, legal, and business questions, these three demonstrate the hallmarks that mark this as a "handle with care" area of reference work.

- The questions are invariably weighty.
- The answers are typically multilevel so that some degree of specialized knowledge becomes necessary.
- A strong code of ethics must govern the answers.
- The resources swallow a significant percent of reference budgets and require constant updates.
- Finally, and most importantly, the reference librarian who is trained in the art and science of answering questions must be constantly aware that they are nonspecialists and should calibrate their responses accordingly.

A careful balance that requires preestablished parameters of appropriate service combined with in-depth knowledge of available reference resources and referrals is the responsibility of every reference librarian. The American Library Association (ALA) recognizes this responsibility, so that in 1992 a set of specific guidelines for medical, legal, and business responses was prepared and subsequently updated. It is a useful reminder that the stated role of the reference staff is a vital first step in organizing reference services in these areas. *"Libraries should develop written disclaimers. . . . The level of assistance and interpretation provided to users should reflect differing degrees of subject expertise between specialists and non-specialists"* (ALA—updated 2001).

Why is the line between the specialist and the nonspecialist so important in these areas? After all, librarians have unflinchingly responded to questions about SQml, Kantian metaphysics, electrical codes, and pointillism without any specialized knowledge of computer science, philosophy, construction, or art. The answer lies in the nature of the beast.

How Medical, Legal, and Business Resources Are Used

The Nature of the Beast

Medical, legal, and business questions are of a different order based on seven characteristics distinctive of these three areas of research.

Criticality

The psychologist Abraham Maslow had argued that there was a hierarchy of needs so humans would fulfill their wish to be a ballerina, for example, only if they had first fulfilled their need for basic security. So also, there is a hierarchy of criticality in providing the right reference resource. In all probability, the obsolete cancer resource has far more of a negative impact than an obsolete book of linguistics. The right resource for the pro se litigant battling for child custody is potentially more critical than the right resource for dining etiquette. Medical, legal, and business issues, while not always of dramatically inflated consequence, have a powerful built-in predilection for criticality. The issues they cover can conceivably fall into Maslow's first level of need (health, financial, and civic security) and must be recognized as such.

Knowledge

A medical doctor takes approximately six years to complete a professional education, and a lawyer is ready to face the bar after three years of specialized study. The level of professionalism is marked by a distinctive and highly specialized vocabulary. Given the density, even consumerist keys to the information can require further decoding. The traditional crutches used by reference librarians while searching in unfamiliar territory, namely the index, table of contents, or "About" icons on a Web site, are sometimes not enough, so that *"staff must have the knowledge and preparation appropriate to meet the routine legal, medical, and business information needs of their clientele"* (ALA Guidelines 2001). It helps, for example, to know how a bill passes into public law, so that when a user wants to know more about a citation preceded by "P.L." rather than "H.R.," the librarian is clear about looking into laws rather than resolutions. A crash course in basic legal structure is possible through publications like *Legal Research In a Nutshell* or *Legal Research for Beginners*. Business resources such as investment reports can be deciphered after a quick study of guides such as *Business Information: How to Find It, How to Use It*.

Restraint

However knowledgeable the librarians, they can only play "doctor on television." Even lawyers who have become librarians, of whom there appear to be an appreciable number, must show restraint in the dispensing of legal advice. Instead, the role of providing guidance to resources and instruction in the use of resources must be adopted both formally as a written directive and behaviorally. The latter can be very hard to do given the neediness and urgency of many users. A strong referral system and relevant pathfinders are both a necessary antidote and a mandatory addition to medical, legal, and business reference services.

Ethics

The "guess what" quotient of medical, legal and business questions can be high. "Guess what, that woman is going through a messy divorce . . . that teen wants a book on the treatment of syphilis . . . that man wants to invest in Saudi oil." Questions can be of a highly personal nature, and confidentiality must be consciously maintained. Additionally, the best possible resource recommendation is dependent on a successful interview, so that tact in conducting the interview is a necessity. The user must feel comfortable about providing the fullest possible information relevant to the question.

Volume

It is no accident that there are specialized libraries devoted to medical, legal, and business collections. The demand for this information is high. As the hapless pages in even nonspecialized public libraries will attest, it is the 300 and the 600 section of the collection that is in never-ending need of shelving and shelf alignment. 300s and 600s are the meat of public libraries primarily because the volume of questions is significant. Publishers, too, have realized this, as attested by the staggering 7,382 medical consumer books published in 2004. A survey conducted by Pew in 2005 also corroborated consumer interest in health with the statistic that eight out of ten Internet users have looked for medical information at some point (Danford 2005, 30).

Updating

Given the premium on currency of resources in these areas, an inordinate number of publications are loose-leaf, or require inserts and pocket parts, or are supplemented by regular updates. Reference librarians will need to set clear guidelines on discarding procedures and updating schedules, as well as monitor the correct placement of inserts and loose-leaf substitutions, pocket parts, or additions. The individual nature of these weekly, monthly, bimonthly, or quarterly additions, so unlike the simple edition updates of other reference material, further sets apart these three fields as a more specialized area of reference. Users who do not have to fumble through bloated *Value Line* binders that show no signs of the weekly inserts having been discarded; or miss out on an updated law because the annotated insert is not placed in the back pocket; or face rows of dusty *Mergent's Bond Records* because staff is not sure whether they are of "some use" are users who will appreciate the librarian's recognition that these resources require informed attention.

Expense
Once again, given the depth of information and overriding need for currency, a significant portion of reference budgets must be kept aside for medical, legal, and business resources. A single volume of *Weiss Ratings' Guides*, for example, may be between $250 and $300. However, the volume is redundant in four months, when a new quarterly appears.

Questions Answered by Medical, Legal, and Business Resources

The need to understand the nature of the beast is not so that the reference librarian shirks responsibility in tackling such questions, but approaches such questions with a full awareness of its necessary limiters.

- *"Can you find any recommendations for a Dr. Mount E. Bank, with whom I have a colonoscopy scheduled?"*
  I could certainly find you a biographical sketch instead, that lists his certifications and specialty background in the *Official ABMS Directory of Board Certified Medical Specialists*.
- *"I am suing my contractor for bad faith. He claims it is a case of negligence. What is the difference and does it mean he can get away with shoddy construction?"*
  West's Encyclopedia of American Law explains the difference between bad faith and negligence, but you do need professional legal representation to ensure your rights in the matter.
- *"Who are the five largest private employers in the United States and are they financially secure?"*
  The U.S. Postal Service, Burger King, Express Personnel, Carlson, and Blue Cross are the five largest according to *Hoover's Handbook of Private Companies 2005*. You could analyze their financial viability by checking the revenue history, net incomes, background information, and structure as given in the *Handbook*.
- *"Are there any contraindications to the drug Coumadin?"*
  Consult the latest copy of the *Physicians Desk Reference* for information, and then I would suggest double-checking with your doctor or pharmacist.
- *"My lawyer left a message to say that inheriting my grandfather's mansion could be 'damnosa hereditas.' Is that good or bad?"*
  Bad! "An injurious inheritance" is the definition given by *Black's Law Dictionary*, so you may want to check into the costs of inheriting it.

Clarity in defining the limits of what can and cannot be answered is critical to these areas of reference. A thorough knowledge of existing medical, legal, and business resources, such as the ones described below, goes a long way in encouraging clarity when faced with a user's real-life question.

Major Health Resources Used in Reference Work

The days of the family doctor who made house calls sounds like a long-forgotten myth in today's frenetic world of specialists and insurance-sensitive health systems. For better or for worse, consumer empowerment in health decisions is the order of the day and replaces the old unthinking reliance on the family doctor. Given this climate of empowerment, both the demand for and the supply of health information has reached epic proportions. The reference librarian therefore plays a vital role in slimming down the large amounts of information published and offering an improved selection of comprehensive and comprehensible medical information.

Medical Dictionaries

Inopexia and pallidotomy, cirrhonosus and amusia—the involved language created to describe the vast functions and malfunctions of the human body is almost mystical in its incomprehensibility. For a prosaic understanding of it, however, a stellar dictionary that can bridge the gap between professional terminology and amateur understanding is vital. Even comprehensible words must be checked in a medical dictionary if the context is one of health. For example, an innocuous word like "bay" that may mean an estuary or a barking sound or a leaf in the nonmedical world is, in anatomy, a recess containing fluid.

- A resource that has provided a bridge for many years is *Stedman's Medical Dictionary*. With over 107,000 terms accompanied by graphics and photographs, the dictionary is used by both health professionals and the layperson. User-friendly features include, but are not limited to, a separate listing of "high profile terms"; synonyms distinguished by blue print; all subentries positioned on a new line so that there is more visual simplicity; densely labeled illustrations; and a detailed index. A free online version is available at www.stedmans.com and can be searched by keyword with wildcard capabilities. A CD-ROM supplement has a medical spellchecker, as well as videos, animations, four-color images, and the ability to keep a record of search histories. The dictionary is also available for PDAs with searches through headwords and multiple hyperlinks.
- First published as a pocket medical dictionary in 1898, *Dorland's Illustrated Medical Dictionary 30th Edition* currently defines more than 125,000 terms supplemented with over 1,100 color plates. The dictionary is invaluable for its clean line drawings, photographs, and radiographic images. In the most recent edition, the dramatic inclusion of color graphics after more than 100 years of black and white images has further enhanced the usability of the reference, as has the addition of over 800 complementary and alternative medical terms. Color boxes, tables for complex information, and medical terms printed in bright red to enhance readability all contribute to a resource that is both user-friendly and comprehensive. The authority of the resource can be testified by the National Library of Medicine, which uses it to establish MeSH®, its own controlled vocabulary of subject headings. The dictionary is available on CD-ROM, and can also be accessed freely at www.dorlands.com.

Medical Encyclopedias

Thompson Gale, Omnigraphics, and Facts On File publish health series that are comprehensive, authoritative, and user-friendly.

General

- With the cautionary principle that "memory is treacherous" guiding its publication, the *Merck Manual of Diagnosis and Therapy* has been an aid to physicians since 1899, when a slim version was first published. Albert Schweitzer is said to have carried a copy to Africa in 1913 and Admiral Byrd to the South Pole in 1829. The layman's version of the Merck was published as recently as 1997, titled *The Merck Manual of Medical Information—Home Edition*. Based on the original Merck, the home edition uses everyday language to give in-depth information on a complete range of disorders. The information is supplemented with original graphics. While the table of contents lists all entries under various disorders, the detailed index guides the user so that it is not necessary to know what disorder contains the word abetalipoproteinemia. Marketed as a "not-for-profit" service to the global community, the home manual is freely available at www.merck.com. The site can be searched by keyword, an alphabetical index, or through a subject section such as "blood disorders" or "infections." Once linked, the page displays a navigation area clearly stating the section, chapter, and topic that has been selected. Relevant hyperlinks and diagrams are also included.
- The *Gale Encyclopedia of Medicine* and the *Gale Encyclopedia of Alternative Medicine* are reliable general encyclopedias. The five-volume "one-stop" work on human diseases, disorders, syndromes, procedures, therapies, and drugs, the *Encyclopedia of Medicine* was first published to rave reviews in 1999. The third edition, due in 2006, aims to continue the format of alphabetical entries covering a range of diseases with information on causes, symptoms, diagnosis, prognosis, treatment, and prevention included. The structure of information is standardized, so that looking up information on unfamiliar topics becomes relatively easy. Graphics supplement many of the entries in the second edition, and a detailed index with a cross-referencing system aids usage.
- With a national statistic that claims more than one-third of adults in the United States use complementary and alternative medicine, the four-volume *Encyclopedia of Alternative Medicine* is a useful addition to reference collections. It presents forty types of alternative medicine, from ancient Indian ayurveda to the modern Feldenkrais Method of healing. The information is careful to avoid any bias. Resource lists of printed information and relevant institutions are also given. Color photographs of medicinal plants provide an invaluable key to identifying obscure herbs. Side effects and general acceptance levels for each entry are also included.

Specialized

- The *Gale Encyclopedia of Children's Health* is a four-volume compilation of pediatric diseases and disorders aimed primarily for children under the age of four years.

In addition to a catalog of diseases, the encyclopedia also covers developmental issues, immunizations, and drugs. The volumes are also available as an e-book through the Gale Virtual Reference Library. The *Gale Encyclopedia of Surgery* covers 265 surgical procedures. The information is enhanced with much-needed descriptions of the diagnostic procedure for each type of surgery as well as the aftercare that will be required. Morbidity and mortality rates and alternate techniques are included. The encyclopedia is aimed directly at patients and caregivers, as evident in the defining of medical jargon, the use of second opinions, lists of questions to ask doctors, procedures for hospital admission and presurgery, and an extensive bibliography of support organizations, associations, and literature on the subject.

- A comprehensive and widely respected source of information for over 4,000 drugs, the *Physicians Desk Reference—PDR®* is a staple of all health collections. Drugs can be located by manufacturer, as well as by product or generic name and category. Usage information includes warnings, dosages, overdosages, contraindications, and use-in-pregnancy ratings. The print edition is published annually and can be updated during the year with two supplements published in July and October. Photographs of over 2,000 drugs are included, even though they are inserted as a group rather than as accompaniments to the written descriptions. The free online version, available at www.pdrhealth.com, on the other hand, includes photos with the description, which is written in lay terms. The Web site also provides information on herbal medicine such as Echinacea; over the counter drugs such as Alka-Seltzer; and nutritional supplements such as vitamins. A collation of *PDR®* and related sources is available on CD-ROM as well.

- Published primarily as a diagnostic tool, the *DSM-IV-TR* (*Diagnostic and Statistical Manual of Mental Disorders*) is published by the American Psychiatric Association. It has become a fixture in libraries because of its unique coverage of psychiatric illnesses and its authority as a source for standard nomenclature of all mental disorders. Prevalence, genetic predisposition, age, gender, culture, and other features are included for each disorder. The presentation is dense and aimed at the professional rather than the lay user. The fourth edition is available for use on PDAs and Smartphones. The original *DSM* of 1952 is a 144-page document that is public domain and available at www.appi.org/pdf/apa_2017.pdf. The recent edition can be searched as a subscription database at www.psychiatryonline.com. The more accessible two-volume *Gale Encyclopedia of Mental Disorders* covers all disorders listed in the *DMV-IV-TR*. It also covers various therapies and medications. All entries are standardized to include, among other things, coverage of definitions, causes, diagnoses, prevention, and additional resources. The language is relatively clear of jargon and entries are complemented by illustrations, photographs, and graphics. Key terms in any description are highlighted in a definition box to simplify understanding of complex issues.

Medical Directories

Locating a particular doctor or hospital; scanning listings for relevant doctors and medical centers in a certain area of specialization; and vetting doctors and hospitals are frequent requests. Medical directories provide answers for this category of questions.

- The annual four-volume *Official ABMS Directory of Board Certified Medical Specialists* has comprehensive biographies of over 600,000 medical specialists in the United States and Canada, who have been certified by the twenty-four medical specialty boards of the American Board of Medical Specialties. Certification is voluntary, so it is not necessary that each qualified physician is in the directory. The directory can be used to locate a physician by specialty and by geographical area. It can also be used to verify a specialist's educational background, professional associations, and general credentials. The CD-ROM version of the directory is updated twice a year and titled *ABMS Medical Specialists PLUS* (Elsevier). The database version, available at www.boardcertifieddocs.com is updated daily and has special features such as "alerts" tailored to specific notifications and downloadable records. A free certification search is accessible at www.abms.org/login.asp, but the user must log in and complete a registration form. Physicians can also be verified by calling the toll-free number, 1-866-ASK-ABMS.
- A popular consumer guide to physicians can be found in Castle Connolly's guide, *America's Top Doctors*. Over 230,000 physicians are surveyed and nominated by their peers so that a total of 4,700 "top doctors" can be found. The procedure is highly subjective but provides a first cut to users looking for a starting point in their search for the right physician. Listings are by area of specialization so that twenty-five specialties and ninety subspecialties can be studied for both institutional and physician listings. The information is also available online for an annual fee at www.castleconnolly.com, though a portion of the database can be accessed free after completing a registration form.
- More than 690,000 fully licensed physicians can be found on the freely available DoctorFinder provided by the American Medical Association at http://webapps .ama-assn.org/doctorfinder/home.html. Physicians who are not fully licensed are best located in the printed *Directory of Physicians in the United States* published by the American Medical Association that currently lists almost 290 additional entries that cover residents, researchers, teachers, administrators, and retired physicians.
- A unique resource that has not been updated since 2000 is the consumer watch publication from Public Citizen, *20,125 Questionable Doctors: Disciplined by State and Federal Governments, National Edition*. The doctors pilloried in the four volumes are from across the nation and collectively account for more than 34,000 disciplinary actions ranging from fines to license suspensions. Detailed information on whether the physician has been disciplined for substance abuse, sex offenses, or incompetence is included. With a majority of the physicians listed continuing to practice, the volumes provide an authoritative resource for users looking for further information on specific doctors. The resource is also available on CD-ROM.
- *DIRLINE*, a comprehensive directory of health organizations, can be found in the free government Web site at http://dirline.nlm.nih.gov. With over 8,000 records of agencies, referral centers, professional organizations, self-help and community groups, and research institutions, the directory can be searched by keyword or a subject search of the disease or condition. The results include an abstract of the organization's aims, history, and budget, as well as complete contact information.

Medical Databases and Indexes

- *PubMed* is both freely accessible and the most extensive bibliographic database for health issues. It covers the information contained in the National Library of Medicine's MEDLINE of twelve million citations dating back to the 1960s; OLDMEDLINE of two million citations ranging between 1950 and 1965; and special out-of-scope citations primarily from the life sciences. The coverage is not limited to North American journals. While full text is not available on *PubMed*, a "Link Out" feature allows the user to access full-text articles from a specific citation. Many of these links, however, require subscriptions or fees to access the full text. Available at www.pubmed.gov, the database has the authority of the National Institute of Health and is invaluable as an index tool for researchers.
- Thomson Gale™ at www.gale.com is responsible for a set of well-known and respected medical databases and indexes to medical journals, newspaper articles, and pamphlets. The two major ones are *Health Reference Center Academic* and the *Health and Wellness Resource Center* available through InfoTrac Web, the online subscription service used by Gale. Similar in content, though different in interface, access, and search strategies, the Gale databases are user-friendly, authoritative, and provide both full-text articles and indexing to additional titles. The index covers articles in books, overviews, pamphlets, and journals.
- EBSCO Information Services at www.ebsco.com parents a host of bibliographic and full-text medical databases of which *Health Source* and *CINAHL* are notable for their coverage and ease in searching. *Health Source* is an extensive database with access to health periodicals, reference books, pamphlets, drug monograph entries, and patient education fact sheets. Full-text documents as well as abstracts and indexes are available, with convenient links that can guide the researcher to more in-depth study. *CINAHL* is less general, but provides the most exhaustive index for issues related to nursing and allied health. Almost 2,000 journals in the nursing field are covered by this database, as well as nursing dissertations, conference proceedings, and standards of practice. Together, there are more than a million records, some of which date back to the early 1980s. Aimed at a more specialized user, full-text articles from almost seventy journals are also available.

Online resources

Changes in medical wisdom have far-reaching effects. The miracle cure of today can become the pariah of tomorrow. Fast changing knowledge of medical research can oftentimes only be available on the Internet, a medium that is capable of handling and disseminating news speedily and globally. Bookmarking at least five to ten valuable Web sites for medical news and updates is a necessity of good health reference service.

- The National Library of Medicine is the largest medical library in the world. *MedlinePlus*, a component of the above-mentioned PubMed, was started in 1998 as the library's consumer health Web site at http://medlineplus.gov with twenty-two health topics. It now covers 687 topics and over 700 diseases and conditions. It is also a strong resource for checking on drugs, clinical trials, hospitals, and physicians.

The information is updated daily and fed by both government agencies and health organizations. A medical dictionary and encyclopedia are included. Some of the sources that cover drug information, such as the USP-DI, give Canadian brand names as well, so that an antihistamine like Sinarest in the United States can be replaced by Sinutab in Canada after a quick check of the Web site.

- While MedlinePlus is a valuable all-purpose site, specialized sites such as www.cancer.gov and www.cancer.org provide authoritative and timely information on specific diseases. Sponsored by the National Cancer Institute and the American Cancer Society respectively, both sites are written in lay terms and cover the various stages faced by cancer patients.

- A valuable site for drug information can be found at www.drugdigest.org/DD/Home which provides the unique Drug Interactions database that allows the user to check for interactions between two drugs. Niggling questions on whether one can take an aspirin for headache while taking a particular prescription drug for diabetes is solved by use of this site. Over 6,000 images of pills also helps users who need to confirm that what they are about to swallow is indeed what they meant to swallow, especially when pill makers change the shape or color of the pills. Freely accessible to all, the Web site also includes data from the subscription database *Clinical Pharmacology*.

- An interesting source for up-to-date medical news articles, with a bias toward news from UK, can be found at http://news.bbc.co.uk/1/hi/health/default.stm. The "Health" section of the BBC news can be checked for current medical stories, as well as searched for archival material by keyword or through an A-Z index.

Health Statistics

The National Center for Health accessible at www.cdc.gov/nchs is the primary source for health statistics. Data collected from birth, death, and medical records as well as through widespread surveys, testing, interviews, and examinations are collated to provide "surveillance information" that can be used to limn the nation's health problems. The site has a simple overview of datasheets so that it is possible to access a rich vein of statistical information with minimal burrowing. Each datasheet has links to a range of additional sources so that more in-depth research is also possible. Hard-to-find statistics on teen pregnancy (425,493 in 2001) or suicide (31,655 in 2002) or persons without health coverage (40.6 million in 2002) can be accessed easily.

Major Legal Resources Used in Reference Work

On January 2, 2003, the Judicial Council of the California County Law Librarians decided to include an icon for 24/7 legal reference help in every page of its site. The effect was immediate. From an average of 100 questions per month, the number of legal queries shot up to an astonishing 2,045 questions. There has never been any doubt that we live in an increasingly litigious society. However, the exponential rise in amateur lawyers and *pro se* litigants has come as a surprise. The person on the street is now potentially able to draw up a living will; expand a home in accordance with local zoning laws; or fight a custody battle. Prohibitive lawyer fees, coupled with extensive access to legal precedent and rules via the Internet, have put the onus of legal responsibility on the common person, and by extension, the neighborhood librarian.

Given this trend, a collection that includes basic printed legal material and access to online resources is a necessary component of reference service in all libraries. While all libraries must have a dictionary to decode legalese and an encyclopedia to cover a breadth of legal topics, more specialized resources such as directories, indexes, and primary and secondary legal material can be acquired based on the needs of the community.

Legal Dictionaries

- Currently in its eighth edition, the invaluable *Black's Law Dictionary* was first published in 1891 under the stewardship of English legalist Henry Campbell Black. It is reportedly the most cited law dictionary in the country and covers more than 43,000 definitions. A large number of the entries are cross-referenced to cases in the *Corpus Juris Secundum* to aid further research. The new edition also provides a useful appendix of more than 4,000 legal abbreviations and another on legal maxims. Pronunciations of arcane legalese such as the feudal "feoffee" are provided, as well as equivalent terms and alternate spellings for over 5,000 terms and senses. A pocket, an abridged, and a deluxe edition of the dictionary are also available. The dictionary is searchable on *WestLaw*.

- With more than 10,000 definitions of over 5,000 legal terms defined with phonetic pronunciations, *Ballantine's Law Dictionary* has been a popular alternative to *Black's*. An all-important case citation, from which a particular definition derives authority, is also supplied, thereby providing a starting point of research for many users. It is particularly useful in its coverage of old Saxon, French, and Latin phrases. The *Ballantine's Law Dictionary and Thesaurus* combines the dictionary with a thesaurus for legal research and writing so that synonyms, antonyms, and parts of speech are also attached to each definition, making for a more exact understanding of each legal term. The appendix includes the *Chicago Manual of Legal Citation* and a guide to doing research.

- Free online legal dictionaries can also be used for quick searches. *Merriam-Webster's Dictionary of Law* can be accessed through FindLaw at http://dictionary .lp.findlaw.com. A basic legal dictionary that can be searched by legal term, by letter of the alphabet, and by all definitions that include the word can be found at http://dictionary.law.com. A historical dictionary of legal terms can be accessed at www.constitution.org/bouv/bouvier.htm, where a copy of the indomitable 1856 *Bouvier's Law Dictionary* provides definitions for such legal entities as "female" (the sex which bears young).

Legal Encyclopedias and Yearbooks

- The word "weal" is defined as the common good or the welfare of the community at large. It is also the motivation and acronym of the preeminent legal encyclopedia, *West's Encyclopedia of American Law*. Formerly published as the *Guide to American Law*, the thirteen-volume set covers 5,000 legal issues. Terms, cases, statutes, documents, issues, forms, time lines, and over 600 biographies are presented without specialized jargon so that it is accessible to the layperson. With a determined focus to provide "legal ease" rather than "legalese," even complex and far-ranging issues such as *Roe vs. Wade* are condensed into understandable packets of knowledge with the inclusion of lawyer arguments, majority and dissenting opinions, and the reasoning of the judges. More current entries such as Internet fraud and movie ratings testify to the currency of the resource. Graphics, cross-references, timelines, and focus boxes enhance the text. The encyclopedia is also available in an e-book format.

- The *American Law Yearbook* is a corollary to *WEAL*. It annually updates the encyclopedia and provides expanded versions of entries in the encyclopedia. Cross-references, time lines, and photographs that accompany the biographies make this a highly user-friendly resource. Each edition carries the U.S. Supreme Court docket as well as other cases not argued at the level of the Supreme Court. The currency of each edition is attested by the 2004 inclusion of the gay marriage issue and the 9/11 Commission report; and the 2005 coverage of the Schiavo case and a biography of Attorney General Alberto Gonzales. It is available in e-book format through Gale Virtual Reference Library.

Legal Directories

- Published for more than 133 years, the *Martindale-Hubbell Law Directory* is an established authority for locating and checking on the credentials of law firms and lawyers. The twenty-six-volume print edition lists more than one million lawyers and firms in 160 countries. The entries are arranged by geographical location so that smaller libraries have the option of purchasing single volumes that cover their own home state. An extensive indexing system allows searches by name as well. The volumes are also available on a two-disc CD-ROM that allows for twenty-seven different search criteria. Search results can be exported to a spreadsheet or database program, with more than one application running at the same time. Free online access is available at www.lawyer.com or via the *Lawyer Locator* at www.martindale.com. Solicitors and law firms in the UK can also be freely accessed at www.lawyerlocator.co.uk. The biographical information provided is also supplemented with peer ratings and reviews, a unique practice begun since the 1896 edition of the directory. The directory is not only a global standard for information on the legal profession; it acts as a marketing or fact-checking tool for lawyers as well. The *Practice Profile* listings can be completed by all lawyers and law firms, so that an unlisted firm or lawyer is invariably considered to be suspect.
- A single-volume directory with almost 2,000 pages packed with information can be found in the annual editions of the *Law and Legal Information Directory*. Over 19,000 legal agencies, programs, institutions, facilities, and services are listed under different categories as diverse as "National and International Organizations" and "Awards and Prizes." Each listing provides a brief description and contact information.

Legal Databases and Indexes

Subscription databases such as Lexis, WestLaw, and LAWCHEK aim to provide a wide range of legal information relevant to the most heavily used areas of legal research.

- Started as early as 1973, *Lexis* was a pioneer in providing full-text legal information. As the *LexisNexis* database, it continues to be the most authoritative index of legal and government documents, as well as a resource for full-text legal material. Various permutations of the master database are available so that custom packages can be created for different levels of libraries, the primary three being corporate, government, and law libraries. Case law, codes, legal analysis, public records of property, news transcripts, and regulations are all part of the powerful array of legal resources provided by *LexisNexis*. Indexes such as H. W. Wilson's *Index to Legal Periodicals* are also part of the array. The database has continued to expand and in 2005 became the exclusive provider of legal content for a major repository of business intelligence, *Factiva*, at www.factiva .com. Given the richness of the database; the endless customization available; and the high costs of purchase, an involved study of each community's legal reference demands must be made before choosing the right package at www.lexis nexis.com.
- *Quicklaw* is the Canadian branch of *LexisNexis* and can be accessed at http://ql .quicklaw.com. Tailored to Canadian legal information needs, the same mix of case law, court and tribunal decisions, procedures, legal news, and commentary are provided for a fee. Legal information can also be found in French and the Web site itself is bilingual.
- *LexisNexis Butterworths* is the UK branch, accessible for a subscription fee at www.lexisnexis.co.uk. With lawyer-locator services, studies and citations of English, Irish, Scottish, Commonwealth, and European cases, all fifty volumes of Halsbury's Laws, tax and pension information, and fully amended texts of statutes, etc., *Butterworths* is a comprehensive legal resource for the United Kingdom. A new initiative to provide online legal service was inaugurated in June 2005.
- *Westlaw* is another powerful provider of legal documents such as case law, statutes with annotations and court corrections, directories, law reviews, and public records such as real property deeds. While aimed at the legal professional, *Westlaw* has introduced user-friendly search aids such as "Smart Tools" that attempts to flag any word or acronym that appears to be spelled incorrectly or appears out of context. So for example, even a "correct" spelling like "statue" is flagged if it mistakenly appears in the context of the term "statute of limitations." Related terms are also suggested to aid the nonprofessional. Directories can be scanned by single word search terms and words are automatically searched along with their plurals, irregular plurals, and possessives. The density of information offered is tempered with these search enhancements, details of which can be found at the Web site, www.westlaw.com.
- *LAWCHEK* was created as a direct result of the 1991 ALA study. It is aimed at the layperson and the reference librarian. Fashioned as a tutorial for twelve selected legal disciplines found to be the most heavily trafficked areas of public research, LAWCHEK provides fee-based access to legal forms, glossaries, guides, letter templates, and legal directories associated with these areas. It is also linked to both state and federal codes and cases. The Web site can be accessed at www.lawchek.com/.

Legal Online Resources

- Winner of the 2005 Webby Awards for best legal Web site, www.findlaw.com is a popular free site for legal professionals, students, and the layperson. Packed with legal links, information, lawyer directories, forms, and news, the site is a rich source for both primary and secondary legal material.
- *Hieros Gamos* is a respected Web site for extensive directory listings of lawyers, law firms, expert witnesses, court reporters, investigators, and process servers both in North America and globally. Legal and bar associations, law libraries around the world, legal events, and news are all part of the site available at www.hg.org.
- In January 1995, *THOMAS* became the first and foremost source for free online information on federal legislation. An invaluable index is supplied by the Congressional Record Index, published every two weeks. Also available are historical documents; summaries of congressional activity; the legislative process; committee reports and information; and bill text, summaries, and status. The utility of the site is indicated by the 2004 average of more than 400,000 files transmitted every day. Accessible at http://thomas.loc.gov, the site is easy to use and provides a valuable resource for any information related to legislation in the United States. Edward Elsner, a Listserv participant, provided the tip that summaries of laws and acts could also be accessed by a Google search with the name of the law in quotation marks followed by the word "summary" (Publib, August 5, 2005).
- Access to global laws is also becoming freely available. For British law a good source is www.interactive-law.co.uk. It provides free access to specialized legal information such as family, property, medical negligence, and personal injury law in the UK. A comprehensive portal to information about Canadian legal resources can be found in the hyperlinks provided by the Harvard Law School at www.law.harvard.edu/library/services/research/guides/international/canada/index.php.

Major Business Resources Used in Reference Work

It is a jungle out there. Business resources run the gamut from tissue-thin pamphlets on personal finance to multivolume works on global marketing. The whys and wherefores and how-tos of making, consolidating, and propagating wealth root into a dense thicket of publications on accounting, taxation, banking, human resources, industrial relations, labor, personal finance, international finance, insurance, advertising, company profiles, product development, biographical directories, commodity statistics, rating guides, statistical overviews, et al. While a set of inclusive business dictionaries, encyclopedias, handbooks, indexes, and directories is required of all reference collections, more in-depth acquisition is required primarily in two of the most heavily trafficked areas of business queries: that of personal finance and business entrepreneurship.

Business Dictionaries

- When users are stumped as to whether they should be putting an "accelerator clause" in their lending document; or whether a "variable markup policy" is advisable for their small business, it is time to consult the Oxford University Press's

A Dictionary of Business. First published in 1990 as a *Concise Dictionary of Business,* the 2004 edition has over 6,500 entries, with a focus on e-commerce terms. The definitions provide pithy background information and are strengthened by a systematic web of cross-references, illustrations, synonyms, and abbreviations.

- The distinct red-covered Economist Series on the *Dictionary of Business* and the *International Dictionary of Finance* provide simple definitions on a wide range of business activity. Brief analyses of business concepts are also provided, along with cross-references, acronyms, and business jargon. More than 2,000 terms are listed in each dictionary. Given the global nature of business, many of the terms included are common to countries other than the United States.
- Libraries that require a more specialized breakdown of dictionary meanings in all the various aspects of business can look into the Barron's Educational Series. Separated into the *Dictionary of Business Terms* with 7,500 entries; the *Dictionary of International Business Terms* with 5,000 entries; the *Dictionary of Marketing Terms* with 4,000 entries, the *Dictionary of Insurance* with 4,200 entries; the *Dictionary of Accounting* with 2,500 entries; the *Dictionary of Finance and Investment Terms* with 5,000 entries, etc., the series is physically small and hard to shelve, but useful and inexpensive.

Directories and Handbooks

- The twenty-volume annual *Thomas Register of American Manufacturers* published since 1906 will cease its print version after 2006. It is the standard authority for finding information such as contact numbers, addresses, subsidiaries, sales offices, and affiliations for over 168,000 American and Canadian manufacturers. There are 72,000 product and service categories listed alphabetically under city and state. Over 8,000 manufacturer catalogs are also printed with all entries verified by editors to ensure accuracy of the resource details. The directory is available on CD-ROM and DVD-ROM, where searches can be limited by state, area code, and zip code. The free online version at www.thomasnet.com is a one-stop source for industrial products, services, and suppliers. Contact information as well as product details are accompanied by drawings of component pieces. Searches can be made via keyword and product category or limited by geographic location. Manufacturing information for the UK can be accessed freely at www.thomasglobal.com through the *Thomas Global Register® Europe.*
- First published in 1928, the two-volume *Standard & Poor's Register of Corporations, Directors and Executives* is a panoptic directory of 75,000 corporations and 290,000 executives across the United States, Canada, and parts of the world. Volume 1 covers corporations with contact information that includes Web site addresses when applicable, as well as a brief listing of key personnel, number of employees, products, total sales, and North American Industry Classification System codes. Volume 2 alphabetically lists officers, directors, trustees, and patrons of business organizations, with both contact information and biographical details such as year and place of birth, college and year of graduation, and noncollege fraternal memberships. The entries are democratic in that Bill Gates is given the same space as an officer of a florist company in Kentucky. An extensive system of cross-references is also provided so that a user can locate companies under NAICS codes, geographical

location, and subsidiary and parent company information. Tracking the ultimate parent company in a corporate family hierarchy, so that the relation between, say, ABC Inc. as a subsidiary of the Walt Disney Company becomes clear elevates this resource to more than just a simple directory. The annual is further updated through cumulative supplements.

- "Who Owns Whom" is the succinct description supporting the title of the extensive eight-volume directory, *Corporate Affiliations*. The directory lists almost 185,000 international and American companies with revenue in excess of $50 million and $10 million respectively. A master index can be used to locate the ownership status, corporate hierarchy, nationality, geographic coverage, personnel, Standard Industrial Classification, and brand name correlations for each company. Users wanting to know if the Bridgestone Corporation is American, or if there are links between the Tokyo office of Bridgestone and the Cobra Tire Company Inc. in Phoenix are well served by the clear nexus provided by this resource. The directory is available both as a CD-ROM titled *CorporateAffiliations PLUS* and as an online subscription at www.corporateaffiliations.com, where the nexus is traced all the way down to the "seventh level of reporting relationships."

- Published in 1991 as a single handbook profiling 500 corporations, Hoover's now publishes multiple handbooks that are updated annually. The *Handbook of American Business* focuses on 750 influential American companies with in-depth coverage of personalities and analyses of successful company strategies. The *Handbook of Private Companies* profiles 900 such companies including hospitals, charities, universities, and cooperatives. The *Handbook of World Business* covers 300 public, private, and state-owned businesses located outside the United States. The *Handbook of Emerging Companies* aims to highlight 600 of the most vibrantly growing small businesses, with in-depth profiles on 200 of them. A combined index to all the Hoover Handbooks is also included in this volume. All four handbooks emerge from a company database of 12 million businesses that allows Hoover's Business Press to offer a dizzying variety of online business resources that can be accessed via subscription at www.hoovers.com.

- *Brands and Their Companies* is a useful directory of more than 400,000 brand names. For users wanting to know which company manufacturers the Frisbee toy (Wham-O Manufacturing Co.); or what the brand Diazinon is (a household pesticide); or whether Big Time candy is still in production (no), this is the directory to consult. The entries are listed alphabetically by brand name and briefly list the product description and the manufacturer or distributor. Brands no longer in production are marked as such, whereas brands that have morphed into generic words such as "Xerox" are also included. Brands not registered with the patent office are also entered, making this a unique resource for hard-to-find information. The directory is also available as part of the Gale Business Resources CD-ROM and database at www.gale.com.

Investment Guides

- In the volatile world of financial investing, a steady guide has been provided by *Value Line Investment Survey*. Published since the 1930s, the survey is a weekly investment advisory that comes in three loose-leaf parts. The main part is the Ratings and Reports section that covers 1,700 stocks. Each stock is analyzed and graded for timeliness, safety, and volatility. Background information on the company is provided along with a graph charting a decade of price ranges. Given the careful mix of recommendation and information, Value Line has become a staple of reference collections.

- Weiss Ratings publishes a series of quarterly investment guides for both the novice and seasoned investor. The beginning user can be directed to the *Ultimate Guided Tour of Stock Investing*, in which a pith-helmeted cartoon safari leader leads the investor through the wilds of stock figures, analyses, and analysts. However, the bulk of publications are aimed at the practicing and amateur investor. There are Weiss Ratings' Guides on *Bonds and Money Markets, Mutual Funds, Brokerage Firms, Stock Mutual Funds, Banks and Thrifts, HMOs and Health Insurance, Life, Health, and Annuity Insurers*. A careful system of ratings is established so that each bond, mutual fund, bank, insurance company, and brokerage firm is analyzed and judged according to a stated set of criteria. Weiss, which has been publishing guides for over thirty years, stresses objectivity so that no compensation is accepted from any of the institutions rated. Libraries have the option of buying one annual issue, or subscribing to the quarterly editions that are published for each guide. Individual rating reports are commercially available at www.weissratings.com.

Business Entrepreneurship Aids

- The 2005 edition of the annual *Market Share Reporter* is a combination of both the North American market and the international market that was previously published as the *World Market Share Reporter*. With more than 3,600 entries arranged under SIC/NAICS codes, the *Reporter* acts a as a unique resource for users interested in comparing and ranking the market share of companies and their products. Products ranging from top disposable diaper brands (Huggies Ultratrim) to the leading aircraft maker for the defense department (Boeing Co.) are listed along with the percentage share of the market and, in some cases, the dollar amounts as well. An alphabetical table of topics is provided along with a table of contents listed in numerical SIC ascending order. Pie and bar charts supplement some of the entries, and each entry cites the source.
- Previously published as the *Source Book of Franchise Opportunities, Bond's Franchise Guide* profiles over one thousand franchises, divided into forty-five business categories such as "recreation and entertainment" and "automotive products and services." Each entry provides contact information. If the information proves to be obsolete, the publishers are ready to update the material if the user can call them at 520.839.5471. The entries are derived from a forty-point questionnaire and are therefore highly detailed, requiring an a priori reading on how to use the data. In addition to contact information, background history, and a description of the business franchisor, criteria for granting a franchise are also given along with legal and financial requirements. Franchise seekers are well served by this resource. A less authoritative resource with far more entries is the *Franchise Annual Directory*. It profiles well over 5,000 franchisors, with separate sections for Canadian and overseas listings. The entries are highly sketchy and best serve those who are in search of nothing more than basic contact information.

Business Databases and Indexes

- A sweeping database with a powerful indexing component, Gale's *Business and Company ProFile ASAP* covers over 200,000 directory listings, full-text public relations newswires for up-to-the-minute information, and thousands of entries from business journals, trade periodicals, and management serials from 1980 to the present. The corollary *Business Index ASAP* is integrated into the *ProFile* so that indexes for the financial section of the *New York Times*, the *Asian Wall Street Journal*, and the *Wall Street Journal* are available. User aids include a controlled vocabulary, a subject guide, cross-references, and customizable search strategies. Subscription information is available at www.gale.com.

- For global business and financial information that includes *Electronic Data Gathering Analysis and Retrieval* filings and *D & B's Million Dollar Directory Plus*; the annual reports of both U.S. public and international companies; financial reports for over 10,000 Canadian and U.S. companies, and insider trading data that records all transactions within a six-month period, *Mergent Online* is an incisive business database. The database provides the tools to compare and analyze up to 200 companies against a set of variables that can be mixed and matched. The ability to create a customized company report is also offered. The database at www.mergentonline.com/ is available with several varieties of configurations and can be adapted to suit the needs of basic business information such as looking up a company to more involved cross-border searches.

- Begun as a graduate project in 1971, *ABI/INFORM* (ProQuest) is a pioneer in the online indexing and abstracting of business information. It currently contains about two million documents, of which approximately half are in full text. The meticulous 150-word abstracts for which it was renowned have also been pared down to a mix of long and short, indicative entries as a wider variety of business sources are being added to the database. Over 60,000 company profiles; full-text journals from academic publishers such as Kluwer, John Wiley, and Palgrave Macmillan; and entries from thousands of local, national, and international management and business publications are offered by *ABI/INFORM* at www.proquest.com/products/pt-product-ABI.shtml.

- EBSCO's *Business Source®* databases come in different packages: *Elite, Premier, Corporate, Complete,* and *Alumni.* The *Premier* and *Complete* include monograph and reference books in addition to articles from serials. A special "business-specific interface" allows for relatively sophisticated fine-tuning of search results so that lists can be limited by preferred sources and search options can be conducted through more than just company name or subject entry. A breakdown of titles available through each database is available at www.ebsco.com/home. EBSCO's user-friendly and standardized search bars, title list management tools, and comprehensive coverage of business resources make it an attractive choice for all levels of libraries.

- Formerly known as Dow Jones Interactive, *Factiva* is an innovative provider of global business content. Indexes, abstracts, and full-text content from over 9,000 resources including *The Wall Street Journal*, the *Financial Times*, television and radio transcripts, individual company reports, the *Dow Jones* and *Reuters* newswires, and publications from 118 countries succeed in providing a content-rich and wide-ranging business database. The content is universally indexed and enables searches in multiple languages. Subscription information is available at www.factiva.com.

Collection Development and Maintenance

Selection and Keeping Current

One of the distinctive aspects of medical, legal, and business resources is that once selected, a large number of the publications tend to fall into the category of a "standing order." Whether it is *Mergent*'s reports, reviews, and handbooks or individual states' annotated statutes, the overriding need for currency fuels a system of constant updating that can only be feasible as a standing order. The onus of decision making, then, is on the initial selection for which there are a few effective ways for identifying new resources.

Published Reviews

In addition to reviews found in mainstream publications such as *Library Journal, Reference and User Services Quarterly, Booklist*, and *Choice*, reviews can also be located in professional journals.

- For health and medicine, the *Medical Reference Services Quarterly* (Book Reviews and From the Literature), *the Journal of the American Medical Association* (Books, Journals, New Media), *and the New England Journal of Medicine* (Book Reviews) are relevant resources.
- For legal resources, reviews are available in the *Law Library Journal* (Keeping up With New Legal Titles). A free monthly online resource can be found in *The Law and Politics Book Review*, sponsored by the Law and Courts Section of the American Political Science Association at www.bsos.umd.edu/gvpt/lpbr.
- A uniquely consolidated update of business resources can be found at the Business Reference and Services Section of the American Library Association. Titled as the *Public Libraries Briefcase*, the quarterly column put out by the section provides an organized bibliographical account of both old and updated resources in all the disparate areas of business.

Publisher Sites

As mentioned earlier, the proclivity to publish series is strong among the publishers of medical, legal, and business resources. Librarians looking for new resources on health, for example, can browse through the Web sites of:

- Omnigraphics Health Reference Series at www.omnigraphics.com;
- Facts on File Library of Health and Living at www.factsonfile.com, and
- Thomson Gale encyclopedias at www.gale.com.

Some legal publications aimed at the layperson are published by:

- West Nutshell series at www.thomson.com;
- Journals and resource series from the American Association of Law Libraries at www.aallnet.org/products;
- Legal products at www.reed-elsevier.com; and
- Nolo legal series at www.nolo.com.

Some business and finance publications can be checked on the following sites:

- Mergent's products at www.mergent.com/publish/products_services.asp
- Financial Services and Business Web pages at www.mcgraw-hill.com; and
- Hoover's Books at www.hoovers.com/free.

Online Catalogs

Given the number of specialized libraries devoted to medicine, law, and business, non-specialist reference librarians need not reinvent the wheel.

- A periodic check of new titles acquired by specialized libraries such as the National Library of Medicine, which lists a column titled *New at the Bookshelf*, is freely accessible at www.ncbi.nlm.nih.gov and can provide timely clues.
- The Harvard Business School brings out a list of new business acquisitions by the fifteenth of each month that are arranged under subject headings. The *New Books at Baker* list can be perused at www.library.hbs.edu/bakerbooks/recent/.
- The *New Law Library Acquisitions* listed monthly by the Lillian Goldman Law Library at Yale Law School provides an alphabetical list that can be accessed at www.law.yale.edu/outside/scr/library/news/index.asp.

Evaluating Medical, Legal, and Business Resources

While scope, accuracy, authority, and cost are basic criteria for evaluating medical, legal, and business resources, of heightened importance are the factors of currency, usability, and utility.

Currency

The urgent need for current information results in a number of publications that have a constant schedule of updates. The type and frequency of these updates must be registered so that older copies are discarded immediately and the processing of updates is done at a priority level. For resources that do not have an updating service, weeding must be punctilious. No information in these three areas is preferable to outdated information. The currency of a publication can be gauged by looking up issues about which new information has been released. What does a 2006 drug reference say about Celebrex or Tamoxifen? Does a legal yearbook document "adjustments" to the Patriot Act? Is the Sanofi-Aventis merger recorded in a directory of companies?

Usability

All three fields are thick with specialized terminology and jargon. Reference resources aimed at the layperson need to be vetted for linguistic and graphic simplicity. Resources that cannot avoid terminology must have boxed definitions, legends, keys, glossaries, highlights, or other aiding devices. The indexes must be infallible as the material is relatively unfamiliar and pattern recognition on the part of the user will play an important part in navigating through the material.

Utility

Given the thousands of titles available in each of these areas, the resources must be evaluated in direct correlation to their use for the given community. Publishers are prone to produce series or sets of health, legal, and finance publications. The series follow a standard format, share a distinctive look, and attempt to cover the most heavily trafficked areas of public demand. For example, the temptation to buy all of Omnigraphics's distinctive red and white hardcover publications on 140 health topics is understandable, but not entirely necessary. A community may need the most updated version of the *Alzheimer's Disease Sourcebook* but not the *Ethnic Diseases Sourcebook* or vice versa. The attractive binders of *Entrepreneur's Business Start-Up Guides* provide a uniform layout to almost fifty different businesses and are a valuable addition to libraries, but again, the *Freight Brokerage Service* may be more useful to some communities and the *Gift Basket Service* to others. Keeping the subject demands of the community in focus is one way of not succumbing to the siren call of professional and well-made series.

Further Considerations

Sources Are Not Enough

In the world of medical, legal, and business resources, despite excellent acquisition skills, a worthy collection, and an acute knowledge of the resources available in multiple formats, there may always be the need to do more. Resources must be supplemented with referrals, research guides, disclaimers, alternate sources, and policies for all kinds of usage.

Alternate Sources

What is considered the ideal source for a general reference question must be approached as just one of the sources for a medical, legal, or business question. There is value in providing alternatives so that the user can make comparisons. This effectively supplants the role of advice and reinforces the role of the nonspecialist librarian as the provider, rather than the interpreter, of information.

Disclaimers

Constant reminders on the currency of the resource must be provided. For example, if the *Physicians Desk Reference* were to be provided as the resource to consult for a certain drug, the user must be reminded to check for currency on a Web site such as www.drugdigest.org, as well as consulting with his or her doctor or pharmacist. An instructive case in point is that the drug *Vioxx* has no mention of any controversy in the 2005 edition of the *PDR* or the *Consumer Drug Reference*.

Research Aids

For popular subject areas, written or online aids in identifying, demystifying, and evaluating medical, legal, and business reference sources are advisable. It is not only of enormous help as a visual crutch to the user who is faced with specialized information, but provides a guard against librarians forgetting to include vital pieces of information while explaining a complex document. Sources such as *Business Information: How to Find It, How to Use It*, despite being an older publication, provides a clear X-ray of the skeletal structure of data-rich financial reports, surveys, and analyses. The data packed into a single page of the *Value Line Investment Survey*, for example, is clearly labeled and explained in the book, so that a condensed key can be prepared by librarians for first-time users of *Value Line*. An online example of an effective aid to understanding Mergent publications can be found in the New York Public Library's *A Guide to the Mergent Manuals* at www.nypl.org/branch/features/index2.cfm?PFID=243.

Referrals

The importance of a referral sheet cannot be underestimated. A list of the nearest law, medical, and business libraries must always be handy, so that the user can be referred to a greater variety and depth of resources if necessary. A directory of lawyers, doctors, and business professionals must also be available so that the user can access professionals for additional information if required. Care must be taken, however, to resist personal recommendations of any one specific professional.

Remote Access Usage

Finally, there must be provisions for remote access usage, especially telephone reference. To inform a user on the telephone that a certain disease reads as being fatal, or to attempt reading aloud the annotations and updates of a certain law is not only awkward but ripe for misunderstanding and liability. Text-based responses must also be handled with care. Emphasis on in-house resources which the user can consult, compare, and interpret is far preferable in most medical, legal, and business queries.

Reference vs. the Radiendocrinator

In the early part of the twentieth century, the entrepreneur William Bailey sold the all-purpose "Radiendocrinator." It professed to cure everything from acne to memory loss by "ionizing the endocrine glands" (Ware 2002, 3). The cost to the user was what would today amount to over $10,000. With scopic medical, legal, and business resources available to users through their libraries, and effective informational roles played by reference librarians, it is hoped there will be a decrease in the sale of modern-day radiendocrinators.

TOP TEN MEDICAL, LEGAL, AND BUSINESS SOURCES

Title	Print	Online
Black's Law Dictionary. 2004. Eagan, MN: Thomson West.	8th ed.	Subscription www.westlaw.com
Hoover's Handbooks. Austin, TX: Hoover's Business Press.	4 vols.	Subscription www.hoovers.com/free/
Martindale-Hubbell Law Directory. 1931– . New York: Martindale Hubbell Law Directory, Inc.	Annual 26 vols.	www.martindale.com www.lawyers.com
The Merck Manual of Medical Information Second Home Edition. 2003. Whitehouse Station, NJ: Merck & Co. Inc.	1 vol.	www.merck.com
Official ABMS Directory of Board Certified Medical Specialists. 1993– . Philadelphia, PA: W. B. Saunders Co.	Annual 4 vols.	Subscription www.boardcertifieddocs.com
Physicians' Desk Reference. 2005. Montvale, NJ: Thomson PDR.	60th ed.	www.pdrhealth.com
Stedman's Medical Dictionary. 2005. Philadelphia, PA: Lippincott Williams & Wilkins.	28th ed.	www.stedmans.com
Thomas Register of American Manufacturers. 1905– . New York: Thomas Publishing.	Annual 33 vols.	www.thomasnet.com
Value Line Investment Survey. New York: Value Line Publications.	Weekly	Subscription www.ec-server.valueline.com/products/web1.html
West's Encyclopedia of American Law. 2005. Farmington Hills, MI: Thomson Gale.	2nd ed. 13 vols.	e-book subscription www.gale.com

Recommended Resources Discussed in this Chapter

Medical

Alzheimer's Disease Sourcebook. 2003. Detroit: Omnigraphics.

America's Top Doctors. 2005. New York: Castle Connolly Medical Ltd.

Cancer. Available at www.cancer.gov and www.cancer.org.

CINAHL. Available at www.cinahl.com.

Clinical Pharmacology. Available at http://cp.gsm.com.

Consumer Drug Reference 2006. 2005. New York: Consumer Reports.

Directory of Physicians in the United States. 2005. Chicago: American Medical Association.

DIRLINE. Available at http://dirline.nlm.nih.gov.

Dorland's Illustrated Medical Dictionary 30ᵗʰ Edition. 2003. Philadelphia, PA: W. B. Saunders Co. (Elsevier).

Drug information. Available at www.drugdigest.org/DD/Home.

DSM-IV-TR (Diagnostic and Statistical Manual of Mental Disorders). 2000. Arlington, VA: American Psychiatric Association.

Ethnic Diseases Sourcebook. 2001. Detroit: Omnigraphics.

Gale Encyclopedia of Alternative Medicine. 2004. Jacqueline L. Longe, ed. Farmington Hills, MI: Thomson Gale.

Gale Encyclopedia of Children's Health. 2005. Kristine Knapp and Jeffrey Wilson, eds. Farmington Hills, MI: Thomson Gale.

Gale Encyclopedia of Medicine. 2006. Jacqueline L. Longe, ed. Farmington Hills, MI: Thomson Gale.

Gale Encyclopedia of Mental Disorders. 2002. Ellen Thackery and Madeline Harris, eds. Farmington Hills, MI: Thomson Gale.

Gale Encyclopedia of Surgery. 2003. Anthony J. Senagore, ed. Farmington Hills, MI: Thomson Gale.

Health Reference Center—Academic. Available on InfoTrac Web or CD-ROM at www.gale.com.

Health Source—Consumer and Nursing/Academic editions. Ipswich, MA: EBSCO Publishing. Available at www.epnet.com.

Health and Wellness Resource Center. Farmington Hills, MI: Thomson Gale. Available at www.gale.com/HealthRC.

JAMA: the Journal of the American Medical Association. 1960– . Chicago: American Medical Association. Available at http://jama.ama-assn.org.

Medical Reference Services Quarterly. 1982– . New York: The Haworth Press. Available at www.haworthpress.com.

MedlinePlus. Available at http://medlineplus.gov.

Merck Manual of Diagnosis and Therapy. 2006. Mark H. Beers and Robert Berkow, eds. Hoboken, NJ: John Wiley & Sons.

The Merck Manual of Medical Information—Home Edition. 2003. Mark H. Beers, ed. White Station, NJ: Merck & Co.

New England Journal of Medicine. 1928– . Waltham, MA: Massachusetts Medical
Society. Available at http://content.nejm.org.
*Official ABMS (American Board of Medical Specialties) Directory of Board Certified Medical
Specialists.* 2006. 38th ed. Philadelphia, PA: W. B. Saunders Company.
Physicians Desk Reference—PDR®. 1974– . Montuale, NJ: Medical Economics Co.
PubMed. 1957– . Bethesda, MD: National Center for Biotechnology Information.
Available at www.pubmed.gov.
Stedman's Medical Dictionary. 2005. Philadelphia, PA: Lippincott Williams & Wilkins.

Legal

American Law Yearbook. 2005. Farmington Hills, MI: Thomson Gale.
Ballantine's Law Dictionary. 1994. New York: Thomson Delmar Learning.
Ballantine's Law Dictionary and Thesaurus. 1995. New York: Thomson Delmar Learning.
Black's Law Dictionary. 5th ed. 2004. Bryan A. Garner, ed. Eagan, MN: Thomson West.
Bouvier, John. 1856. *Bouvier's Law Dictionary.* Jamaica Plain, MA: Boston Book
Company.
Corpus Juris Secundum. Eagan, MN: Thomson West. Copyright varies.
Hieros Gamos. Available at www.hg.org.
Law and Legal Information Directory. 2006. Farmington Hills, MI: Thomson Gale.
Law Library Journal. 1908– .Washington, DC: American Association of Law Libraries.
LAWCHEK. Available at www.lawchek.com.
LexisNexis. Available at www.lexisnexis.com.
LexisNexis Butterworths. Available at www.butterworths.com.
Martindale-Hubbell Law Directory. 1931– . New York: Martindale Hubbell Law
Directory, Inc.
Merriam-Webster's Dictionary of Law. 1996. Linda Picard Wood, ed. Springfield, MA:
Merriam-Webster, Inc.
Quicklaw. Available at http://ql.quicklaw.com.
WestLaw. Available at www.westlaw.com.
West's Encyclopedia of American Law. 2004. Jeffrey Lehman and Shirelle Phelps, eds.
Farmington Hills, MI: Thomson Gale.

Business

ABIINFORM. Available at www.proquest.com.
Bannock, Graham, Evan Davis, Paul Trott, and Mark Uncles. 2003. *Dictionary of
Business.* New York: Bloomberg Press.
Bannock, Graham, and William Manser. 2003. *International Dictionary of Finance.*
London: Profile Books.
Bond's Franchise Guide. 1995. Oakland, CA: Source Book Publications.
Brands and Their Companies. 2006. Farmington Hills, MI: Thomson Gale.
Business and Company ProFiles ASAP. Available at www.gale.com.
Capela, John J., and Stephen W. Hartman. 2004. *Dictionary of International Business
Terms.* New York: Barron's Educational Series.

Corporate Affiliations. 2005. New Providence, NJ: LexisNexis Group.

A Dictionary of Business. 2004. 3rd ed. London: Oxford University Press.

Downes, John, and Jordan Elliott Goodman. 2002. Dictionary of Finance and Investment Terms. New York: Barron's Educational Series.

Factiva. Available at www.factiva.com.

Franchise Annual Directory. 2005. New York: Info Press Inc. Also available at www.infonews.com.

Friedman, Jack P. 2000. Dictionary of Business Terms. New York: Barron's Educational Series.

Hoover's Handbook of American Business. 2005. Austin, TX: Hoover's Business Press.

Hoover's Handbook of Emerging Companies. 2005. Austin, TX: Hoover's Business Press.

Hoover's Handbook of Private Companies. 2005. Austin, TX: Hoover's Business Press.

Hoover's Handbook of World Business. 2005. Austin, TX: Hoover's Business Press.

Imber, Jane, and Betsy-Ann Toffler. 2000. Dictionary of Marketing Terms. New York: Barron's Educational Series.

Market Share Reporter. 2005. Farmington Hills, MI: Thomson Gale.

Mergent's Bond Record. 1999. New York: Mergent FIS.

Mergent Online. Available at www.mergentonline.com.

Standard & Poor's Register of Corporations, Directors and Executives. 2005. New York: McGraw Hill.

Thomas Register of American Manufacturers. 2005. New York: Thomas Publishing. Also available at www.thomaspublishing.com.

Value Line. Available at www.valueline.com.

Value Line Investment Survey. 1995. New York: Value Line Publications.

Weiss Ratings' Guides. Jupiter, FL: Weiss Ratings. Copyright varies.

World Market Share Reporter. 2001. Farmington Hills, MI: Thomson Gale.

Recommendations for Further Reading

American Library Association, Reference and User Services Association, Business Reference and Services Section. Guidelines for Medical, Legal, and Business Responses. Available at www.ala.org/ala/rusa/rusaprotools/referenceguide/guidelinesmedical.htm. A clear set of guidelines prepared for both the specialist and non-specialist reference librarians in dealing with issues on the role of staff, the currency and accuracy of sources, and the special care required for off-site users in need of medical, legal, or business questions.

Ambrogi, Robert J. 2004. The Essential Guide to the Best (and Worst) Legal Sites on the Web. New York: ALM Publishing. The author, who introduced "legal.online," a syndicated column in 1995, has organized relevant legal Web sites into major practice areas. Each site is also rated along a five-star rating system that covers utility, design, content, accessibility and innovativeness.

Anderson, P. F., and Nancy J. Allee, eds. 2004. The Medical Library Association Encyclopedic Guide to Searching and Finding Health Information on the Web. New York: Neal-Schuman Publishers. While relevant Web sites, organizations, and referrals pertinent to health information are provided in this book, it is the focus on developing effective search terms and strategies that make this a unique resource.

Boorkman, Jo Anne, and Fred W. Roper, eds. 2004. *Introduction to Reference Sources in the Health Sciences.* 4th ed. New York: Neal-Schuman Publishers. A comprehensive collection of health resources, the fourth edition of this book continues to pinpoint the major bibliographic and informational sources relevant to health reference collections. Print, electronic, and online formats are all included.

The Directory of Business Information Resources, 2006. 2005. New York: Grey House Publishing. A useful overview of the most relevant business newsletters, trade shows, special associations, trade journals and magazines, industry-specific databases, directories, and Web sites for almost 100 broadly grouped industries.

Encyclopedia of Business Information Sources. 2006. Farmington Hills, MI: Thomson Gale. The 21st edition of this book is a dense compilation of an unusually broad spectrum of print, electronic, and online business resources arranged by subject. Within each subject, types of resources such as indexes, directories, almanacs, and databases are listed with a brief description and complete contact information.

Medical and Health Care Books and Serials In Print. 2005. New York: Bowker. An extensive listing of over 100,000 books and nearly 23,000 serials related to the health and biomedical field. The two-volume set can be searched by subject and title as well as by author and publisher. It is a useful resource to consult for updates in a field where currency is of paramount value.

Moss, Rita W. 2004. *Strauss's Handbook of Business Information.* Westport, CT: Libraries Unlimited. A clear and well organized handbook describing business reference sources and formats. It also covers the tricky area of looseleaf services.

Worley, Loyita. 2006. *BIALL Handbook of Legal Information Management.* Burlington, VT: Ashgate Publishing Company. Though applied to the laws of the United Kingdom, this is an authoritative handbook on critical aspects of law librarianship applicable to all information providers. Search techniques and orga-nization of legal resources along with chapters on the practical management and training of staff in ongoing legal research and ethics, combine to provide a compelling focus on legal information services as a whole.

Bibliography of Works Cited in this Chapter

"Accessing Legal and Regulatory Information in Internet Resources and Documents." 2006. *Journal of Library Administration* 44, 1/2: 263–324.

Cohen, Morris, and Kent C. Olson. *Legal Research In A Nutshell.* 2003. Eagan, MN: Thomson West.

Danford, Natalie. 2005. "Reader, Heal Thyself." *Publishers Weekly* (June 27): 30.

Feldmann, Louise. 2005. "Selected Business Resources on the Web." *Colorado Libraries* 31, no. 3 (Fall): 34–35.

Habermann, Julia. 2005. "Weblogs as a Source of Business News and Information." *Online* 29, no. 5 (September/October): 35–37.

"Health and Medical Resources: Information for the Consumer." 2006. *Journal of Library Administration* 44, 1/2: 395–428.

Hysell, Sharon Graff, associate ed. 2005. *American Reference Books Annual*. Vol. 36. Westport, CT: Libraries Unlimited. Also available online at www.arbaonline.com.

Ketchum, A. M. 2005. "Consumer Health Information Websites: A Survey of Design Elements Found in Sites Developed in Academic Environments." *Journal of the Medical Library Association* 93, no. 4 (October): 496–499.

Larson, Sonja, and John Bourdeau. 1997. *Legal Research For Beginners*. New York: Barron's Educational Series.

Lavin, Michael, R. 1992. *Business Information: How To Find It, How To Use It*. Phoenix, AZ: Oryx Press.

Ojala, Marydee. 2006. "The New Life Cycle of Business Information." *Online* 30, no. 1 (January/February): 48–50.

Ware, Leslie, and editors of Consumer Reports. 2002. *Selling It*. New York: W. W. Norton & Co.

Welch, Jeanie M. 2005. "Silent Partners: Public Libraries and Their Services to Small Businesses and Entrepreneurs." *Public Libraries* 44, no. 5 (September/October): 282–286.

Wells, Karen K., Stephanie Weldon, and Elaine Connell. 2005. "Medical and Public Librarians: Partnering to Make a Difference." *Colorado Libraries* 31, no. 3 (Fall): 29–31.

Whisner, Mary. 2005. "Cool Web Sites." *Law Library Journal* 97, no. 4 (Fall): 721–728.

10

Answering Questions about Geography, Countries, and Travel—Atlases, Gazetteers, Maps, Geographic Information Systems, and Travel Guides

Overview

Geography is an interdisciplinary area of study spanning both earth science (physical geography) and social science (human geography). Today geography "explores the relationship between the earth and its peoples through the study of place, space and environment. Geographers ask the questions where and what; also how and why" (Unwin 1992, 13). "Individuals with diverse interests are tied together through their interest in understanding how places or locations affect activities (human or otherwise), how places are connected, and how those connections facilitate movement between places or cause an event at one location to impact another location" (Johnson 2003, 1).

As our users' perspectives become more global, the importance of geographic information increases, allowing more learning about the world in which we live. The information provided by geographic sources is remarkable and extensive and includes information in print and available electronically. Geographic sources provide information in narrative form through gazetteers and other print resources and visually through maps. Although geographic information is available in other information sources, sources specific to the field provide the most precise and accurate information. For example, in an atlas the user can find not only the location of a country or city but also its latitude and longitude and other pertinent facts.

How Geographic Information Is Used

Geographic information sources are used in a variety of ways. First of all, they can be employed to find the location of towns, rivers, mountains, countries, continents, and so on. Geographic sources make it possible for users to more easily visualize the relationship between countries and continents. They do more than just provide directions; they may show the makeup of a particular land area—its mountains, valleys, rivers, and plains. Other geographic tools show the environmental and climatic or ecological factors in an area so we can better understand how this affects the ability of the area, for example, to develop agriculturally. Geographic sources may deal with the past as well as the present. For example, historical maps and atlases trace changing country boundaries to provide the reader with a way to visualize what has happened in a particular country and how history has been affected by these changes.

Questions Answered by Geographic Information

- What countries surround Turkey?
  This answer can be found by looking at a map of Turkey in an atlas.
- What is the present name of the country called Burma?
  A gazetteer such as the *Columbia Gazetteer of the World Online*, which will cross-reference Burma to its present name, Myanmar, can provide this information.
- Where is Doha located?
  Either an atlas with a good index or a gazetteer can be used to find this answer. It is a city in the country of Qatar.
- What were the boundaries of the countries in Europe in 1848?
  This can be found in *Shepherd's Historical Atlas*.

Major Geographic Information Resources Used in Reference Work

Geographic information sources come in many formats. First of all, there are gazetteers. Gazetteers are text-based sources of information about geographic places and features. They are arranged alphabetically and describe as concisely and precisely as possible where, for example, a particular town or mountain range is located and other pertinent facts about it.

In contrast to gazetteers, maps are a visual way of showing locations of places and land features. The most common types of maps are route and street maps that show the streets and highways so that someone can determine the best route to get from one place to another. Topographic maps show the natural land features through the use of color so that the user can see clearly the mountainous areas, the rivers, and the plains. Political maps show the boundaries of major cities, towns, and villages, and the boundaries of countries. Thematic maps usually deal with a narrow theme such as religion, ethnic diversity, or history, using the visual format of maps to convey information.

The digital revolution has brought new possibilities to mapmaking, but the end of the paper map is not in sight. Although digital mapmaking has made it possible to produce interactive maps, to provide for route finding, to place name searches and convert maps into electronic form, paper maps still have some distinct advantages. First of all, they allow for subtleties of color and text that are not possible with digital maps. Maps that appear on a computer screen are limited by the screen resolution. Paper maps also allow for the user to look at a wider expanse at one time than is possible on a screen (Ashworth 2003, 56). Route maps are particularly useful in electronic format. Such vendors as Mapquest.com and Google Maps (http://maps.google.com) make it possible for the user to type in their starting location and their destination. These programs then provide a map and written directions to the location. Alternately, these programs allow a user to type in a specific address and get a map of that location. In some major metropolitan areas, Web sites such as HopStop.com are being developed to help plan routes on foot and via public transportation.

An atlas is a collection of maps with some unifying theme. Atlases may include a series of maps for a particular country or continent, showing both the overview and more specific areas such as a state, province, city, or a world atlas that covers the entire globe. Atlases offer more than maps since they often include other geographic information such as population, the environment, and statistics on countries, with a detailed index. But there are also collections of historical maps that show the changes in political boundaries through time. Thematic or subject atlases have become popular to show visually a particular subject, for example, an atlas on some aspect of history. A third type of map is a globe. Globes provide a way to see the relationship between continents and land masses and provide a more accurate visualization of the earth. There is less geographic detail on a globe. Another source of geographic information is travel guides. Travel guides come in many forms. Some simply list places to see, restaurants and hotels, while others provide more detailed information about a particular city or country with maps, detailed information on the history and culture of the city or country, and interesting descriptions of historical sites.

Gazetteers and Geographical Dictionaries

"A gazetteer is an alphabetical list of place names with information that can be used to locate the areas that the names are associated with" (Johnson 2003, 49). Often users do not need a map but simply want information about the location of a particular city, town, river, or mountain. For this information, the librarian can turn to a gazetteer or geographical dictionary.

The *Columbia Gazetteer of the World* is a standard source for reference librarians. This three-volume set contains 160,000 detailed entries listing geographical sites worldwide. Now updated by the *Columbia Gazetteer of the World Online* (www.columbiagazetteer.org) it includes 165,000 entries as well as the 2000 U.S. census figures and is available by subscription.

Merriam-Webster's Geographical Dictionary, 3rd edition revised, is a one-volume gazetteer and a good choice for libraries not needing the more extensive *Columbia Gazetteer of the World*. There are over 54,000 brief entries with economic, political, and physical data and 250 black-and-white maps. Countries, cities, natural features, and historical sites are listed.

The *Getty Thesaurus of Geographic Names Online* (www.getty.edu/research/tools/vocabulary/tgn) is a free online gazetteer developed by the Getty Research Institute. Listing nearly 1 million place names, it provides information about the preferred name for a place (a place could be a city, a village, or a land feature such as a mountain) and all variants by language and through history. The latitude and longitude is given for each place as well as its hierarchical position. For example, Milan's hierarchical position is World (facet), Europe (continent), Italy (nation), Lombardy (region), Milano (province), Milan (inhabited place). It also places Milan in its historical hierarchy and adds a note about its history. Sources of information for this thesaurus are listed and include the *Columbia Lippincott Gazetteer*, *Webster's Geographical Dictionary*, and the *Encyclopaedia Britannica*.

Geographic Names Information System (GNIS) (geonames.usgs.gov/index.html) lists over 2 million physical and cultural geographic names in the United States, the U.S. territories, and Antarctica. It was developed in cooperation with the U.S. Board of Geographic Names. Users can search for names of towns, rivers, streams, valleys, airports, schools, and much more. For example, the search for a town will give the user the elevation, the population, history notes, and the latitude and longitude, as well as a link to the Topozone (see p. 190) map of the town.

GEOnet Names Server (www.nga.mil/gns/html/index.html), a database of 5.5 million foreign place-names, is hosted by the National Geospatial-Intelligence Agency. This is the official source for all names of foreign geographic features and places.

The U.S. Bureau of the Census's *U.S. Gazetteer* (www.census.gov/cgi-bin/gazetteer) provides detailed maps of all incorporated towns, counties, and county subdivisions in the United States. The user can search by place-name or zip code. There is a link to a Topographically Integrated Geograhic Encoding and Referencing System map. Unfortunately, they are still using the 1990 census.

Worldmark Encyclopedia of the Nations, also available online, is a good source of information on over 200 countries and dependencies around the world. In addition to the detailed information on each country, there are biographical essays on national leaders.

Maps and Atlases

Mapmaking has a long history. Even in ancient times the Babylonians drew maps on clay tablets. The Greeks were among the early mapmakers. The maps of Ptolemy were still being used in the fifteenth century when his book *Geography* was published in 1482 in Latin.

The European discovery of America and the explorations of Africa and Asia diminished the importance of Ptolemy's works. Geographers from all over Europe contributed new information and corrected the maps of Ptolemy during the sixteenth century. Among those mapmakers were two Dutchmen, Abraham Ortelius and Gerard Mercator. The invention of printing coincided with these explorations so new maps could be more easily produced and distributed. "Governments began to use maps as tools not only for foreign conquests and economic exploitation but to establish control at home and for purposes of national defense" (info@maphistory.info).

Called by *Booklist* the "pinnacle of atlases," *The Times Atlas of the World* is the highest quality world atlas available. The maps are the work of John G. Barthlomew of Edinburgh, Scotland. It has 248 pages of digitally produced maps that have light but easy to distinguish colors and a readable typeface. This atlas has tried to provide a balanced coverage of all parts of the world and includes extensive mapping of all continents with at least ten maps per continent. Eight thematic world maps covering such topics as climate, population, and minerals are included. *The Times Atlas* pays careful attention to detail and uses easy-to-read symbols. Its excellent index lists place names at latitude/longitude coordinates and can serve as a gazetteer. *The Times Atlas* does, however, lack city maps.

The New International World Atlas is another excellent world atlas that includes world thematic maps, continental maps, and regional maps. The text is provided in five languages (English, French, German, Spanish, and Portuguese). The index includes 160,000 entries and uses longitude and latitude as the means to find locations. A separate section provides sixty-five city maps.

The *National Geographic Atlas of the World*, though smaller that the *Times Atlas* with fewer pages, maps, and index entries, is nevertheless a very good atlas that particularly excels in U.S. maps. There are city maps for each continent with the largest number from the United States. Completely revised, it contains the latest information on political and natural changes. A group of thematic world maps provide information on climate, biodiversity, the economy, and other issues. A companion Web site is available for owners of the print atlas that provides updated information and the ability to customize maps.

Many of the publishers of atlases publish a series of atlases in various sizes and at different prices.

Medium-sized Atlases

Although there is no comparison to the *Times Atlas of the World*, there are many atlases in the medium-sized category that provide good coverage at a moderate price and are very useful in a library.

The *Times of London Concise Atlas of the World* is a smaller version of the *Times Atlas*. It includes the usual Bartholomew maps, the detailed index, and a list of countries with concise information on each country and a picture of the flag.

The *Hammond World Atlas* is one of a series of Hammond atlases. The new edition of this medium-sized atlas has 181 physical and political maps, a sixty-four page "Thematic Section," and a forty-eight page "Satellite Photo Section." The physical maps are from digital elevation data. The index features 110,000 entries. Major metropolitan areas are dealt with as insets rather than in the section on city centers. The *Hammond World Atlas* uses smaller scale for countries other than the United States, which makes comparisons difficult. Nevertheless, it is an excellent atlas for its size and price.

The *Oxford Atlas of the World*, which is revised annually, includes 176 pages of full-color, computer-generated maps with an index of 75,000 entries. The major part of this atlas is devoted to maps of the continents including physical maps, political maps, and maps of specific regions. There is a separate section with sixty-seven major metropolitan areas and thirty-eight city centers with its own index. A thirty-two-page gazetteer that provides ready-reference information is arranged alphabetically with country summaries and official flags. The index uses the latitude and longitude as well as a letter/figure grid reference.

The *HarperCollins New World Atlas* also features Bartholomew maps. It provides a new approach to an atlas with a variety of maps for each continent on such subjects as countries, issues, and environments, and a number of excellent physical/political maps covering all parts of the continent. The index of 80,000 place names is particularly useful.

A newly revised edition of Reader's Digest's *Illustrated World Atlas* provides ninety-five full-page topographical maps and twenty-four world thematic maps. Recent geopolitical changes are reflected in this revised edition. The index features more than 80,000 entries for countries, cities, and geographical features. There is a profile box for each country with the official name, area, capital, organizations, population growth rate, life expectancy, languages, literacy, currency, Gross Domestic Product, and per capita GDP. This atlas is a good and reasonable choice for libraries.

Desk and Student Atlases

Smaller atlases are also published by the same publishers. Though not as detailed as larger atlases, they are often useful to students. *Goode's World Atlas* is an excellent compact atlas with world thematic maps, physical/political regional maps, and an index and geographic tables. It is highly recommended. In addition, Hammond publishes the *Hammond Citation World Atlas*, Oxford publishes the *Oxford New Concise World Atlas* and National Geographic publishes *National Geographic Concise Atlas of the World.*

Children's Atlases

Some atlases are specifically designed for children. Two examples of children's atlases are the following:

The *National Geographic World Atlas for Young Explorers* provides twenty-five thematic maps. The maps throughout the atlas are of good quality and easy to use. The flags and facts about each country including population, the capital and language are provided. An interesting feature is the fifteen pages devoted to the oceans.

The *Reader's Digest Children's Atlas of the World* divides the world into thirty countries and regions. Most of the maps are of the United States, with fewer maps for other continents.

For online sources appropriate for children and young adults, consult Ann Jason Kenney's article, "More Than Just Maps," published in *School Library Journal's Net Connect.*

Historical Atlases

Maps provide information about the past as well as the present. They can be arranged by theme or by date. *Shepherd's Historical Atlas* is a rich source of historical maps, especially European maps. *Shepherd's* shows the changes in boundaries throughout the ages, providing the user with an understanding of the impact of wars and treaties on the face of Europe.

David Rumsey and Edith M. Punt have produced *Cartographica Extraordinaire: The Historical Map Transformed.* This work reflects the way even historical maps are being transformed by geographic information systems (GIS). The maps in this work are also available on Rumsey's Web site (www.davidrumsey.com). The David Rumsey Map Collection also provides 11,000 free of copyright maps specializing in eighteenth- and nineteenth-century maps, focusing on the Western Hemisphere but including historic maps of other continents as well. These maps can be search by country, state, publication author, or keyword and can be printed.

Other sources of historical maps online are the History of Cartography Gateway (www.maphistory.info) that links to map sources and the Library of Congress American Memory Collection (http//lcweb2.loc.gov/ammem/gmdhtml/gmdhome.html), which features mostly U.S. maps from 1544 to 2004 in the public domain. Users can search the American Memory Collection by cities and towns or by subject, e.g., conservation and environment, discovery and exploration, cultural landscapes, military battles and campaigns, and transportation and communication. Yale University provides on its Web site a selection of maps from its historical map collection. This is a good source of antiquarian maps and historical city maps (www.library.yale.edu/MapColl/index.html).

Road Atlases

The best-known road atlas is the *Rand McNally Road Atlas*. This atlas, updated annually, provides maps of every state in the United States, every Canadian province, and a map of Mexico. There are also maps of 300 cities and twenty U.S. national parks. A list of town names by state is available at the end of the atlas as well as a nationwide mileage chart and a map showing interstate mileage and drive time. This atlas is used by people needing to determine the best route to a destination. It is integrated with www.randmcnally.com via codes on the map pages.

Thematic Atlases

The atlas format is used for thematic maps, which may or may not depend on geography. These atlases usually deal with a narrow theme. Some examples of thematic atlases are the following:

Times History of the World, edited by Richard Overy, begins with a twelve-page "Chronology of World History." It presents a balanced view of world history, including information on social history and on the cultural achievements of the various civilizations.

The *Atlas of World History* provides a series of maps combined with a narrative and photographs for each time period, beginning with the Ancient World and continuing to the year 2000. There is also an alphabetical list of events, people, and places. This atlas provides an added dimension to our understanding of world history through its visual approach.

The *Historical Atlas of the U.S.* provides a visual approach to U.S. history. It alternates the thematic sections, e.g., land, people, boundaries, economy, networks, and communities, with the five chronological sections—1400–1606, 1607–1788, 1789–1860, 1861–1916, and 1917–1988. The atlas includes time lines of U.S. history along with text and photographs. A bibliography includes the sources of the maps and illustrations as well as additional sources of information and an index.

The *Historical Atlas of Canada* is a three-volume interdisciplinary effort to capture the history of Canada—both of the indigenous people and the Europeans. The three volumes are *From the Beginning to 1800*, *The Land Transformed, 1800–1891*, and *Addressing the Twentieth Century, 1891–1961*. The maps range over a wide variety of subjects from population, workforce, and transportation to trade, agriculture, and fishing. This atlas presents its material in clear, easy-to-read maps with accompanying text. There is no index, but there is a detailed table of contents.

Oxford New Historical Atlas of Religion in America, edited by Edwin Gausted, is an excellent atlas using maps to show by century and region the growth of each religion. There are bibliographical references at the end of each section.

The *Barrington Atlas of the Greek and Roman World* by William Rand Kenan, Jr., is a comprehensive atlas of the classical world that includes all the regions that the Greeks and Romans penetrated between 1000 BC and 640 AD. It is an attempt to recreate the landscape of that time.

Rand McNally Commercial Atlas and Marketing Guide (annual) has been to date produced only in book form. But as of 2005 is also an electronic resource. This atlas provides maps for 123,000 places in the United States with information on population, the economy and economic activity, and transportation and communications. It is an excellent business planning tool. The electronic version requires a learning curve for both librarians and users.

Maps

Individual maps are often needed by users. The following are some of the sources of individual maps, both current and historic.

The Perry-Castenada Library, University of Texas, Web site (www.lib.utexas.edu/maps/index.html) provides 5,000 digitized maps country by country from the library's collection. It is strong in historical maps and is a good source for printing out a small-scale map.

The National Geographic Society provides some free maps, and many for purchase from its Web site (www.nationalgeographic.com/maps).

The United Nations also has a growing collection of country maps that can be accessed at www.un.org/depts/dhl/maplib/maplib.htm.

Topozone (www.topozone.com) features interactive topographic maps from the U.S. Geological Survey with exact longitude and latitude for the United States. The user can search by place name, location, and state.

Terraserver (www.terraserver.microsoft.com) provides public access to maps and aerial photographs of the United States. Users can look at their own neighborhood or at some famous place such as a national park.

National Atlas of the United States (www.nationalatlas.gov) is an interactive geological and topographical map that provides a wealth of information about the United States on a variety of topics from agriculture to government. Users can access over 400 data layers. Many files require GIS software, but it is, on the whole, a user-friendly site.

The Atlas of Canada is a bilingual online product. There are many interesting thematic maps showing both current and historic information in visual form on such subjects as the environment, the economy, history, climate, and health (atlas.gc.ca).

Mapquest (www.mapquest.com), a popular Web site, provides the user with directions to locations even beyond the U.S. borders, and locations of a particular address.

A more recent addition to online maps is Google's maps. At http://maps.google.com the user can find a map for a particular location, find a map to locate a business, or get directions from one location to another. In addition to these maps, Google Earth at http://earth.google.com provides satellite maps.

The American Fact Finder, located on the U.S. Census site (www.census.gov), provides maps based on historical information. There are both reference and thematic maps that have been developed using census data.

Oddens's Bookmarks: The Fascinating World of Maps and Mapping (http://oddens

.geog.uu.nl) provides over 4,000 links to map collections and cartography resources on the Web. Users can search under a variety of subjects including maps and atlases, sellers of cartographic materials, departments of cartography, and libraries.

Infomine (http://infomine.ucr.edu/cgi-bin/search?maps), a site developed by librarians, has a selective list of map links primarily of the United States.

For British maps a good place to start is the British Library Map Collection (www.bl.uk/collections/maps.html), which includes old and new maps. This site links to other important map collections in the United Kingdom including the Bodleian Library at Oxford University, the National Library of Scotland, the National Library of Wales, and the Royal Geographic Society.

Librarians will want to buy road and street maps for their community, county, and state. Many good local and regional map companies exist and can be located through the Yellow Pages of local telephone directories. Maps are also produced by city, county, and state governments.

U.S. Government Publications and Maps

Maps are available from many departments of the U.S. government. The largest number of maps is produced by the U.S. Geological Survey (www.usgs.gov). They include geological maps, topographical maps, and GIS maps on a wide range of topics including agriculture and farming, atmosphere and climate, and health and disease. They make aerial photographs available for purchase through EROS (Earth Resources Observation Systems) Data Center (http://edc.usgs.gov).

From the U.S. Bureau of the Census (www.census.gov/geo/www/maps) there are maps that enable the user to visualize the information in the census. The Bureau of the Census also provides online mapping resources of U.S. locations through the TIGER mapping service. The Environmental Protection Agency (EPA) has developed EnviroMapper (www.epa.gov/enviro/html/em/index.html), which provides maps by location showing eligibility for the Superfund monies and information about such issues as hazardous wastes and toxic emissions. Federal Emergency Management Agency (www.hazardmap.gov/atlas.php) provides multiple hazard maps showing locations vulnerable to floods, landslides, tornedoes, and hurricanes.

The *CIA World Factbook* (www.cia.gov/cia/publications/factbook/index.html) provides maps and some general information about 267 countries. This excellent free source, which includes information on geography, people, government, economy, communications, transportation, military, and transnational issues is current and quite extensive.

Background Notes (www.state.gov) are published and updated by the U.S. State Department. These publications provide concise information about countries, including the land, people, history, government, political conditions, the economy, foreign relations, and travel and business. They are updated frequently, and some are for sale in print.

The Geography and Map Division of the Library of Congress (http://lcweb2.loc.gov/ammem/gmdhtml/cnsvhome.html) provides both historic and more recent maps showing changes in the U.S. landscape, e.g., maps showing the growth and development of the U.S. National Parks.

Topographic maps in Canada are produced by the Centre for Topographic Information of Natural Resources Canada (CTI) (http://maps.nrcan.gc.ca/search/index.html).

GIS Sources

Geographic Information Systems (GIS) use "computer hardware, software, data and people combined to answer spatially based questions and to provide new ways of looking at geographic information to find solutions or make decisions" (Johnson 2003, 177). GIS has added a whole new dimension to the study of geography, going far beyond the study and use of maps. Using GIS software requires advanced study or training. Some of the sites providing GIS products are:

U.S. Geological Survey's GIS Web site (erg.usgs.gov/isb/pubs/gis_poster), the Census Bureau's American Factfinder and EPA's EnviroMapper.

There are a number of companies providing GIS software including ESRI (www.esri.com), which has a suite of GIS software (ArcExplorer, ArcIMS, ArcPad, ArcView, ArcInfo), Microsoft (Map Point), and Caliper (Mapitude 4.7) (Cline 1005, 27).

Travel Guides

An often overlooked geographic source is travel guides. Travel guides are available from a diverse array of authors and publishers. Although some may seem too subjective to be used as a reference source, others provide a great deal of factual, up-to-date information on cities and countries. Some of the most factual of the guide books are the Michelin Green Guides, the Baedeker Guides, the Rough Guides, Lonely Planet, and Moon Handbooks. All of these guidebooks provide detailed information about the history of a city or country and information about museums and other cultural sites. They often provide maps of the interiors of museums and noted buildings and detailed descriptions of important rooms within these buildings.

There are also useful specialized travel guides providing information on such subjects as accessibility, guides to special kinds of sites such as the national parks, Native American landmarks, and ecotourism sites. In addition to these there are guides to campgrounds, Woodall's *Campground Directory*, and the *OAG Frequent Flyer* for airline schedules.

Collection Development and Maintenance

Selection and Keeping Current

Information about geographical sources as well as reviews of new monographs and online information sources help the librarian to identify new and updated materials. Geographical sources are regularly reviewed in *Booklist, Choice, Library Journal*, and *American Reference Books Annual*.

The U.S. government remains a key source of information producing a wide variety of maps. The TIGER mapping service from the U.S. Bureau of the Census produces detailed maps of locations throughout the United States using census data. Other maps are produced by the National Oceanic and Atmospheric Administration (NOAA), the U.S. Geological Survey (USGS), the U.S. Department of Housing and Urban Development (HUD), the U.S. Department of Defense's National Imagery and Mapping Agency (NIMA), the Environmental Protection Agency (EPA), and others.

Information about new geographic sources is available through the American Library Association's Map and Geography Round Table (MAGERT) newsletter, *base line*, and its Listserv, maps-l; the *Information Bulletin* of the Western Association of Map Librarians; and the *Bulletin* of the Association of Canadian Map Libraries and Archives. There are also numerous monographs including Mary Lynette Larsgaard's *Map Librarianship: An Introduction* and Barbara Farrell and Aileen Desbarats's *Guide for a Small Map Collection* that provide information on map librarianship.

In addition to some of the geographic sources listed in this chapter, ALA's Map and Geography Round Table has suggested in its publication "Helpful Hints for Small Map Collections" that libraries acquire topographic maps of their county and state, city maps of nearby cities, and aerial photographs of their area. These can be acquired through commercial map dealers or through the U.S. Geological Survey (geography. usgs.gov). Libraries needing to acquire maps should look at the catalogs or Web sites of the major publishers of maps including Rand McNally, C. S. Hammond, National Geographic Society, Michelin (France), and Oxford University Press, as well as publishers of electronic maps including DeLorme and GIS firms such as ESRI.

Evaluating Geographic Resources

The criteria for good-quality accessible maps includes currency and accuracy, authority, legibility, scale and projection, color, symbols, format, index, and price.

The currency of the maps must be a primary consideration. Boundaries continue to change and even place names change. Maps must be current in order to be useful. Before purchasing geographic sources, the currency of the source should be verified by checking to see if current boundaries of countries are shown and to see that it reflects changes in names of cities and countries.

Accuracy is essential for a good-quality map. Accuracy and currency are closely linked, since a large part of accuracy has to do with being up-to-date.

Authority is particularly important to mapmaking. The major publishers of maps and atlases are Rand McNally, C. S. Hammond, the National Geographic Society, and Oxford University Press. Other publishers are known for the quality of their maps. Among them are John G. Bartholomew (Edinburgh) and George Philip & Sons, Ltd. in the United Kingdom and Michelin in France.

Legibility and readability of the map is crucial. This may be influenced by the scale of the map, the color contrast of the map, and the way symbols are used to indicate certain features of the map. "Scale is the ratio of distance on the map to linear distance on the earth" (Monmonier and Schnell 1988, 15). Scale can be represented as a ratio 1:10,000 or 1/10,000 or it can be represented as a bar scale or a verbal scale "one inch equals 64 miles."

Color is often a subtle but important part of mapmaking. A well-done map will be pleasant to look at and yet offer enough contrast to understand the different kinds of land areas. Symbols are used to distinguish between geographic features and make them easier to locate. Symbols must have a good legend and be adequately explained. The use of a good type style is needed to enable the user to easily find the desired information.

Atlases should display a balanced coverage of the world or a balanced approach to the continents or countries that they cover. Mary Lynette Larsgaard suggests determining the number of pages in an atlas and then counting the number of pages devoted to the United States and the number of pages devoted to Africa as a way to ascertain whether the atlas is providing balanced coverage (Larsgaard 1998, 113). Larsgaard also suggests comparing the same area in two or more atlases to determine which atlases are providing the best treatment (Larsgaard 1998, 114).

As much as possible, the same scale should be used throughout an atlas. In this way it is possible to compare the size of countries or continents. "Map projection is the method employed to transfer a curved area—a section of earth—to the flat, two-dimensional plane of the page" (*Encyclopedias, Atlases & Dictionaries* 1995, 164). All flat maps distort to some extent the shapes and areas. The larger the area covered by the map, the greater is the distortion; the smaller the area, the less distortion there will be. Various methods of projection are used to lessen the distortion. The kind of projection used depends on the use of the map. Within an atlas different map projections are often used to best capture a particular area.

Atlases need to be accessible. This involves both the arrangement of the atlas as it moves from area to area, the need for a clear and easy-to-understand legend, and finally a comprehensive index with both cross-references to other names or spellings and a good grid system. Many indexes use latitude and longitude to describe the location of a particular place while others use a grid system. If it is hard to find specific places after locating them in the index, then the indexing has failed.

Because there are maps that are now produced both on paper and electronically, it is necessary to evaluate whether the format serves the source well. Is this, for example, an appropriate map for an electronic format or would it be better in paper? Sometimes the purpose of the source will dictate which format is more appropriate. If the format is paper, it is important to note the ease of handling the atlas, the convenience of use and the binding and whether some of the maps fall into the book's gutter, making them hard to read.

Price is the final consideration for any atlas. It may pay to have fewer atlases and purchase those of high quality.

Further Consideration

For many reasons users need geographic information. They may want to see a map of a particular area of the world to better understand what is happening there. They may want to know where Saudi Arabia is in relation to Iraq or they may want to know where Bali is in relation to Penang. Maps often provide an understanding of how events affect other countries in a region.

People planning a trip want maps and guidebooks to chart their trip. For example, they might be planning a trip to Thailand and want to know what other countries they could easily visit. Maybe friends have given them names of towns to visit, and they need to see where they are.

A businessperson has just been told that he is being sent to Kiev in the Ukraine. He is researching Kiev to find out about the area, the temperature for the time of year he is going, what he can expect in terms of access to e-mail, and whether he can expect to be able to use a wireless laptop. Maps and guidebooks will provide him with a great deal of information, as will Web sites.

THE TOP 10 GEOGRAPHIC INFORMATION SOURCES

Title	Print	Online
2005 Commercial Atlas and Marketing Guide. Chicago: Rand McNally.	Annual	
American Fact Finder.		www.census.gov
CIA World Factbook.		www.cia.gov/cia/publications/factbook/index.html
Columbia Gazetteer of the World Online.		Subscription www.columbiagazetteer.org
Hammond World Atlas. 2003. Union, NJ: Hammond.	4th ed.	
National Geographic Atlas of the World. 2004. Washington, DC: National Geographic Society.	8th ed.	
Mapquest.		www.mapquest.com
The New International World Atlas. 1999. Chicago: Rand McNally.	25th ed.	
Rand McNally Road Atlas. Chicago: Rand McNally.	Annual	
Times Atlas of the World. 1999. New York: Times.	10th ed.	

Recommended Resources Discussed in this Chapter

American Library Association. 1981– . *Base line: a Newsletter of the Map and Geography Round Table.*
Association of Canadian Map Libraries and Archives. 1968. *Bulletin.* Ottawa, ON, 1968– . Triannual.
Atlas of Canada. Available at http://atlas.gc.ca.
Atlas of World History. 2002. New York: Oxford University Press.
British Library Map Collection. Available at www.bl.uk/collections/maps.html.

Centre for Topographic Information of Natural Resources Canada. Available at http://maps.nrcan.gc.ca/search/index.html.

CIA World Factbook. Available at www.odci.gov/cia/publications/factbook.

Columbia Gazetteer of the World. 1998. 3 vols. New York: Columbia University Press.

Columbia Gazetteer of the World Online. Available at www.columbiagazetteer.org.

Environment Protection Agency. *EnviroMapper.* Available at http://maps.epa.gov/enviro/mod/enviromapper/index.html.

FEMA Maps. Available at www.hazardmap.gov/atlas.php.

Geographic Names Information System (GNIS). Available at http://geonames.usgs.gov/index.html.

GEOnet Names Server. Available at http://164.214.59/gns/html/index.html.

Getty Thesaurus of Geographic Names Online. Available at www.getty.edu/research/tools/vocabulary/tgn.

Goode's World Atlas. 2002. Chicago: Rand McNally.

Hammond Citation World Atlas. 2000. Maplewood, NJ: Hammond.

Hammond World Atlas. 2003. 4th ed. Spring House, PA: Hammond.

HarperCollins New World Atlas. 2001. New York: HarperCollins.

Historical Atlas of Canada. 1987–1993. 3 vols. Toronto: University of Toronto Press.

Historical Atlas of the U.S. 1988. Rev. ed. Washington, DC: National Geographic Society.

History of Cartography Gateway. Available at www.maphistory.info.

Infomine. Available at www.infomine.ucr.edu/cgi-bin/search?maps.

Kenan, William Rand, Jr. 2000. *Barrington Atlas of the Greek and Roman World.* Princeton, NJ: Princeton University Press.

Library of Congress. *American Memory Collection.* Available at http://lcweb2.loc.gov/ammem/gmdhtml/gmdhome.html.

Library of Congress. Geography and Map Division. Available at http://lcweb2.loc.gov/ammem/gmdhtml/cnsvhome.html.

Mapquest. Available at www.mapquest.com.

Merriam-Webster's Geographical Dictionary. 2001. 3rd ed. Rev. Springfield, MA: Merriam-Webster.

National Atlas of Canada. Available at http://atlas.gc.ca.

National Atlas of the United States. Available at www.nationalatlas.gov.

National Geographic Atlas of the World. 2004. 8th ed. Washington, DC: National Geographic Society.

National Geographic Concise Atlas of the World. 1997. Washington, DC: National Geographic Society.

National Geographic Society. *Maps.* Available at www.nationalgeographic.com/maps.

National Geographic World Atlas for Young Explorers. 2003. Washington, DC: National Geographic Society.

New International World Atlas. 1999. 25th ed. Chicago: Rand McNally.

OAG Frequent Flyer. 1989– . Oak Brook, IL: Official Airline Guide, Travel Magazine Division. Monthly.

Oddens's Bookmarks: The Fascinating World of Maps and Mapping. Available at http://oddens.geog.uu.nl.

Oxford Atlas of the World. 2004. 12th ed. New York: Oxford University Press.

Oxford New Concise World Atlas. New York: Oxford University Press. Annual.

Oxford New Historical Atlas of Religion in America. 2001. Edwin Gausted, ed. New York: Oxford University Press.

Perry-Castañeda Library Map Collection. Available at www.lib.utexas.edu/maps/index.html.

Rand McNally Road Atlas. Chicago: Rand McNally. Annual.

Rand McNally's New International World Atlas. 1999. Chicago: Rand McNally.

Reader's Digest. 2004. *Illustrated World Atlas.* Pleasantville, NY: Reader's Digest.

Reader's Digest Children's Atlas of the World. 2003. 3rd ed. Pleasantville, NY: Reader's Digest.

Rumsey, David, and Edith M. Punt. 2004. *Cartographica Extraordinaire: The Historical Map Transformed.* ESRI. Available at www.davidrumsey.com.

Shepherd's Historical Atlas. 1980. 9th ed. Rev & updated. Totowa, NJ: Barnes & Noble.

Terraserver. Available at www.terraserver.microsoft.com.

Times Atlas of the World. 1999. 10th ed. New York: Times Books.

Times History of the World. 1999. Richard Overy, ed. 5th ed. New York: Times Books.

Times of London Concise Atlas of the World. 2000. 8th ed. New York: Crown.

2005 Commercial Atlas and Marketing Guide. Chicago: Rand McNally. Annual.

United Nations Map Library. Available at www.un.org/depts/dhl/maplib/maplib.htm.

U.S. Bureau of the Census. Available at www.census.gov/geo/www/maps.

U.S. Bureau of the Census. *American Fact Finder.* Available at www.census.govcheck.

U.S. Bureau of the Census. *U.S. Gazetteer.* Available at www.census.gov/cgi-bin/gazetteer.

U.S. Department of State. *Background Notes.* Available at www.state.gov.

U.S. Geological Survey. Available at www.usgs.gov.

U.S. Geological Survey. *EROS (Earth Resources Observation Systems) Data Center.* Available at http://edc.usgs.gov.

U.S. Geological Survey. Topozone. Available at www.topozone.com.

Western Association of Map Librarians. 1970– . *Information Bulletin.* Triannual.

Woodall's North American Campground Directory. Guilford, CT: Globe Pequot. Annual.

Worldmark Encyclopedia of the Nations. 2003. 11th ed. Farmington Hills, MI: Gale.

Yale University Map Collection. Available at www.library.yale.edu/MapColl/index.html.

Recommendations for Further Reading

Berenstein, Paula. 2006. "Location, Location, Location: Online Maps for the Masses." *Searcher* 14, no. 1 (January): 16–25. A discussion of new online maps including Google maps, Google Earth, and Yahoo maps.

McDermott, I. 2002. "Where Was I? Maps on the Web." *Searcher* 10, 6: 75–78. A guide to map sources on the Web.

Mitchell, Susan. 2003. "Where in the World? An Online Guide to Gazetteers, Atlases and Other Map Resources." *Internet Reference Services Quarterly* 8, 1/2: 183–194. An annotated guide to map resources on the Web.

Smith, Linda C., and Myke Gluck. 1996. *Geographic Information Systems and Libraries: Patrons, Maps and Spatial Information.* Urbana, IL: University of Illinois. Graduate

School of Library and Information Science. Papers from the 32nd Annual Clinic on Library Applications of Data Processing addressing accessing spatial data use of GIS systems and related issues.

Tenner, Elka, and Katherine H. Weimer. 1998. "Reference Service for Maps: Access and the Catalog Record." *Reference & User Services Quarterly* 38, 2: 181–186. A discussion of the cataloging of maps. Tenner states that subject analysis is the most important access point. Digital format may necessitate changes in cataloging to emphasize intellectual content.

Weessies, Kathleen. 2001. "Electronic Maps: Sources and Techniques." *Reference Services Review* 31, 3: 248–256. This article focuses on how to work with electronic maps including saving them to a disk, pasting them into PowerPoint, and cropping them.

Bibliography of Works Cited in this Chapter

Ashworth, Mick. 2003. "Paper or Pixels: Where to Next for Maps?" *Geographical* (December): 56–60.

Cline, Michael E. 2005. "Mapping Solutions Under $500." *Online* (May/June): 27–30.

Cobb, David. 1990. *A Guide to U.S. Map Resources.* 2nd ed. Chicago: American Library Association. (A new edition is planned.)

Encyclopedias, Atlases & Dictionaries. 1995. Marion Sader and Amy Lewis, eds. New Providence, NJ: R. R. Bowker.

Farrell, Barbara, and Aileen Desbarats. 1981. *Guide for a Small Map Collection.* Ottawa: Association of Canadian Map Libraries.

Johnson, Jenny Marie. 2003. *Geographic Information: How to Find It, How to Use It.* Westport, CT: Greenwood Press.

Kenny, Ann Jason. 2002. "More Than Just Maps." *School Library Journal. Net Connect* (Fall): 45–47.

Larsgaard, Mary Lynette. 1998. *Map Librarianship: An Introduction.* 3rd ed. Englewood, CO: Libraries Unlimited, Inc.

Map History of Cartography: THE Gateway to the Subject. www.maphistory.info or info@maphistory.info.

Monmonier, Mark, and George A. Schnell. 1988. *Map Appreciation.* Englewood Cliffs, NJ: Prentice Hall.

Unwin, Tim. 1992. *The Place of Geography.* Burnt Mill, England: Longman Scientific and Technical Press.

Wood, Denis, with John Fels. 1992. *The Power of Maps.* New York: Guilford Press.

11

Answering Questions about the Lives of People—Biographical Information Sources

Many reference questions are about well-known people. Where were they born? How old are they? How many times were they married? How many children do they have? Biographical sources answer these and many more questions. Although biographical information is widely available in many other reference sources, biographical resources provide more extensive and often more accurate information about people who are important historically and people who are presently in the news. To these ends, a wealth of biographical sources exists. Some are published by major publishers and others by small, sometimes vanity, presses.

How Biographical Resources Are Used

Biographical sources provide information about the lives of both living and deceased people; these print and electronic resources may concentrate on one country, such as *Who's Who in America*, or on people in a certain field, such as *American Men and Women of Science*. The information may be brief—such as, correct name, dates of birth and death, the field of work of the person, and the person's nationality—or may be more extensive, discussing in great detail the person's life and accomplishments.

Since biographical sources are a source of information about people, they are of use to the user who is simply seeking minimal information about a person, including what their field of work is or was, dates of birth and maybe death, and nationality. Sometimes biographical sources are used to determine that the user has the correct person if there is more than one person with the same or a similar name. On the other hand, the user may be looking for more extensive information on a person and should be directed to a source that provides a lengthy biography and perhaps a list of sources for more information. Sometimes biographical sources are used to find well-known people in a certain field such as engineers, jazz musicians, or philosophers. For this reason, some biographical sources have an index by profession.

Questions Answered by Biographical Resources

- When did Marian Anderson die?
  The answer can be found in the *American National Biography*.
- What are the birth and death dates for Laurence Olivier?
  This can be found in *Oxford Dictionary of National Biography*.
- How can I find articles about Twyla Tharp?
  Biography Index is a good source to check for articles on contemporary people.
- Where can I find a biography of the present king of Morocco?
  Biography Resource Center can be searched by occupation and nationality to find this information.

Major Biographical Resources Used in Reference Work

Indexes

Indexes are a good place to begin when you are uncertain where the biography of a certain person will be found. Two indexes can be helpful, particularly if biographical information on a person is difficult to locate. One, the *Biography and Genealogy Master Index*, indexes over 1,000 biographical reference sources such as biographical dictionaries, Who's Who, indexes, and literary criticism with biographical information. Fifteen million biographical sketches of persons, both living and deceased, from every field and from all areas of the world are included in this index. Each reference work where you can find biographical information on a certain person is listed. This index is particularly useful when it is not obvious which biographical source would have information. This index is available online and in print. The print index is issued annually with a cumulation every five years.

The second, *Biography Index*, indexes biographical material in 3,000 periodicals indexed in other Wilson databases and in 2,000 books per year. The online coverage is from 1984 to the present. The value of this index is that it provides access to biographical material on contemporary people that would not be easily found elsewhere.

Biographies of Contemporary People

For concise information about contemporary people, the user can turn to the Marquis Who's Who series of publications. *Who's Who in America* is perhaps the best known of the series. This annual publication, now in its 59th edition (2005), provides current autobiographical information about 120,000 noteworthy Americans. Some of the entries are new listings, while many are updated entries. Questionnaires are sent to those listed to update their information annually. A typical entry includes the person's name, occupation, date of birth, family information, education, career summary, publications, civic and political activities, memberships, and address. This valuable biographical source includes a geographic index, a professional index, a retiree list, and a necrology for those deceased since the last edition.

Marquis also publishes regional Who's Who for each part of the United States, such as *Who's Who in the East, Who's Who in the Midwest, Who's Who in the West,* as well as other Who's Who such as *Who's Who of American Women* and professional Who's Who, such as *Who's Who in American Education* and *Who's Who in American Politics.* The format for all the print *Who's Who* is similar. *Marquis Who's Who on the Web* provides access to over one million biographies. This online database allows the user to search by such criteria as name, gender, occupation, education, hobbies and interests, or a combination thereof. According to the publisher, the online database is updated daily.

Who's Who is the British resource listing contemporary people of note—mostly British but a few Americans as well. With over 30,000 biographies, this resource follows the typical pattern of listing the name, present position, date of birth, family details, education, career in order of date, publications, recreations, and address. *Who's Who* is updated through a questionnaire to the people listed. There is also an obituary section with the death date.

Although *Canadian Who's Who* began in 1910, it did not become an annual reference work until 1980. Questionnaires are sent out annually to update the 14,000 biographical sketches in this work. For each person, the date and place of birth, address, family details, education, career information, memberships, and awards or other achievements are listed.

The *International Who's Who* includes information on more than 20,000 noteworthy men and women from all professions and from all parts of the world based on questionnaires filled out by the people included. A typical entry includes the person's name, nationality, profession, date and place of birth, family information, education, career summary, awards, publications, hobbies, address, phone, fax, and e-mail address. There is an obituary section with death dates and a section that lists all the reigning royal families in the world. An online version is also available that allows the user to search by name, nationality, place and date of birth, and profession. It includes biographies of people who have died recently.

Europa also produces a series of Who's Who by profession such as *International Who's Who in International Affairs* and *International Who's Who in Classical Music.*

Current Biography provides biographical information on people in the news. Each of its eleven issues a year provides profiles of eighteen to twenty people from art, politics, literature, sports, film, and television, as well as obituaries of people previously profiled. This well-written biographical source is useful for students as well as adults. The articles are 2,000 to 3,500 words in length and include a photograph of the person and a bibliography of additional sources of information. An annual volume is published compiling the individual issues for the year. *Current Biography Illustrated* is the online version of *Current Biography.* In this format users can search the entire database from 1940 to the present by name, profession, place of origin, birth or death date, ethnicity, and gender.

A recent publication, *Current Biography International Yearbook*, began in 2002. This annual focuses on people outside the United States making international news and history. The yearbook includes profiles of about two hundred people, covering a wide range of professions. Each article includes the subject's own opinions and the observations of journalists and colleagues. Photographs and a bibliography are included.

Newsmakers: The People Behind Today's Headlines is similar to *Current Biography*. Each biography of 1,500 to 3,000 words includes the person's address, date of birth, family details, education, career summary, awards, writings and a biographical essay. A photo of each person and a bibliography of additional sources of information are included. People listed in each issue come from all walks of life including business, television and film, entertainment, science, literature, politics and government, and science. There are indexes by nationality, occupation, and subject as well as an obituary section. In addition to the four issues published annually, there is an annual cumulative volume.

Biography Resource Center is an extensive online database providing biographical information about persons currently in the news and those deceased. Each profile includes personal information, career information, the person's writings, "sidelights," and a bibliography for further readings about the person. This Gale resource includes full text from *The Complete Marquis Who's Who*, 250 periodicals, and other Gale biographical resources including *Encyclopedia of World Biography*, *Dictionary of American Biography*, and *Scribner's Encyclopedia of American Lives*. Nearly 415,000 biographies of more than 320,000 people from over 840 volumes of more than 135 Gale resources are included, as well as full-text articles from more than 265 magazines. Searches can be done by name, occupation, year of birth, nationality, ethnicity, or place of birth.

Biography Reference Bank combines several Wilson databases into one biography database. This database includes *Wilson Biographies Plus Illustrated*, *Biography Index*, and links to other full text from Wilson publications including *Current Biography*. More than 450,000 people are listed in this database, which can be searched by name, profession, place of origin, gender, ethnicity, birth and death dates, titles of works, and keyword.

Biography.com is a free database that includes 25,000 biographies of well-known people from ancient times to the present. Each entry includes birth and death dates, career information, and often a photograph, list of works, and related Web links. Information for this Web site comes from *Cambridge Dictionary of American Biography* and *Cambridge Encyclopedia Database* as well as information from the cable station, A&E. It is probably the most extensive free database providing biographical information.

Retrospective Biography

American National Biography is a recent work published in print and available online that is a companion to the *Dictionary of American Biography*. It is a completely new work "that resulted in the more expansive understanding of who is a notable American" (Bryant 1999, 82). There are 17,500 lengthy biographies that include more women, minorities, and people from other countries who have lived in the United States and made contributions to it than the original *DAB*. Not all people in the *Dictionary of American Biography* are included in the new *American National Biography*. As in the *Dictionary of American Biography* all persons listed are deceased. This new work is updated quarterly online and can be searched by name, occupation, gender, birth and death dates, birth place, and ethnic heritage. Entries include a photograph of the person and a bibliography. A useful feature is the hyperlinks to related biographies.

The *Dictionary of American Biography* was commissioned by the American Council of Learned Societies. It has been for many decades the premier source of American biography. The last supplement was published in 1985 and includes people who died before 1980. A total of 19,000 biographies are included in the volumes of this work.

Oxford Dictionary of National Biography, published in 2004, is a major revision of the *Dictionary of National Biography (DNB)*, which was completed in 1900. Available both in print and online, this new version includes both 55,000 new biographies and rewritten or revised biographies of the lives of people included in the thirty-three volumes of the original *DNB* and its supplements. The coverage includes Britons from all walks of life who have made their mark in Great Britain or elsewhere, as well as people from other countries who have played a role in British history and life. As in the original *DNB*, people listed in this work are all deceased. Searching online can be done by person, place, dates, fields of interest. There are three updates online each year.

The original *Dictionary of National Biography* covered 29,333 people. It was reissued in 1908–1909 in twenty-two volumes. Additional supplements were published between 1912 and 1996. As is the case with the *DAB*, the *DNB* has been the primary source of biographical information about people of British origin.

The *Dictionary of Canadian Biography* states in the introduction that those omitted are those "who have not set forth in what is now Canada, or at least approached its shores" (*DCB* 1966, xvi). The volumes are arranged in chronological order as determined by the person's death date. Volume 1 covers 1000 to 1700. Each biographical sketch is 400–1200 words. There is a general bibliography and an index at the end of each volume. Fourteen volumes have been published to date. The dictionary is also available in French. The *Dictionary of Canadian Biography Online* is the online version of the *Dictionary of Canadian Biography*, which also includes some of the biographical sketches for the upcoming volume.

World Biographical Information System (WBIS Online) compiles biographical articles from printed reference works published from the sixteenth to the twentieth century and provides facsimiles of the original documents online. This online tool includes 2.28 million digitized biographical articles and is available in German, Spanish, English, French, and Italian. Searches can be done by name, gender, year of birth or death, occupation, and country.

Who Was Who and *Who Was Who in America* are the retrospective versions of *Who's Who* and *Who's Who in America*. Once a person is deceased he or she becomes part of the retrospective version. *Who Was Who* is grouped in four-year segments. Volume 10, for example, contains the entries of people who died between 1996 and 2000. The entries are as they appeared in *Who's Who* with the death date added as well as posthumous publications. There is also a *Who Was Who, A Cumulated Index 1897–2000* that provides easy access to the ten volumes of *Who Was Who*, listing the person's name, birth and death years, and the volume number. *Who Was Who in America* now has thirteen volumes beginning in 1897 and continuing through 2000. There is also a historical volume covering the years 1607–1896. This is a specially compiled volume since *Who's Who in America* did not begin until 1899.

The *National Cyclopedia of American Biography* is subtitled "Being the History of the U.S. as illustrated in the lives of the founders, builders and defenders of the Republic and of the men and women who are doing the work and moulding the thought of the present time." The volumes are groupings of individuals and not in alphabetical order. Each person has a fairly lengthy biography and a photo or line drawing as well. Many of these people were alive when the volume was published. Because the listings are not in alphabetical order, each volume has an index. The uniqueness of this biographical source is that it lists many people who are not in other biographical sources such as prominent business people, clergy, etc.

The Scribner Encyclopedia of American Lives presents very readable signed biographies of deceased people with a photo of each person and a bibliography. Each volume is arranged in alphabetical order with an occupations index. The latest volume includes people who died between 2000 and 2002. These volumes are supplements to the *Dictionary of American Biography*.

Encyclopedia of World Biography 2nd edition, a multivolume work, includes in depth portraits of over 7,000 persons, both living and deceased, from all time periods and all walks of life both living and deceased. The biographies are very readable and include a bibliography and often a photograph or drawing of the person. Because of the emphasis on the international, it is a good place to find information on persons from other countries such as government officials.

One-Volume Biographical Dictionaries

Chambers Biographical Dictionary is a large one-volume biographical dictionary (1650 pages) that includes "people who have shaped, and continue to shape, the world in which we live" (preface). In a user-friendly format, the dictionary provides short biographical sketches of people both living and deceased. The entry is written in prose describing the achievements of the person. For a few select people the biographical sketch is highlighted in a box with an appropriate quote by or about the person. It is also published under the title *The Cambridge Biographical Dictionary*.

Merriam-Webster's Biographical Dictionary is a compact one-volume biographical dictionary listing concise biographical information about 30,000 deceased persons from ancient times to the present day. It is useful as a ready reference source.

Obituaries

Obituaries are often requested by library users searching for details of someone's life. Although with such easy access to the retrospective issues of the *New York Times*, it is not necessary to have separate volumes with obituaries; however, these two print volumes can be quite useful and easy to check. The *New York Times Obituaries Index, 1885–1968* and *New York Times Obituaries Index 1969–1978* are an accumulation of their obituaries for these periods of time. It is rather interesting to note that there have been different policies throughout the decades about murders and suicides; volume 2 does cover these deaths. Newsbank has also developed an online obituaries database, *America's Obituaries and Death Notices*, which includes information from newspapers throughout the United States.

Subject-based Biographical Tools

Contemporary Authors is an excellent source of information on current authors, especially nonfiction writers whose biographical information can be hard to find. Available in print and electronic formats, it includes a wide range of authors publishing fiction, nonfiction, poetry, etc. The information provided includes personal information, career information, awards, "sidelights" which are essays about the author's work, writings by the author, and writings about the author. Periodically these biographies are updated. Over 120,000 authors are included.

Contemporary Authors is included in *Gale's Literature Resource Center*, which also contains *Contemporary Literary Criticism Select* and the *Dictionary of Literary Biography Online*. The *Dictionary of Literary Biography Online* contains more than 10,000 biocritical essays on authors and their works. This information has been compiled from other Gale publications and from 260 literary journals. The user can search by name, ethnicity, nationality, genre, literary theme, and literary movement. Web sites on the author's life and work are included.

Voices from the Gaps: Women Artists and Writers of Color (http://voices.cla.umn.edu) is maintained and updated by the English Department of the University of Minnesota. This site provides biographical information on North American women artists and writers of color. Users can search by name, birthplace or geographical location, racial/ethnic background, or significant dates.

The *Directory of American Scholars* provides short biographical sketches similar to those found in *Who's Who in America*. Each of the five volumes covers specific disciplines: History; English, Speech, and Drama; Foreign Languages, Linguistics, and Philology; Philosophy, Religion, and Law; and Social Sciences. There is a separate index volume that includes an alphabetical index, discipline index, institutional index, and geographical index. This resource provides information about many in the academic world not easily found in other biographical sources.

American Men and Women of Science: A Biographical Directory of Today's Leaders in Physical, Biological and Related Sciences is an invaluable source of information about contemporary scientists in both the United States and Canada who have made significant contributions in their field. The information is provided in a concise format and includes birth date, birth place, citizenship, family details, field of specialty, education, honorary degrees, professional experience, honors and awards, memberships, research information, address, and e-mail. There are seven volumes of biographical information with a eighth volume devoted to a discipline index organized by field of activity, and within each subject the names are arranged by state. Volume 1 also lists the winners of various scientific prizes.

A free biographical Web site on mathematicians (www.history.mcs.st-andrews.ac.uk/history) has been produced and kept up to date by the School of Mathematics and Statistics of the University of St. Andrews, Scotland. The biographies are quite extensive and are signed.

Biographies of philosophers can be found on a free Web site, http://plato.stanford.edu. It provides extensive signed biographies of philosophers.

The *Biographical Directory of the United States Congress, 1774 to Present* is now available online (http://bioguide.congress.gov/biosearch/biosearch.asp). Users can search by name, position in Congress (senator, representative, Speaker of the House, etc.) state, party, etc. Photos of recent members of Congress are included.

Major Modern and Contemporary Visual Artists (www.the-artists.org) can be searched by the name of the artist or by art movement, style, or medium in this free Web site. The listings provide information about the artists and their work.

The Union List of Artist Names (ULAN) is produced at the Getty Museum in California (www.getty.edu/research/tools/vocabulary/ulan). It lists over 220,000 names of artists. Its scope is global, and it covers antiquity to the present. Each record includes variations of the artist's name, dates of birth and death, geographic locations, relationships such as student–teacher relationships, biographical notes, and the source of the information.

Biographical information on people in the movies can be found on the Internet Movie Database site (www.imdb.com). Another Internet site, www.what-a-character.com, lists biographical information on character actors with photos and lists of their film and TV roles.

An alphabetical list of biographical information on jazz musicians can be found at www.pbs.org/jazz/biography.

Biographical Resources Featuring Ethnic/Culture Heritage

Who's Who among African Americans provides biographical sketches of prominent African Americans. The main part of this reference work lists each person's personal data, occupation, educational background, career information, organizational affiliations, honors or awards, special achievements, and military service. There are geographical and occupational indexes as well as an obituaries section for people who are recently deceased. This resource is also available as an e-book through the Gale Virtual Reference Library. *African American Lives*, edited by Henry Louis Gates, Jr., and Evelyn Brooks Higginbotham, is an excellent recent publication that contains biographical information on more than 600 African Americans who have had an impact on American society and culture. The biographies are well written, running one to three pages in length, and often include a photo or line drawing of the person. A short bibliography is also included. Persons both living and deceased are represented.

The most recent biographical resource for Hispanic Americans is the *Biographical Dictionary of Hispanic Americans* by Nicholas E. Meyer. With 250 profiles, it is aimed at middle school through high school. For Asian Americans there is *Asian American Biographies*, edited by Helen Zia and Susan B. Gail. This two-volume work includes 150 biographies; each biography is two to five pages with a photograph. There are indexes by biographee, subject, and field of endeavor.

Collection Development and Maintenance

Selection and Keeping Current on Biographical Sources

Biographical sources are reviewed by the journals that review reference materials. The librarian can find new biographical resources reviewed in *Library Journal*, *Booklist*, *Choice*, and *American Reference Book Annual*. Standard titles are discussed in Balay and in Walford. Recent biographical resources are listed in the *ARBA Guide to Biographical Resources 1986–1997*, which includes international sources arranged by country and sources of biographies in professional fields organized by profession.

Evaluating Biographical Resources

Criteria for evaluating biographical resources include the following:

- Scope;
- Accuracy;
- Length of entry;
- Criteria for inclusion;
- Audience;
- Authority;
- Frequency of updates;
- Photo; and
- References for further reading.

Scope is particularly important in biographical sources. Does the resource cover both living and deceased people? Does it only cover certain professions or certain countries? What are the parameters of its coverage? In a library's collection the librarian will want to have biographical sources that describe the lives of well-known people of the past, called retrospective biography, as well as sources that describe the lives of people who are alive today, called current biography. The collection will also want to have resources with information on people from other countries as well as the United States. Sometimes biographical sources include people from many different parts of the world, while others provide information on people from a region or a country.

Attention to accuracy is needed in biographical resources. Check the dates of birth and death against another credible source to check for accuracy. Read some entries in the reference source to see if they are objective and comprehensive within the parameters of the entries.

The length of the entry is important because sometimes users need a short biographical sketch and sometimes they need lengthy, more detailed information. Libraries will want resources with short biographies and longer ones.

Criteria for inclusion is of great interest. Perhaps those included filled out a questionnaire or perhaps the author made an effort to find everyone who fit his criteria for inclusion. This is often explained in the preface or introduction to the biographical resource. If, however, it appears that everyone in the book was required to pay to be included, this may not be a very objective source.

The audience for the resource should be noted. Determine the reading level of the biographical source. Is it for students or for adults?

The authority of the work must be examined, which may be either the publisher or the author. Not all biographical sources are published by major publishers. This does not mean they are not useful additions to a library collection. But it does mean that the librarian should review these resources more carefully.

Determine how often the publisher plans to update the book, especially if most of the people listed are currently alive. Many biographical sources are updated annually. If online, the biographical source can be expected to be updated more regularly.

Note whether the biographical source includes a photograph of the person. Many sources do not, but it is extremely useful to have biographical sources with photographs since many users are interested in knowing what the person looks or looked like.

Finally, it can be useful for the biographical source to include a bibliography of other sources of information about the person to assist the user in doing more extensive research.

Further Considerations

Biographical information is both easy and difficult to find. Well-known people are listed in many different biographical resources. However, some people can be very hard to locate in biographical resources. It can be useful to narrow the kinds of biographical resources that would possibly be relevant by attempting to categorize the person, assuming the user has some information. First of all, try to determine whether the person is living or dead. If the person is living, for example, you can then eliminate the biographical resources that only include persons that are deceased. Then try to determine the nationality of the person. This can definitely narrow the number of possible sources since, not all biographical sources are international. If the user knows the profession of the person, this can also be useful. It can also be helpful to try large comprehensive resources such as *Biography and Genealogy Master Index*, or if the person has only recently become newsworthy, *Biography Index* could be checked. Sometimes it is necessary to go beyond these biographical sources and try some of the periodical and newspaper databases for information on people currently in the news.

THE TOP 10 BIOGRAPHICAL SOURCES		
Title	**Print**	**Online**
American National Biography. 1999. New York: Oxford University Press.	24 vols.	Subscription www.anb.org
Biography and Genealogy Master Index. 19XX– . Farmington Hills, MI: Gale.	Biannual	Subscription www.gale.com
Biography Index. 1946– . Bronx, NY: H. W. Wilson.	Quarterly	Subscription www.hwwilson.com/ databases/bioind.htm
Biography Resource Center. Farmington Hills, MI: Gale.		Subscription www.gale.com/ BiographyRC/
Current Biography. 1940– . New York: H. W. Wilson. Online, *Current Biography Illustrated.*	Monthly	Subscription www.hwwilson.com/ databases/cbillus.htm

International Who's Who. 19XX– . Independence, KY: Europa Publications Distributed by Taylor & Francis.	Annual	Subscription www.worldwhoswho.com
Literature Resource Center. Farmington Hills, MI: Gale.		www.gale.com/LitRC/
Oxford Dictionary of National Biography. 2004. New York: Oxford University Press.	60 vols.	Subscription www.oxfordonline.com/online/odnb
Who's Who. 1897– . New York: St. Martin's Press.	Annual	
Who's Who in America. 19XX– . New Providence, NJ: Marquis Who's Who	Annual	Subscription www.marquiswhoswho.com

Recommended Resources Discussed in this Chapter

African American Lives. 2004. Edited by Henry Louis Gates, Jr., and Evelyn Brooks Higginbotham. New York: Oxford University Press.

American Men and Women of Science: A Biographical Directory of Today's Leaders in Physical, Biological and Related Sciences. 2005. 22nd ed. Farmington Hills, MI: Gale.

American National Biography. 1999. 24 vols. New York: Oxford University Press. Available at www.anb.org.

ARBA Guide to Biographical Resources, 1986–1997. 1998. Edited by Robert L. Wick and Terry Ann Mood. Englewood, CO: Libraries Unlimited.

Asian American Biographies. 2004. Edited by Helen Zia and Susan B. Gail. 2nd ed. Farmington Hills, MI: UXL/Gale.

Biographical Dictionary of Hispanic Americans. 2001. Edited by Nicholas E. Meyer. 2nd ed. New York: Facts on File.

Biographical Directory of the United States Congress, 1774 to present. Available at http://bioguide.congress.gov/biosearch/biosearch.asp.

Biography and Genealogy Master Index. Farmington Hills, MI: Gale. Annual. Also available online.

Biography.com (www.biography.com).

Biography Index. 1946– . Bronx, NY: H. W. Wilson. Quarterly with annual cumulations. Also available online.

Biography Reference Bank. New York: H. W. Wilson. Available online.

Biography Resource Center. Farmington Hills, MI: Gale. Available online.

Canadian Who's Who. 1980– . Toronto: University of Toronto Press.

Chambers Biographical Dictionary. 2002. 7th ed. Edinburgh: Chambers.

Contemporary Authors. 1962. Farmington Hills, MI: Gale. Available online as part of the *Literature Resource Center.*

Current Biography. 1940. New York: H. W. Wilson. Monthly with an annual cumulative volume. Online version, *Current Biography Illustrated,* available.

Dictionary of American Biography. 1927–1936. 20 vols. and index. New York: Scribner. Supplements, 1944–1980 with index, 1996.

Dictionary of Canadian Biography. 1966. 14 vols. and index. Toronto: University of Toronto Press. Also published in French. Also available online at www.biographi.ca/EN/index.html.

Dictionary of National Biography. 1885–1900. London: Smith, Elder. Supplements 1912–1996.

Directory of American Scholars. 2001. 5 vols. Farmington Hills, MI: Gale.

Encyclopedia of World Biography. 1998. 2nd ed. Farmington Hills, MI: Gale.

International Who's Who. Independence, KY: Europa Publications, distributed by Taylor & Francis. Annual.

Internet Movie Database (www.imdb).

Jazz Musicians (www.pbs.org/jazz/biography).

Literature Resource Center. Farmington Hills, MI: Gale. Available online.

Major Modern and Contemporary Visual Artists (www.the-artists.org).

Marquis Who's Who on the Web. Available at http://marquiswhoswho.com.

Merriam-Webster's Biographical Dictionary. 1995. Springfield, MA: Merriam-Webster.

National Cyclopedia of American Biography. 1898–1984. New York: White.

New York Times Obituaries Index, 1885–1968. 1970. New York: New York Times.

New York Times Obituaries Index, 1969–1978. 1980. New York: New York Times.

Newsmakers: The People Behind Today's Headlines. Farmington Hills, MI: Gale. Quarterly.

Oxford Dictionary of National Biography. 2004. 60 vols. New York: Oxford University Press. Available at www.oxfordonline.com/online/odnb.

Philosophers (http://plato.stanford.edu).

School of Mathematics and Statistics, University of St. Andrews, Scotland www.history.mcs.st-andrews.ac.uk/history.

Scribner Encyclopedia of American Lives. 1998– . New York: Scribner. Biennial.

Union List of Artist Names (ULAN). Available at www.getty.edu/research/tools/vocbulary/ulan/.

Voices from the Gaps: Women Artists and Writers of Color (http://voices.cla.umn.edu).

What a Character database (www.what-a-character.com).

Who Was Who. 1897. London: A&C Black, with a cumulated index 1897–2000.

Who's Who. 1897– . New York: St. Martin's Press. Annual.

Who's Who Among African Americans. 2006. 19th ed. Farmington Hills, MI: Gale.

Who Was Who in America. 1897– . Chicago: Marquis Who's Who. Historical volume, 1607–1896.

Who's Who in America. 1899. New Providence, NJ: Marquis Who's Who. Annual.

World Biographical Information System (WBIS Online). Farmington Hills, MI: K. G. Saur, distributed by Gale. Available online.

Recommendations for Further Reading

Aycock, Anthony. 2006. "Where's Waldo: A Primer on People-Searching Online." *Online* 30, no. 1 (January/February): 28–33. A guide to using the Internet to locate information on people.

Bridge, Noeline. 2003. "Verifying Personal Names on the Web." *The Indexer* 23, no. 3 (April): 149–156. A guide to indexes on verifying personal names serves as a good guide to biographical resources.

Ojala, Marydee. 1994. "The Never-ending Search for People." *Online* 18 (Setptember/October): 105–109. Resources for finding biographical information on business executives.

Schreiner, Susan A., and Michael A. Somers. 2002. "Biography Resources: Finding Information on the Famous, Infamous, and Obscure." *College and Research Libraries News* 63, no. 1 (January): 32–36, 39. An interesting review of biographical Web resources from specific fields of study.

Thomsen, Elizabeth. 2000. "When You Need to Know Who's Who: Biographical Resources on the Web." *Collection Building* 19, 2: 76–77. A listing of biographical resources on the Web.

Bibliography of Works Cited in this Chapter

Bryant, Eric. 1999. "Assessing American National Biography." *Library Journal* 122 (July): 82.

Fialkoff, Francine. 1998. "Dueling Dictionaries." *Library Journal* 123 (November 15): 54.

LaGuardia, Cheryl. 2005. "Oxford Sets the Bar High." *Library Journal* 129 (October 15): 24–25.

McDermott, Irene E. 2003. "What's What With Who's Who on the Web." *Searcher* 11 (July/August): 49–51.

Quinn, Mary Ellen. 1998. "Brief Lives." *Booklist* 95 (September 1): 164.

Rollyson, Carl E. 1997. "Biography as a Genre." *Choice* 35 (October): 249–258.

Schreiner, Susan A., and Michael A. Somers. 2002. "Biography Resources: Finding Information on the Famous, Infamous and Obscure." *College and Research Libraries News* 63 (January): 32–35, 39.

Thomsen, Elizabeth. 2000. "When You Need to Know Who's Who: Biographical Resources on the Web." *Collection Building* 19, 2: 76–77.

Whiteley, Sandy. 2005. "An Undertaking of Exceptional Magnitude." *Booklist* 101 (January 1–15): 901.

12

Answering Questions about Governments—Government Information Sources

Overview

Every level of government, from federal agencies to the local municipal authorities, publishes. Perhaps unsurprisingly these works are often referred to, in reference services and beyond, as "government documents." In the U.S. government publications are defined as "informational matter which is published as an individual document at government expense, or as required by law" (44 U.S. Code 1901). This definition encompasses records of government administrations, research publications including statistics and other data, and popular sources of information on such subjects as nutrition, health, jobs, and travel. They are as varied as "Celebrating a Century of Flight," from the National Aeronautics and Space Administration, "Measuring America: The Decennial Censuses from 1790 to 2000," from the U.S. Census Bureau, "Eyes on the Bay," from the Maryland Department of Natural Resources and "Social Safety Nets for Women," from the United Nations. These publications come in many formats: books, CD-ROMs, periodicals, pamphlets, films, maps, and online publications. Every country produces its own government publications, and international organizations such as the United Nations and the World Bank also produce many publications.

How Government Publications Are Used

Government publications are an excellent source of information about many important issues. In fact, information on some subjects is only available from government publications. If one looks at the array of subjects covered by government departments and agencies, it becomes apparent that the government deals with nearly every part of a citizen's life. For this reason it is important to know about government publications and how to organize, access, and then add them to a library's collection.

Questions Answered by Government Publications

- How can I get a National Parks Pass?

    Go to the National Parks System site (www.nps.gov), and you will find that the pass costs $50 and can be purchased online.
- Do I need a visa to go to Romania?

    Go to the State Department site (http://travel.state.gov), and you will find that you do not need a visa to go to Romania for less than ninety days.
- How can I find information about the cleanliness of beaches in New Jersey?

    Go to the Environmental Protection Agency site (www.epa.gov), and you will find information on beach advisories and closings.
- How can I find information on financial aid for education?

    Go to the Department of Education site (www.ed.gov), and you will find information on what financial aid is available and how to apply.

The U.S. Government Printing Office and Its Future

The U.S. Government Printing Office (GPO) is "the largest information processing, printing and distribution facility in the world" (www.gpo.gov/factsheet/index.html). It produces an enormous number of publications annually on every conceivable subject, e.g., census information, reports on education, information on immigration procedures and on environmental issues. The Government Printing Office has begun to make a sea change in the way it publishes and distributes publications. First of all, in an effort to cut costs, the U.S. Government Printing Office will in the future be basically an online publisher. A selected number of publications will remain in print, but most publications will only be available online. This is a huge adjustment for libraries that have housed vast print collections of government publications. For users it means they can access free of charge most government publications as long as they have a computer and preferably a printer. Second, the government has put more responsibility on government agencies. The E-Government Act of 2002 has mandated agencies to improve public access to their information resources. "Agencies will have to follow standards in organizing information and making it easily searchable, and to provide basic information on agency mission, structure, and strategic plans" (Hernon, Dugan, and Shuler 2003, 9). Finally, in May 2002 the Office of Management and Budget (OMB) "indicated that when the private sector can provide the better combination of cost, quality and timely delivery, agencies should contract with the private sector" (Drake 2005, 46). This has produced many questions from librarians since if government information can be printed by private publishers, will these publications be part of the government's publications, or only available through the private publisher, thus increasing the cost?

All in all, the face of government publishing is drastically changing. With this new online world the public and libraries alike must become adept at searching and accessing the information they need. In the long term this will no doubt work quite well, but the transition will be challenging.

Depository Libraries

Depository libraries were established in their present form by the Printing Act of 1895 in order to keep the citizenry informed and to provide a way to distribute the publications to all parts of the country. These depository libraries receive government information from the Government Printing Office without charge with the agreement that they will provide free access to the public. There are two kinds of depository libraries, regional depository libraries and selective depository libraries. The regional libraries receive all items distributed to the depository system, while the selective depository libraries can receive the materials that meet their needs. Each state can have two regional depository libraries and each congressional district can have two selective depository libraries. There are about 1,300 federal depository libraries including public libraries, academic libraries, and special libraries. The list of depository libraries is available at www.gpoaccess.gov/libraries.html.

Most depository libraries arrange their publications according to the Superintendent of Publications (SuDoc) classification numbers. These numbers are based on an abbreviation system that identifies the name of the agency, the subagency, the publication type, and a cutter number that represents the title. For example, if a publication had the classification C3.134/2:C83/2/994, the C would indicate that it was a Department of Commerce publication, the 3 would indicate that it is a Census Bureau publication, the numbers after the decimal point would indicate the type of publication, and the numbers after the colon would be the individual cutter number of the publication.

Since the majority of government publications are now available online, the role of the depository libraries is in doubt. It is possible that they may take on an enhanced role and that there may not be as many depository libraries. The fate of the depository library program is currently being discussed by the Depository Library Council. Charles A. Seavey wrote recently that "we are moving into an era when every library in the country has the potential to become a depository in the sense that each one could potentially provide users with access to government information at a level previously unavailable (Seavey 2005, 44).

Major Government Publication Resources Used in Reference Work

Guides to the U.S. Government

Fewer books have been published about government publications in recent years, perhaps due to fast pace of change. Judith Schiek Robinson's *Tapping the Government Grapevine: the User-friendly Guide to U.S Government Information Sources* remains a useful text. More indicative of the new direction of government publications is Peter Hernon et al., *U.S. Government on the Web: Getting the Information You Need* (Libraries Unlimited 2003), which deals with government publications as they appear on the Web.

In addition to books, there are many good Web sites that link the librarian to a wealth of information on government publications. Core Documents of U.S. Democracy can be found at www.gpoaccess.gov/coredocs.html. This site leads the user to the Declaration of Independence, the U.S. Constitution, and the Emancipation Proclamation, as well as to the search page for the U.S. Code, the Congressional Record, Supreme Court decisions, and many other key documents. Housed at Vanderbilt University (www.library.vanderbilt.edu/romans/fdtf) is an excellent site with a good subject guide to help the librarian or user to find pertinent publications on a wide variety of subjects. Another Web site is housed at the University of Michigan and can be found at www.lib.umich.edu/govdocs/. Both are very complete and a good starting place for researching not only U.S. government publications but also state and international publications. Google Uncle Sam (www.google.com/unclesam) is another source of government information where the user can conduct a subject search and find both federal and state legislation on the same subject.

CQ Encyclopedia of American Government is a new fee-based online resource providing concise information on all aspects of U.S. government, the presidency, the Supreme Court, Congress and elections. It includes information about the organization and powers of each branch of government as well as current and past presidents, justices, and members of Congress.

Directories

The *U.S. Government Manual* is the best single source of information about the various branches and agencies in the Federal Government. It provides basic information about each government department and agency and quasi-government agencies including chief officials, addresses, phone numbers, and a summary of the areas of responsibility. It is available in print and online at www.gpoaccess.gov/gmanual/index.html. The commercial version of this manual is the *Washington Information Directory* (Congressional Quarterly), an annual publication available in print and online that provides contact information and a brief description for each government agency or congressional committee. It also includes information on nongovernmental agencies such as associations, lobbying organizations, and foundations.

Each branch of government has its own directory. For Congress there is the *Congressional Directory* (www.gpoaccess.gov/cdirectory/index.html), published by the GPO. The *Congressional Staff Directory*, the *Federal Staff Directory* for the Executive Branch and the *Judicial Staff Directory* for the Judicial Branch are published by Congressional Quarterly Press three times a year with an annual volume. They are all available in paper and online.

Periodicals and Their Indexes

The U.S. government is a prolific publisher of periodicals. These periodicals are indexed in the *Government Periodicals Index*, published by LexisNexis, to provide access to articles in over 175 federal government publications. This quarterly index is published in print and online and can be searched by keyword. The U.S. government periodicals indexed include *FDA Consumer, Export America, Environmental Health Perspective, Science and Technology Review*, and *Occupational Outlook Quarterly*.

Two other fee-based indexes provide access to government publications. *PAIS International* indexes governmental as well as many nongovernmental publications in the areas of its coverage. *LexisNexis* also indexes government material and provides the full text of many government publications online. (See Chapter 8 for more information.)

U.S. Government Publications

In order to understand the organization of government publications, it is necessary to understand the organization of the U.S. government. The U.S. government has three branches: Legislative Branch, Executive Branch and Judicial Branch. Each branch has many agencies within it. The branches of the U.S. government and their publications are described in the sections that follow.

Legislative Branch Publications

The Legislative Branch consists of Congress—the Senate and House of Representatives—and its supporting agencies that include the Library of Congress, the Government Printing Office, the General Accounting Office, and Congressional Budget Office. The legislative branch of government produces a huge number of publications as it moves from Congressional bills to committee hearings and reports to House or Senate publications to discussions and votes on the floor of the House and Senate and then to the public laws that are eventually written into the *United States Code*. At each step of the way there is a document that is being discussed and often revised. All the information about the actions of the U.S. Congress can be found on GPO Access (www.gpoaccess.gov). It provides the history of bills, the text of all Congressional bills, the Committee reports, and the text of the laws. The most important document is the *Congressional Record* (www .gpoaccess.gov/crecord/index.html) which is the official record of what takes place on the floor of the House and the Senate. There is also a *Congressional Record Index* that is available on GPO Access from 1992 to date.

This legislative process is documented by THOMAS (http://thomas.loc.gov), a Web site of the Library of Congress named for Thomas Jefferson. With THOMAS the user can easily follow the progress of a bill. THOMAS provides the text of the bill, its status, committee schedules and reports, the debate in either house of Congress as documented by the *Congressional Record*, the roll call vote, and the text of the public law when passed. Users can search by keyword or bill number. Within the *Congressional Record* users can search by subject or by member of Congress. THOMAS also provides information about the legislative process and the text of historical publications such as the Constitution of the United States and the Declaration of Independence.

There are a number of commercially produced publications that document the progress of bills through Congress. The *CIS/Index to Publications of the United States Congress* is the most comprehensive index to bills and resolutions, committee prints, and congressional hearings. It indexes the publications of House, Senate, and joint committees and subcommittees. Each monthly issue has an index volume and an abstract volume. The index volume indexes publications by subject, name, title, bill number, and publication number. The abstract volume provides bibliographic information, SuDoc numbers, and summaries of the contents, including such detail as the names of witnesses and their affiliations. This index is published monthly in paper with a cumulation at the end of the year. It is also available online through *LexisNexis Congressional*, where it links to related congressional publications. Since 1984 Congressional Information Service (CIS) has also published an annual legislative history volume with material indexed by subjects and names. CQ Press publishes numerous guides to Congress. *CQ Weekly*, an online resource, reports on a weekly basis on the activities of Congress. Flexible searching allows the user to search by keyword, date, etc. This database has recently expanded to include coverage of the executive branch and government regulations. *CQ Congress Collection*, another online resource, integrates a large amount of information into one database including information on legislation, members of Congress, key floor votes as far back as 1945, and other information about the legislative branch of government. The *U.S. Serial Set* and the *American State Papers*, available through *LexisNexis Congressional*, provide researchers with access to the Congressional legislative history documents from 1789 to 1969. *CQ Researcher* and *CQ Researcher en espanol*, available in print and online, provide reports on individual topics such as social, political, environmental, and health issues. Each report is about 13,000 words. There are forty-four issues a year.

Executive Branch Publications

The Executive Branch includes the Office of the President and many agencies that report directly to the president, such as the Council of Economic Advisors, the Office of Management and Budget, the National Security Council, and the Domestic Policy Council. The cabinet-level departments, i.e., Department of Commerce, Department of Defense, Department of Education, Department of Health and Human Services, Department of State, and others, are also part of the Executive Branch, as well as a number of independent government agencies such as Environmental Protection Agency, Federal Reserve, National Commission on Libraries and Information Science, the Peace Corps, and the National Science Foundation.

Many excellent publications on the presidency have been published. A recent one is *Encyclopedia of the American Presidency* by Michael Genovese (Facts on File 2004), which provides information on many aspects of the American presidency from George Washington to the present president. Information is included on the relationship between the presidency and other branches of government and on court cases, elections, and scandals. Another source is the Presidential Library System Web site, which can be found at www.archives.gov/presidential_libraries/index.html.

The Federal Register (www.gpoaccess.gov/fr/index.html), produced by the National Archives and Records Administration, is this branch's most important publication. It provides information on a daily basis about presidential publications such as executive orders and proclamations, rules, proposed rules, and notices from agencies. This is a good place to look for the guidelines for government-funded programs. The database can be searched by subject or by agency. There is also a *Federal Register Index*. *The Code of Federal Regulations* (www.gpoaccess.gov/cfr/index.html) codifies the rules into public laws. Many rules and regulations are now published on the agencies' Web sites as a result of the E-Government Act of 2002.

The cabinet-level departments of the Federal Government are located in the Executive Branch. Each has its own Web site. These Web sites are gold mines of information. Sometimes it takes some hunting to find certain resources. The following is a description of a selection of government departments to provide the reader with a sense of the vast amount of information on these departmental Web sites.

Department of Education

Through the Department of Education Web site (www.ed.gov) one can find information on the latest education policies, financial aid information, education publications, grants, and, of course, ERIC, the Educational Resources Information Center, which is found at www.eric.ed.gov (see Chapter 8). A couple of interesting features are the Gateway to Educational Materials, which provides lesson plans, curriculum units, and other educational resources, and the National Center for Education Statistics (http://nces.ed.gov), which provides nationwide statistics on education.

Department of Labor

Through the Department of Labor Web site (www.dol.gov), one can find information on safety and health standards (OSHA), wage, hour, and other workplace standards, labor statistics, information about job seeking (America's Job Bank) and careers (*Occupational Outlook Handbook*), and information for working women from the Women's Bureau. The Bureau of Labor Statistics (www.bls.gov) is a source of local data and includes the Consumer Price Index.

Department of Interior

Through the Department of Interior Web site (www.doi.gov) one can find information on fish and wildlife, including endangered species and wildlife refuges (United States Fish and Wildlife Service), maps from the U.S. Geological Survey, and information from the National Park Service about each National Park.

Department of Health and Human Services

The Web site of the Department of Health and Human Services (www.os.dhhs.gov) provides a wealth of information on diseases and conditions, safety and wellness, drugs and food, as well as information on aging issues, family issues, and issues for specific populations. This well-organized Web site provides easy access to many important resources. The Department of Health and Human Services includes the Centers for Disease Control and Prevention, Centers for Medicare and Medicaid Services, Food and Drug Administration, and the National Institutes of Health, which publishes MEDLINEplus, an important source of consumer health information.

The Department of Commerce

The Department of Commerce (www.commerce.gov) includes the Bureau of Economic Analysis, which publishes the journal *Survey of Current Business*, as well as the International Trade Administration, which provides reports on U.S. trade and the U.S. industry and trade outlook. The Minority Business Development Agency resides here as does NOAA (National Oceanic and Atmospheric Administration). On the NOAA site one can find all kinds of weather and climate information including hurricane information and other kinds of weather advisories. The National Technical Information Service is also housed in this department. This clearinghouse for government-funded engineering, scientific, technical, and business related information has an online library and bookstore.

The Department of State

The State Department (www.state.gov) provides information on U.S. embassies and consulates, travel information, and information on international issues. *Background Notes* are published and updated by the U.S. State Department. These publications provide concise information about countries including the land, people, history, government, political conditions, economy, foreign relations, and travel and business. They are updated frequently, and some are for sale in print.

Central Intelligence Agency

The CIA publishes the *CIA World Factbook*, which provides maps and some general information about 267 countries (www.cia.gov/cia/publications/factbook/index.html). This excellent free source, which includes information on geography, people, government, economy, communications, transportation, military, and transnational issues, is current and quite extensive.

Library of Congress

The Library of Congress (www.loc.gov) is often treated as a national library, but it is actually the research arm of Congress. The Library's Web site states as its mission "to make its resources available and useful to Congress and the American people and to sustain and preserve a universal collection of knowledge and creativity for future generations." It houses the THOMAS Web site and the Congressional Research Service, which works for Congress. On the Library of Congress Web site there are resources especially for librarians, researchers, publishers, kids and families, and teachers. The Copyright Office is of interest to many. Here one can find out how to register a copyright or how to search copyright records. The American Memory project provides a wealth of digitized text and images on many aspects of American history, e.g., women's history, African American history, immigration, and culture and folk life.

Judicial Branch Publications

The Judicial Branch consists of the Federal Courts, including the Supreme Court and special courts such as the Court of International Trade. There are also administrative units of the Judicial Branch such as the Federal Judicial Center. The Web site for the U.S. Supreme Court is www.supremecourtus.gov. Here one can find the history of the court, biographies of past and present members of the Supreme Court, and even speeches by members of the Supreme Court. Opinions of the Supreme Court can be found at http://supremecourtus.gov/opinions/opinions.html.

The Findlaw.com site provides a free searchable database for Supreme Court decisions since 1985. Other sources of court decisions can be found in the fee-based databases of *Westlaw* and *LexisNexis*. A recent print source is *CQ Guide to the Supreme Court* 4th edition, which includes information on the history of the Supreme Court, important cases, and the impact of these decisions on American life.

Statistical Resources

All libraries receive many questions about statistics on population, jobs, education, health, crime, income, and much more. Since so many statistics are collected by government entities, this is often a good place to start.

Statistical Abstract of the United States (www.census.gov/compendia/statab/), published by the Bureau of the Census annually in paper and online, is a compilation of tables and graphs of statistics from every government agency about the United States. Sources for each table and graph are noted. When U.S. government statistics are not available, statistics from other reliable national organizations are used. This source covers such areas as population, health and nutrition, vital statistics, education, labor, agriculture, law enforcement, manufacturing, trade, and housing. FEDSTATS (www.fedstats.gov/), maintained by the Federal Interagency Council on Statistical Policy, provides links to federal statistics by topics and agencies. There are links to agency databases such as the Bureau of Labor Statistics and the Center for Education Statistics. One can also search by state or by subject and then by state or city. It also possible to search across agency Web sites. American Fact Finder is a user-friendly Web site from the Bureau of the Census (factfinder.census.gov/home/ saff/main.html?_lang=eng). This Web site provides statistics on population, housing, economic, and geographic data. In addition to the data from the last census, it provides information from the annual American Community Survey, information from the Economic Census that is taken every five years, and population estimates that are done between censuses.

Three indexes are produced that cover statistics at the federal, state, and international levels. They are all published by LexisNexis. *American Statistical Index (ASI)* provides statistics from publications in all parts of the federal government. Published monthly, it includes an index and abstracts with an annual cumulation. It is available in paper and on *LexisNexis Statistical*. *Statistical Reference Index (SRI)* includes sources of statistics from private-sector organizations and state governments. Over one thousand sources are included. This publication is produced monthly in an annual cumulation with an index and abstracts. It is available in paper and on *LexisNexis Statistical*. *Index to International Statistics (IIS)* includes all kinds of statistical publications from over one hundred international intergovernmental organizations including all major Intergovernmental Organizations (such as the United Nations, European Union, Organization of Economic Co-operation and Development, and Organization of American States). It is published monthly with an index and abstracts and with an annual cumulation and is also available on *LexisNexis Statistical*.

Business and economic statistics are available from several sources. Bureau of Economic Analysis (www.bea.gov) provides statistics such as the gross domestic product, the balance of payments, international trade, and personal income. STAT-USA (www.stat-usa.gov), a publication of the U.S. Department of Commerce, is "one stop for business, trade and economic information." Individuals can subscribe to it for a fee or can use it at no cost at a depository library. Bureau of Labor Statistics (www.bls.gov) provides a wealth of labor statistics. Here one can find the consumer price index, import/export indexes, wage statistics, demographics about the work force, and career information. There is also statistical information on a state-by-state basis. National Center for Health Statistics (www.cdc.gov/nchs) provides health statistics on all kinds of health issues nationwide.

Government Publications by Subject

The government has also made it possible to access information by subject. The overall Web site is FirstGov.gov, which was designed to provide access to government publications for the general public. This portal provides gateways for citizens, businesses, and government employees. Users can search for information by topic such as health, jobs, education, money, or recreation or by department or agency, can download forms for jobs, benefits, passports, social security, etc. and can even receive an e-mail newsletter. There are a large number of subject-specific Web sites that the public or the librarian can also access. They include www.consumer.gov, www.science.gov, www.disabilityinfo.gov, www.seniors.gov, and www.recreation.gov. Each site is tailored to the needs of the target group or subject area.

Maps

The U.S. government produces many maps. Among the agencies producing maps are the U.S. Geological Survey, the Bureau of the Census, the National Park Service, and the National Oceanic and Atmospheric Administration. These are described in more detail in Chapter 10.

Information on Elections

Elections have become an important part of our national life, as they are in other countries. There are many places to look for information on current and historical elections. FirstGov.gov, which provides a great deal of user-friendly information, is a good place to start. There is also the Federal Election Commission Media Guide, available at www.fec.gov. Other sites of interest include America Votes (www.americavotes.org), Congress.org, funded by Capital Advantage, Project Vote Smart (www.vote-smart.org), the League of Women Voters Democracy Net (www.dnet.org), and the U.S. Election Atlas (uselectionatlas.org).

Historical Data

Historical Statistics of the United States has recently been updated by Cambridge University Press and is now available in print and online. It includes historical statistics on every aspect of American society from colonial times to the present including population, labor and employment, agriculture, manufacturing, and transportation. Another historical series of great interest is the U.S. Congressional Set, which includes the House and Senate documents and House and Senate reports, bound by session of Congress, beginning with the first session of the 15th Congress in 1817. The earlier records are found in the *American State Papers*.

The States

State governments also produce a wide array of interesting and essential publications. They usually have a Web site that can be checked to find their publications either in print or online. Two useful Web sites are State and Local Government on the Net (www.statelocalgov.net), which is arranged by state and by topic, e.g., arts, aging, health, education, and libraries; and FirstGov.gov, which has a link to local government information. A state-by-state list of links to state publications can be found at www.library.uiuc.edu/doc/statelist/check/check.htm. There is also a Web site for information on state depository library systems at www.dpo.uab.edu/~dweather/SLDTFDepSys.htm.

The Book of the States, published by the Council of State Governments, provides data about state government including articles on trends and issues in state constitutions, the three branches of state governments and major policies and programs, information about legislatures, governors, and other state officials, information on agricultural policy, women in government, environmental spending, education, mental health, etc. *City and County Data Book*, a supplement to *Statistical Abstract*, includes statistics for 1,078 cities, all U.S. counties, and places with 2,500 or more inhabitants and provides a way to make comparisons among cities and counties.

CQ State Fact Finder (2005) is a commercially published book on the states. It includes tables comparing the states in such areas education, health, crime/law enforcement, welfare, and taxes.

For Kids

Ben's Guide to U.S. Government for Kids has been added to GPO Access. Divided into three different grade levels, it provides basic information about the federal government. In addition many government agencies such as the EPA, CIA, FBI, Federal Trade Commission, and the Forest Service have developed clever, well-designed Kids' Pages. Access to them is available through www.kids.gov.

International Resources

Although the United Nations is the first organization that comes to mind when we say international, there are many international organizations, including the many agencies that are part of the United Nations and the many other international organizations worldwide.

The United Nations has made its official publications available for free at www.un.org/Pubs/onlinepubs.htm. The majority of the publications in this database are from 1993 onwards, but older publications are added all the time. The Official Publications of the United Nations (ODS) "provides access to the resolutions of the General

Assembly, Security Council, Economic and Social Council and the Trusteeship Council from 1946 onwards" (Web site). It does not include the UN Treaty Series or the UN Sales Publications.

The *Statistical Yearbook* of the United Nations provides data on the world economy, its structure and major trends, population and social statistics, economic activity and international economic relations. It is published in English and French. The *Demographic Yearbook*, published by the United Nations, is an international source of statistics that provides basic statistical data on over two hundred countries. The information, presented in tables, includes basic demographic statistics such as population trends and size, fertility, mortality, marriage and divorce, migration. This yearbook is published in English and French.

UN publications have a similar organization system to the Superintendent of Publications. They are arranged by the issuing body and any subordinate body, the form and a number for a specific publication.

Canadian Publications

The Canadian government's Web site for publications can be found at http://Canada.gc.ca/publications/publications_e.html. This site provides information about Canadian government publications. Users can search by topic, by title, or by keyword in a database that lists all kinds of government publications. Users can also access a list of best sellers, recent releases, and information guides. A Weekly Checklist of new publications is available online. The only full-text publication is the *Canada Gazette*, the official paper of the government of Canada. This publication, begun in 1841, publishes weekly information on new statutes and regulations, decisions of administrative boards, government notices, and public notices from the private sector.

Like the United States, Canada has a library Depository Service Program. Established in 1927 to provide access to federal government information, there are presently 680 depository libraries in public and academic libraries. Of these depository libraries only fifty-two are full depositories and the rest are selective depository libraries. A list of these libraries can be found at http://dsp-psd.pwgsc.gc.ca/Depo/table-e.html. The selective depositories select their publications from the Weekly Checklist.

Government Publications in the UK

The Office of the Public Sector Information (www.opsi.gov.uk) manages and provides access to UK government information. Their Web site (www.ukop.co.uk) houses the catalog of official UK publications since 1980. Another Web site (www.officialdocuments.co.uk) points users to all Command Papers and House of Commons Papers since May 2005, as well as Departmental Papers. Command Papers are those presented by a government minister "by Command of Her Majesty." Some selected Command Papers for 2004 and House of Commons papers from 2002 to date are also available. Copies of all government publications can be purchased from the Stationery Office, Ltd. Public libraries may receive a 50 percent discount on some government publications. Further information on the UK government is available through Directgov (www.direct.gov.uk/Homepage/fs/en).

Collection Development and Maintenance

Selection and Keeping Current

The primary access point for U.S. government publications is GPO Access (www .gpoaccess.gov). This portal provides free access to federal publications produced by the various government departments and agencies. Users can search by branch of government, i.e., legislative, executive, or judicial, or can search by title or topic.

Starting in 2006, the *Online Public Access Catalog* (OPAC) for GPO's Integrated Library System, called "Franklin," provides the user with many points of access to government publications. The OPAC replaces the *Catalog of U.S. Government Publications*, an online index that included bibliographic records from 1994 to 2005. The print version of the catalog, begun in 1895, was called the *Monthly Catalog of U.S. Government Publications* and is the major access point for pre-1976 documents. Government publications can also be access through *WorldCat*, which includes all items from the *Monthly Catalog* and its successors since July 1976.

In order to purchase government publications, one can turn to the U.S. Government Online Bookstore (bookstore.gpo.gov) which allows searching by subject. There is a weekly list of new publications. Libraries can purchase publications from the GPO by setting up a deposit account or paying by credit card or check. Federal publications can also be purchased from the Federal Citizen Information Center (www.pueblo.gsa.gov). These are mostly low-cost or free publications on such subjects as education, small business, health, and employment.

The Government Documents Round Table (GODORT) in the American Library Association has an excellent Web site at http://sunsite.berkeley.edu/GODORT, linking the librarian to many good Web sites on government publications. It is the best place to start for the beginner and the experienced librarian. GODORT produces guides to government publications and up-to-date information on the status of the Government Printing Office and the Government Depository Library Program.

Evaluating Government Documents

Because government documents are published by a governmental body, they are assumed to provide accurate, reliable, and up-to-date information. For this reason there is no need to apply the usual evaluation criteria. However, since some government information is also published by trade publishers, librarians will want to compare the products to see which will be the most useful to their clientele. For example, material published by a trade publisher might be easier to use, easier to search, or have a more acceptable layout. Cost will enter into the librarian's decision, since government publications tend to be less expensive than those published by a trade publisher. Format will continue to be an issue. Librarians should pay attention to which documents remain in print, since at least for U.S. documents, it has been stated that only a small number will continue in print format. The access issue will remain. If important information is not available for a reasonable cost or online, librarians must make a case for access. Or if information is made available and is then withdrawn, librarians must call that to the attention of appropriate officials. Even with government information some evaluation criteria will apply, and librarians must be alert to these issues.

Further Considerations

Having so much accessible on the Internet has made searching for government publications much easier. Efforts are being made to digitize older material. The new OPAC of the GPO is the way to begin, since one can search from a number of access points. However, having some rudimentary knowledge of the organization of the U.S. government will still come in very handy in finding the document needed. Getting familiar with the Web sites of departments and agencies will also be useful. They are not equally user friendly, and many times the user needs some knowledge to make use of them. The *U.S. Government Manual* is helpful in finding out where a particular agency is housed. This is a time of change in the area of government publications. Everyone is learning together and, in fact, must learn, since any library will be able to help their users with the online publications.

TOP 10 GOVERNMENT PUBLICATIONS		
Title	**Print**	**Online**
Bureau of the Census		www.census.gov
Congressional Record		www.gpoaccess.gov/ crecord/index.html
Federal Register		www.gpoaccess.gov/ cfr/index.html
FirstGov		www.firstgov.gov
GPO Access		www.gpoaccess.gov
GPO's Online Public Access Catalog "Franklin"		www.gpoaccess.gov
Library of Congress		www.loc.gov
Statistical Abstract of the United States	Annual	www.census.gov/ Statab/www
THOMAS		http://thomas.loc.gov
U.S. Government Manual		www.gpoaccess.gov/ gmanual/index.html

Recommended Resources Discussed in this Chapter

America Votes. Available at www.americavotes.org.

American Statistical Index. New York: LexisNexis. Published monthly with an annual cumulation. Available online through *LexisNexis Statistical.*

Ben's Guide to U.S. Government for Kids. Available at www.kids.gov.

The Book of the States. 1965– . Lexington, KY: Council of State Governments. Annual.

Canada. Depository libraries. Available at http://dsp-psd.pwgsc.gc.ca/Depo/table-e .html.

Canada. Publications. Available at http://Canada.gc.ca/publications/publications_e .html.

Central Intelligence Agency. CIA World Factbook. Available at www.odci.gov/cia/ publications/factbook.

CIS/Index to Publications of the United States Congress. 1970– . New York: Congressional Information Service/LexisNexis. Published monthly with an annual volume. Also available online through *LexisNexis Congressional.*

City and County Data Book 2000. 2001. Washington, DC: Government Printing Office.

Code of Federal Regulations. Available at www.gpoaccess.gov/cfr/index.html.

Congressional Directory. Washington, DC: Government Printing Office. Also available at www.gpoaccess.gov/cdirectory/index.html.

Congressional Record. Available at www.gpoaccess.gov/crecord/index.html.

Congressional Record Index. Available at www.gpoaccess.gov.

Congressional Staff Directory. Washington, DC: CQ Press. Published three times a year with an annual volume. Also available online.

Core Documents of U.S. Democracy. Available at www.gpoaccess.gov/coredocs.html.

CQ Congress Collection. Washington, DC: CQ Press. Available online.

CQ Encyclopedia of American Government. Washington, DC: CQ Press. Available online.

CQ Guide to the Supreme Court. 2004. 4th ed. 2 vols. Washington, DC: CQ Press.

CQ Researcher and *CQ Researcher en Español.* Washington, DC: CQ Press. Forty-four issues a year and an annual volume. Also available online.

CQ State Fact Finder. Washington, DC: CQ Press. Annual.

CQ Weekly. 1983– . Washington, DC: CQ Press. Available online.

ERIC (Educational Resources Information Center). Available at www.eric.ed.gov.

Federal Citizen Information Center. Available at www.pueblo.gsa.gov.

Federal Register. Available at www.gpoaccess.gov/fr/index.html.

Federal Staff Directory. Washington, DC: CQ Press. Published three times a year with an annual volume. Also available online.

FEDSTATS. Available at www.fedstats.gov.

Findlaw.com. Available at www.findlaw.com.

FirstGov.gov. Available at www.firstgov.gov.

Genovese, Michael. 2004. *Encyclopedia of the American Presidency.* New York: Facts on File.

Google Uncle Sam. Available at www.google.com/unclesam.

Government Documents Round Table (GODORT). Available at http://sunsite.berkeley .edu/GODORT.

Government Periodicals Index. 1988– . New York: LexisNexis. Quarterly. Also available online.

GPO Access. www.gpoaccess.gov.
Historical Statistics of the United States. 2006. New York: Cambridge University Press. Also available online.
Index to International Statistics. New York: LexisNexis. Published monthly with an annual cumulations. Also available online through *LexisNexis Statistical.*
Judicial Staff Directory. Washington, DC: CQ Press. Published three time a year with an annual volume. Also available online.
League of Women Voters Democracy Net. Available at www.dnet.org.
Library of Congress. Available at www.loc.gov.
National Center for Education Statistics. Available at http://nces.ed.gov.
National Center for Health Statistics. Available at www.cdc.gov/nchs.
Presidential Library System. Available at www.archives.gov/presidential_libraries/index.html.
Project Vote Smart. Available at http://vote-smart.org.
STAT-USA. Available at www.stat-usa.gov.
State and Local Government on the Net. Available at www.statelocalgov.net.
State depository library systems. Available at www.dpo.uab.edu/~dweather/SLDTFDepSys.htm.
State publications. Available at www.library.uiuc.edu/doc/statelist/check/check.htm.
Statistical Abstract of the United States. Washington, DC: Government Printing Office. Annual. Also available at www.census/gov/Statab/www.
Statistical Reference Index. New York: LexisNexis. Published monthly with an annual cumulation. Also available online through *LexisNexis Statistical.*
Statistical Universe. New York: LexisNexis. Available online.
THOMAS. Available at http://thomas.loc.gov.
United Kingdom. Command Papers and House of Commons papers. Available at www.official-documents.co.uk.
United Kingdom. Directgov. Available at www.direct.gov.uk/Homepage/fs/en.
United Kingdom. Office of the Public Sector Information. Available at www.opsi. gov.uk.
United Kingdom. Publications. Available at www.ukop.co.uk.
United Nations. *Demographic Yearbook.* New York: United Nations. Annual.
United Nations publications. Available at www.un.org/Pubs/onlinepubs.htm.
United Nations. *Statistical Yearbook of the United Nations.* New York: United Nations. Annual.
United States. Depository libraries. Available at www.gpoaccess.gov/libraries.html.
University of Michigan Government Documents Web site. Available at www.lib.umich.edu/govdocs/godort.html.
U.S. Bureau of the Census. *American Factfinder.* Available at http://factfinder.census.gov/home/saff/main.html?_lang=eng.
U.S. Bureau of Economic Analysis. Available at www.bea.gov.
U.S. Bureau of Labor Statistics. Available at www.bls.gov.
U.S. Department of Commerce. Available at www.commerce.gov.
U.S. Department of Health and Human Services. Available at www.os.dhhs.gov.
U.S. Department of the Interior. Available at www.doi.gov.
U.S. Department of Labor. Available at www.dol.gov.
U.S. Department of State. *Background Notes.* Available at www.state.gov.

U.S. Election Atlas. Available at http://uselectionatlas.org.
U.S. Government Manual. Washington, DC: Government Printing Office. Annual. Also available at www.gpoaccess.gov/gmanual/index.html.
U.S. Government Online Bookstore. Available at http://bookstore.gpo.gov.
U.S. Serial Set Digital Collection. New York: LexisNexis.
U.S. Supreme Court. Available at www.supremecourtus.gov.
U.S. Supreme Court. Opinions. Available at http://supremecourtus.gov/opinions/opinions.html.
Vanderbilt University Government Documents Web site. Available at www.library.vanderbilt.edu/romans/fdtf.
Washington Information Directory. Washington, DC: CQ Press. Annual. Also available online.

Recommendations for Further Reading

Evans, Donna, and David C. Yen. 2005. "E-Government: An Analysis for Implementation; Framework for Understanding Cultural and Social Impact." *Government Information Quarterly* 22, 3: 354–373. This article explores the implications of e-government for U.S. citizens and the international community.

Fagan, Jody Condit, and Bryan Fagan. 2004. "An Accessibility Study of State Legislative Web Sites." *Government Information Quarterly* 21, 1: 65–85. A study of the barriers to state legislative Web sites for users of assistive technology.

Jacobs, James A. James R. Jacobs, and Shinjoung Yeo. 2005. "Government Information in the Digital Age: The Once and Future Federal Depository Library Program." *The Journal of Academic Librarianship* 31, 3: 198–208. The authors argue that the even with the technological changes in the delivery of government documents, the Federal Depository Library Program is still needed.

Liptak, Deborah A. 2005. "Congressional Research Service Reports Revealed." *Online* 29, no. 6 (November/December): 23–26. Information on where to find the Congressional Research Service Reports that are written for Congress on such subjects as copyright, global climate change, AIDS, and stem cell research.

Mann, Wendy, and Theresa R. McDevitt, eds. 2003. *Government Publications Unmasked: Teaching Government Information Resources in the 21st Century.* Pittsburgh: Library Instruction Publications. An excellent guide to teaching government publications.

Martin, Mary, ed. 2005. *Local and Regional Government Information: How to Find It, How to Use It.* Westport, CT: Greenwood Press. A recent guide to local and regional government information online and in print.

Prophet, Mary, Megan Fitch, and Joy He. 2004. "Ohio5 Government Documents." *Against the Grain* 16, no. 3 (June): 38–39. Describes a cooperative arrangement among five college libraries in Ohio who are all Federal Depository libraries.

Reddick, Christopher G. 2005. "Citizen Interaction with E-government: From the Streets to the Servers." *Government Information Quarterly* 22, 1: 38–57. A study of the demand of citizens for e-government.

Rogers, Michael. 2005. "Illinois Libraries/OCLC Tackle Government Information Online." *Library Journal* 130, no. 10 (June 1): 35–36. Discussion of the development of an Illinois State Library, the University of Illinois at Chicago and OCLC sponsored virtual reference desk for government information using thirty librarians from federal depository libraries.

Shuler, John A. 2004. "New Economic Models for the Federal Depository System—Why Is It So Hard to Get the Question Answered?" *The Journal of Academic Librarianship* 30, no. 3 (May): 243–249. A discussion of the need for a new economic model that will enable the Government Printing Office to survive and the future role of depository libraries.

Singer, Carol A. 2003. "The Transition of U.S. Government Publications from Paper to the Internet: A Chronology." *Internet Reference Services Quarterly* 8, 3: 29–35. A year by year chronology of the transition of U.S. government publications to the Internet.

Wilson, Yvonne, and Deborah Richey. 2005. "State and Local Documents Roundup. A Basic Primer on Collecting Government Publications." *Documents to the People* 33, no. 4 (Winter): 9–11. Includes information on collecting financial reports, annual reports, statistical surveys, municipal codes, and planning documents, etc.

Bibliography of Works Cited in this Chapter

Drake, Miriam A. 2005. "The Federal Depository Library Program: Safety Net for Access." *Searcher* 13, no. 1 (January): 46.

Herman, Edward. 1997. *Locating United States Government Information: A Guide to Sources.* 2nd ed. Buffalo, NY: William S. Hein.

Hernon, Peter, Robert E. Dugan, and John A. Shuler. 2003. *U.S. Government on the Web: Getting the Information You Need.* 3rd ed. Westport, CT: Libraries Unlimited.

Johnson, Linda B. 2004. "Electronic Moves Center Stage." *Library Journal* (May 15): 52–57.

Robinson, Judith Schiek. 1998. *Tapping the Government Grapevine: The User-friendly Guide to U.S. Government Information Sources.* 3rd ed. Phoenix, AZ: Oryx Press.

Seavey, Charles A. 2005. "Publications to the People." *American Libraries* 36, no. 7 (August): 42–44.

Smith, Diane H., ed. 1993. *Management of Government Information Resources in Libraries.* Englewood, CO: Libraries Unlimited.

Smith, Lori L., Daniel C. Barkley, Daniel D. Cornwall, Eric W. Johnson, and J. Louise Malcomb. 2003. *Tapping State Government Information Sources.* Westport, CT: Greenwood Press.

Wilson, Paula. 2003. "Electronic Publications to the People." *Public Libraries* 42, no. 6 (November–December): 362–363.

Part 3
Special Topics in Reference and Information Work

13

When and How to Use the Internet as a Reference Tool

The Facts

The most seductive and ubiquitous reference resource to emerge in the twentieth century was the Internet. Virtually unknown to the general population till the advent of the World Wide Web in 1990, the explosion of Internet use in little more than a dozen years has been nothing short of spectacular. It took many centuries for an encyclopedia to be viewed as an all-purpose resource accessible to the common man. In contrast, it has taken less than a decade for 95 percent of libraries in postsecondary degree-granting institutions to establish open access to the Internet. As of today, almost 99 percent of public libraries and a little over 90 percent of school media centers have Internet access (ALA Fact Sheet 26). This access can feed off a stratospheric 4.3 billion IP addresses (ISC Internet Domain Survey). With so much material and access freely available, usage statistics are also high. 80 percent of eighteen-to-twenty-four-year-olds use the Internet on a regular basis and according to a Generational Media Study, the Internet has predominated as "the medium of choice" (Greenspan 2004). It seems clear then that the Internet is here to stay, perchance to flourish.

The Puzzle

Yet reference librarians have been curiously sluggish in wholly claiming, organizing, and charting the course of Internet research.

On September 30, 2005, the *Chronicle of Higher Education* published a special segment on "Libraries." The articles in the issue, whether dealing with buildings, pedagogy, or the future, unanimously testified to the centrality of Internet-based research. The "doom" view expressed at the scheduled opening of a $15 million library building was "It's a shame we spent all that money . . . now that everything is on the Internet," the article went on to refute. The article on reference pedagogy acknowledged at the start that it was "no exaggeration to say that most student research projects [began] with a Google search," but that librarians were there to help sort out the subsequent "50 million hits." The final article, tellingly written by a recent library graduate, was the only one to extend the centrality of Internet research. As written by Elizabeth Breakstone, "librarians not only participate in the information revolution but help direct its course" ("Libraries" 2005). The active role demanded by "directing the course" of Internet research has not found widespread recognition or acceptance among reference librarians. In fact, at the start of the twenty-first century, a fascinating and important study by Ross and Nilsen found that reference librarians "seem to regard the Internet as an external resource that users can search independently . . . but not as a full-fledged reference tool for which reference librarians have a responsibility to help users search and evaluate" (2000).

Much like the canonical Hausfrau, the Internet is being used in any number of ways by reference librarians, without being given the necessary recognition or attention due to a "full-fledged reference tool." Various applications of Internet protocol such as electronic mail, chat, remote login, and file transfer are being appropriated by reference librarians to conduct e-mail reference, chat reference, and instant messaging reference, as well as remote access to reference databases. So in addition to the ubiquitous use of Web sites and search engines, the larger technological domain covered by the Internet is also being used in dynamic and ever-increasing ways. While some reference librarians are more immersed in Internet reference than others, there is no librarian who can claim complete immunity.

The Solution

Rather than holding on to the tail of the Internet tiger and bumping along wherever it goes, Internet reference must be recognized as a "full-fledged reference tool" so that reference librarians can "help direct its course." This can be achieved through an understanding of the nature of the beast and a considered blueprint for actual use.

Nature of Internet Reference

The portable book was invented in the Middle Ages; in all these centuries we have developed a visceral acceptance of the strengths and weaknesses of the format. With the Internet, this has yet to happen. Both paeans and dirges are sung with equal passion and sincerity as we grapple with the possibilities and ramifications of the format. A spotlight on the major strengths and weaknesses of the Internet is a step toward understanding the best ways to use the medium to its most effective advantage.

Strengths

- Ease

    Intuitively, the act of plugging into a universe of information, 24/7, at the click of a finger is enticing. Despite all the wrong or unfiltered information for which the Internet is known, the number of right answers for information that would otherwise have taken extended time, energy, and resources is impressive. The process of getting these right answers is not only trivial, but instantaneous and handy.

For example, a question like *"Who is the person listed at 708.555.1212?"* could potentially have been time-consuming for a user. The knowledge that a criss-cross directory existed, followed by the search for a library that subscribed to a printed criss-cross directory for the 708 area, followed by a study of the arrangement of the directory, would be the minimum requirement. A reverse lookup in any of the online directories is accomplished in a matter of a minute.

In a 1999 study it was found that fully one-third of the traditional reference questions used as class assignments for library students had to be discarded because finding an answer required neither logic nor knowledge of sources. Instead, the answers were available with a minute's worth of Googling (Ross and Nilsen 2000, 148). Ease of use and the potential instant gratification of needs contribute greatly to the perceived strengths of Internet research.

- Currency

  Internet resources are stereotypically valued for their currency. Print resources, by definition, have built-in time delays to accommodate the vetting and printing process. Even a newspaper takes twenty-four hours to print the day's news. The Internet, on the other hand, can potentially update news as it is made.

  The print directory listing new Congress members, for example, was published as the *Congressional Directory* in August 2005, more than six months after the inaugural session of the 109th Congress. In the interim, users wanting to contact a Congressman or browse the roster had little choice but to consult Web sites such as www.senate.gov.

- Audiovisual

  Useful or even critical to some research is the need for audiovisual information. The Internet has the capability to provide it in composite forms that can include text, visual, and audio packages. A reference question on the unique positions of Sirius, Mirzam, Wezen, and Adhara, the major stars of the Canis Major constellation, could be partially answered with a print resource. However, their positions at changing times, dates, and latitudes could only be answered with the interactive simulations of a sky chart provided online by www.outerbody.com/stargazer. In children's reference, recurring school projects on country or ethnic studies, for example, gain immeasurably when textual descriptions are enhanced by a rendering of the national anthem of the country, or by videos of the celebration of local festivals and cultural programs. A student presenting a project on Pueblo tribes in southwestern America was able to dress and present a truncated kachina dance of the Hopi tribe based on a streaming video found online.

- Exclusivity

  Given the ease in both entering and accessing information, there are an increasing number of publications, proceedings, transcripts, and data that are available only on the Internet. Conference proceedings, government documents, state job listings and application forms, news blogs, and even professional communications can be found exclusively on the Internet.

  The most dramatic example of exclusivity appeared in 1991, when Paul Ginsparg, a physicist at the Los Alamos National Laboratory, launched an online archive of preprint research communications that would, in effect, circumvent print publications. The initiative, currently owned, operated, and funded by Cornell

University, has proven to be wildly successful. Acknowledged as a leader in "e-print" service, *arXiv* as it is known currently attracts monthly submissions numbering over 4,000, a big jump from the less than 500 submissions received in 1991–1992. Reference questions dealing with the cutting edge of physics must frequently be referred to the Web site at http://arxiv.org.

- Interactive

    Print information is information that informs, but rarely "listens." Internet information has the capability to be interactive. Discussion groups, Listservs, e-mail newsletters, live interviews, and ongoing comment pages are possible so that an information dialogue can be created. Interactivity in research is quite possibly one of the most dynamic areas of future development in reference librarianship.

    Even as major initiatives such as *Q&A NJ* in New Jersey, *AskNow* in California and *ASKaLibrarian* in Florida are maturing at a hectic pace, instant messaging (IM) reference is taking shape as a less costly and more personalized alternative. According to a 2004 survey, eighty million Americans are using instant messaging on a regular basis, so that it is possible to extend the likelihood that IM will not remain an unfamiliar technology for long (Houghton and Schmidt 2005, 26–30). Teens are particularly involved in IM techniques and are the "targeted group" for new IM ventures such as the one begun in 2005 at the Marin County Free Library (Houghton 2005, 192–193).

    Another area where interactivity is playing a major role is in statistical information (Foudy 2000, 49–53). Web sites are beginning to offer data in formats that permit users to transpose data directly on to spreadsheets or Excel and Access programs; to create graphs; or extract selective line data. The National Economics Accounts at the U.S. Department of Commerce, for example, provides "Interactive Access" for all of its tables. A reference question on changes in the market value of goods and services in the American economy before and after the 9/11 terrorist attack could require multiple printed resources, relatively difficult to locate. With the "Interactive Access" tables, however, changes in current-dollar Gross Domestic Product can be tailored to fit any selected range of years with the frequency of data tweaked to present annual, quarterly, or monthly figures.

- Mass convenience

    Unlike single book sources, Internet information is accessible to multiple users at the same time. A user spending hours over the *Occupational Outlook* need not be disturbed if Internet access is available for the twenty high school students with career assignments who can access the same resource online at www.bls.gov/oco.

- Scope

    There are reportedly three new pages added to the Internet every second of the day. That is a lot of material. Then again, there are a lot of print resources published every day as well; so why is "scope" treated so holistically for the Internet? The reason lies in the different form of access to print versus Internet resources. The clicking of the same mouse to switch almost instantaneously from one resource to another gives the admittedly misleading impression that the scope of the Internet is one vast composite whole. In reality, the criterion for scope should be applied to each individual site, much as is done for each individual book. However, in terms of the appeal of Internet research, the perception of scope, voiced as "you can find everything," is powerful.

Weaknesses

Given the scope, accessibility, ease, currency, convenience, and value-added features of Internet use, it is curious that the Internet is taking so long to be treated as a full-fledged reference tool. The explanation for this time lag can reasonably be located in the following vulnerabilities peculiar to Internet research.

- Quality Control

  Both the attraction and the detraction of Internet research is that for any and every reason, anyone can write anything, from anywhere in the world, and leave it for any amount of time for anyone to read. With the insouciant littering of information and wisdom, knowledge and factoids, learning and vitriol flung haphazardly into Everyman's existence, it is no wonder that librarians, with their trained beliefs and classical training in classification and subclassification, have indulged in nervous speculation that the end of the information world was imminent (Crawford and Gorman 1995; Anhang 2002). Without any checks on authorship, reliability, accuracy, currency, or validity, information can quite literally run amok. The fast developing Internet religion of the "pastafarians," followers of the Flying Spaghetti Monster, a parodist creation originally designed to mock the inclusion of intelligent design in Kansas school curricula, is a case in point. It can be accessed at http://venganza.org.

- Evaluation

  Given the absolute lack of quality control, the onus of evaluating sites falls squarely on the shoulders of the user. Evaluation, as librarians are aware, is a complex undertaking, requiring both the awareness and the skills to navigate between trustworthy and untrustworthy sites. Since users are conditioned to accept all printed material as valid information, the pitfalls of Internet-generated research become more acute. Public librarians faced with the directive to "print something from that Internet"; and undergraduates laboring under the IKIA (I Know It Already) syndrome (Wilder 2005) are daily examples of users unaware about the fallible nature of Internet information.

- Lack of overview

  Thomas Mann, the venerable reference librarian at the Library of Congress, describes how scholarship can be affected in the way information is presented. Direct and physical access to subject-classified shelves can result in information that may not be possible through digital access dependent on the use of keywords. This is because:

  a. Researchers invariably do not have all the exact keywords prior to starting the research, but do recognize the information when it is "immediately in front of them within a manageably segregated group of likely sources."

b. Even with the right keywords specified in advance, results cannot "build bridges *among* multiple sets" so that an overview of the research topic becomes difficult (Mann 2005).

While Mann has a valid point and has voiced, in more learned terms, the book librarians' angst over the change in serendipitous shelf browsing, there are skills that can establish keywords, link words, and search terms to circumvent the apparent lack of an overview. This will be outlined further in the chapter.

- Delusive

  Oftentimes, the Internet is just not the right resource. Given the powerful belief that all information is available on the Internet, much time can be wasted in looking for information that can be found far more efficiently through other formats. In addition to the waste of time engendered by choosing the wrong resource, time can be wasted in sifting reliable from unreliable material; or getting caught in the hop-skip-and-jump allure of hyperlinks.

- Free full text

  Full-text articles from journals are also not always free to the Internet user. Research-quality articles have traditionally clustered under expensive subscription databases. This would not ordinarily be considered a "weakness." After all, full-text articles in print journals are also available only through purchase. However, Internet research has accrued the impression of being free. As Joe Thompson of the Baltimore County Public library laments, "Good information still costs money, and people forget that" (Selingo 2004). The cost of information, accepted as normal for print, is paid unwillingly for Internet sources, fueled no doubt by the lurking suspicion that the information might indeed be free "somewhere" on the Internet. Increasingly, however, with projects such as Google Scholar and its Print Library Project, as well as the Open Content Alliance scheduled to run Yahoo's library digitization venture, the extent of open-access journals will probably increase.

- Spotty coverage of historical material

  The presence of historical material on the Internet is limited. Even databases usually do not go far back into archival material so that journal articles prior to the 1980s are hard to find via the Internet. If included, historical coverage tends to be spotty, almost as if it is included only if and when time and personal interest permit such inclusions.

- Volatility

  With content being added, modified, deleted, or forgotten, there is a constant level of volatility built into the medium. What was vetted yesterday as being a "good" site will have to be vetted again today before it is used, because it might have changed. Internet Yellow Pages that become partially obsolete within the first year of publication are prime exhibits of this volatility. Documenting the Web site to the last letter or number of the URL (Uniform Resource Locator) address is one way of coping with the mercurial quality of Internet-generated answers. While it does not retrieve a lost site, it both testifies and provides clues to the earlier structure of a site. The Internet Archive at www.archive.org can also be consulted with its storehouse of more than thirty billion dead Web sites and extinct pages.

Five Steps to Successful Internet Reference

The Internet is surfed. It should be searched. To chart a logical reference course rather than crest every passing information wave, the following five steps should prove instructive.

Step 1: Ask Yourself if the Internet is the Right Medium

"Type first and think later" has been the instinctive reaction to using the Internet. The considered reaction should be:

- Is it the best resource to use?
- Is it the only resource to use?

Clarity in the advantages and disadvantages of Internet use is a necessary first step. Being open to a combination of formats can also pay dividends. For example, on the morning of August 29, 2005, when the hurricane Katrina struck the Gulf Coast region of the United States, the Web site for the American Red Cross was jammed. Loading the page took an average of 25–55 minutes, if it opened at all. By contrast, referring users to the information for Disaster Relief at the American Red Cross headquarters, found in print resources such as the *Washington Information Directory*, took a minute. Picking up the telephone or consulting a colleague can also prove to be more efficient in certain situations. The first step, then, involves a clear choice of using the Internet in tandem, or in preference, to print or other information mediums.

Step 2: Select the Right Internet Tool

The second step is using the most efficient Internet search tool—a search engine, a meta-search engine, or a subject directory.

- Search Engines
  If the question requires a broad overview, single keywords or phrases typed into a search box can provide a flood of hits. This option requires eyeballing a list of random resources that may or may not be productive, but at minimum, helps formulate the research query. General search engine technology, yet in its relative toddlerhood, is growing in leaps and bounds so that various tools are now available to fine-tune the keyword search. Some of the more popular search engines are Yahoo! Search, Google, MSN Search, Ask (formerly known as Ask Jeeves), WiseNut, Gigablast, AOL, iWon, EarthLink, and MyWay. A brief overview of some of the major general engines available to users can be seen in Table 1.
  For seven-to-twelve-year-old users, child-friendly search engines are available. They typically provide a mix of information and ready entertainment. The page is

Table 1 SAMPLE GENERAL SEARCH ENGINES

	GOOGLE	YAHOO!	TEOMA
DEBUT YEAR	1998	1994	2000
SITE	www.google.com	www.yahoo.com	www.teoma.com
NAME ETYMOLOGY	From "googol," a number represented by 100 zeros following the numeral 1	Acronym for: "Yet Another Hierarchical Officious Oracle"	Gaelic for "expert"
INDEXED PAGES	Over 8 billion	Over 4 billion	Over 1.5 billion
TRAFFIC	81.9 million unique users per month as of June 2003	Average of 2.4 billion page views per day as of March 2004	1 million unique users as of April 2002
BOOLEAN	Capitalized OR; Default AND	Capitalized AND; OR; AND NOT; NOT	Capitalized OR; Default AND
UNIQUE FEATURES	1. At least 24 special search features such as local business listings in the U.S., UK, and Canada	1. Both a general search engine and a directory that can be used in tandem	1. Can refine search results through word filters and stated suggestions
	2. Special tools such as blogging and services such as "froogle" shopping	2. Signature exclamation mark directs user to specific service so that "travel!" for example, goes to Yahoo! Travel	2. Results show context of search terms
	3. Sites "cached" so that if page is unavailable, original page can be displayed	3. Communication services such as chat and commerce services such as auctions	3. Editorial comments on Web links are often provided
RANKING ALGORITHM	Page Rank™—general popularity usage calculated from over 100 factors	Relevancy— through keyword density	Subject Specific Popularity— number of same subject pages that reference a site

bright and loaded with contrasting colors and graphics. The sites are usually geared to providing both directories and search engine capabilities. The highly popular Ask for Kids, available at www.askforkids.com, uses natural language technology so the importance of keywords is lessened. It only accepts links that are "G-rated" and written specifically for children. There is no option for chat. Yahooligans! on the other hand, available at http://yahooligans.yahoo.com, provides safe surfing guidelines and places the onus of responsibility on parents and the child.

New ways to display results are also appearing so that the new "Grokker" system, available at www.grokker.com, can organize over 150 results into a single pictorial that can be previewed by the user to gauge what might be the most relevant groups of results. Brainboost, at www.brainboost.com, sells itself as an "answer engine" as opposed to a search engine. It provides answers to natural language questions along with ranked sites that provide the answers.

- Meta-search engines

  Meta-search engines produce far more results, given that they collate sites from multiple search engines. Searches can be overwhelming and search statements can be read differently so that meta-searches are best used when a very broad overview of a subject is required. Some of the best known meta-search engines are Ixquick, ez2find, Queryserver, KartOO, Clusty, and Dogpile. A brief overview of the last two is provided in Table 2.

- Subject directories

  Since directories employ subject headings based on standardized vocabulary, organized by human rather than robotic logic, specific questions can benefit from a directory. Conversely, if users are unclear about search terms within a subject area, the directory supplies terms, much as a thesaurus supplies synonyms. The Web sites are relatively vetted and therefore produce a more limited, yet pertinent set of results. The directory is also useful in mining the "invisible web," those sites such as specialized searchable databases that are typically not locatable in a general search engine (Sherman and Price 2001). An overview of three subject directories is given in Table 3.

If the past is a true predictor of the future, the above search engines, meta-search engines, and directories will morph into sleeker technology and different ranking and selecting systems. Search engine names such as Lycos, Hotbot, and Excite are no longer what they were a few short years ago. Sudden death or transpositions of engine technology and ownership is the order of the day, so that the tables provide a brief, time-bound snapshot of ways to synopsize a tool as and when it appears on the search horizon.

Step 3: The Right Search Terms

The third step, possibly the most critical in establishing the difference between a wild surfing session and a professional search strategy, is in constructing the most effective search terms. To succumb to the siren call of typing in terms as they pop

Table 2 SAMPLE METASEARCH ENGINES

	DOGPILE	VIVISIMO/CLUSTY
SITE	www.dogpile.com	www.clusty.com
DEBUT YEAR	1996	2004
NAME ETYMOLOGY	Term used to describe players piling on top of one another to celebrate	Vivísimo is Spanish for "bright, lively, and intelligent"
META-SEARCHES	Google, Yahoo!Search, MSN, Ask, About, LookSmart, MIVA, and more	LookSmart, Lycos, MSN, Open Directory, Teoma, Gigablast, Wisenut. Advanced Search crawls through specialized sites such as FirstGov and PubMed
UNIQUE FEATURES	1. Comparison View tool allows side-by-side viewing of difference search engine results	1. Clustering by Topic, Source, or URL that includes co.uk
	2. Sites found by only one engine are highlighted	2. Overview of 200–500 results on the first page
	3. Live news ticker with hyperlinked headlines from ABC and Fox	3. Users have option of customizing display tabs and inserting new tabs of their choice
	4. Can give customized information if ZIP code and birth date are supplied	4. Clusty Blog Search allows for search of blog engines such as Blogdigger and Technorati
	5. Radio button for audio, video, images, news, and directories	5. "Details" tab in the results page allows user to check all engines searched

like flashbulbs in one's head is to be vulnerable to a lengthy and possibly frustrating search.

• Instead, the trained response should be to pick up a pencil and draw up a list. Starting with a democratic strategy allows all words and phrases associated with the question to be jotted down in two categories that differentiate between key representative terms and related terms. Once the brainstorming of words is over, a hierarchy needs to be imposed, however tentative the ranking. Stratification would help to both structure preresearch thinking and save an immense amount of time and energy as the research proceeds. Dubious leads can be tweaked and search terms revised based on this list. Repetition can be avoided and time saved. The

Table 3 SAMPLE SUBJECT DIRECTORIES

	INFOMINE	LIBRARIANS' INTERNET INDEX	RESOURCE DISCOVERY NETWORK
DEBUT YEAR	1994	1993	1998
SITE	http://infomine.ucr.edu	www.lii.org	www.rdn.ac.uk
LINKS	Over 100,000 links, of which 26,000 are by librarians and the rest by robots/crawlers	Over 16,000 Web sites	More than 100,000 linked resources
TRAFFIC	Current figures not known—over 20,000 accesses in 3/1996	24,102,513 accesses Jan.–Sept. 19, 2005	3,547,630 searches performed between 8/02–7/03
BOOLEAN	NEAR, NOT, AND, OR are executed in that order	Default AND; NOT and OR can be used	Default AND; OR and minus sign for NOT is used
UNIQUE FEATURES	1. University level research with sites vetted by librarians from the University of California, Wake Forest University, California State University, and others	1. Free of advertising	1. A collaboration of over 70 education and research organizations in the UK aimed at higher level research
	2. Rich resource for the "invisible web" of databases, electronic journals and books, and bulletin boards	2. Sites vetted by permanent staff and 100 contributors from libraries in California and Washington	2. Eight "hubs" that focus on a subject specialty; within a hub are subspecialties
	3. Nine major subject headings	3. Free weekly newspaper for resource updates	3. Highly useful interactive Web tutorials
	4. Concise descriptions for each record	4. Fifteen primary subject headings and many subheadings	4. A set of online case studies provided for each hub
			5. Live RSS feed for "Behind the Headlines" news service

Zen insight of finding equal importance in absence as in presence is also instructive in that dead end terms can throw critical light on the relative relevance of different aspects of a research topic. For example:

Query:
"I need to research separatist movements in Sri Lanka"

Representative search terms:
Sri Lanka, Sri Lanka and politics, Sri Lanka and separatists, Sri Lanka and ethnic conflict

Related terms:
Ceylon Tamils, Tamils and Sinhalese, LTTE, Tamil Tigers, TULF, PLOTE, EPRLF, Thimpu Talks, Prabhakaran/Pirabhakaran, Sri Lanka and India, eelam, Jayewardene, Kumaratunga

Hierarchy:
1. *Sri Lanka politics*
2. *Sri Lanka and ethnic conflict*
3. *Liberation Tigers of Tamil Eelam*

Free online tutorials on developing list skills can be found at www.vts .rdn.ac.uk, a national initiative in the UK that presents wonderfully detailed tutorials designed for subject areas ranging widely from engineering to gardening.

- In addition to setting up a hierarchy of search terms, an awareness of the syntax, spelling, and alternate spelling of terms can both ease and enhance a search. For example, an Internet search on the history of Myanmar, the Democratic Republic of Congo, or Surinam may be incomplete without using the recently discarded names of Burma, Zaire, and Dutch Guiana. While existing awareness of alternatives is not necessary, it is necessary to be aware of the possibility of alternatives so that clues offered in one search string can be hoarded for another search.
- Vague or generic keywords and search terms can result in a frustrating, never-ending, or dead-end search. If a word is generic, the trick to relieve it of its anonymity is to use combination terms that establish the context of the word. For example, a user wanting biographical information on the singer formerly known as Prince cannot type a search term as generic as "prince." The results would no doubt cover the singer, but the information would be embedded within millions of sites on the scions of Great Britain, Monaco, the Netherlands, and various African countries; the history of Russia and the Indian subcontinent; bestsellers from today's Rowling and yesterday's Machiavelli; counties in Maryland and Virginia; and fond owner descriptions of dogs answering to that name. Combining the term "prince" with "singer," or even searching the notorious phrase "formerly known as prince" provides the necessary limiters to coalesce the search.

Step 4: Use the Right Search Operators

Having established the best possible hierarchy of productive search terms, considera-tion of the most effective search operators is the logical corollary. In theory, Boolean operators, truncations, wild cards, quotation marks, and proximity matrices are help-ful tools that can streamline the search process or extend it in the right direction. The inclusion of the Boolean "and" between two terms narrows an over-large search result. If the results are too limited, the use of the Boolean "or" can expand it.

In practice, however, search operators vary from site to site so that Gigablast, for ex-ample, accepts Boolean operators AND, OR, NOT, parentheses, and plus and minus signs, while WiseNut uses only the minus sign. The best way to take control over idio-syncratic operator acceptance is to check the "Help," "About," or "Tip" icons included on each Web site, directory, or search engine. A comparative chart on the various oper-ators allowed and disallowed by major search engines is provided in effective detail by Greg Notess at http://searchenginesshowdown.com/features; by Danny Sullivan at http://searchenginewatch.com; and by Joe Barker at http://infopeople.org/search/chart.html. With most searchers favoring one engine over another, it is expedient to be wholly familiar with the effective and time-saving tips provided by each engine. Even trivial shortcuts, such as hitting the "Return" key rather than clicking on the "Search" button as suggested by Google, can shave away search time.

Step 5: Evaluate the Search Results

The moment of truth is at hand. Carefully selected search terms are rewarded with a clutch of sites that can number anywhere from a few pages to thousands. How best to pick the best sites and evaluate them in more detail?

Given the complete absolution from traditional vetting agencies such as personal name accountability, publisher standards, editorial expertise, or professional evalua-tion, all Internet information must be treated as "guilty unless proven authoritative." This sounds harsher than it is. It merely reminds the Internet user to establish the va-lidity of each informational site using some of the same criteria used for print evalua-tion, along with recognition of the working mechanics of the Internet medium. The need for this is greater when providing Internet reference for minors. A comprehensive checklist of Web site evaluation for kids can be found at www.ala.org/ala/alsc/greatwebsites/greatwebsitesforkids/greatwebsites.htm.

- Authority

    Placing authorship is a traditional way of establishing the authority of any piece of information. It is no different in the Internet medium, though the ways of gauging the author's repute may require keener detection.

    - Who is the author? Is the work signed, and if so, is the name familiar or well-regarded in the field?
    - If the name is unfamiliar, is there more detailed contact information about the author? Open accountability can usually be regarded as a sign, though not a guarantee, of reliability.

- Is there any professional review or affiliation of the author provided on the site? Affiliations can provide clues to author validity.
- Is the link that led to this site one that can be trusted? Most trustworthy sites feel responsible about the hyperlinks they allow and thereby act as a vetting agent. Links from libraries are a classic example.
- What appears to be the motive of the author? Is there any indication that the author might be biased? If so, is the bias a necessary part of the research angle or liable to skew the research?
- Does the author exhibit a grasp of the subject, provide an overview of the field, or allude to existing theories in the field? While known authors are reviewed and slotted into comfortable perception fields, unknown Web authors must prove their expertise in the field and these exhibits provide some indicators of the level of expertise.

- Reliability
  - Is the site sponsored by a known organization or institution?
  - If unknown, what does the "About Us" icon say about the organization?
  - Are clear contact details provided? Once again, accountability can vouch for some degree of reliability.
  - Is the URL indicative? For example, when researching for information on Winston Churchill, the reliability of a URL such as www.chu.cam.ac.uk/churchill_papers/biography can be considered very high, even without actually delving into the site. Why is that? Because of URL clues such as "uk," which stands for the United Kingdom, home to Churchill; the "ac," which stands for academia much as "edu" does in the United States; and "cam," which stands for the prestigious University of Cambridge. A URL with a tilde (~) could be a highly useful source of information, but needs a more critical eye as it is the personal site of an individual rather than a known institution.
  - The URL is also valuable in establishing the context of the resource. An account of the relevance of insurance ratings by various companies as presented on the Weiss Web site will quite naturally present a point of view that is favorable to the Weiss ratings system. This is perfectly valid information but must be recognized as information that has a vested interest.
  - Another prominent aspect of reliability is accuracy. This is gauged much as it is in print. Is there a bibliography or hyperlinks to other resources with which the searcher is familiar? Does the link seem like a good choice? Is the literature overview or the factual information used correct in the areas with which the user is familiar? If the background research is solid, it is an indication that the rest of the information may be reliable.
  - Are quotations, referrals, graphics, or statistical data well documented and fully cited? If statistical data is presented, does it provide solid data or does it resort to dubious phrases such as "a majority of" or "a large percentage" or "a significant amount" without any real numbers?

- Are there typos, spelling mistakes, or egregious grammar errors evident throughout the document?

- Currency

   Relative to print resources, Internet reference is most valued for providing the kind of currency that print formats cannot possibly supply. Minute-by-minute game plays, hourly stock updates, daily foreign news updates, weekly conference proceedings, monthly cost-of-living estimates—the scope of instant communication of information as provided by the Internet is breathtaking. The relevance of checking for currency in areas where it is required can therefore pose a very important part of evaluation. In order to check for currency

   - Scroll down to the bottom of the page where a "last updated" message may be provided.
   - If unavailable, check the site directory to see the "last modified" date.
   - Check for copyright dates.
   - Check for statements that verify that the data will be updated on a recurring basis according to a set schedule.
   - If no obvious statements of currency are available, check for more subtle signs such as whether a current event or statistic you are sure about has been included.
   - Check for giveaway statements that mention the date such as "According to a 2006 study . . ."; or even such as "Next week, the 110th Congress will open. . . ."
   - Check for multiple dead links, a sure sign that the site has been abandoned for some time.

In general, if information found on the Internet appears suspicious or dubious, it probably is. Erring on the side of caution is recommended. However, the power of Internet research is irresistible and need not be resisted. Librarians must learn to evaluate resources speedily and effectively so that snap judgements on the millions of available sites become second nature. With this skill, the nature of the medium is accepted, absorbed, and engaged. In addition, establishing a conscientious system of bookmarking favorite Web sites and creating a "Web-based reference desk" (Sauers 2001) is an effective way of adding on source-specific searches that are more akin to print research.

Practicing with the excellent *Virtual Training Suite* of free, interactive tutorials provided by the UK's *Resource Discovery Network* is a good way to develop evaluation skills. Available at www.vts.rdn.ac.uk, the site has sixty-six tutorials in various subject areas. Developing a content evaluation tool such as the one given below (figure 13-1) is another way to practice appraising a site with consistency.

WWW CYBERGUIDE RATINGS FOR CONTENT EVALUATION

Site Title: _____ Subject: _____

URL: _____ Audience: _____

Purpose for exploring this site:

_____

Notes on possible uses of this site and URLs for useful linked sites:

_____

_____

_____

To determine the worth of the Web site you are considering, evaluate its content according to the criteria described below. Circle "Y" for "Yes," "N" for "No," "NA" for "Not Applicable."

1. First look

A. User is able to quickly determine the basic content of the site.	Y	N	NA
B. User is able to determine the intended audience of the site.	Y	N	NA

2. Information Providers

A. The author(s) of the material on the site is clearly identified.	Y	N	NA
B. Information about the author(s) is available.	Y	N	NA
C. According to the info given, author(s) appears qualified to present information on this topic.	Y	N	NA
D. The sponsor of the site is clearly identified.	Y	N	NA
E. A contact person or address is available so the user can ask questions or verify information.	Y	N	NA

3. Information Currency

A. Latest revision date is provided. Date last revised_____	Y	N	NA
B. Latest revision date is appropriate to material.	Y	N	NA
C. Content is updated frequently.	Y	N	NA
D. Links to other sites are current and working properly.	Y	N	NA

4. Information Quality

A. The purpose of this site is clear: business/commercial— entertainment—informational-news—personal page— persuasion	Y	N	NA
B. The content achieves this intended purpose effectively.	Y	N	NA
C. The content appears to be complete (no "under construction" signs, for example)	Y	N	NA
D. The content of this site is well organized.	Y	N	NA
E. The information in this site is easy to understand.	Y	N	NA

F. This site offers sufficient information related to my needs/purposes.	Y	N	NA
G. The content is free of bias, or the bias can be easily detected.	Y	N	NA
H. This site provides interactivity that increases its value.	Y	N	NA
I. The information appears to be accurate based on user's previous knowledge of subject.	Y	N	NA
J. The information is consistent with similar information in other sources.	Y	N	NA
K. Grammar and spelling are correct.	Y	N	NA

5. Further Information

A. There are links to other sites that are related to my needs/purposes.	Y	N	NA
B. The content of linked sites is worthwhile and appropriate to my needs/purposes.	Y	N	NA

Totals

Based on the total of "yes" and "no" answers and your overall observations, rate the content of this site as:

____Very useful for my information needs ____Worth bookmarking for future reference____Not worth coming back to

Figure 13-1 Content Evaluation Guide, Karen McLachlan, 2002 (used with permission)

Recommendations for Further Reading

Bell, David A. 2005. "The Bookless Future." *The New Republic* (May 2–9): 27–33. The ever-elegant Bell writes a supremely cogent treatise on both the "democratizing effects" of Internet research, as well as its associated risks and ways of dealing with it. Ideas, arguments, and language come together seamlessly to provide a thought-provoking and pleasurable read.

Boyd, Rhonda S. 2005. "Assessing the True Nature of Information Transactions at a Suburban Library." *Public Libraries* (July/August): 234–240. While the article deals with far broader issues than just the assessment of transactions as suggested by the title, it offers a strong quantitative argument on the impact of Internet research on reference services and the reference staffing model best suited to accommodate this impact.

Bradley, Phil. 2004. *The Advanced Internet Searcher's Handbook, 3rd ed.* London: Facet Publishing. The strength of this title, in a long list of titles that hope to enhance the process of Web research, is its inclusion of real-life examples for all the techniques provided. Different types of search engines are analyzed by structure to help choose according to individual engine strengths. Tips for searching for multimedia information, the "hidden" Web, blogs, and information gateways are also provided along with fifty tips for better searching such as suggestions for truncating an unwieldy URL.

Hacker, Diana. 2006. *Research and Documentation in the Electronic Age, 4th edition.* Boston, MA: Bedford/St. Martins. The author, recently deceased, was able to complete a final update to this classic guide to finding, understanding, and evaluating online resources. Distinguishing between "narrow," "challenging," and "grounded" research questions, Hacker introduces the text with suggestions for mapping out an appropriate search strategy, and concludes with an extensive annotated bibliography of specialized library and Web resources.

Henninger, Maureen. 2004. *The Hidden Web: Finding Quality Information on the Net.* Sydney: University of New South Wales Press. This is a more specialized guide to Internet research in that it aims to uncover "hidden" information tucked into the folds of an HTML document, or one deeply embedded into a Web site, or a full-text document that does not require subscription to a database.

Janes, Joseph. 2003. *Introduction to Reference Work In the Digital Age.* New York: Neal-Schuman. This book is a formal study of emerging reference strategies, couched in a deceptively informal tone. It focuses on the importance of identifying user needs and utilizing new, hybrid formats and technology to supply those reference needs.

Radford, Marie L., Susan B. Barnes, and Linda R. Barr. 2005. *Web Research: Selecting, Evaluating, and Citing, 2nd ed.* Boston, MA: Allyn and Bacon. The authors provide a comprehensive and valuable overview of initiating research on the Web, mining for the best resources, and concluding Web searches with the most appropriate citations. The sensitive issue of Web copyright is also addressed.

The Scout Report. Available at http://scout.wisc.edu. Published by the reputable Internet Scout Project, the weekly report provides an update of new and evolving Internet resources that can be accessed on the Web or via direct e-mail. Each resource is annotated. The Report is a handy way to keep abreast of new and noteworthy Web sites.

Sherman, Chris. 2005. *Google Power: Unleash the Full Potential of Google.* Emeryville, CA: McGraw-Hill/Osborne Media. Recognizing that "googling" is fast evolving into a regular verb, the author provides a hands-on study of different search techniques that can enhance the results from this search engine. Some of the lesser known charms of Google, such as retrieving information from dead links and setting up automated search tool mechanisms are also outlined.

Bibliography of Works Cited in this Chapter

American Library Association. *ALA Fact Sheet Number 26: Internet Use In Libraries.* Available at www.ala.org.

Anhang, Abe. 2002. "Be It Resolved that Reference Librarians are Toast." *American Libraries* 33, no. 3 (March): 50–51.

Crawford, Walt, and Michael Gorman. 1995. *Future Libraries: Dreams, Madness, and Reality.* Chicago: American Library Association.

Foudy, Geraldine. 2000. "Wide, Wide World of Statistics: International Statistics on the Internet." *EContent* 23, no. 3 (June–July): 49–53.

Greenspan, Robyn. 2004. "OPA: Online Most Favored of All Media." (September 21). Available at www.clickz.com.

Hock, Randolph. 2004. *The Extreme Searcher's Internet Handbook: A Guide for the Serious Searcher*. Medford, NJ: CyberAge Books.

Houghton, Sarah. 2005. "Instant Messaging: Quick and Dirty Reference for Teens and Others." *Public Libraries* 44, no. 4 (July–August): 192–193.

Houghton, Sarah, and Aaron Schmidt. 2005. "Web-Based Chat vs. Instant Messaging: Who Wins?" *Online* 29, no. 4 (July–August): 26–30.

Internet Systems Consortium. *ISC Internet Domain Survey Background*. Available at www.isc.org.

"Libraries." 2005. *Chronicle of Higher Education*, Section B, September 30.

Mann, Thomas. 2005. "Google Print vs. Onsite Collections." *American Libraries* (August): 45–46.

Ross, Catherine Sheldrick, and Kirsti Nilsen. 2000. "Has the Internet Changed Anything in Reference? The Library Visit Study, Phase 2." *Reference & User Services Quarterly* (Winter): 147–155.

Sauers, Michael P. 2001. *Using the Internet as a Reference Tool*. New York: Neal-Schuman.

Selingo, Jeffrey. 2004. "When a Search Engine Isn't Enough, Call a Librarian." *New York Times*, February 5.

Sherman, Chris, and Gary Price. 2001. *The Invisible Web: Uncovering Information Sources Search Engines Can't See*. Medford, NJ: CyberAge Books.

Wilder, Larry. 2005. "Changes in Reference Service in Academic Libraries." *Illinois Library Association Reporter* 23, 1: 9.

14

Reader's Advisory Work

Mary K. Chelton

Reader's Advisory and Reference: A Marriage of Convenience

Reader's Advisory (RA) services encompass more in practice and concept than is usually included in the conventional scope of reference/information services. The latter is often defined as a method of information retrieval by a person needing utilitarian information from an information system of some kind, with or without the help of an intermediary. Consequently, reference as such tends to focus on individual service, especially on determining the specification of the user's question and the development of his or her information literacy skills. RA services, on the other hand, also reaches out to a broader audience, including casual browsers and groups, using displays, lists, formal presentations, and discussions. Further, it is as much concerned with the potential for enjoyment as it is with the rationale of a user's needs. Organizationally, RA service can be situated in other library departments, such as adult, children's, or young adult services. School libraries, especially at the elementary level, often emphasize RA service to enhance literacy development. Regardless of this distinction, however, the fact remains that in most libraries RA is delivered face to face with adults as a part of reference, making it a crucial element of this volume.

The inclusion of RA within reference flies in the face of the false dichotomy that exists, both within our profession and the larger culture, between "information" and "entertainment." "Information" supposedly encompasses useful knowledge, whereas "entertainment" is purely frivolous. Fiction ostensibly falls into the second category and skills in retrieving or suggesting fiction to readers have, as a result, been marginalized to the point that they can literally be forgotten in discussions of core services (Wiegand 2000). This is bad enough when adults are the clientele, having driven many of them to bookstores prior to interactive reader Web sites on the Internet, but it is particularly problematic for youth services, where language and literacy development are emphasized and prized. Under such circumstances, the degradation of any form of readerly engagement is to be avoided at all costs. In addition, many youth reference queries are at least partially RA. For example, students required by a teacher to read a historical novel set in certain period in U.S. history, or in some instances just to read a novel, might need to take advantage of the reference department.

Catherine Ross (1999a) has looked at what information readers get from fiction in "Finding Without Seeking: The Information Encounter in the Context of Reading for Pleasure," in which she lists the non-goal-oriented information (i.e., problem-solving information) encountered by readers in their interactions with texts. She also directly challenges the prevalent cognitive model of information seeking in the profession and reiterates the importance of an affective dimension in finding information:

> Constructing the searcher/reader as a rational, goal-directed individual who is engaged primarily in problem-solving downplays the role played by feeling. The reported research with pleasure-readers suggests that the affective dimension is involved throughout the process, from choosing a book according to mood to valuing a book for its emotional support in providing confirmation, reassurance, courage or self-acceptance. What readers said about risk-taking—that the choice of familiar and unchallenging vs. novel and challenging materials depends on the level of stress in the rest of their life—may turn out to be generalizable to goal-directed information seeking situations as well.

Ross's research with readers, like Kuhlthau's on the information search process (2004), makes the point that information seeking has both cognitive and affective dimensions, and that the affective dimension is particularly important for pleasure readers who do find information in their reading.

Jessica Moyer (2004), following Ross's lead, examines the educational outcomes of reading fiction, hypothesizing that reading a book can have both educational and recreational outcomes. Based on a factor analysis of her interview data, she finds such outcomes in four categories: people and relationships; other countries, cultures, and time periods; enriching one's life; and gaining access to different perspectives.

While such research is sparser than would be desired, the fact that information science actually has a term for it—"incidental information" (Williamson 1998)—suggests that pleasure readers are relegated too easily to the "entertainment" and opposite side of the false dichotomy between "information" and "entertainment." In RA services, librarians must understand that both information and entertainment are involved in reading when they help readers locate books. The arrival of the computer does not mean that all information and learning is now electronic.

Common RA Questions

Nearly every practicing librarian has, at some point in his or her career, received any one of three variants on a common question. Some users are content to simply ask, "Can you recommend a good book to read?" Others, aiming for the personal, go further, querying, "What have you read lately that's good?" A few more tend toward the specific with requests such as "I just read Jodi Picoult's book, My Sister's Keeper and loved it. Could you recommend another one like it?"

These three questions are *all* variations on the same theme, namely what the user means by a "good book." In addition, the first two questions are deceptive because "good book" does not necessarily mean "of high literary quality." Nor do they appeal to the librarian's own definition of "good." The reference librarian needs to find out what "good book" means to the person asking. It is helpful to ask the person to tell you about a book he or she has enjoyed or loathed; once that is understood, find out whether they are in the mood for the same kind of "good" book or something different, and if the latter, how different. Depending on whether the user has given an author or title, one can use *NoveList*'s "Search Our Database" > "Find a favorite author (or title)" > "Find similar books" feature to answer this question. If the person cannot remember a specific title, the librarian can ask them to describe an ideal story and use *NoveList*'s (www.epnet.com) "Search Our Database" > "Describe a Plot" feature to pull up likely titles. If the library does not have NoveList, try another tool, such as a book like *Genreflecting* or *What Do I Read Next?* although such printed volumes are rarely as versatile as a truly dynamic database.

For the third question, the reference librarian needs to find out what the person liked about the book, whether he or she might like to try another one by the same author who, in this case, tends always to write compelling stories with the same appeal, or a different author. In other words, find out why the person thinks this title is a "good book," and depending on what the person says, proceed exactly as in the first question with *NoveList*.

I've been put in charge of our book club group for our next meeting and have no clue what to do. Can you help me?

The reference librarian needs to find out more about the book group, whether they have already picked a title for discussion, and what the person wants specifically. If the group has picked a title, check *NoveList* under "For Readers" > "Book Discussion Guides" if the person needs questions for discussion. If nothing appropriate is found there, a variety of online resources are available, such as www.readinggroupchoices.com and ReadingGroupGuides.com. Many major book publishers also have book group guides available on their Web sites (e.g., www.randomhouse.com/reader_resources/browsetitle or www.harpercollins.com/hc/readers/index.asp) as do the major online bookstores (amazon and Barnes and Noble). If no guide already exists, or if the group has not yet selected a title, the person should be directed to one of the many books on organizing book discussion groups, such as the *New York Public Library Guide to Reading Groups*, or *What to Read: The Essential Guide for Reading Group Members and Other Book Lovers*.

Unfortunately, many reader's advisory questions go unasked. It is important to realize that many people looking for something "good" to read will never approach a reference librarian to ask anything, but rather, will browse displays and shelves. It is important to watch for and offer help to these people when they exhaust their own resources. Setting up appropriate displays is another means of helping them; although such activities are usually not discussed in this context, there are books on reader's advisory services that explain how to do this.

The Reader's Advisory Interview

Once the encounter with a patron seeking reader's advisory help has begun, it is crucial that the librarian determine as much information as possible about the user's needs and interests. Most people call this dialogue the "RA Interview," but the word "interview" usually implies a question and answer forum, an interrogation that would be controlled by the librarian from the outset. Such an approach is better suited for the retrieval of facts for information seekers than for discovering what someone likes to read. In RA interactions, where mapping moods and attitudes is more important than determining how much factual information is needed and how it is to be used, another strategy is called for.

Consider the example of two different kinds of reference requests about travel. If someone is planning a trip to Australia, the classic reference interview format is sufficient, insofar as it allows the librarian to determine what the user needs to know. If, on the other hand, their interest is in vicarious journeys, it is important to seek out clues that will reveal the tone of the texts they enjoy, as opposed to the amount of raw information they need. Getting the user to reveal, for example, that he or she loves funny travel books, regardless of where they take place, meaning that he or she is an ideal reader for Bill Bryson's books, is less straightforward. The other aspect of the RA encounter that distinguishes it from the reference interview is that even within the limitations of this kind of assessment, there is no immediate way to assess the aptness of a recommendation until the user actually sits down and reads it. Accuracy, in fact, is irrelevant to many fiction readers who want to escape from mundane reality.

Saricks (2005), in *Readers' Advisory Services in the Public Library*, suggests that the librarian start the RA encounter like a conversation by asking the person to tell about a book that he or she has recently read and enjoyed. Most people cannot say specifically what kind of story they want except for the vague "good book," which is meaningless in RA terms without knowing what they mean by it; but they can usually talk about a title they have liked or disliked and why. With knowledge of appeal factors, the librarian can then listen for descriptors that suggest whether a person may like plot- or character-driven books, contemporary or historical or fantastic settings, male or female narrators, or any other such distinguishing information. The librarian can also listen for rejection factors such as the common ones of "too much sex and violence," or "alternating viewpoints."

A failure to understand appeal factors can lead to a mistake where books are suggested based only on theme, topic, or some subcategory similarity such as "legal thriller," when the authors themselves handle the themes or subcategories quite differently in terms of appeal. This is not to say that some readers are not varied in their tastes, nor omnivorous in terms of a subcategory, but the range of their interests cannot be automatically assumed. One such mistake of this kind would be to offer books on serial killers as a topical readalike for those who enjoyed *The Lovely Bones*, a book that is really about a family's healing from the unimaginable loss of their daughter, simply because the protagonist in it is murdered by a serial killer.

Ross (1999b) and Ross and Chelton (2001) suggest that one of the most important factors for avid adult readers in selecting books is what reading experience they are in the mood for. They may be looking for something different from the title they have just described, regardless of whether they remember enjoying it or not, so the librarian should ask them about their current needs before starting to look for possible reading suggestions. Ross describes mood preferences along six dimensions: 1) familiarity vs. novelty; 2) safety vs. risk; 3) easy vs. challenging; 4) upbeat and positive vs. hard-hitting/ironical/cynical; 5) reassuring vs. stimulating/frightening/amazing; and 6) confirming of beliefs and values vs. challenging them. Mood, of course, varies. When readers are busy or under stress, they often want safety, reassurance, and confirmation. They will reread old favorites or read new books by trusted authors. When life is less stressful, they can afford to take more risks and may want to be amazed by something unpredictable.

Common Mistakes in the RA Encounter

Poor Interpersonal Communication

As with the other forms of reference service described throughout this text, poor communication can severely mar the process, making it an unsatisfactory experience for the user. The first interpersonal mistake librarians make is to lose eye contact with the reader. This avoidance behavior is often compounded by the pretense that everything the librarian is doing on the computer is some sort of secret ritual that the user should just accept without explanation. Continuing to pay attention to users and inviting them to look at the computer while the librarian searches and explains what he or she is doing is more appropriate. Failing to provide such information and attention can leave the user confused, uncertain whether a service is actually being providing. This sense of bafflement also occurs when librarians leave the desk to search for specific books or colleagues to help answer the query without providing some indication as to where they are going or inviting the user to come along.

Beyond increasing the user's comfort, observation of his or her nonverbal reactions can let the librarian know if he or she is on the right track. Listening to the reader's unsolicited as well as solicited comments can be useful to the librarian. The user has to be regarded as the primary source of information in a reader's advisory interaction, just as they are in a classic reference interview.

Before the interaction with patrons begins, librarians often do not appear "askable," nor do they always greet users. Users occasionally have to interrupt conversations between librarians at the desk, a move with which many may not be comfortable. Other patrons have to calm librarians visibly upset because they don't know how to answer RA questions, are unfamiliar with sources when they do use them, or are annoyed with the users because it is too close to closing time. Often, service librarians fail to greet readers with a "hello," and visibly reveal their irritation with users who have RA questions. This is bad service regardless of whether it involves reader's advisory or classic reference. Needless to say, none of these scenarios are desirable or result in positive user experiences.

Inappropriate OPAC Use

Foreclosing—the premature assumption that the librarian knows what the person wants before he or she has finished explaining or before the librarian has finished eliciting enough information to understand the question—is as common in RA work as in conventional reference. Many librarians turn immediately to Online Public Access Catalogs to identify other titles by the same author before asking the reader whether he or she had read other books by the author, or what the reader likes about the particular book. This problem is now rampant in public libraries, and an increased computer dependence of staff combined with a lack of background in popular reading seems to be making it worse. Worse still, these librarians never tell or show the user what they are doing on the computer, making it all look hermetic, magical, and obscure.

Looking up other books by the same author in an OPAC gives the librarian something to do, but it is rarely correct. Instead, the librarian should continue the interaction with the reader until certain of what the person wants. Since good subject headings for fiction are not specific enough in traditionally catalogued OPAC databases, and keyword searching may be just a sort of "scattershot" approach, first resorting to an OPAC before talking more to the reader and consulting RA reference tools is usually not helpful. Librarians who do not read popular fiction or know anything about the genre being described by the user should remember that many authors write books of different categories. Assuming that another title by the same author will have the same appeal is therefore often a mistake.

Query Avoidance and Lack of Follow-up

It is generally not considered ethical for reference librarians to refuse to answer a question about which they have no personal knowledge. The same is true of reader's advisors, but it seems almost the norm when librarians are asked RA questions about a genre they do not read personally. Excusing one's own ignorance is not the same as answering the user's question, nor is it professional behavior. A librarian asked about cancer would never dream of saying, "I have never had cancer, so I cannot answer that," but many feel no problem with saying, "I do not read that kind of book," and ending the interview there.

Reference librarians are obliged to document the sources for the information they provide and avoid off-the-cuff responses, and reader's advising practice demands no less. The numerous reference tools devoted to books in general as well as to specific genres should be consulted before checking availability in an OPAC. One of the biggest myths among librarians about RA services is that the librarian must have read the book personally to suggest it, without resorting to any reference sources. At an absolute minimum, librarians should be familiar with the top ten RA Resources listed below. Tempting as they are, the auto-recommendation lists generated by amazon.com and Barnes and Noble online (bn.com) should be avoided. While these suggestions do pick up readalikes, they are generated through patterns of associative buying, not designed by a careful analysis of the appeal factors of particular books and, depending on the query, can be as misleading as helpful. Instead, librarians should look to the appropriate professional resources when met with the unknown.

When readers are referred to shelves to search for themselves, it is important to follow up and see if they find anything. Often librarians act as if their job is sending everyone off to help themselves, assuming that they will find what they want. At a minimum, the librarian should tell the user to come back if he or she does not find anything, a simple suggestion that is almost never implemented. If a library has few sources like displays and lists available to readers in addition to staff, referring users to shelves arranged in alphabetical order, spine out, makes follow-up is even more important, since browsing is more difficult under those circumstances.

Reader's Advisory Reference Tools

The ideal RA tool should have multiple access points, be linked to a library or library system's holdings, and be indexed by those factors that most appeal to readers, such as pacing and characterization, in addition to more traditional index terms such as genre, setting, historical period, award category (if any), and gender or occupation of the protagonist. Such a tool would have to be digital, featuring flexibility of access in searching, and the combination of both natural language and controlled vocabulary in its search options. Unfortunately, such a perfect tool does not yet exist, and formal cataloging for OPACs does little to rectify the situation, despite some overdue attention given to genre subject headings a few years ago in a project cosponsored by ALA's Association for Library Collections & Technical Services division and Online Computer Library Center. Annalise Petersen has done pioneering work of this kind in Denmark, but it has not been replicated in the North American context.

The usefulness of any RA tool will vary based on the kinds of questions asked, but RA tools generally fall into and should be evaluated against reference needs in five categories: content (general or specific), scope (time period covered, genre or mainstream, adult or juvenile, in print or out of print), originator (librarian or librarian/fan or fan/non-librarian), format (print or electronic), and purpose (reader's guide or collection development tool). All tools are only as good as their currency, the expertise of their creators, the way they are indexed and may be searched, and their relevance to local library collections. Identifying something a reader wants, only to have to borrow it from another library on interlibrary loan, unless the reader is a diehard fan of whatever is requested, can be a frustrating experience, solved when reference librarians can suggest more than one item to fit the reader's mood and interests.

The Top Ten RA Tools

1. *NoveList/Book Index to Reviews (BIR)*
    The nearest thing to the ideal tool, and the one that librarians should be most familiar with, is *NoveList*, a licensed searchable fiction database of over 125,000 titles (soon to include popular nonfiction) from EBSCO Publishing. Developed initially by Duncan Smith and Roger Rohweder, the tool allows searching by author, title, series, a variety of traditional index terms, natural language terms or phrases, and Boolean combinations. The latter are particularly important because the elusive appeal and mood factors are more often captured in a reviewer's or reader's own words and adjectives, than in more formally assigned subject headings. Saricks calls this "the vocabulary of appeal" (2005). Using the Boolean search function, you can also search for reviews that mention when a title is written much like "so and so's book" or in the same style as "so and so's book" and then use NOT to exclude the titles by that author. The "Learning Center" section of *NoveList* includes self-help sections to teach users how to search the database and also how to take advantage of the customized content added to the database at the Browse Lists, For Readers, Reader's Advisory, and School Resources tabs. This content (such as Author Read-alikes, What We're Reading, book discussions, and more) is developed especially for *NoveList* and its customers. Citations in *NoveList* also include

links to author Web sites and to the value-added content in the database itself, such as readalike lists, feature articles, annotated lists from selected readers, etc.

The creators of *NoveList* have developed a companion product called *Book Index to Reviews* (*BIR*), also published by EBSCO, which allows users to search the Baker & Taylor inventory database to find lists of books on topics of interest. *BIR* offers a wide variety of search terms, many of them relevant for RA, such as publication date, reading level, audience level, whether the user wants fiction or nonfiction, and limits on the number of pages. There is also a browsing function. *BIR* includes both fiction and nonfiction. There are many other RA tools besides *NoveList* and *BIR*, although none as generally useful for so many purposes, or as flexible in terms of search options.

2. *BookSpot.com.*
BookSpot is a compendium of news about books, publishing, authors, and awards, covering all ages, with numerous reviews and a great deal of genre-specific information. Also including links to the book review pages of major U.S. newspapers and to book excerpts, this site is enormously useful, though reference librarians need to be familiar with it to use it well. The excerpts are particularly important because first paragraphs or selections of text allow readers to sense the "feel" or "frame" of a story to get an idea of whether they might like it or not. This site provides direct access to *Publishers Weekly*. After *NoveList*, *BookSpot.com* offers more one-stop looking.

3. *AllReaders.com*
While this Web site duplicates the previous two resources, what makes it so useful is its Gordonator Precision Search Function for genre categories, which allows searchers to match many appeal characteristics such as "difficult/unusual lover" for romance, or "spying/terrorism" for thrillers, etc. Searchers can even specify the age of the character. An examination of the requirements for reviews shows how this is possible, because reviewers are asked to specify certain things about the books they review.

4. *What Do I Read Next?*
Started by a Gale editor who worked part-time in a used-book store, this series is organized to help librarians make suggestions and, as the name suggest, readers to decide what to read next. Each entry describes a separate book, listing everything readers need to know to make selections. Arranged by author within six genre sections, detailed entries provide: Title, publisher, and publication date, series, names and descriptions of characters, time period and geographical setting, review citations, story types, brief plot summaries, selected other books by the author, and similar books by different authors. Author, title, series, character name, character description, time period, geographic setting and genre/sub-genre indexes are included to facilitate research. While the print versions are annual volumes, they are all combined into a licensed database called *What Do I Read Next?*

5. *Genreflecting*
Not a single text, but a set of tools produced in the Genreflecting series from Libraries Unlimited/Greenwood, these books include the signature title, *Genreflecting:*

A Guide to Reading Interests in Genre Fiction and at least thirteen other genre-specific guides plus a Web site (www.genreflecting.com) with links to other RA resources and a new newsletter on RA services. Well edited and written by experts, these annotated guides are indispensable for many RA questions, their only weakness being that they are not yet wholly electronic.

6. *FictionDB.com*

    Started in 1999 with the intention of providing "accurate and reliable information for readers of genre fiction," this subscription site (although the first month is free) offers reviews, author pseudonyms, series and upcoming releases information, author Web sites and a way to buy and sell books to keep track of your own reading. There are also links to other related genre and publisher sites.

7. *Fiction_L*

    Started by Roberta Johnson while she was still a library school student and working at the Morton Grove Public Library in Illinois, the Fiction_L Listserv is a godsend for many librarians doing RA work because it functions as a communal mind of collegial professional helpers. Many posts begin with, "I have a patron who . . ." followed by further elaboration about desired readalikes, queries about forgotten titles of favorite books, and so on. While one often wishes that all the list subscribers did better RA interviews before going online, at least frantic reference librarians are guaranteed some level of help very quickly. The list is housed on the MGPL home Web site, along with all the member-generated readalike lists. Beside readalike and title identification assistance, the list members identify and comment on useful tools, discuss titles and discussion guides for library-based reading groups, and even discuss briefly books that they have read. A staple is the "Best Books of the Year" list.

8. *What's Next*

    One of the more frustrating reference RA questions can be finding a single title or all the titles in a series in order. To help rectify this, the Kent District Library (www.kdl.org) has created a research database called *What's Next*, which can be searched by author, title, or series under the "research tools" category on their home page.

9. *www.audiofilemagazine.com/audiofileplus.html*

    The popularity of audiobooks, especially in new downloadable formats, necessitates knowledge of and attention to what is going on in the industry, and there is no place better than the expanded version of *AudioFile Magazine* online. Besides discussions of industry trends, the "golden-voiced" narrators who read the books, the award winners in various genre and age categories, as well as reviews of current and forthcoming audiobooks, the expanded electronic version offers access to 17,000 archived reviews, links to audiobook publishers, a reference guide to the industry, and search capability.

10. *Reader's Guide to Genre Fiction*

    Based on the work that Joyce Saricks and her staff at the Downer's Grove Public Library did in their "genre studies," this book lists key authors and titles in specific genres, explains the appeal of the genre and its subgenres, and provides lists for people coming into or willing to leave a favorite genre to try something new.

The book should probably be at every reference desk for helping users and self-training during down times.

Other RA tools are listed at the end of this chapter.

Collection Development and Maintenance

Selection and Keeping Current

Reading genre fan magazines and Web sites, such as *Romantic Times Book Club* and www.rwanational.com for romance and romance hybrids, or *Locus* and www.sfsite.com/home.htm for science fiction, fantasy, and horror, or *Deadly Pleasures* and cluelass.com for mysteries, especially for awards, features, and author profiles, is helpful for name recognition, as are the feature articles and author interviews in *Publishers Weekly*. Since *NoveList*/EBSCO, ALA Editions, Thompson/Gale and Greenwood/Libraries Unlimited are the main publishers of RA tools, looking at their Web sites for new offerings regularly will help identify both new tools such as *NoveList*'s readalike lists, and updates of old favorites, such as Libraries Unlimited's *Genreflecting*.BookSpot.com offers information about publishing, awards, bestsellers, the book review sections of major papers, etc., in one place.

Both the Public Library Association (PLA) and the Reference and User Services Association (RUSA), divisions of ALA, have standing committees devoted to RA services, so their publications, *Public Libraries* from PLA and *RUSA Quarterly* from RUSA usually include articles on RA services and reviews of tools. Both divisions offer programs at ALA's annual and divisional regional conferences on RA topics. The other way of staying current at the local level is to use part of every staff meeting to share new questions (and answers) and new tools with each other, and to know about and use colleagues' expertise for mini-workshops on particular questions about what they know best.

Bibliography of Works Cited in this Chapter

Kuhlthau, Carol Collier. 2004. *Seeking Meaning: A Process Approach to Library and Information Services*. 2nd ed. Westport, CT: Libraries Unlimited.

Moyer, Jessica E. 2004. "Learning from Leisure Reading: Educational and Recreational Outcomes of Leisure Reading—A Study of Adult Public Library Patrons." (Certificate of Advanced Study Project Report), Urbana-Champaign: University of Illinois, September 21.

Pejtersen, Annelise Mark, and Jutta Austin. 1983. "Fiction retrieval: Experimental Design and Evaluation of a Search System Based on Users' Value Criteria. Part 1." *Journal of Documentation* 39, no. 4 (December): 230–246.

———. 1984. "Fiction Retrieval: Experimental Design and Evaluation of a Search System Based on Users' Value Criteria. Part 2." *Journal of Documentation* 40, no. 1 (March): 25–35.

Ross, Catherine Sheldrick. 1999a. "Finding without Seeking: The Information Encounter in the Context of Reading for Pleasure." *Information Processing and Management* 35, no. 6 (November): 783–799.

———. 1999b. *A Model for the Process of Choosing a Book For Pleasure.* Handout. Public Library Association Spring Symposium.

Ross, Catherine Sheldrick, and Mary K. Chelton. 2001. "Reader's Advisory: Matching Mood and Material." *Library Journal* 126, no. 2 (February 1): 52–56.

Saricks, Joyce G. 2005. *Readers' Advisory Service in the Public Library.* 3rd ed. Chicago: American Library Association.

Wiegand, Wayne. 2000. "Librarians Ignore the Value of Stories." *Chronicle of Higher Education* 47, no. 9 (October 27): B20.

Williamson, Kirsty. 1998. "Discovered by Chance: The Role of Incidental Information Acquisition in an Ecological Model of Information Use." *Library & Information Science Research* 20, 1: 23–40.

15

Reference Work with Children and Young Adults

Mary K. Chelton

Introduction

Young people are a special reference audience for several reasons. First of all, they are a major clientele in public libraries, where librarians themselves report that 60 percent of the users are under eighteen (NCES 1995), and in school libraries they *are* the primary clientele. While they have personal information needs and interests like anyone else, young people usually use library reference services primarily for homework assignments that have been imposed on them by adults. These "imposed queries" (Gross 1995) pose interesting problems for reference librarians because of the difficulty inherent in interviewing someone who does not know or care enough about what he or she needs. Clarifying the question without forcing an answer is difficult, and, even in the best of circumstances, is hardly the ideal situation for a good reference interview. Many children and adolescents are given the same assignments at the same time, stretching resources beyond what they may have been intended for. Further, parents coming to "help" their children with homework queries often add to the confusion as they tend to know even less about what is needed than the young person does.

Librarians sometimes mistakenly assume that every assignment is intended to teach students how to do research. Alternately, others believe that kids have been taught how to do it by someone else. Compounding this possible confusion, teachers are often clueless about how much research and resources are needed to do something they regard as a simple assignment. All of this can make reference service to youth a very frustrating experience for everyone concerned unless the stakes are understood at the outset and necessary precautions are put into place.

Information Literacy Instruction and Youth Information-Seeking Behavior

Information literacy, which will be discussed in greater detail in the next chapter, is the ability to access, evaluate, and use information responsibly (American Association of School Librarians 1998). Whether or not the instructional role is mandated—as it is in school libraries through national professional standards—librarians doing reference work with young people in today's highly technological library environments need to make information literacy instruction a large part of their interactions with kids. Since most reference librarians feel that their job is either to locate information for people or help them locate it for themselves, they need to understand that many youngsters lack even the experience needed to evaluate and synthesize the information they find into something meaningful. Even clarifying the question for these users places the reference librarian in the role of an instructor of information literacy, even if only by the questions asked. Locating information comes at the end of a process that is unknown to many youths, and good reference librarians understand this.

A New York City school librarian is fond of relating the story of a middle school student who needed a picture of Mary Todd Lincoln, and typed "Mrs. Lincoln" into Google's search field, printed out the photo of a New Jersey woman in full wedding regalia from her wedding photos on the Web. Only upon questioning by the librarian did she decide that Abraham Lincoln's wife probably had not looked or dressed that way. The idea of broadening or narrowing a topic, using quotes to join words together in a search, or using Boolean logic to join or exclude terms and concepts, to give just three examples, are largely unknown among most youth. Likewise, few young students have been taught to evaluate the materials they find in their research efforts for quality, relevance, and authority. If a word they find matches the word in an assignment, they print it out, going no further. They also do not know what to do when they get stuck during a search with no idea what to do next, are unaware of simple navigation commands to shortcut the search process, and are easily distracted by essentially meaningless visuals (see Shenton and Dixon 2004 for an overview of research in this area). A knowledge, not only of the common mistakes in information-seeking behavior by kids, but also of specialized search engines geared toward their needs (Haycock et al. 2003) is essential.

Finally, the idea of intellectual property is alien to kids used to cutting and pasting their way around the Internet in the belief that all of it is free for the taking. All of these problematic behaviors (also shared by many adults), have a silver lining in that they present eminently teachable moments for information literacy instruction by good school and academic librarians, as eloquently discussed by Harris (2005). Unfortunately, they can also be an endless source of annoyance to overworked public librarians inundated with kids after school.

Developmental Barriers and Perceptions of Helpfulness

Developmentally, young people often lack the vocabulary to generate synonyms or the specialized vocabulary for a new subject they are still learning. Lacking hypothetical thinking strategies, they wait until the last minute to do dreaded assignments. They can also lack background knowledge on topics they are asked to research, and many do not understand that surfing the Web is not the same as searching for specific information using well-defined search strategies. Worst of all, they do not perceive many adult reference librarians as helpful because they have long experience of being treated shabbily by librarians and many other adults who act as though they do not want them around. The following quote from a harried public library reference librarian is an example of a common attitude toward adolescents:

I'll be happy to tell you why I find this age group "problematic." So many come to the reference desk with no idea of why they are there. They shove a sheet of paper in my face and say "this is my homework. Where I can I find this?" When I ask them what the assignment is, they appear to be looking at it for the very first time. Or they simply mumble "I don't know." It's the total lack of concern and the assumption that I'll figure it all out for them and go fetch the materials that irritates me.

We have OPACS, and many of these patrons won't even go near them. When I ask them if they've checked the catalog, they reply they don't know how to use it. They will ask for staples, paper, directions, permission to use the phone, but they won't ask for help using the OPACS. They don't come to library for any other purpose than to socialize and bother patrons who have legitimate business in the library. We're across the street from a high school. At 2:45, it's like a parade that crosses the street and enters the library. We hired a monitor to do nothing else but to keep order in the library when the teenagers are here. In contrast to those who won't use the OPACS are the ones who love to bring a terminal down by screwing around in the DOS program. We have security features, but some have figured this out. One will bring it to my attention that a terminal is down, then two or three of his friends eagerly wait for me to log back on so they can watch. (I'm wise to this.)

I know I sound "negative" but so many patrons in this age group don't need the services of the library or the librarians. They simply want a place to hang out until their parents pick them up. I love helping a kid find stuff for a tough research project. I enjoy taking vague questions and formulating reference questions. But having homework assignments and reading lists shoved in my face by healthy, intelligent, able-bodied young people who have no interest in their own homework just plain "bugs" me. (Chelton 1997, 2002)

This perception of unhelpfulness carries over beyond homework help to everyday personal information seeking. For example, Julien (1998, 1999) noted that libraries were rarely seen as a source of information by teenagers in career decision making.

Research and Assignment Topics

Since so many youth research or report topics are determined by school curricula, there is a seasonal redundancy that allows reference librarians to anticipate demands, so they are not caught off guard. A recent query to relevant professional Listservs came up with the following repeated cyclical list, which varied by grade level: explorers, *Romeo and Juliet*, civil rights, aspects of life for someone in the Middle Ages, gangs, banned books, cloning, legalization of marijuana, science fair projects, famous buildings, ancient

Egypt, biomes, American presidents and states, countries, mammals, the Civil War, elements, ancient civilizations, scientists, inventions and inventors, hurricanes, Native American legends, famous African Americans (in February) and women (in March), endangered species, the Holocaust, engineered food, saints, leaf identification, careers, drugs, alcohol, and smoking, diseases (such as bubonic plague, AIDS, STDs), rainforests, literary criticism, dinosaurs, solar system, and animals.

Many topics that are self-chosen by students within teacher-mandated parameters can be on controversial topics. They hear about the topics on the news and want to know more. On other occasions, well-intentioned social studies teachers assign debate questions, or the students are told to write something rhetorical about a topic from a specific point of view. These choices make the *Opposing Viewpoints* series and accompanying database published by Greenhaven Press, a division of Thomson Gale, particularly valuable for reference work with youth. Now over ninety volumes, the *Opposing Viewpoints* series, as the publisher says, "offers divergent points of view on controversial social, political, and economic issues. By using primary sources presented in a pro/con format, the *Opposing Viewpoints* series offers high school students an invaluable tool for conducting research and sharpening their critical thinking skills" (www .galegroup.com/greenhaven/about.htm).

Solutions to Common Problems in Reference Work with Youth

Mass Assignments

While it would be nice if mass assignments disappeared, they probably will not, because curricula determine that a certain number of children or adolescents must cover certain topics in a specific order during the year. Asking teachers to customize each report or research project for the convenience of librarians is as unrealistic as it is misguided for librarians to vilify teachers for not doing so. Being familiar with local school curricula topics and sequencing should help reference librarians plan better responses through strategies like acquiring duplicate materials in advance of assignment deadlines, creating temporary reserve lists of relevant circulating materials, and creating reference pathfinders on repeated topics. In schools, collaboration with classroom teachers in the design of assignments also helps.

School and public librarians should keep in touch with each other about both upcoming assignments and those that become problematic. A reminder to faculty at the beginning of each semester to state in writing on assignments that librarians are allowed to offer alternatives when all resources are out or in use averts student frustration. Librarians can also distribute teacher alert forms and business cards with contact information in order to improve the early warning system. Should things get especially bad, the use of some sort of standard notification form to teachers might be helpful if the tone is right. Examples of such forms from *Connecting Young Adults and Libraries* (Jones 2004) appear below. Mass assignments will never go away entirely, but the frustration they cause librarians, parents, and students can be managed with good communication, anticipation, and preparation. Reference librarians should remember that if they were notified of every assignment in advance, they would have time to do

Assignment Alert Form

Dear Media Specialist,

As you know, often students will use the public library to find resources to complete assignments. Help us help them by alerting us as soon as possible to assignments which require library use. Together, we can help students use the wide variety of resources available in libraries, both school and public.

MEDIA SPECIALIST:_____ DATE:_____

SCHOOL:_____ TEACHER:_____

GRADE:_____ CLASS:_____ #STUDENTS:_____

ASSIGNMENT:_____

_____

DATE ASSIGNMENT IS DUE:_____

SPECIAL REQUIREMENTS (# OF SOURCES, LIMITS, ETC):

_____

_____

Letter to Teacher

Dear Teacher,

During the past week, I've been able to help several students from your _____ class work on their homework assignment/term paper. I'm delighted to see that you have encouraged them to use our library. Thank you.

There is one thing that you could do to help us help your students learn even more. Some students won't ask for assistance, and others simply won't come to the library. You could help us help your students by:

• Arranging for them to visit the library as a group to receive library instruction

• Notifying us (and your school librarian) at least a week in advance of assignments so we may gather materials for them

• Allowing us to prepare pathfinders or other handouts which would help them help themselves

Again, I'm pleased to see so many of your students in our library. Please contact me so we can arrange the activities mentioned above to benefit your students. In this "information age," it is important that all students learn how to access the vast amount of information available to them; that is why we're here and we'd like the opportunity to work with your students at your convenience.

Sincerely,

Materials Unavailable Card

LIBRARY:_____ DATE:____

Dear Teacher,

Your student _____came to the library today to find materials on
_____. We are sorry to report that we were
unable to help your student because:

_____ All materials were checked out

_____ A reasonable search failed to find materials.

_____ Materials are for "in library" use only

_____ Clarification of request is needed

_____ Other:_____

If you have any questions, please contact me. Often we can better help students and reduce their frustration in using libraries when we are notified in advance about school assignments like this one. Then, we can provide instruction and gather materials and other services to benefit all of your students.

LIBRARIAN:_____ PHONE#:_____ EMAIL_____

nothing else, making universal notification an ideal that ultimately leads to its own frustrations.

Parents Doing Homework

Public librarians can get very moralistic about parents who come in to get materials for a child's report, and this second-hand interview with someone who is even more distant from the query can lead to total confusion. That being said, such professional judgments are self-defeating and do nothing make the "problem" go away. The solution is to do the best job possible under the circumstances and leave the person with the impression that the librarian has been helpful. Whatever family situation prompts the parent to act as proxy for a child, it is neither of the librarian's making nor within his or her purview to change. Since there is usually some confusion in such encounters, offering to take follow-up calls, e-mails, or visits to clarify the assignment further is necessary, as is offering multiple options to answer the query so the parent does not leave with just one possibly incorrect resource.

If the child or adolescent is with the parent, try to talk directly to the young person, although this can be difficult, because inevitably the parent answers. Usually, if they are there together, it is because the youth is clueless and the parent is frustrated already, so the best the librarian can do is "no harm."

Reader's Advisory Questions in Youth Reference Services

Many youth reference questions arrive as reader's advisory questions, such as being assigned to read a novel about a period in history or one that has won an award. Reference librarians should stock and consult one of the many youth references sources designed to help with such queries. Examples include titles like *American Historical Fiction: An Annotated Guide to Novels for Adults and Young Adults* by Lynda G. Adamson; *Middle Ages in Literature for Youth: A Guide and Resource Book* by Rebecca Barnhouse; *World's Best Thin Books: Or What to Read When Your Book Report is Due Tomorrow* by Joni Bodart; *Guide to Collective Biographies for Children and Young Adults* by Sue Barancik; or ALA's *Newbery and Caldecott Awards: A Guide to the Medal and Honor Books*.

Conclusion

It seems silly to remind reference librarians that children and adolescents are worthy of their professional assistance, but unfortunately, it is a point that needs repeating. Too many people attracted to reference service for the intellectual thrill of playing information detective fail to develop a strong service orientation grounded in the needs of real users. Fortunately, the needs of contemporary youth—informational as well as social—are well documented in library and information science research literature. The real question is whether librarians' attitudes can adjust to meet those kids who deserve—and need—more from reference librarians than impatience and neglect. Whether they remain an underserved group or are tapped as an ideal audience for formative instruction and assistance depends greatly on the attitudes of the librarians they encounter.

Bibliography of Works Cited in this Chapter

American Association of School Librarians and Association for Educational Communications and Technology. 1998. *Information Power: Building Partnerships for Learning*. Chicago: American Library Association.

Chelton, Mary K. 1997. *Adult-Adolescent Service Encounters: The Library Context.* Brunswick, NJ: Rutgers University. Doctoral dissertation.

———. 2002. "The 'Problem Patron' Public Libraries Created." *Reference Librarian,* nos. 75–76 (June): 23–33.

Fidel, Raya, Rachel K. Davies, and Mary H. Douglas. 1999. "Visit to the Information Mall: Web Searching Behavior of High School Students." *Journal of the American Society for Information Science* 50, 24–37.

Greenhaven Press. *Homepage.* Available at www.galegroup.com/greenhaven/about.htm.

Gross, Melissa. 1995. "Imposed Query." *RQ* 35, 1: 236–243.

Harris, Frances Jacobsen. 2005. *I Found It on the Internet: Coming of Age Online.* Chicago: American Library Association.

Haycock, Ken, Michele Dober, and Barbara Edwards. 2003. *Neal-Schuman Authoritative Guide to Kids' Search Engines, Subject Directories, and Portals.* New York: Neal-Schuman.

Jones, Patrick, Michele Gorman, and Tricia Suellentrop. 2004. *Connecting Young Adults and Libraries*. 3rd ed. New York: Neal-Schuman.

Julien, Heidi. 1998. "Adolescent Career Decision Making and the Potential Role of the Public Library." *Public Libraries* (November–December): 376–381.

———. 1999. "Adolescents' Information Seeking for Career Decision Making." *Journal of the American Society for Information Science* 50, no. 1 (January): 38–48.

National Center for Education Statistics. 1995. *Services for Children and Young Adults in Public Libraries*. (NCES 95-731). Washington, DC: U.S. Government Printing Office.

Shenton, Andrew K, and Pat Dixon. 2004. "Issues Arising from Youngsters' Information-seeking Behavior," *Library & Information Science Research* 26, no. 2 (Spring): 177–200.

16

User Instruction in the Reference Department

Modern libraries—whether public, academic, special, or otherwise—are far more than mere storehouses for books and magazines. The dusty monastic scriptoriums of the ancient past, in which volumes were literally chained to the shelves and kept from all but a select few, have all but vanished. With few exceptions, today's libraries exist as spaces of dynamic learning in which we actively engage with the products and processes of our culture, exploring the associations and connections between the disparate elements of our changing world. To do so, however, we first need to understand how to use the resources available to us. Many users, daunted by the complexity of our information organizations, give up before reaching this point, content to find what they are looking for on a bookstore's bestseller tables or with a quick Google search. Faced with such despair, passionate librarians have an obligation to make the library a less forbidding space.

Reference services are one of the most ideal means to make the library a non-threatening environment because it is here that we have the opportunity to teach our users how the library really works. This may seem a surprising proposition at first. After all, isn't the primary function of the reference librarian to point the user to the information they seek? To some extent, this is, in fact, the case, but reference is also teaching users how to make sense of the library for themselves—encouraging them to become self-directed, critical thinkers. As has been suggested elsewhere in this book, the reference librarian should be the user's guide on the quest for knowledge, not his or her proxy. We can walk beside our users, but it is rarely a good idea to walk the road for them. In leading them on their path, we can help them find their own sense of direction, developing the skills known as information literacy.

Information literacy is defined as a set of abilities enabling individuals to "recognize when information is needed and have the capacity to locate, evaluate, and use effectively the needed information" (ALA 1989). Instruction in these activities evolved from Bibliographic Instruction (BI), which sought to "meet basic needs and at the same time teach skills that users can transfer to new situations, new information tools, and new environments to help them learn how to learn" (Grassian 2004). Typical activities of BI included orientations to the library, classes, tours, pathfinders, credit courses, and development of new instructional materials and guides to using reference tools; it also included experiments in integrating bibliographic instruction into the curriculum. Two pioneers in this area were Evan Farber at Earlham College in Indiana and Patricia Knapp with the Monteith College Library Experiment (Knapp 1966). Information literacy encompasses and expands the concepts of bibliographic instruction to include outreach, collaboration, and sequenced learning beyond the library (Grassian 2004).

The American Library Association (ALA) turned its attention to information literacy in 1989, creating a Presidential Task Force on Information Literacy. This led to the creation of the definition cited above and further resulted in the creation of the National Forum on Information Literacy, an organization of over seventy-five national organizations. Nine years later, ALA issued "A Progress Report: An Update on the ALA Presidential Committee on Information Literacy: A Final Report." This report discussed the activities of the National Forum on Information Literacy.

Education organizations and agencies have also been concerned with information literacy, particularly in relation to new technologies. The National Research Council produced a report on this topic entitled *Being Fluent with Information Technology*. The term FIT (fluent with information technology) was used to describe people who have achieved a sufficient degree of mastery to use information for problem solving and for critical thinking (Committee on Information Technology Literacy 1999). The National Council for the Accreditation of Teacher Education has also included information literacy competencies in their standards, as have many other accrediting agencies including the Middle States Commission on Higher Education and the Commission on Colleges and Universities of the Northwest Association of Schools and Colleges.

In the past few decades, a consciousness of the need to foster universal information literacy has been central to libraries' approaches to user orientation. Instead of focusing only on content, libraries now focus on user outcomes and the need to connect users to knowledge. Whether this involves working one-on-one with users, developing online tutorials, presenting information in classroom situations, or working with teachers and faculty to integrate information literacy skills into their lesson plans, the library has a major role to play in information literacy. In the process, the face of information literacy has changed from simply teaching skills to placing an emphasis on encouraging curiosity and creativity. The ability to think and to evaluate information is at the core of this new information literacy. Randy Burke Hensley expresses this well, stating "fostering an individual's sense of curiosity and creativity in tandem with developing his ability to find, locate, and evaluate information is the essence of information literacy" (Hensley 2004, 35).

Standards for Information Literacy

In the past decade many organizations have developed standards for information literacy. The first were developed by the American Association of School Librarians (AASL) and the Association of Educational Communications and Technology (AECT) in 1998. "Information Literacy Standards for Student Learning," part of the publication *Information Power*, provided standards grouped by competency area for students in K–12 including standards for information literacy, independent learning, and social responsibility. Each standard suggests indicators that the students must display in order to demonstrate their competency. The three indicators are:

1. The student who is information literate accesses information efficiently and effectively.
2. The student who is information literate evaluates information critically and competently.
3. The student who is information literate uses information accurately and creatively. (AASL and AECT 1998)

The Association of College and Research Libraries (ACRL) in its 2000 publication *Information Literacy Competency Standards for Higher Education* defined information literacy as the basis for lifelong learning. These standards were instrumental in providing a framework for a discussion of information literacy within higher education (Arp and Woodward 2002). The standards define an information literate person as able to:

1. Determine the extent of information needed;
2. Access the needed information effectively and efficiently;
3. Evaluate information and its sources critically and incorporate selected information into one's knowledge base;
4. Use information effectively to accomplish a specific purpose; and
5. Understand the economic, legal, and social issues surrounding the use of information, and use information ethically and legally. (ACRL 2000)

Approaches to Information Literacy

Many have outlined the components involved in teaching information literacy. One approach is the Big6, which was proposed by Eisenberg and Berkowitz (2000) and is now available on a Web site, www.big6.com. The authors outlined a practical six-step strategy for working with learners that could be applied equally well to the reference interaction:

*   Defining the information problem;
*   Determining the possible sources;
*   Locating the sources;
*   Using the information and extracting the information needed;
*   Organizing the material and presenting it; and
*   Evaluating the product and process. (Eisenberg and Berkowitz 2000)

Another strategy was proposed by Cunningham and Lanning, who presented various approaches for librarians working with faculty to integrate information literacy into the curriculum including information literacy presentations in a class, working as a liaison with an academic department, and providing workshops for faculty (Cunningham and Lanning 2002) Conceptual frameworks for instruction were defined by Kobelski and Reichel and included methods such as teaching systematic literature searching, teaching about primary and secondary sources, understanding citation patterns, understanding how different forms of publications are designed, and understanding index structure and how it is designed to describe content (Kobelski and Reichel 1987, 3–12).

Reporting on the ACRL Institute for Information Literacy, Susan Barnes Whyte states that "when we teach, we need to think less about the right way to do research, the right databases. We need to think more about who we're teaching. Ask them what they think they need to know. . . . I think that teaching is a succession of minor epiphanies. . . . It cannot be accomplished in one session or in one year of education. Build upon those epiphanies!" (Whyte 2001, 2). This approach is further supported by Carol Collier Kuhlthau, who writes that a user's needs are best fulfilled by a series of instructional sessions over a period of time rather than just one session. She describes the need for the librarian to intervene and help the user when and where the user's need arises and asserts that this is an individual need (Kuhlthau 1999).

Information Literacy by Type of Library

Information Literacy in School Media Centers

School media centers try to provide a structured approach to teaching students how to do research in order to prepare them for lifelong learning and for academic research. School media specialists have found that collaborating with teachers is very important to success and that students are best taught using real examples from their school assignments. School media specialists and teachers work together to help students learn to evaluate information sources and to develop search strategies. School media specialists have also found it useful to take high school seniors to a university library and introduce them to the library and its resources. In addition to the AASL standards, school librarians continue to develop and share their strategies for integrating information literacy into new education programs.

Information Literacy in the Academic Library

The academic library is responsible for helping the student to make the transition to more structured research, e.g., researching an assigned topic. The reference librarian must begin wherever the school library left off, continuing to blend the skills of structured information seeking with independent information seeking (Hinchliffe 2003). In order to do this successfully, the librarian must work with the faculty so that the students learn through subject-specific content rather than just through abstract presentations. As is the case with elementary and high school students, the teachable moment is important. The best time for a student to learn is when he or she has a topic to research. In order to make information literacy sustainable in the university setting, librarians must encourage the faculty to take ownership of information literacy (Bridgeland and Whitehead 2005, 59).

Information Literacy in the Public Library

The public library is often the first library the child encounters. Here the child learns how to use a library and how to use the information technology independently or with the help of the librarian. The introduction may be one-to-one or may be a class visit to the library. The public library provides for children or adults a continuing experience in independent learning. Here they can explore and grow on their own (Hinchliffe 2003). Public libraries have become more interested in developing their own approaches to information literacy in recent years. A library advocacy program developed in 2000 by the ALA continued the articulation of information literacy in the public library with the statement: "Librarians will partner with government, education, business, and other organizations to create models for information literate communities" (*Library Advocacy Now! Action Pack* 2000). Public libraries have developed structured programs to introduce users to the use of computers and online databases. Literature in this area of public library information literacy is still sparse but will no doubt continue to increase.

Information Literacy in the Special Library

The special library provides information literacy on a one-on-one basis. Many users of special libraries have already gained some information literacy from public, school, or academic libraries. Because special libraries vary widely, the librarian must introduce the user to the library individually (Hinchliffe 2003).

Carmel O'Sullivan points out the need for information literacy in a corporate setting. She states that many of the skills needed by workers are part of information literacy including advocacy and inquiry, the ability to learn, networking, resource investigation, IT skills, problem solving, and the ability to review risks, opportunities, and successes (O'Sullivan 2002, 12). She also points out that the librarian must move beyond the walls of the library and "apply corporate terminology to relevant information concepts" in order to work successfully with employees. Just as in schools and universities, librarians in a special library setting must make their information literacy relevant to the employees.

Social and Ethical Uses of Information

Plagiarism has become one of the greatest problems in the use of information. Real information literacy is more than the simple ability to find what one is looking for; it is the ability to parse, recombine, and make use of such knowledge. Those who simply appropriate materials without thinking critically about them do not understand how to use information. One of ACRL's standards states that students should be able to "understand the economic, legal, and social issues surrounding the use of information, and access and use information ethically and legally" (ACRL 2000). The *Information Literacy Standards for Student Learning* also address the social responsibilities of students. Standard 8 states: "The student who contributes positively to the learning community and to society is information literate and practices ethical behavior in regard to information and information technology." This standard goes on to say that the student "respects the principles of intellectual freedom and the rights of producers of intellectual property . . . [and] applies these principles across the range of information formats—print, nonprint, and electronic."

Lynn D. Lampert has pointed out some of the issues surrounding plagiarism. Often there is no consistent approach by faculty, so the student does not have good guidelines.

In other circumstances, it is not clear who is responsible for enforcing plagiarism guidelines, so no one puts them into practice. Finally, Lampert says it is not clear whether the faculty are teaching students to integrate and cite information sources they have used and incorporated into their writing (Lampert 2004, 349). Arp and Woodward point out that "technology has blurred the once clearly delineated and separate processes of the use of information and its creation. Cutting, pasting, and cropping are simple keystrokes. The knowledge of when these actions are appropriate or inappropriate is not so easily imparted" (Arp and Woodward 2002, 130). Librarians can improve this situation by teaching how to deal with exact quotations and with paraphrasing and by providing the faculty with resources for explaining what constitutes plagiarism. Many academic libraries provide information on quoting and paraphrasing on their Web sites. Rutgers University has a good example of an online tutorial on plagiarism at www.scc.rutgers .edu/douglass/sal/plagiarism/intro.html, which uses real-life case studies.

One-on-One Instruction

Although we may think of information literacy as a group activity, librarians have traditionally done a great deal of information literacy instruction on a one-on-one basis. In many library situations, librarians use the opportunity of a reference question to provide some individualized library instruction. At times, the help they provide may be as simple as teaching the user how to search the catalog. Where circumstances permit, they may then move on to instruct the user in how to query a particular index or construct a Boolean search string. Alternately, they might be called on to provide a more in-depth research consultation, allowing them the space and time to educate the user about obscure but important elements of the collection.

Those who recommend making instruction a part of the reference encounter advise that the librarian find out what the user already knows to avoid pedantically reteaching familiar skills. The librarian should query the user as to whether he or she would like to learn more about a database or catalog before proceeding, so as to allow the user to learn at his or her own pace. Beck and Turner (2001) recommend that librarians prepare mini-lessons that they can teach at the reference desk, supplementing them with handouts. Confronted with those unwilling to listen to more formal lessons, librarians can verbalize the search process so that the user understands the steps the librarian is taking and the decisions the librarian is making.

Asking questions along the way also helps keep the user engaged in his or her research, thereby demonstrating that the process is as important as the answer. Lisa A. Ellis describes a topic development exercise that is used in her institution to help students think about their paper topic. This exercise can be done via chat or e-mail. In this exercise, questions are asked about the topic in an effort to further its development. The questions center on what the student already knows and what the student needs to know about the topic. This process helps the student to refine and narrow his or her topic (Ellis 2004). Jeanne Galvin suggests that the library should take advantage of out-of-class opportunities to promote and support information literacy. She discusses the use of library pathfinders, individual instruction at the reference desk, instruction in the virtual reference environment, and library Web pages. Galvin points out that the use of assignment-specific pathfinders that are readable and accessible and that can be used by students for completing assignments are more useful than more general pathfinders (Galvin 2005).

For virtual reference, the librarian can develop short scripted messages to include in the interview or to attach to the information that they provide to the user in order to instruct as they answer the question (Beck and Turner 2001). "Instruction via chat reference is a prime example of 'learning at the point of need' and librarians have found users very open to learning in the chat reference situation" (Alternative Strategies 2005, 4).

The librarian can also use the library's Web site as a way to introduce the students to library resources. They can provide Web tutorials or other kinds of Web-based instruction, or list good free Web sites that have been evaluated by the library staff. "A well-constructed and carefully maintained portal would be a good vehicle for breaking down the border between the free Internet resources favored by students and authoritative, scholarly databases not available via Google" (Alternative Strategies 2005, 5).

Information Literacy in a Classroom Setting

School and college libraries and to a lesser extent public libraries have tried to integrate information literacy into the classroom. They have worked with teachers and faculty to teach information literacy at the moment when the student most needs it in order to complete a project. By providing this instruction at such a turning point in the research process teachers can maximize the learning experience for the students and guide them to appropriate resources. The teacher or librarian must ask the "why" questions such as "Why would I use one source rather than another?" The openness of such questions forces students to settle on their own answers, ensuring that they will develop the information literacy strategies most suited to their own characters.

Molly R. Flaspohler studied the effectiveness of an instruction program at a four-year liberal arts college. In this study, librarians, working with faculty who taught an introductory course, taught three library sessions focused on active learning and aimed at improving the students' ability to use library resources including online indexes, and to evaluate and identify appropriate periodical literature. This study showed improvement in the ability of the students to use quality academic resources when information literacy skills are integrated into the curriculum.

Many promote the idea of an across-the-curriculum model in which information literacy is fully integrated into the curriculum. In this way, students learn about research and problem solving as part of whatever subject they are learning. The framework should include:

- Recognizing the need for information;
- Developing skills in using information technologies;
- Accessing information from appropriate sources;
- Critically analyzing and evaluating information;
- Processing and organizing information;
- Applying information for effective and creative decision making;
- Effectively communicating information and knowledge;

- Understanding and respecting the ethical, legal, and sociopolitical aspects of information and its technologies; and
- Developing an appreciation of lifelong learning. (Orr, Appleton, and Wallin 2001, 459)

D'Angelo and Maid reported on an information literacy program at Arizona State University. In a collaboration between the Multimedia Writing and Technical Communications (MWTC) program and the library at Arizona State University East, D'Angelo and Maid described a three-credit course "InfoGlut: Deal with It" that emphasized how to incorporate new information; how to effectively select information; and how to understand issues related to information, including economic, legal, and ethical issues. They reported that students advocated for the inclusion of information literacy in their program; as a result, other courses were identified in which an information literacy component would be added (D'Angelo and Maid 2004).

Impact of New Technology on the Teaching of Information Literacy

Through the rise of information technology we have taken great steps to expanding and universalizing our access to knowledge. To many, the way the World Wide Web and other innovations have leveled the playing field seems almost like a Utopia, a better world in which all are potentially equal. We must remember, though, that the word *utopia* literally means "no place." The price we pay for living in such a world is the obligation to shape it ourselves, making meaning out of the inchoate mass of information with which we are met. As a result, it has become much more important to be able to critically evaluate information sources in order to select the best. The librarian is challenged daily to present to the user information about reliable sources and the differences between leased electronic resources and sources on the Internet.

Information literacy instruction's purpose is to change the way students approach the search for information and to teach them more complex research methods and strategies. This can be done through a variety of instructional approaches including online tutorials (Bloom and Deyrup 2003, 238). Southeastern Oklahoma State University has developed an interactive tutorial (www.sosu.edu/lib/searchpath/yoursearchpath/choice.html) of just this kind that helps students to write a paper. It covers areas such as:

- The types of sources available, such as magazines, books, newspapers, indexes, and the World Wide Web;
- Selecting sources, including the difference between library sources and Internet information;
- Topic selection and how to narrow the topic;
- How to search the catalog; and
- How to search an index.

A similar interactive model was developed at the University of Texas and can be found at http://tilt.lib.utsystem.edu.

The University of California at Berkeley Library has developed a tutorial for its students to use in evaluating Web pages. Located at www.lib.berkeley.edu/TeachingLib/Guides/Internet/Evaluate.html, it encourages the student to ask questions that will help him or her evaluate a Web page and decide whether it is a reliable source of information. They suggest:

- Examining the URL to see what it reveals about the site—for example, whether it ends in .edu, .org, or .com;
- Examining who the author is, whether it is current, and the author's credentials; and
- Looking for indicators of quality information such as footnotes, permissions to reproduce or copyright information, links to other resources, and what other sites link to this resource.

This tutorial shows how complicated it is to examine a site and decide whether it is a good reference to use.

Assessment and Evaluation of Information Literacy

Teaching assessment and evaluation is equally as important as teaching the basic research skills found in information literacy programs. In order to judge the effectiveness of the program, the learning outcomes must be determined. These outcomes are influenced by the environment, that is, the type of educational institution or library. The use of multiple assessment tools is recommended, including surveys, focus groups, and assessment built into the assignments.

ACRL's *Characteristics of Programs of Information Literacy that Illustrate Best Practices* states that the ideal information literacy program is one that "establishes a process for assessment at the outset" (*Characteristics of Programs of Information Literacy* 2003). In the Assessment/Evaluation section it identifies both outcomes for program evaluation and student outcomes. For program evaluation, it recommends using multiple methods for assessment/evaluation, including formative and summative evaluation and short-term and longitudinal evaluation. For student outcomes, it recommends using a variety of appropriate outcome measures, such as portfolio assessment, oral defense, quizzes, essays, direct observation, anecdotal, peer, and self-review, and experience to allow for differences in learning and teaching styles (*Characteristics of Programs of Information Literacy* 2003).

Molly R. Flaspohler describes three assessment tools used in her study of the information literacy project conducted at Concordia College. She used an information literacy questionnaire developed by the UCLA libraries, a comparison of the bibliographies of the pilot groups and the control groups to see if the instruction had been successful, and a start/stop exercise that asked the students to write "what they will start doing in the library and what they will stop doing as a result of their session with a librarian" (Flaspohler 2003, 133). This is a good example of using multiple assessment methods in order to have more than one perspective on the gains achieved.

Information Seeking Behavior

In order to assist users, it is important to understand the stages of the information seeking process. Carol Kuhlthau's important research into the information seeking process has been key to understanding these stages. She describes the user process from the time they become aware of needing information, to their selection of a topic, their exploration of the topic and its various facets, their formulation of a more focused topic based on their exploration, their actual collection of information for their project, and finally their presentation of the results of their findings (Kuhlthau 1993, 170–72). In order to successfully help a user, the librarian must try to understand where the user is in their information seeking. Kuhlthau further defines the various degrees of assistance the librarian can offer as they interact with the user from simply organizing the materials in order for the user to work on their own to actual counseling of the user in need of more assistance as they progress in the search process (Kuhlthau 1993, 175).

Further Considerations

Information literacy is an ongoing topic of interest, one that is no more likely to go away than the books we store on our shelves. Staying at the cutting edge of this fundamental part of our professional activities, especially as it applies to reference services, is a near obligation. Fortunately, many of the leading library publications have taken up the call to provide this information: The *Reference and User Services Quarterly* includes a regular column on information literacy edited by Lori Arp and Beth S. Woodward. The journal *Reference Services Review* publishes an annual issue on information literacy, including a bibliography of articles published during the previous year. Articles can also be found in *Knowledge Quest* and *School Library Journal*. The American Association of School Librarians and the Association of College and Research Libraries have recently started an information literacy Listserv.

Thinking on information literacy has changed. It has gone from a concentration on content to a concentration on how people learn. The ideas of presenting information about the library and research in small amounts and of integrating it into the curriculum are important new directions for this vital service. Finding quality information can be challenging for the user. Librarians can help the user identify high-quality information sources through well-thought-out information literacy programs.

Recommendations for Further Reading

Brier, David J., and Vickery Kaye Lebbin. 2004. "Teaching Information Literacy Using the Short Story." *Reference Services Review* 32, 4: 383–387. An approach to information literacy through the use of short stories. Provides course instructors with examples of how to use the short story to discuss information literacy standards.

Brown, Cecelia, Teri J. Murphy, and Mark Nanny. 2003. "Turning Techno-Savvy into Info-Savvy: Authentically Integrating Information Literacy into the College Curriculum." *The Journal of Academic Librarianship* 29, no. 6 (November): 386–398. Describes an approach to information literacy that combines the traditional instruction with novel approaches that appeal to college student's reliance on Internet search engines.

Bury, Sophie, and Joanne Oud. 2005. "Usability Testing of an Online Information Literacy Tutorial." *Reference Services Review* 33, 1: 54–65. Discusses the usability testing of an online information literacy tutorial designed for freshman undergraduates at the Wilfrid Laurier University Library. The findings were useful in making revisions and enhancements to the tutorial.

Buschman, John, and Dorothy A. Warner. 2005. "Researching and Shaping Information Literacy Initiative in Relation to the Web: Some Framework Problems and Needs." *Journal of Academic Librarianship* 31, no. 1 (January): 12–18. A discussion of the need to develop other frameworks of analysis to in order to shape our knowledge of academic information seeking and the Web.

Davis-Kahl, Stephanie, and Lisa Payne. 2003. "Teaching, Learning and Research: Linking High School Teachers to Information Literacy." *Reference Services Review* 31, 4: 313–319. Teacher professional development, and university and library outreach activities and influences are described to provide an overview of the Compton Teacher Information Literacy Institute curriculum development. Curriculum remodeling after a mid-year assessment is also discussed.

Hoffman, Paul S. 2002. "The Development and Evolution of a University-Based Online Library Instruction Course." *Reference Services Review* 30, 3: 198–211. Describes the development and evolution of an introduction to library research course into an online course that integrated information literacy into the curriculum through the general education program at the University of Nebraska.

Johnson, Anna Marie. 2003. "Library Instruction and Information Literacy." *Reference Services Review* 31, 4: 385–418. An annotated bibliography of literature on library instruction and information literacy for all types of libraries. Most articles are from 2002.

Johnson, Anna Marie, and Sarah Jent. 2004. "Library Instruction and Information Literacy—2003." *Reference Services Review* 32, 4: 413–442. An annotated bibliography of literature recently published on the topic of library instruction and information literacy in academic, school, public, and special libraries.

Lenholt, Rob, Barbara Costello, and Judson Stryker. 2003. "Utilizing Blackboard to Provide Library Instruction: Uploading MS Word Handouts with Links to Course Specific Resources." *Reference Services Review* 31, 3: 212–218. Librarians at Stetson University describe how they integrated library instruction materials into the course management system.

Lindauer, Bonnie Gratch. 2004. "The Three Arenas of Information Literacy Assessment." *Reference & User Services Quarterly* 44, no. 2 (Winter): 122–129. A solid article on information literacy assessment that includes organizations and resources dealing with this area.

Malenfant, Chuck, and Nora Egan Demers. 2004. "Collaboration for Point-Of-Need Library Instruction." *Reference Services Review* 32, 3: 264–273. Describes a project in which the librarian and member of the teaching faculty collaborated on an advanced information literacy experience. They found that offering advanced information literacy to upper-class students at their point of need increased their interest and participation in the program.

McMillen, Paula S., Bryan Miyagishima, and Laurel S. Maughan. 2002. "Lessons Learned About Developing and Coordinating an Instruction Program with Freshman Composition." *Reference Services Review* 30, 4: 288–299. Describes a collaboration between the Oregon State University Libraries and the university's freshman composition program. The article outlines the process followed by the coordinators of the instruction program and the important role they can play.

Owusu-Ansah, Edward K. 2004. "Information Literacy and High Education: Placing the Academic Library in the Center of a Comprehensive Solution." *The Journal of Academic Librarianship* 30, no. 1 (January): 3–16. The author suggests a comprehensive approach to help all students will receive instruction in information literacy.

Phillips, Lori, and Jamie Kearley. 2003. "TIP: Tutorial for Information Power and Campus-Wide Information Literacy." *Reference Services Review* 31, 4: 351–358. A description of the Web tutorial developed by the University of Wyoming Libraries focused on the ACRL Information Literacy Competency Standards.

Seamans, Nancy H. 2002. "Student Perceptions of Information Literacy: Insights for Librarians." *Reference Services Review* 30, 2: 112–123. First-year students at Virginia Tech were questioned about their use of information using both e-mail questioning and face-to-face interviews. The data collected resulted in ways to improve library services for first-year students.

Sharkey, Jennifer K., and F. Bartow Culp. 2005. "Cyberplagiarism and the Library: Issues and Solutions." *The Reference Librarian* 91/92, 103–116. Deals with plagiarism in academic institutions influenced by the easy availability of online resources.

Somerville, Mary M., and Frank Virotto. 2005. "If You Build It With Them, They Will Come: Digital Research Portal Design and Development Strategies." *Internet Reference Services Review* 10, 1: 77–94. A pilot that builds information literacy into academic curricula of agribusiness through the portal Web-based design process.

Wood, Gail. 2004. "Academic Original Sin: Plagiarism, the Internet, and Libraries." *The Journal of Academic Librarianship* 30, no. 3 (May): 237–242. Describes an information literacy and integrity model to help students distinguish between their own ideas and those of others.

Bibliography of Works Cited in this Chapter

American Association of School Libraries and the Association of Educational Communications and Technology. 1998. *Information Power: Building Partnerships for Learning*. Chicago: ALA. Available at www.ala.org/ala/aaslproftools/informationpower/informationliteracy.htm.

American Library Association. 1989. *Presidential Committee on Information Literacy*. Chicago: ALA.

Arp, Lori, and Beth S. Woodward. 2002. "Recent Trends in Information Literacy and Instruction." *Reference & User Services Quarterly* 42, no. 2 (Winter): 124–132.

Association of College and Research Libraries. 2000. *Information Literacy Competency Standards for Higher Education*. Chicago: ACRL. Available at www.ala.org/ala/acrl/acrlstandards/informationliteracycompetency.htm.

Beck, Susan E., and Nancy B. Turner. 2001. "On the Fly BI: Reaching and Teaching from the Reference Desk." *The Reference Librarian* 72, 83–96.

Bloom, Beth, and Marta Deyrup. 2003. "Information Literacy Across the Wired University." *Reference Services Review* 31, 3: 237–247.

Bridgeland, Angela, and Martha Whitehead. 2005. "Information Literacy in the 'E' Environment: An Approach for Sustainability." *Journal of Academic Librarianship* 31, no. 1 (January): 54–59.

Characteristics of Programs of Information Literacy that Illustrate Best Practices: A Guideline. 2003. Chicago: ACRL.

Committee on Information Technology Literacy. 1999. *Being Fluent with Information Technology.* Washington, DC: National Academies Press. Available at www.nap.edu/catalog/6482.html.

Cunningham, Thomas H., and Scott Lanning. 2002. "New Frontier Trail Guides: Faculty-Librarian Collaboration on Information Literacy." *Reference Services Review* 30, 4: 343–348.

D'Angelo, Barbara J., and Barry M. Maid. 2004. "Moving Beyond Definitions: Implementing Information Literacy Across the Curriculum." *Journal of Academic Librarianship* 30, no. 3 (May): 212–217.

Eisenberg, M. B., and R. E. Berkowitz. 2000. *Teaching Information and Technology Skills: The Big 6 in Secondary Schools.* Worthington, OH: Linworth Publishing.

Ellis, Lisa A. 2004. "Approaches to Teaching through Digital Reference." *Reference Services Review* 32, 2: 107.

Flaspohler, Molly R. 2003. "Information Literacy Program Assessment: One Small College Takes the Big Plunge." *Reference Services Review* 31, 2: 129–140.

Galvin, Jeanne. 2005. "Alternate Strategies for Promoting Information Literacy." *Journal of Academic Librarianship* 31, 4: 352–357.

Grassian, Esther. 2004. "Building on Bibliographic Instruction." *American Libraries* 35 (October): 51–53.

Hensley, Randy Burke. 2004. "Curiosity and Creativity as Attributes of Information Literacy." *Reference & User Services Quarterly* 44, no. 1 (Fall): 31–36.

Hinchliffe, Lisa Janicke. 2003. "Examining the Context, New Voices Reflect on Information Literacy." *Reference & User Services Quarterly* 42, no. 4 (Summer): 311–317.

Knapp, Patricia. 1966. *The Monteith College Library Experiment.* Metuchen, NJ: Scarecrow Press.

Kobelski, Pamela, and Mary Reichel. 1987. "Conceptual Frameworks for Bibliographic Instruction." In *Conceptual Frameworks for Bibliographic Education: Theory into Practice*, edited by Mary Reichel and Mary Ann Ramey. Littleton, CO: Libraries Unlimited, Inc.

Kulthau, Carol Collier. 1993. *Seeking Meaning: A Process Approach to Library and Information Services.* Norwood, NJ: Ablex Publishing Corp.

———. 1999. "Accommodating the User's Information Search Process: Challenges for Information Retrieval System Designers." *Bulletin of the American Society for Information Science* 25, no. 3 (February–March): 12–17.

Lampert, Lynn D. 2004. "Integrating Discipline-Based Anti-plagiarism Instruction." *Reference Services Review* 32, 4: 347–355.

Library Advocacy Now! Action Pack: A Library Advocate's Guide to Building Information Literate Communities. 2000. Chicago: ALA.

Orr, Debbie, Margaret Appleton, and Margie Wallin. 2001. "Information Literacy and Flexible Delivery: Creating a Conceptual Framework and Model." *Journal of Academic Librarianship* 27, no. 6 (November): 457–463.

O'Sullivan, Carmel. 2002. "Is Information Literacy Relevant in the Real World?" *Reference Services Review* 30, 1: 7–14.

Whyte, Susan Barnes. 2001. "From BL to IL: The ACRL Institute for Information Literacy." *OLA Quarterly* 7, no. 2 (Summer): 14–15.

Woodward, Beth S. 2005. "One-on-One Instruction: From the Reference Desk to Online Chat." *Reference and User Services Quarterly* 44, no. 3 (Spring): 203–209.

Part 4
Developing and Managing Reference Collections and Services

17

Selecting and Evaluating Reference Materials

Of all the sections of a library, the reference collection must be the most focused, specific, and selective. Although far smaller than circulating collections, the works they contain are often far more expensive than those found elsewhere. Consequently, developing a reference collection is a sort of tightrope performance for the librarian, each step requiring great thoughtfulness and care. To stay balanced and keep the collection from toppling over into the abyss of redundancy and irrelevance, the book buyer must combine knowledge and experience to great effect. Each choice must be made with care, allowing the library to best leverage its resources and ensuring that neither money nor shelf space goes to waste. As has been suggested in the previous chapters, thoughtful evaluation of relevance and currency is crucial with each individual purchase, but those responsible for development must also possess:

- Knowledge of the library's community of users and their needs and interests;
- Knowledge of how different types and formats of reference materials are used;
- Knowledge of subject areas; and
- Knowledge of how to evaluate reference materials.

More often than not, these areas are interdependent. Note, for example, that an understanding of the library's users often goes hand in hand with the type of library and the educational level of the community it serves.

The takeaway point here is that buyers must be willing to think out of the box and look beyond their immediate spheres of influence. Thus, academic librarians must take the various disciplines studied at their university or college into account when considering purchases. The needs and interests of this community are defined by the college or university's curriculum as well as the research needs of both students and faculty. As the curriculum changes, the academic library must respond by adding new reference materials that will meet these new needs. Likewise, public libraries respond to the requests for information from members of their communities, reflecting their users' wide-ranging information needs and interests from educational and career interests to hobbies and leisure reading. Public libraries have the most diverse user body to serve. Their audience includes children, teens, and adults of all ages and all backgrounds.

Consequently, reference collection development must take into account the widest possible range of users. School libraries serve a community of students and faculty. They tailor their collections to the subject areas being taught in the school as well as the interests of their user group. Special libraries serve the needs of their community of users, be they museum curators, hospital employees, business people, or others. Their users have very specific information needs and interests that may change over time.

The ways in which knowledge is sought out and used by a library's patrons also plays a crucial part in the shaping of the reference collection. If the users tend toward factual information, the library may collect a large number of ready reference materials or build a ready reference section on its Web site. If queries tend more toward in-depth research, the library should concentrate on indexes and other reference sources that lead the user to full-text information. Sometimes libraries will need specialized materials such as maps or government documents. Alternatively, they may need collections of directories to meet certain kinds of requests.

By understanding characteristics of specific types of materials the libraries can tailor their collections to meet user needs. Formats of reference materials are much more important than ever before. In particular, libraries must decide how to balance print and electronic acquisitions. This may be based on the way the library's users request and utilize materials or the most suitable format for particular types of material. Resources may, for example, be bought on CD-ROM or microform if they are necessary, but rarely used, guaranteeing patron access while freeing up shelf-space. Alternate media may also be selected in some circumstances if they provide a more inexpensive way to provide access to the information they contain.

A comprehensive knowledge of relevant subject areas will help the librarian decide how much material is needed to fully cover any given topic. Again, it is helpful here to think in terms of what users need and want. Sometimes, if demand is low, a single book or database is sufficient coverage for a given subject area, while in others multiple titles are needed to support the user requests. Further, titles about subjects in flux will have to be weeded and replaced with much greater rapidity, meaning that those responsible for reference collection development must stay abreast of changes in the field. Returning to the question of formats, note that especially frequent developments may call for the purchase of or subscription to online resources that are regularly updated.

Finally, as should by now be obvious, knowing how to evaluate reference materials is key to the success of a reference department. This requires both knowledge of how reference materials are used and knowledge of the subjects of the materials. Careful examination of the many important criteria is essential, as well as deciding for a particular work what the most important characteristics are. For many subject areas there may be more than one choice. By knowing the library's users the librarian can select the materials best suited to this particular audience.

Although reference collection development may appear to be one-dimensional, it actually includes a number of different tasks:

- Identifying, selecting, and evaluating new reference materials;
- Management of the reference budget, including approval plans, standing orders, exchange agreements, and cooperative collection development;
- Ongoing assessment of the reference collection;

- Weeding the reference collection;
- Writing and updating a reference collection development policy; and
- Promoting and marketing new reference materials to the library's users.

Identifying, Selecting, and Evaluating New Reference Materials

Many reference materials are published both in print format and as an electronic database, while some are available in only one of these formats. Since most reference collections can acquire only a selection of the available titles, all decisions must be made thoughtfully. Reference materials should be selected either through personal examination, reference to literature produced by the publisher, reading of reviews, or some combination of the three.

Sources of Reviews

Reviews are one way of obtaining information about reference materials. *Booklist, Library Journal, School Library Journal, Choice,* and *Reference & User Services Quarterly* are the review sources most frequently consulted by librarians searching for reviews of new reference titles.

Booklist is published by the American Library Association twice monthly September through June and monthly in July and August. The purpose of *Booklist* is "to provide a guide to current library materials in many formats appropriate for use in public libraries and school library media centers. Materials are recommended for reasons relating to both quality and demand." "Reference Books Bulletin," a section of each issue of *Booklist*, reviews "reference sources designed by their arrangement and treatment to be consulted for specific items of information rather than to be read consecutively . . . that would be of interest primarily to public libraries and school media centers" (www.ala .org/ala/booklist/insidebooklist/booklistpolicy/booklistselection.htm). The reviews in "Reference Books Bulletin" are prepared and critiqued by members of the editorial board and by contributing reviewers and represent the board's collective judgment. Each issue includes an introductory essay that discusses titles reviewed in the issue and reviews of about fifteen titles, meaning that it covers approximately 500 reference books and electronic resources annually. "Reference on the Web" reviews Web sites on a particular theme. All reviews are well written and thorough. Occasional special sections on types of material such as an annual review of encyclopedias are among the best to be found. This review source is online as of 2005.

Reference & User Services Quarterly is published by the Reference and User Services Association of the American Library Association. This journal is devoted to articles on all aspects of reference services. Each issue includes a "Reference Books" column that reviews twenty-five to thirty reference titles. The signed reviews both describe and critically evaluate each work.

Library Journal, a publication of Reed Business Information, is released twice a month. A "Reference Reviews" section in each issue looks at about fifteen reference titles and makes recommendations about the relative value of each title and in what library settings it would be appropriate. Also included in this section are analyses of Web and CD resources as well as more conventional print resources.

School Library Journal, also published by Reed Business Information, is a magazine for librarians who work with young people in schools or in public libraries. About twenty reference books and several databases are reviewed six times a year. Suggestions as to which titles should be purchased are also clearly made.

Choice is published monthly by the Association of College and Research Libraries except in July and August, when it is bimonthly. It is a book review service designed to support undergraduate library collections. *Choice's* section reviewing reference titles is divided into General, Humanities, Science & Technology, and Social & Behavioral Sciences. Among these four categories, over sixty reference titles are reviewed in each issue. These reviews are written by academic scholars and librarians and, like the other titles discussed above, include a recommendation as to whether the text should be purchased and the types of libraries for which it is recommended. Electronic resource reviews are integrated with the print material reviews. *Choice* reviews are also available online at www.choicereviews.org.

ARBA (American Reference Books Annual), published by Libraries Unlimited, reviews all new reference works in print, online, or on CD-ROM published in the United States and Canada during the year. The reviews are arranged by four broad subject categories—general reference, social sciences, humanities, and science and technology. It is an important source of information about reference materials and includes some professional materials. This reference tool is also available online. The online version covers 1997 to date and is updated monthly with 150–200 additional reviews.

In addition to the publications described above, a number of annual lists of recommended reference titles are produced by committees and publications. These include a list compiled annually by a RUSA committee and published in May in *American Libraries* and an annual list compiled by *Library Journal* and published in the April issue. Reference reviews also appear on the Gale site (www.gale.com/free_resources/reference/index.htm) under the "Free Resources" section. They include "Peter's Digital Reference Shelf," where Peter Jacso reviews online and CD-ROM products; a review of public and academic reference resources by John R. M. Lawrence called "Lawrence Looks at Books"; "Reference for Students" by Blanche Woolls and David Loertscher; and a "Reference Reviews Archive."

Other retrospective guides to reference materials include *Guide to Reference Books* 11th edition, edited by Robert Balay; *The New Walford Guide to Reference Resources* (three volumes); *Recommended Reference Books for Small and Medium-sized Libraries and Media Centers*; and Scott E. Kennedy's, *Reference Sources for Small and Medium-Size Libraries* 6th edition. For further information about these titles, please see the bibliographic list at the end of this chapter.

Evaluation Criteria

In order to determine which reference materials to purchase, the materials must meet certain evaluation criteria. In general, these criteria apply to both print and electronic materials:

- Scope;
- Quality of content;
- Accuracy of content;
- Currency;
- Authority of author and/or publisher;
- Ease of use including usability, searching capabilities, and response time (for electronic resources);
- Arrangement of material;
- Appropriateness to the audience/meeting of user needs;
- Format; and
- Cost

Criteria	For print materials	For electronic materials
Scope	•	•
Quality of content	•	•
Accuracy	•	•
Currency	•	•
Authority	•	•
Ease of use		•
Arrangement	•	
Appropriateness		
for users	•	•
Format	•	•
Cost	•	•

In order to evaluate a reference work, it is important to understand its scope. In printed works the author usually discusses this in the preface or introduction. This should include a discussion of what the work covers, including topics such as how comprehensive it is, whether it covers allied fields, the dates covered, and whether the work includes only information from the United States or is international in scope. Reference to this information will give the librarian a way to compare this work with similar reference works on the same subject and to decide if this one is a necessary addition to the collection. Determining the scope of an electronic database is often more difficult, as there is rarely a direct equivalent to the preface, and access to nonsubscribers may be limited. Often the printed material from the publisher describing the electronic database includes information on scope, and the Web site of the company may also be a source of information. In electronic versions of print resources, coverage is still an issue, as it is important to determine whether the digital version offers anything newer than the print version and, if so, what time period it covers. Questions of duplication are critical, since most libraries cannot afford to have print and electronic resources that are identical.

The quality of the content has become particularly important in electronic resources since the librarian appears to have less control over what content the publisher chooses. Quantity is not as important as quality here. Quality content can be defined as accurate, up-to-date information of sufficient depth for the intended audience.

The authority of the reference work is indexed by the qualifications of the author or the publisher. The author may be someone known for authoring reference materials.

Some publishers have a good track record in a certain area of reference material, meaning that the selector can begin the examination of the work with some confidence that the publisher will produce a credible work. Remember, though, that even the most seemingly authoritative work still needs to be examined for accuracy and currency. Accuracy can be tested by comparing it to other works on the same topic. Currency can be tested by checking to see if recent information on a specific topic is included in the work and checking the dates of resources cited. It is also important to note when the cutoff date was in relation to the publication date for this reference work. In the case of electronic databases, choose a current topic or a recent world event and see how fresh the information on that topic is.

Electronic resources should be examined for usability. Here, the most relevant factors are whether the program is easy to search and how quickly it responds to commands and queries. These issues of maneuvering the database are one set of criteria that applies exclusively to electronic resources.

Examining the arrangement of the reference work will determine whether its sections are organized and indexed in such a way as to facilitate easy access to the information it contains. Good organization separates a truly useful reference work from a text or simply a well-written work on a subject. The print reference work needs to have good page layout with many headings to make it easy to scan the pages. A sufficient amount of white space is needed, and a typeface that is clear and easy to read. The reference work must also have a good table of contents and index with cross-references where appropriate. An electronic work should use a thesaurus or accepted list of subject headings such as the Library of Congress Subject Headings as well as cross-references to enable the user to find the information easily. An easily intelligible interface and searchable help files are equally significant ways to enable the user to understand how to search the database easily.

Because choices must often be made about in which format materials should be purchased, it is important to consider the form that will best convey a title's content. Some information is still appropriately in print format, while other material lends itself to electronic format. If the content changes often, it may be best in electronic format since the changes are easily made online. Indexes for periodicals and newspapers are far superior in electronic format since new material is being indexed constantly. Directories are another good candidate for the electronic format since addresses, phone numbers, e-mail addresses, etc. are constantly changing. Other reference works may be best or very acceptable in print. These include atlases, some ready reference materials, and handbooks.

The audience for the reference work must be considered in purchasing. A good reference work that is not for the audience of a particular library is not a good purchase. For example, a science handbook that is aimed at a university or professional audience will not be appropriate in a high school library. There are usually reference works on the same subject on a variety of levels so that there is an appropriate title for the library's audience. On this account, it may be helpful to consider where in the professional literature a work has been reviewed. A text spotlighted in school library publication will probably be inappropriate for the main research library of a large university. An astute purchaser should be able to determine this information on his or her own, however, as it should be clear on consideration of the text.

Given the diversity of reference titles on almost every subject imaginable, librarians must try to distinguish between the good and the bad. A close examination of a title will reveal whether the title has material that is not found in other similar titles or presents the material in a unique way. This would be a good reason for purchasing this title.

Cost may be the final determination as to whether to purchase a specific reference work. For most subjects there are several reference works available and the librarian can choose based on any or all of the criteria above. But in the end—all other factors being equal—price may be the determining concern. With electronic resources the library may want to be part of a consortium that can share costs in order to afford the more expensive electronic resources.

Choosing between Print and Electronic Resources

Many factors go into the decision as to which format to buy. Usually it is a decision based on the library's own needs. Some factors that may influence a library's decision are how often the resource is updated, whether everything in the print version is included in the electronic version, the years of coverage, the ease of use, and whether the resource is compatible with the library's technology infrastructure. For many academic libraries electronic resources are the best choice for many materials since students want to use the resources outside of the library and at any hour. In public libraries the choice may not be so clear, since most public libraries have a wide range of users—many of whom are probably not accustomed to doing all their research electronically or simply prefer print resources. Sometimes the decision must be to duplicate the resource in print and electronically since it is so heavily used that it makes sense to have both. Encyclopedias in a public library are an example of a resource that is useful to have both in print format and electronically, as the print set will accommodate more users at one time. Some reference materials are really still best in print, since not all digital conversions are as good as their original sources. Materials where visual browsing within the text is useful are still best in print. Although there is not a large place for CD-ROMs in the library today, there may still be occasions when it makes sense to buy a CD-ROM. Some examples of this might be a seldom updated bibliography or a dictionary.

Management of the Reference Budget

Librarians must learn to manage and maximize the library's reference budget. Reference departments typically have a specific annual budget. Depending on the size and administrative complexity of the institution this may be one budget or may be divided into a number of categories such as print, electronic, approval plans, standing orders, and specific subject areas. Either way, the staff must make a plan at the beginning of the year as to how the budget will be distributed. In academic and large public libraries approval plans and standing orders play a major role in the reference budget. Money must be allocated at the beginning of the year to pay for these plans. Reference works may come as part of a larger library approval plan or the library may set up approval plans with reference publishers. Electronic resources may include contracts paid for by the library and cooperative arrangements with library consortia. Most libraries have found it economical to join or form consortia for the purpose of purchasing electronic resources. This has made it possible to buy more titles for a more reasonable price. Another way to build collections without spending more money is to develop exchange agreements with other institutions and libraries. Some institutions publish quality journals as a way of being able to exchange with other institutions.

Ongoing Assessment of Reference Collections

Collections should be assessed on a regular basis to ascertain whether the materials meet the needs of the users and whether the selections are worth the cost. This is a two-pronged process that involves both determining gaps in the existing collection and evaluating the quality of available resources. On the former count, the library might want to look at the questions it received and could not answer and the interlibrary loans placed because the material was not available at the library. In addition to this, it is wise to browse the shelves to see if the collection appears balanced in relation to the current interests of the library's users. Is there too much material on subjects no longer of interest to the users? Is more material needed on subjects that have recently become more popular?

There are a number of ways to assess a collection. For example, the staff could check the collection against standard lists such as the *Best Reference Books, Recommended Reference Books for Small and Medium-sized Libraries and Media Centers, Reference Sources for Small and Medium-sized Libraries, Choice's Outstanding Academic Titles 1998–2002,* or *Best Books for Academic Libraries.* Alternatively, the staff could use the conspectus approach to evaluate the level of materials in each subject area and whether the level reflects the emphasis and interest in the subject area as reflected in the use of the materials. Third, the library could compare its holdings with a comparable library using either OCLC or Research Libraries Information Network.

User satisfaction can also be ascertained by questionnaires to the library's users—in person, by mail or e-mail, through interviews, and through feedback at the reference desk.

Weeding the Reference Collection

Weeding or deselection is an important part of reference collection development. Reference collections by their very nature must have the most current information in order to accurately answer the users' questions. Anything less than the most current information possible is simply not acceptable. Accordingly, removing dated materials from the collection must take high priority. Current thinking dictates that print reference collections should be smaller since many materials are available electronically and are much more suitable in that form.

The criteria for weeding reference materials in any type of library are:

- The content is no longer up-to-date or accurate.
- A new edition is available.
- The reference work is seldom used.
- The information is duplicated in another reference work.
- The book is worn out.

Libraries may want to use the same guidelines for weeding reference texts as for circulating nonfiction. Libraries will want to identify subjects that date quickly and weed those areas more often. History, art, literature, philosophy, and religion are seldom weeded, whereas science, medicine, and some of the social sciences require continual updating. Libraries do not necessarily replace all annuals each year. Because of the cost considerations some annuals are replaced every two or three years. Encyclopedias are often rotated out of the collection; five years is the longest an encyclopedia should be kept in a reference collection. (Nolan 1998, 162–163.) Cumulative sets are usually maintained such as *Current Biography* unless they become available online at an affordable price.

It is useful to have an organized approach to weeding so that within a particular time period all materials have been reviewed. A weeding team is a good approach so that materials in question can be discussed and decisions made as to whether to discard, move to the circulating collection, or put in storage.

Writing a Reference Collection Development Policy

Reference collection development policies provide a way to document current practices in a reference department and to set directions for their future development. This is useful for guiding the present staff in their work, orienting new staff, and providing information to the users. It also provides consistency and continuity within the library as staff changes. Although the reference collection development policy need not repeat details about collection development that have already been documented in the library's overall collection development policy, it does help to document separately the collection development activities of the reference department, especially as it reflects some practices that differ from the rest of the library. The primary parts of this policy should be:

- Introduction that describes the library, its clientele and its areas of research or reference service;
- Description of the scope and size of the collection;
- Formats of materials collected, with a separate section on electronic resources;
- Collecting levels by subject;
- Types of reference materials collected;
- Description of the responsibilities of staff and others for selection;
- Criteria for selection, assessment, and weeding;
- Sources of funding; and
- External relationships with other libraries, consortial arrangements, and resource sharing.

In the introduction the policy should describe briefly the library, its goals, and its clientele. This introduction should also provide an overarching statement about the goals of the reference collection, which might be to provide accurate, up-to-date information or to support educational and informational needs. If others use the library who are not the primary clientele, this should be mentioned, as well as how the library serves them. For example, some university libraries are open to the general public as well as to the school's employees and students. With the increase in distance learning the policy might want to discuss how the library serves this part of its users.

In the description of the scope and size of the collection the library will want to describe the subject areas covered by the reference collection. This may be different from the circulating collection or may mirror it. In any case, it is important to describe what the collection includes and what it does not. For example, the library may not buy textbooks or may not purchase materials in certain subject areas. The size of the collection is equally important. Today the size must include both print and electronic resources so the description may begin to differ from previous policies.

The formats of materials collected should be outlined. Here the library will want to discuss how it decides whether to buy a reference work in print or in an electronic format and when it might buy both. It is also important to state whether microform collections continue to be maintained and whether CD-ROMs continue to be purchased. This area of electronic resources has become an important part of the collection. Guidelines must be set up to help staff and users understand how these decisions are being made. Some of the issues that need discussion are whether electronic resources will be offered for remote use, criteria for purchase of electronic resources, and consortial relationships. Future plans for electronic resources might be outlined here.

Subject collecting levels and the types of reference materials collected reflect the use of the reference collection. The subject levels might be explained using the Research Library Group system or another system that describes subject levels. The library might also want to list some specific types of reference materials it collects, such as government documents, maps, etc. The reference collection is developed and maintained based on user requests and interests. This can change over time as user needs move in new directions.

Staff usually has specific collection development responsibilities. Each staff member may be responsible for a certain area of the collection. In an academic library the faculty as well as the library staff may have some responsibility for collection development. Some libraries use committees to discuss proposed additions to the reference collection. This may be particularly true for electronic resources, since their cost is so much greater than that of a reference book.

The library will want to outline the criteria that they use for selection and for weeding. General guidelines are discussed elsewhere in this chapter. It can be helpful to discuss in general terms the funding of the library's collection. Many people have no idea of how a library is funded and the limits of its budget. Finally, the policy should discuss relationships that the library has with other libraries, such as the consortia agreements between academic institutions discussed throughout this chapter. The policy will document whatever agreement has been developed with other libraries, whether for print or electronic materials.

An example of a general statement about the reference collection is the following:

> The reference collection supports primarily the research needs of IPFW (Indiana University-Purdue University Fort Wayne) undergraduates, graduate students, and faculty. It contains, but is not limited to, encyclopedias, dictionaries, atlases, directories, indexes, bibliographies, statistical compilations, and handbooks. Items for the

reference collection are selected by the librarians. Though items selected for this collection support primarily the academic programs offered at IPFW, core academic reference works published in other subject areas are also selected when they provide fundamental bibliographic access to, or an introductory overview of, an academic discipline, items in the reference collection normally do not circulate. The reference collection is reviewed by the librarians on a regular basis to insure currency and accuracy. (www.lib.ipfw.edu/index.php?id=682)

Promoting and Marketing Reference Materials to the Library's Users

Promoting and marketing reference materials have recently become much more important topics because of the advent of electronic resources. These new resources often remain hidden from users unless they are making extensive use of the library's Web site. Most libraries feel that their electronic resources are underutilized by their users. In the hopes of rectifying this situation, many have begun to take more active steps to increase the visibility of these resources among library users.

There are two important areas to address in promoting these resources. The first is the staff themselves. Many electronic resources were added to the collection in a short period of time so that the staff did not have a lot of time to get acquainted with them. Now it is important to go back and refresh the staff's knowledge of these databases. Some libraries send out a write-up on a different database each week or month. Others ask staff members to each study a particular database and then make a presentation to the staff. For the users the library can feature a database of the week or month on the library's Web site. They can feature databases in newsletters and on bookmarks. And they can encourage staff to tell users about the electronic databases.

Regardless of the approach taken, it is crucial that the contents of the collection be advertised to the library's users. Reference work is, after all, predicated on service, and unless the collection is put to use in real, practical scenarios it does little good.

Recommendations for Further Reading

Bradford, Jane T. 2005. "What's Coming Off the Shelves? A Reference Use Study Analyzing Print Reference Sources Used in a University Library." *The Journal of Academic Librarianship* 31, no. 6 (November): 546–558. A four month study of print materials at the Stetson University Library concluded that the reference collection was too large and was not well used.

Clendenning, Lynda Fuller, J. Kay Martin, and Gail McKenzie. 2005. "Secrets for Managing Materials Budget Allocations: A Brief Guide for Collection Managers." *Collections, Acquisitions & Technical Services* 29, 1: 99–108. A step-by-step guide to managing individual funds within a library's materials budget.

Doll, Carol A., and Pamela Petrick Barron. 2002. *Managing and Analyzing Your Collection; a Practical Guide for Small Libraries and School Media Centers*. Chicago: American Library Association. An easy-to-use guide to collection analysis and weeding.

Johnson, Peggy. 2004. *Fundamentals of Collection Development and Management.* Chicago: American Library Association. An excellent recent addition to the literature on collection development.

Samson, Sue, Sebastian Derry, and Holly Eggleston. 2004. "Networked Resources, Assessment and Collection Development." *Journal of Academic Librarianship* 30, no. 6 (November): 476–481. An evaluation of networked resources as they relate to the library's collection development policy.

Tucker, James Cory, and Matt Torence. 2004. "Collection Development for New Librarians: Advice from the Trenches." *Library Collections, Acquisitions & Technical Services* 28, 4: 397–409. Practical advice on collection development for the new librarian.

Twait, Michelle. 2005. "Undergraduate Students." Source Selection Criteria: A Qualitative Study." *The Journal of Academic Librarianship* 31, no. 6 (November): 567–573. Twait studied a group of undergraduate students to determine what criteria they used in selecting sources to use.

Tyckson, David. 2005. "Reference Classics Ahead of Their Time." *Against the Grain* 17, no. 4 (September): 22–28. Based on an ALA program in 2005 that discussed what makes a reference classic.

Wilkinson, Frances C., and Linda K. Lewis. 2005. "Reference eBooks: Does an eBook on the Screen Beat One on the Shelf?; Discussion on Electronic Reference Books with Seven Academic Librarians." *Against the Grain* 17, no. 4 (September): 1, 18, 20, 22. This article explores the rapidly changing world of reference books—the ways that electronic reference books are being selected, purchased, and budgeted. (p. 1)

Wu, Michelle M. 2005. "Why Print and Electronic Resources Are Essential to the Academic Law Library." *Law Library Journal* 97, no. 2 (Spring): 233–256. The author argues that both print and electronic resources are needed.

Sources Cited

Balay, Robert, ed. 1996. *Guide to Reference Books.* 11th ed. Chicago: ALA.

Best Books for Academic Libraries. 2003. Temecula, CA: Best Books.

Best Reference Books, 1970–1980: Titles of Lasting Value Selected from American Reference Books Annual. 1981. Edited by Susan Holte and Bohdan S. Wynar. Englewood, CO: Libraries Unlimited.

Best Reference Books, 1981–1985: Titles of Lasting Value Selected from American Reference Books Annual. 1986. Edited by Bohdan S. Wynar. Englewood, CO: Libraries Unlimited.

Best Reference Books, 1986–1990: Titles of Lasting Value Selected from American Reference Books Annual. 1992. Edited by G. Kim Dority and Bohdan S. Wynar. Englewood, CO: Libraries Unlimited.

Choice's Outstanding Academic Titles 1998–2002. 2003. Chicago: ACRL.

Kennedy, Scott E. 1999. *Reference Sources for Small and Medium-size Libraries.* 6th ed. Chicago: ALA.

The New Walford's Guide to Reference Resources. 2005. 3 vols. London: Facet; distr. by Neal-Schuman.

Recommended Reference Books for Small and Medium-sized Libraries and Media Centers. 1981. Englewood, CO: Libraries Unlimited. Annual.

Resources for College Libraries. 2006. 3rd edition. New Providence, NJ: ACRL/CHOICE and R. R. Bowker.

Bibliography of Works Cited in this Chapter

Bates, Marcia J. 1986. "What is a Reference Book: A Theoretical and Empirical Analysis." *RQ* 28 (Fall): 40–43.

Doll, Carol A., and Pamela Petrick Barron. 2002. *Managing and Analyzing Your Collection: A Practical Guide for Small Libraries and School Media Centers.* Chicago: ALA.

Gwinnett County Public Library. 1998. *Weeding Guidelines.* Chicago: Public Library Association.

Nolan, Christopher W. 1998. *Managing the Reference Collection.* Chicago: ALA. Occasional Paper #27. Chicago: ALA.

Perez, Alice J. 2004. *Reference Collection Development: A Manual.* 2nd ed. RUSA.

18

Managing Reference Departments

Of Car Designs and Learning Styles

Just prior to the Thanksgiving holiday of 2005, General Motors, once the largest employer in the United States, had the thankless job of announcing the layoff of 30,000 workers. Many of those workers, according to a commentator, *"were its best and most productive. Their bosses simply couldn't give them a car to build that Americans really wanted to buy"* (Bai 2005). In other words, despite stellar staff and a conscientiously produced product, it was management that had failed in its primary duty of making effective business decisions. The fallibility of their decision making was further traced to an inability or unwillingness to *"let consumers drive its designs."* Library management has traditionally looked to corporate management for guidance. For reference managers of the twenty-first century there is a clear cautionary tale to be salvaged from GM's managerial pileup.

The consumers of reference services are information seekers, and information is mined according to their individual learning styles. Do information seekers of the twenty-first century have learning styles that are intrinsically different from the past? If we peer through the mists of time, we can see Socrates surrounded by a group of students who have presumably traveled from many directions to quite literally be at the feet of the master in their search for answers. If we flip forward two and a half millennia to the Simon Fraser University in Canada or Harvard University in Boston, we see reference librarians toting laptop computers, primed to instantaneously assist students in their search for answers. So yes, the "design" has changed and there is such a thing as a twenty-first-century learning style.

It is a style that has developed a muscular expectation for rapid and on-demand information. Fueled by this expectation, the organization of reference delivery and access has been, and is continuing to, change in many ways. The reference manager of the twenty-first century must not only be acutely sensitized to the evolving environment, but must be prepared to ably administer and manage dramatic new service models, information delivery systems, and innovative staff configurations. All this must be done while grace-fully accepting the additional new roles thrust upon them by the continuing changes.

Organizing Reference Departments

Traditionally, the management of reference departments has cohered to a hierarchical principle that upholds a scalar chain of command. While elements of that chain con-tinue, the hierarchy is perforce flattening out to accommodate the vibrant new roles and services necessitated by the new learning style.

Table 1 Changing Paradigms in Management

Traditional Models	⟹	Emerging Models
Hierarchical	*Organization*	Flattened
Stationary	*Service Delivery*	Spatial
Specialized	*Staffing*	Multidisciplinary
Isolated	*Work*	Integrated
Independent	*Structure*	Interdependent
Inductive	*Logic*	Deductive
Materials	*Mission Focus*	Users

Self-directed or team-based management is quite rapidly making inroads into tradi-tional hierarchies. Since 1998 the Ohio State University Health Sciences Library has in-stituted the Reference and Information Services Team (RIST), a "self-regulating management team" that has adopted a system of rotating coordinators rather than a head of reference to manage the team. All members of the team are given the opportu-nity to learn each other's jobs with the idea of making reference services more inte-grated (Bradigan and Powell 2004). The Valley Library at Oregon State University has also subscribed to "team-based management" that employs workgroups and coordi-nating advisory councils to replace top-down decision making (McMillen 2003). The University Library at the University of Albany has a "Reference Team" that annually selects a rotating team leader. Though initially developed in response to the loss of multiple supervisory staff, the team approach was continued due to its obvious suc-cesses (Young 2004).

Various persuasive analyses have been offered attesting to the intrinsic value of self-managed teams. It has been argued that "members feel a moral sense to make the ap-proach work so as not to let down other members" (Young 2004); there is flexibility in being able to respond quickly to problems without consulting a chain of authority (Poon-Richards 1995); and the opportunity exists to provide professional development for a wider swathe of reference librarians (McMillen 2003).

However, these are all perceived advantages accruing to nonhierarchical adminis-trative models in any scenario, not specifically the one facing the twenty-first-century reference manager. The reason these models are appearing in the current environment is *because* of the current environment. The explosion of changing technology requires a far more diverse body of talents and experience. As James Neal points out in his presentation at the ACRL (Association of College and Research Libraries) Twelfth National Conference, there is a "new generation of feral professionals" brought about by the "expanding number of positions in functional specialist, computer systems, and administrative services" (2005). Additionally, the rapid change in service needs demands a higher degree of coordination and "synergistic problem-solving" (Kelly 1998, 8). It is these that have combined to limn the advantages of flexibility, dimensionality, and personal motivation inherent to self-directed management.

By logical extension, once the environment is not marked by such intense flux and changing expectations, the relevance of self-directed teams could dim. This in fact already holds true for smaller public libraries, where the change in user needs and the induction of technological innovations is more gradual. The emergence of self-directed teams is, not surprisingly, dominant in academic libraries, where both the expectation and delivery of changing technologies is most insistent. In a study covering changes in the role of academic librarians, it was found that the highest percentage of change in both job activities and reference tools was a spin-off of changes in technology. Electronic collection development, e-mail reference, online searching, and designing Web pages marked the largest change in job activity. Online databases, the World Wide Web, e-mail, and electronic dictionaries and indexes counted for the most dramatic change in reference tools used (Cardina and Wicks 2004).

Organizing Staff

Given that staff costs account for 50–80 percent of a public library's operating budget (Goodrich 2005), the onus of providing the wisest possible allocation of staff time lies heavily on the head of the reference manager. According to an earlier time management analysis, *"the allocation of staff time to the reference desk is one of the most important library personnel issues"* (Dennison 1999).

The Reference Desk

In 1967, a minimum standard for staffing public libraries was published by the American Library Association so that x number of staff, y number of books, and z square footage of building per capita was deemed as necessary. The kind of logic girding this prescriptive and quantitative model did not prove very effective. Currently, and in the foreseeable future, the staffing of reference derives from the kind of deductive logic provided by confirmed user needs. At the Winona State University Library, for example, data on actual usage of the reference desk was recorded for both the number of requests and the level of difficulty in answering the requests. Based on this data, suggestions for double-staffing the desk at particular times of the day and designating on-call reference librarians were proposed (Dennison 1999). "Staffing for Results," published as part of the PLA (Public Librarian Association) Planning for Results series, also subscribes to deductive principles of staffing so that the number and type of staff is a function of proven local needs and priorities rather than a formulaic allocation based on a priori assumptions.

Reference Consultation

In many cases, the primacy of the reference desk as the nexus for all information needs is being consciously muted. As Karyle Butcher states, "The physical reference desk has become the place where librarians catch their breath between patrons. It is less and less the place where actual reference service takes place" (1999, 351).

In the academic libraries of York College, Pennsylvania, and Northwest Missouri State University, for example, the reference desk has been completely phased out and reference librarians are seen by appointment. Ready reference questions are handled at a general-purpose desk that covers circulation and the more basic technological problems faced by users. This model has taken on different shades of variation in different institutions. The medical library at the Johns Hopkins University and the Arizona State University West libraries staff the all-purpose desk with paraprofessionals. Brandeis University libraries employ graduate students. The University of North Carolina at Charlotte uses both paraprofessionals and student assistants to staff a "first point of service," complemented by referrals to more in-depth research by professional reference librarians (Bailey and Tierney 2002).

The model of an "information commons" aims to integrate all reference activities into a one-stop shop, so that students and faculty are provided with a "seamless continuum . . . from planning and research through presentation into final product" (Bailey and Tierney 2002, 284). Further discussion on how such models feed into a viable picture of the future of reference can be found in Chapter 20.

Management of Service Delivery

Service delivery has undergone perhaps the most dramatic transformations. With the growing pervasiveness of digitized information, electronic databases, the all-consuming Internet, IM (instant messaging), podcasting, blogging, RSS (Really Simple Syndication), and virtual and chat reference, teamed with the ubiquity of desktop and laptop computers, wireless networking, and cell phones with IM capability, the delivery of reference services is at a whole new level.

Roving or Mobile Services

Traditionally, the term *roving reference* implied a model whereby reference librarians were encouraged to be less stationary in their traditional posts behind a reference desk and more proactive in approaching users. As Suzanne Tronier, the manager of the East Millcreek Library of the Salt Lake County Library System succinctly explained in a Publib Listserv exchange, "Our librarians are expected to contact people in the library during the first part of their roving shift, helping as needed. After that they provide back up for the reference desk, put out new arrivals and straighten displays; they can weed or do other projects in the stacks and otherwise make themselves available for questions. In some areas of the library . . . just working in that area will invite questions" (12/22/2005).

A more dramatic interpretation of roving librarians has them ranging far beyond the confines not only of the desk, but of the library building as well. At Harvard

University, the Roving Librarian provides "reference on the road" by strategically roving the undergraduate student center with laptop in hand. Given the wealth of electronic databases and online resources available, these librarians are able to either answer or direct a large part of the research interests of the students milling around the center. Similarly, the "Ask Us Here!" initiative at the Bennett Library of the Simon Fraser University in Canada has two choice "service locations" with a "high volume of pedestrian traffic" (Wong and O'Shea 2004, 91) where the research needs of students are either referred appropriately or answered by reference librarians with wireless laptops.

Virtual

The successful integration of remote access to reference information and services has created an important additional responsibility for reference managers. Hiring or training staff to provide this service, apportioning staff time; effectively evaluating the services provided, and staying on top of the quicksilver advances in remote access technology must all become part of the management environment.

24/7 Access

The most robust form of virtual reference has been in the creating of live, 24/7 access—chat reference. Recent literature on the provision of this form of virtual reference suggests that its cost effectiveness can vary dramatically from one institution to another. While individual libraries that provide virtual reference can pay up to $12,000 annually for merely retaining the infrastructure, consortial arrangements can whittle down the cost to $3,000 (Bailey-Hainer 2005). A thought-provoking study by Steve Coffman and Linda Arret (2004) questioning the viability of chat reference has been answered by equally convincing proponents of its cost effectiveness (Tenopir 2004). Reference managers following the debate may also want to track the developments of various national and statewide collaborations, some of which are listed in Table 2.

The attraction of virtual reference collaborations can also be traced internationally. *Virtual ReferenceCanada* is a Canadian bilingual service inaugurated in 2003 to answer reference questions from libraries, rather than the public. The *People's Network Enquire* is a UK initiative that has been put together by over eighty public libraries under the sponsorship of the Museums, Libraries and Archives Council. The *ZLB (Zentral-und Landesbibliothek)* of Berlin provides e-mail reference in German, English, French, and Turkish through active partnerships with other libraries in Europe (IFLA 2005). These collaborative ventures, then, appear to be the most viable models of 24/7 virtual reference access (Bailey-Hainer 2005).

Reference managers wanting to organize virtual reference services for their institution can refer to ALA's guidelines at www.ala.org/ala/rusa/rusaprotocols/referenceguide/virtrefguidelines.htm. Helpful survey planning documents marking the initiation of these services can also be found at the URLs given below. Project management software tools such as MSP2000 (Microsoft Project) are handy organizers available to both scope and monitor the introduction of such services. An example of the use of this tool is to be found in the study by Zhang and Bishop (2005).

Table 2 Select Examples of Collaborative Virtual Reference Services

Service	URL	Area	Activated	Libraries
ASK a Librarian	http://askalibrarian.org	Florida	2003	85
QandANJ	www.qandanj.org	New Jersey	2001	45
NCknows	www.ncknows.org	North Carolina	2004	58*
L-net	www.oregonlibraries.net	Oregon	2003	21
KnowItNow	www.knowitnow.org	Ohio	2004	51
AskUsNow	www.askusnow.info	Maryland	2003	26*
AskColorado	www.askcolorado.org	Colorado	2003	43
QuestionPoint— 24/7 Reference	www.questionpoint.org	National	2001 (merger 2005)	1500+

Libraries subscribing to 24/7 Reference as well.

"Ask A" Services

In addition to virtual reference offering both e-mail and live reference services through statewide collaboration, a dizzying variety of individual initiatives are available to the reference manager.

- Michigan State University, for example, has installed a Trillian-based IM service with the idea that it enhanced virtual reference by providing "convenience" to the many users who already used IM (Behm 2005).
- The Schreyer Business Library at Pennsylvania State University has also embraced IM as a potentially high-use addition to its virtual services (Zabel 2005).
- The Orange County Library Systems were the first public library system to adopt RSS (Really Simple Syndication) to enhance its content distribution.
- Discussions on including special enhancements to Web contact center software such as VoIP (Voice Over Internet Protocol) that allows for vocal interaction; "knowledgebases" that hold frequently asked questions and answers; and improved cobrowsing even with proprietary databases hint at future trends in virtual reference (Coffman 2001).

Increasingly, all libraries, be they academic, public, corporate, special, or school libraries, are setting up Web sites with some form of "Ask a Librarian" service.

New Roles

In a study of the Executive Leadership Institute instituted by the Urban Libraries Council to develop strong future managers, the authors found that successful participants were, among other things, "intrigued by recreating libraries through new business models" and "comfortable with messy, complex partnerships" (Nicely and Dempsey 2005, 300). As outlined above, new business models marked by a flattening of the hierarchy, multi-professional staffing, and innovative service delivery systems unrestricted by stationary physical locations are par for the course being followed by reference managers of the twenty-first century. In addition, though, is the recognized value of getting comfortable with "messy partnerships." Some recurring areas requiring reference managers to get "messy" are in the field of electronic resource management, Web management, and reference marketing.

Electronic Resource Management

"Buying electronic information is more expensive and more complicated than purchasing print information" (Butcher 1999). That truism must leap out to the reference manager who must plan, choose, negotiate, and finally budget for every database that is purchased. Guidelines for implementing collection development policies, such as whether a print resource needs to be replaced or complemented with an electronic counterpart, must be prepared. Given that academic libraries reportedly budget 61 percent of their resources on electronic material (Albanese 2004), planning a reflective and judicious budget can be a demanding task, requiring a change in traditionally held collection policies.

Vendor negotiation and site licensing agreements have evolved into art forms demanding far greater sophistication on the part of the reference manager. The variety and scope for negotiation tends to fracture into as many possibilities as vendors available to provide them. Given this, decisions on whether and how to join the simplifying construct of a consortium become relevant (Hiremath 2001). Consortial initiatives such as the International Coalition of Library Consortia at www.library.yale.edu/consortia; the Washington Research Library Consortium at www.wrlc.org; or the Statewide California Electronic Library Consortium at http://scelc.org, to name just a few, have the potential to exponentially power both the breadth and depth of access to electronic databases for individual libraries. Legal issues of copyright compliance need to be mastered and conveyed to users in effective ways, even as these issues continue to get "more complex and more blurred" (Wamken 2004).

Web Management

A library's Web site has become both the introductory façade to the institution and the user's first step to dipping into the library's reference services and tools. It is no wonder then that the responsibility of Web site content invariably falls on the reference department. Managers of the twenty-first century must be geared to either take on—or at minimum, share—the task of developing and maintaining Web sites.

A 2001 survey of the 122 members of the American Research Libraries found that 98 percent of reference librarians worked at "developing, editing, revising, and updating" Web content (Ragsdale 2001). Depending on the size, structure, and motivations of the library, the management of Web projects can take on many permutations, from the employment of a single Webmaster to a Web committee, to a distributed system involving input and coordination with collection development staff, catalogers, and bibliographers. The reference manager must also prepare for messier strains of Web responsibilities. As pointed out by Butcher, with the digitization of information becoming a rising expectation, "faculty look to librarians to participate in campus partnerships concerning the storage and retrieval of information" (1999, 351).

Reference Marketing

Although nonprofits have been using marketing techniques in recent decades, libraries have been slow to realize the need to market reference resources and services. The invisibility of electronic resources and services, however, have alerted librarians to making sure that their users are more aware of what they have available. Marketing is a broad term that includes public relations, advertising, contacts with community groups, and more. Marketing can involve a cost to the library or can be almost cost free.

Developing a plan for the reference marketing project is the first step. It will be necessary to define a target audience, which might include students, senior citizens, teachers, business people, freelancers, government officials, professionals, etc., for a public library and faculty; students and administrators for an academic library. The library's market could also be defined by demographics such as age, gender, income, education, occupation, ethnicity, etc. The next step is to list the reference resources and services that the library offers and wishes to promote to their users. This could include electronic databases, the library's virtual reference service, or the library's e-book collection. There are many strategies that can be used to promote these resources and services. Consider both the low-cost and more costly possibilities. These range from brochures, newsletters, newspaper articles, newspaper ads, direct mail, radio and TV advertising, and promotion on the Internet. For potential users, the library could develop subject pathfinders in print or on the Web that will bring an awareness of relevant and available electronic databases. Information on any reference resource or service can be highlighted on the library's home page. The Web is an inexpensive and powerful way to provide information to the library's users, such as online newsletters that can be sent to them on a regular basis. A simple bookmark with information about reference resources and services can also serve as a reminder to library users. The library's public relations office may want to place news stories or articles about the library's reference resources and services. Staff can promote reference resources by making presentations to community groups, faculty or student groups, or to the employees of local institutions and organizations. With a budget for paid advertising, the library can promote its reference services and resources through newspaper ads and radio or TV spots. Define what results are being sought before beginning, so there is a way to measure success.

Although general marketing of services and resources is effective, libraries can also consider the techniques of niche marketing, which is designed to aim the marketing at a specific audience such as senior citizens, students, business people, etc. By using niche marketing the message can be made more detailed and specific. To do this, the reference manager will need to focus on a particular resource or service (or a group of them) and consider who might benefit from these resources and services (Walters

2004). For example, a message aimed at the business community could talk about the kinds of information available through electronic databases that identify new places to advertise, new audiences for their products, and new advertising techniques that are cost effective.

Relationship marketing is another technique that reference managers should consider. This kind of marketing goes a step beyond traditional marketing by developing interactive programs with the customers. This is an excellent technique for reference libraries since it allows for long-term partnerships based on listening closely to user needs and developing strategies that respond to those needs. In this kind of marketing, all staff play a role in carrying the library's message to the users. Relationship marketing involves a greater degree of flexibility and creativity in meeting the user's needs and interests (Walters 2004), but is ideally suited to the marketing of reference resources and services.

Virtual Reference Service Evaluation

In addition to evaluating traditional reference services, one of the new duties demanded of the reference manager is to administer and evaluate the many permutations of virtual reference services. While in-person reference transactions quite naturally focus on the reference interview and answer, virtual reference has a dual focus. Both human interaction and digital competency vie for attention. A successful virtual reference transaction is highly dependent on effective chat software, bandwidth speed, and a robust workstation.

The ability to co-browse so that the librarian can directly demonstrate a search to the user; page-pushing software that can transfer files and screen shots without cutting and pasting; file sharing from proprietary databases; the ability to archive pages; concurrent usage with more than one user at a time; customizable user and library information; queuing options such as call selection; scripted messages; transference of active sessions; provision of final transcripts with hyperlinks; in-built statistical assessment tools and surveys; and troubleshooting assistance are just some of the cogs that keep the wheels of virtual reference moving smoothly. These are also some of the criteria for initial selection of software technology.

In addition to the choosing, assessing, and constant upgrading of virtual technology, managers are responsible for relatively involved logistical factors. Collaborative virtual services, such as those listed earlier in this chapter, are increasingly becoming the norm. The parameters of individual contribution have to be decided, effective liaison procedures need to be instituted, and the scheduling of staff time, training, and evaluation slotted into place.

Further Considerations

In their study of the management of libraries and information centers, Stueart and Moran present five "functions common to all managers" (2002):

- Planning
- Organizing

- Staffing
- Directing
- Controlling

For reference managers, technological innovations of tsunami proportions have compulsively created changes in all five functions. Planning of both strategic and long-term reference services and tools must necessarily incorporate the expectations of a demanding new learning style typical of users of the twenty-first century. The learning style, in turn, has fed into new experiments with the organization of reference departments so that a variety of models leaning toward lateral coordination can facilitate quick information services, rather than pyramidical hierarchies that are typically less flexible. Staffing must necessarily be more multidisciplinary to cater to different varieties of reference service delivery ranging from traditional in-person desk reference to 24/7 remote access services. Reference managers, faced with rapid changes, must be motivated to take on new and unexpected roles that could involve "messy partnerships" with players as varied as Web developers, electronic database vendors, and statewide consortia. Finally, the control of reference services is best maintained through a canny mix of effective marketing and vigilant evaluation.

Recommendations for Further Reading

Arthur, Gwen, ed. 2000. *Get Them Talking: Managing Change through Case Studies and Case Study Discussion.* Illinois: American Library Association. Published as *RUSA Occasional Paper # 25*, this hands-on approach to management problems regularly faced by reference departments in both academic and public libraries is useful to help managers think through the recurring challenges brought about by change.

Buff, Hirko, and Mary Bucher Ross. 2004. *Virtual Reference Training: the Complete Guide to Providing Anytime, Anywhere Answers.* Illinois: American Library Association. With the increasing prominence of virtual reference, this book not only provides an in-depth review of Washington's Statewide Virtual Reference Project, but supplies the reference manager with an easy-to-follow program for training virtual staffers, developing policies, and assessing effectiveness.

Gandhi, Smita. 2004. "Knowledge Management and Reference Services." *The Journal of Academic Librarianship* 30, no. 5, (Summer): 368–381. This article provides a clear and compelling argument for reference managers to embrace the corporate reliance on knowledge management (KM), whereby cumulative staff knowledge is retrievable. KM initiatives such as Refquest and Common Knowledge Database that already exist in some academic libraries are also reviewed.

Neal, James G. 2005. "Raised by Wolves: The New Generation of Feral Professionals In the Academic Library." Paper presented at the ACRL Twelfth National Conference, Minneapolis, MN, April 7–10. Available at www.ala.org/ala/acrl/acrlevents/neal2-05.pdf. In this article, the author poses interesting questions on the organization, training, and overall management of academic library staff with formal training in disciplines other than library science.

Sarkodie-Mensah, Kwasi, ed. 2003. *Managing the Twenty-First Century Reference Department: Challenges and Prospects*. New York: The Haworth Press, Inc. With a stellar collection of articles selected from the 2003 issue of *The Reference Librarian*, this resource brings focus to management as it pertains specifically to reference departments in libraries. From training a new head of reference, to core competencies required for a leader, to managing an academic reference department, and collaborative leadership the collection is informative.

Bibliography of Works Cited in this Chapter

Albanese, Richard Andrew. 2004. "The Reference Evolution." *Library Journal* 129, no. 19 (November 15): 10–12, 14.

Bai, Matt. 2005. "New World Economy." *New York Times Magazine* (December 18): 15.

Bailey, Russell, and Barbara Tierney. 2002. "Information Commons Redux: Concept, Evolution, and Transcending the Tragedy of the Commons." *Journal of Academic Librarianship* 28, no. 5 (September): 277–286.

Bailey-Hainer, Brenda. 2005. "Virtual Reference: Alive & Well." *Library Journal* 130, no. 1 (January 15).

Behm, Leslie. 2005. "Adoption of Instant Messaging for Chat at a Research Library in Conjunction with the Formal Chat Software Used." Presented at the Virtual Reference Desk Conference, November 15. Available at http://librarianinblack.typepad.com/librarianinblack/2005/11/adoption_of_ins.html.

Bradigan, Pamela S., and Carol A. Powell. 2004. "The Reference and Information Services Team." *Reference & User Services Quarterly* 44, no. 2 (Winter): 143–149.

Butcher, Karyle. 1999. "Reflections on Academic Librarianship." *Journal of Academic Librarianship* 25, no. 5 (September): 350–354.

Cardina, Christen, and Donald Wicks. 2004. "The Changing Roles of Academic Reference Librarians Over a Ten-Year Period." *Reference & User Services Quarterly* 44, no. 2 (Winter): 133–142.

Casell, Kay Ann. 1999. *Developing Reference Collections and Services in an Electronic Age: A How-To-Do-It Manual for Librarians*. New York: Neal-Schuman.

Coffman, Steve. 2001. "Distance Education and Virtual Reference: Where Are We Headed?" *Computers In Libraries* 21, no. 4 (April): 20.

Coffman, Steve, and Linda Arret. 2004. "To Chat or Not to Chat." *Searcher* 12, no. 8 (September): 49–56.

Dennison, Russell F. 1999. "Usage-based Staffing of the Reference Desk: A Statistical Approach." *Reference & User Services Quarterly* 39, no. 2 (Winter): 158–165.

Goodrich, Jeanne. 2005. "Staffing Public Libraries: Are There Models or Best Practices?" *Public Libraries* 44, no. 5 (September–October): 277–281.

Grahame, Vicki, and Tim McAdam. 2004. *SPEC Kit 282: Managing Electronic Resources*. Washington, DC: Association of Research Libraries.

Hiremath, Uma. 2001. "Electronic Consortia: Resource Sharing in the Digital Age." *Collection Building* 20, 2: 80–88.

IFLA (International Federation of Library Associations and Institutions). 2005. "Think Globally, Act Locally: Building National and International Cooperative Virtual

Reference Networks." Meeting at the annual 71st IFLA General Conference and Council, Oslo, Norway (August 16).

Kelly, Graham. 1998. *Team Leadership: Five Interactive Management Adventures.* Hampshire, UK: Gower.

McMillen, Paula, and Loretta Rielly. 2003. "It Takes a Village to Manage the 21st Century Reference Department." *Reference Librarian* 39, no. 81 (January): 71–87.

Nicely, Donna, with Beth Dempsey. 2005. "Building a Culture of Leadership." *Public Libraries* 44, no. 5 (September–October): 297–300.

Poon-Richards, Craig. 1996. "Self-Managed Teams for Library Management: Increasing Employee Participation via Empowerment." *Journal of Library Administration* 22, no. 1 (April): 67–84.

Ragsdale, Kate. 2001. *SPEC Lit 266: Staffing the Library Website.* Washington, DC: ARL Publications.

Stueart, Robert D., and Barbara B. Moran. 2002. *Library and Information Center Management.* Englewood, CO: Libraries Unlimited.

Tenopir, Carol. 2004. "Chat's Positive Side." *Library Journal* 129, no. 28 (December): 42.

Walters, Suzanne. 2004. *Library Marketing That Works!* New York: Neal-Schuman.

Wamken, Paula. 2004. "New Technologies and Constant Change: Managing the Process." *Journal of Academic Librarianship* 30, no. 4 (July): 322–327.

Wong, Sandra, and Anne O'Shea. 2004. "Librarians Have Left the Building: Ask Us HERE at Simon Fraser University." *Feliciter* 3, 90–92. Also available through the Canadian Library Association Web site at www.cla.ca.

Young, William F. 2004. "Reference Team Self-Management at the University at Albany." *Library Administration & Management* 18, no. 4 (Fall): 185–191.

Zabel, Diane. 2005. "Trends in Reference and Public Services Librarianship and the Role of RUSA." *Reference & User Services Quarterly* 45, no. 1 (Fall): 7–10.

Zhang, Ying, and Corinne Bishop. 2005. "Project Management Tools for Libraries: A Planning and Implementation Model Using Microsoft Project 2000." *Information Technology and Libraries* 24, no. 3 (September): 147–152.

19

Assessing and Improving Reference Services

Why Assess

There is an unwritten assumption that libraries, like Mom and apple pie, will always be there. One of the more impressive buildings in an academic campus, for example, is invariably the library building. With an estimated 117,859 libraries in the country, even Anytown, USA usually has a town hall, a post office, and yes, a library. In Canada, the ubiquity of libraries is advertised by the fact that the 3,153 libraries in the country constitute three times the number of McDonald's restaurants. In the United Kingdom, public libraries have existed for over 150 years and currently number 4,610, not counting the national, academic, specialized, and school libraries.

However, times are changing and the very existence of physical libraries is being questioned, even as funding for libraries is habitually finding a position at the bottom of the totem pole. At the end of 2004, more than $82 million had been cut from library budgets nationally, according to the American Library Association. An unsettling parallel development is the quantum increase in funding resources required for erupting electronic information formats and resources essential to every modern library institution. Caught between spiraling costs and continued funding invisibility, library managers are fast jumping into the ethos of the business world. Words like "ROI" or return-on-investment, "performance indicators," "institutional accountability," and "outcome based evaluations" are finding expression through increasingly sophisticated tools of survey and multivariate analysis.

Traditionally, library feedback has been strong in the realm of library material and usage. Circulation statistics and turnstile counts are an integral part of many libraries. Both provide direct indicators of the number of people entering a library and borrowing material from the library collection. Libraries have been content with these few areas of quantification. The value quotient of a library has drawn legitimacy from these numbers. This is no longer enough.

In 1993, the U.S. government passed the Government Performance and Results Act, which mandates federal agencies to "establish specific objective, quantifiable and measurable performance goals," thus setting the goal of accountability for all institutions. Academic libraries are increasingly accountable to regional accrediting agencies. Corporate libraries must demonstrate ROI on a recurring basis. Public libraries are also finding it beneficial to establish an ROI on every dollar spent; Florida recently published a study claiming a return of $6.54 for every $1, similar to a study by the British Library that pegged the return to 4.4 times the investment (Oder 2005). Even school libraries are feeling the need to rely on more than historical precedent to justify their existence. Statistical truths and the institutional reliance on numbers are being used by all kinds of libraries across the nation both as validation and as a way to support changes, modifications, and additions to library services. Reference rooms do not have the backing of circulation statistics and are particularly vulnerable to marginalization if no clear mandate for their purpose and performance is readily available.

What to Assess

There are three aspects to every reference environment that can and should be evaluated:

- Reference collection;
- Reference staff; and
- Reference services.

Given the time and commitment levels required, the question naturally arises: is the assessment of a reference environment really necessary? Most town libraries, for example, tend to rely on multitasking librarians so that a day in the life of a reference librarian could involve computer troubleshooting, calming disturbed patrons, sorting personnel problems, mopping unfortunate spills, conducting diplomatic conversations with unexpected visitors from Town Hall, and pretzeling over an antique copier tweezing out inky papers accordioned in the machine. In the midst of such busy days, is it any wonder that service assessment is more a theory than a practice?

Traditionally, reference staff has also relied heavily on the accuracy of a strong reference collection. The process of building up a good reference collection has been established in the field. Library literature is replete with monthly broadcasts of "best of" lists and "core collection" choices. But for who are these collections "best" and to what end? Do the small town public library and the large college library choose their selections because they are, after all, "the best of reference" or because their customers have a proven need for these specific materials? "A measure of library quality based solely on collections has become obsolete" (Hernon and Dugan 2001).

Additionally, the formats in which collections are being accessed are multiplying at a dizzying rate. Do users prefer electronic to print resources? Is remote access to sources essential? A pressing challenge for each reference librarian today is to align quality of reference materials, formats, and service so that the fundamentals of what constitutes a "core" reference collection are constantly being questioned and molded in accordance with reference needs. To benefit from feedback, a reliable reference services assessment is essential.

Finally, the funds for setting up and supporting a reference room are increasingly propelled by an assessment of achievement levels in the provision of reference services. If the actuary can convert the value of missing eyes, limbs, and even thumbs to specific dollar amounts so that it is now beyond the realm of human shock and well within the purview of community understanding, surely the library can convert the value of reference services into calculable numbers—or so seems to be the thinking of the day.

How to Assess

The evaluation of reference services is of predominant importance simply because it gauges the satisfaction of the end user, with the collection and the staff as the critical means to attain satisfying end-user service. In that sense, an assessment of reference services encompasses the collection and the staff as well.

The evaluation of services is also the most abstract. The multidimensionality of reference services requires multidimensional approaches for a reliable assessment. In many cases, there are little or no direct tracings of service activity so that evaluative indexes have to be devised to accurately reflect user satisfaction. Given the need to establish convincing evaluative techniques, a number of strategies have evolved over the past few decades. It is incumbent on each reference manager to be familiar with all the following techniques so that the right combination of techniques can be selected, appropriate to the assessment at hand. The most prominently used methods are listed below along a continuum of simple to complex requirements.

> Suggestion boxes > Observation > Surveys > Focus Groups > Case studies

Suggestion Box

The most basic attempt at assessment is via feedback channels such as the humble suggestion box. Whether a generic container with a slot for slipping in suggestions; a book for writing in suggestions and comments; an online box for keyboarding in suggestions; or an e-mail address for sending in suggestions, the intent is the same. "Tell us what you think, or want, or hate, or love about anything and everything" is the simple appeal of the ubiquitous "box."

The advantages of this method are ease of access for the user and simplicity of design and implementation for cash-strapped reference managers. John Lubans, Jr., for example, introduced his wildly popular "Suggestion Answer Book" at both the University of Colorado and Duke University. In his experience, the thousands of suggestions entered in the book were used to leverage "improvements in facilities, services, policies, and staffing." Equally importantly, he notes, the "desire to help . . . was made manifest" to the users (Lubans 2001, 240–245).

The strictures of the format are the lack of accountability inherent in answering random suggestions. The very randomness of the suggestions tends to feed more easily into tweaking improvements, rather than any systemic planning. Idiosyncratic feedback can spark insights, but is less amenable to detecting a pattern or trend in general reference user needs and assessments. While the importance of user needs and assessment is openly and consistently upheld with the provision of an ongoing feedback channel, a more formalized format would need to be instituted for a reference assessment requiring depth.

Surveys

One such format is the age-old survey method. A survey is simply a set of questions asked of a defined community in order to get a quantitative handle on community values, activities, qualities, or perceptions. Since the purpose of a survey is to tap into people's individual preferences, the method is most appropriate when personal information is required: "Were YOU satisfied with the help you received today?" or "Did YOU find the information you wanted?" or "Do YOU think the reference room should be open on Sundays?" Surveys are also helpful when information is required about community characteristics. Demographic information, the mainstay of collection developers, is, after all, derivative of the king of all surveys, the U.S. census. Age, education, ethnicity, and affluence are critical survey results that undergird the shaping of library collections.

While the rules of logic suggest that a response to survey questions provides a direct and effective way of assessing reference services, the reality and complexity of human behavior suggests otherwise. Users who answered they were "very satisfied" with the help they received at the reference desk may still not have found the answer to their question, but are responding instead to the strenuous efforts of a charming reference librarian. The seemingly innocuous structuring of survey questions so as to elicit the desired area of response is a tricky business. Users who want "more hours" available at reference may be users who never really utilize those extra hours. The chasm between stated perceptions and actual behavior is well documented. Surveys then are an intuitive, age-old method of collecting data on a community of users, but they gain in value when supported with collaborating data on observed behavior or when teamed with reasoned treatises.

Once conducted, surveys tend to develop a life of their own. They act as powerful, persuasive, and recurrent sources of justification for arguments, additions, or modifications made in the library world. The whole idea for roving reference librarians, for example, emerged when surveys showed that users were reluctant to walk up to a reference desk. Hernon and McClure's survey, which claimed that the average percentage of reference questions answered correctly in a library was 55 percent, has clung onto professional memory long after it was undermined on several counts and by several authorities (Richardson 2002). Given the power of surveys, a number of formats have emerged through which a survey can be conducted. The primary choice of the twenty-first century appears to be the online survey, but a brief list of formats in use by libraries is given below.

In-house

In-house surveys have been the most common method utilized by libraries. The advantage of such surveys is that they are relatively inexpensive and can be administered by staff as part of their daily routine. The staff of the Leavey Library at the

University of Southern California, for example, describes an in-house survey that cost less than $250 (Eng and Gardner 2005, 38–39). According to the results of a College Library Information Packet Note venture that studied 214 colleges, "the most common instrument developed in college libraries is the self-administered user satisfaction survey" (Adams and Beck 1995). Since they are administered on the spot, the rates of response are high. The assessments given out following an Internet instruction session, or after concluding a reference transaction, or using a new electronic database are all commonly used surveys. The Yuba County Library's Reference Department, for example, has conducted various in-house surveys to gauge patron satisfaction and collection usage. Below is an example of a survey conducted in 2005 (Figure 19-1).

Telephone

Ironically, the advantages of telephone surveys appear suspiciously close to their disadvantages. The telephone indisputably provides direct and instant entry into every household, qualities that appeal to every serious surveyor. However, that very aspect can lead to criticism from those being surveyed (for being too intrusive), and result in unwilling or less-than-sincere responses. The nature of the format also defines and limits the depth and breadth of questions. By definition, telephone surveys would be limited to relatively shorter questions and responses that require minimal or no relative rankings. While this increases the speed of responses, it limits the depth and variety of questions. Telephone surveys, while widely used in the past, enjoy less legitimacy in the aftermath of intrusive telemarketing and the subsequent law allowing households to block calls or monitor incoming calls through caller identification.

Mailed Questionnaires

Mailed questionnaires are the most nonintrusive way of conducting surveys. The time to fill out a survey and the inclination to complete one are left entirely up to the respondent. However, this could lead to low response rates as well as slow return rates. The cost required for postage is also relatively higher than other formats, especially since self-addressed, stamped envelopes are usually included in a survey package to encourage a return from the chosen respondent.

E-mail/Online

The online survey is indisputably becoming the primary tool of choice, especially for academic and corporate libraries. When the library at the University of Louisiana–Lafayette needed to survey the attitudes of library staff, Perennial Survey, a professional survey firm, prepared a list of thirty-one questions specifically for online use. The survey was then posted on the University Web site for eleven days with links provided to four popular Listservs. Only one response per IP (Internet Protocol) address was permitted. Subsequent data was then analyzed using SAS System software (Goetting 2004, 12–17). Overall, the survey method is advantageous in that "information is gathered, summarized, analyzed, and put to use in a short amount of time" (Everhart 1998).

Yuba County Library
Reference Department

Please take a few minutes to complete this survey so that we can enhance our services. All individual answers will be combined with others, thus remaining confidential.

1. Have you ever used any of the Reference department's services?

    ___Yes   ___No*   *If no, please stop here

2. Which of the services have you used in the past year?

    ___Reference Librarian   ___Brochures and fliers at the Reference desk

    ___Small Business Resources   ___Reference collection

    ___Nolo press legal references   ___Law Library computers

    ___Buzz newsletter   ___Ping newsletter

    ___ALP newsletter   ___Adult Literacy

3. If you have made use of the Reference Librarian's services, how was your "case" handled?

    ___In person   ___Email   ___Phone

4. Overall, what is your impression of the Reference Librarian and her service?

    ___Poor   ___Adequate   ___Good   ___Excellent

5. If you used any of the brochures and fliers available at the Reference desk, please list as many as you can remember, on the back.

6. If you used the Small Business Resources collection, please give your evaluation by filling out the last page of this survey.

7. If you used our Reference collection this past year, please give us your overall opinion of the quality and usefulness.

    ___Poor   ___Adequate   ___Good   ___Excellent

8. If you used our Reference collection, what materials or subject areas do you feel need improvement?

9. Have you ever used our collection of Nolo press legal materials?

    ___Yes   ___No

If yes, which materials?

10. Have you ever used our Law Library computers?

    ___Yes   ___No

If yes, what is your general opinion of the computers, their programs, etc.?

11. Have you ever seen a copy of the Buzz newsletter? If you have, please fill out the last page of this survey.

    ___Yes   ___No

12. Have you ever seen a copy of the Ping newsletter?

    ___Yes   ___No

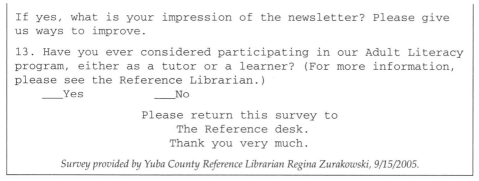

If yes, what is your impression of the newsletter? Please give
us ways to improve.

13. Have you ever considered participating in our Adult Literacy
program, either as a tutor or a learner? (For more information,
please see the Reference Librarian.)
    ___Yes   ___No

Please return this survey to
The Reference desk.
Thank you very much.

Survey provided by Yuba County Reference Librarian Regina Zurakowski, 9/15/2005.

Figure 19-1 Reference Department Survey

Surveys that require data to be gathered from human subjects are mandated by Federal Regulations to undergo a review process both before and during the survey process. This is typically undertaken in academic institutions by "an appropriately constituted group" commonly referred to as the Institutional Review Board (IRB). Libraries that are less familiar with the review process can refer to the specific code (45CFR46.116) available at www.hhs.gov/ohrp/humansubjects/guidance/45cfr46.htm.

Observations

An observation is the seemingly simple act of recording what took place. Did the reference librarian answer the question correctly? Did the reference user approach the desk for assistance? Are reference sources easily accessible to the user? A live transaction is recorded and evaluated in accordance with preset questions and expectations. The method is most applicable when actual behavior as opposed to values and perceptions is the required area of assessment. Whatever the area of assessment, there are three distinct types of observational methods.

Direct Observation

The most intuitive method is through direct observation. An activity or service is monitored and the observations are recorded. However, as Newton's humble apple can testify, the simple recording of an activity can lend itself to relevance only if it is placed within a context of well-developed suppositions and expectations. In the case of reference assessments, a set of clear questions needs to establish the grounds for observation. A sampling plan needs to set the periodicity of the observation. Finally, a plan for analyzing the data gathered through observation must be in place so that the criteria for observation are fully answered.

The Pennsylvania State University Libraries, for example, undertook direct observational analysis of the usability of a new online catalog introduced in 2001 and known as The CAT. A clear set of questions and rationale for analysis was prepared in advance. As can be seen in the box below, in order to add more dimension to the observations, users were not only observed, but were also asked to "think aloud" as they searched.

The method has much to offer. It is relatively simple and the results resonate with the sincerity of direct observation. On the negative side, the procedure can be intrusive, with reference staff or reference users constantly aware they are being watched. The observations can be potentially colored by the biases and idiosyncratic perceptions of

---

A PROTOCOL ANALYSIS STUDY

1. A friend recommends that you read a book called *History by Hollywood*. Does the Penn State Libraries have this book?

Question Rationale: To examine how users search for known items and whether they could locate a book when they knew the title. The title was chosen so that the broadest keyword search resulted in fewer than fifty matches.

2. Please use the library catalog to ask for a copy of the book *History by Hollywood*.

Question Rationale: This task was designed to see if users could determine how to use the "I Want It" button in The CAT to request materials. Analysis of e-mail queries revealed that many users were unable to determine how to request materials.

3. The article you need is in the journal *Kansas Law Review*, volume 49, issue 5, June 2001. Is this issue of the journal in the Penn State libraries? If so, where is it?

Question Rationale: A unique title was chosen so that users retrieved only one match regardless of which search type was selected (keyword or browse). The research team was interested in determining how users interpreted a serials record.

4. Another article you need is in a journal called *Civil Engineering*. Specifically, you need volume 70, December 2000. Is a copy for this year available on the University Park campus? If so, which library can it be found in?

Question Rationale: To see how users navigated a potentially complex search. The default keyword search options results in over 2,000 matches. The record display includes multiple holdings, with the UP copy at the bottom of a very long record.

5. You have been assigned to write a paper on the topic "Efforts to combat teen smoking." For this paper, you need to find four books at the Penn State Libraries. Please note the call numbers and locations of four books on this topic.

Question Rationale: To see how users search for materials on a subject. The topic was constructed so as to make it likely that multiple strategies would be required. Teen smoking as a keyword only retrieves two of the necessary four matches. The LC subject heading is Teenagers-United States-Tobacco-Use-Prevention, but other keywords would also work: teens, adolescents, smokers, and so on.

Source: Eric Novotny, "I Don't Think I Click: A Protocol Analysis Study of Use of a Library Online Catalog in the Internet Age." College & Research Libraries 65, no. 6 (November 2004): 537.

---

the all-too-fallible human observer. The quality of the questions and the strictures of plan analysis methods can skew observational studies. Relying on a tried and tested question plan can dilute some of the methodology angst.

Hidden Observation

A variation on direct observation is the method of the hidden observer. A frequently used method, the modus operandi is inculcated right from library school, when students are asked to observe and record reference interviews being conducted by librarians at their neighborhood library. In this method, the same need for a set of predetermined questions and plan of analysis need to be in place, but the staff is unaware that they are under scrutiny. The rationale is that the results would mirror more typical behavior, much as naturalist portrait photography claims to a more profound presentation of the "true" person, than does a formal studio photograph.

For example, between 1998 and 1999 the University of Arizona libraries evaluated reference service as a function of both approachability and reliability, through a three-step approach involving a survey questionnaire, observation, and focus groups. According to the coordinator of this assessment, "most of the important information the team uncovered was from the unobtrusive observation." The questions structuring the observation are given below as an example of how hidden observations can be planned (Figure 19-2).

While the claim of veracity might make this a more appealing form of observation, the use of this method must be tempered by questions of ethics and accuracy. Staff that is subsequently told they were under observation may feel embarrassed or upset. Proxy questions that required staff time in research may be considered a waste of time and energy and engender hostility. Studies that have circumvented this problem have typically involved large, multibranch libraries where the identity of the observed librarians can be kept anonymous.

Online reference transactions that apply hidden observation techniques are also relatively easier, given the invisibility of the assessor. In 2001, for example, a set of specific assessment questions were sent to 111 sites of the Association of Research Libraries that offered e-mail reference services. The unobtrusive study allowed for comparisons across institutions and could lend itself to a wider and more comprehensive assessment of e-mail reference in general. Timeliness, scope of answer, and policy statements versus actual delivery were some of the aspects of e-mail service that were studied through this method (Stacy-Bates 2003, 59–70). When a study of such scale is required, unobtrusive online observation can be the best method available.

Self-imposed Observation

Transaction diaries, journals, preset forms, and reference activity notebooks, are all examples of self-imposed observations. The most basic observation is the number and general type of reference question answered. Almost all libraries have or should have a recording of this. The hash mark denoting reference, directional, or technological queries was instrumental in providing the foundation for the innovative Brandeis Model of reference service whereby staff were apportioned to graded levels of service.

Unobtrusive Observation Worksheet (Questions)

1. Observe the reference desk for approximately two to five minutes (incognito).
What are the reference staff members doing? (Write down everything.)

Do they look approachable?

Yes   No

                   1   2   3   4   5

2. How long is the average wait for service?
3. Which person are you going to approach? Why?
4. What is your research question? (Write down the general idea.)
5. What did the person say when you initially asked the question?
6. What was the person's attitude while you explained the problem?
7. Which resources did the person recommend?
8. Did you find the resources useful?

Yes   No

                   1   2   3   4   5

9. Did the sources directly answer your question?

Yes   No

                   1   2   3   4   5

10. Would you approach the same person again? Why?
11. Did the person follow up to see if you needed additional help?
Take this time out to list two strengths and two ideas for improvement about the
reference/service.

*Source: Elaina Norlin, "Reference Evaluation: A Three-Step Approach—Surveys, Unobtrusive
Observations, and Focus Groups." College & Research Libraries 61, no. 6 (November 2000): 546–553.*

Figure 19-2 Unobtrusive Observation Worksheet

A more intensive format for self-imposed observation is a preset transactional form
that not only records the number and type of questions but also provides information
on how the question was answered or referred. Such observational data can be highly
useful in a number of assessment scenarios. The reliance on one format over another,
the efficacy or inefficacy of one source over another, and the success of one reference
librarian's search strategy over another are all areas where preset transactional forms
can throw evaluative light.

DAY	TELEPHONE	IN PERSON	COMPUTER
MONDAY			
TUESDAY			
WEDNESDAY			
THURSDAY			
FRIDAY			
SATURDAY			
SUNDAY			

COMMENTS:

Figure 19-3 Reference Transaction Diary

Monday, 4/18/2005

- Bergen's *Record*
- Ledger—March 27th—*Detailer* ad?
- T-bills—tax considerations
- Out of print books—how to purchase?
- Assertiveness training
- Math review for aptitude test
- How to teach an adult to ride a bicycle
- Fashion during Harlem renaissance
- Business plan for screen script
- Microsoft Publisher
- Jane Watson—nursing?
- Writing a screenplay
- Reviews of Guare—six degrees of sep.
- e-mail reviews of Gilead to xxxxxxxx
- Lemony Snicket pseudonym
- Japanese population in NJ
- Montessori
- Slavery in north vs. south
- Johnnie Cochran—bio
- Scholarly articles on HIV/AIDS
- Historic real estate values
- AIDS in Africa

Source: Transcript of page from the Reference Notebook of the West Orange Public Library, New Jersey.

Figure 19-4 Reference Desk Notebook, Sample Page

Many librarians also use unformatted reference activity notebooks. Given hectic schedules at a reference desk, a hurried scrawl on the text of a question is sometimes the only record that a librarian is physically able to manage. While analyzing such notebooks is far more challenging, there is great utility in such books, since the reference manager has more than individual memory to back up a statement like "we get a lot of health questions during winter." Above is the transcript of a page from the reference desk notebook of a public library (Figure 19-4).

Diaries and journals are the hardest self-observation tools to institute, decipher, and present as a consolidated finding. However, they are rich sources of information that can supplement or fill in the blanks left by other more succinct modes of observation.

Focus Groups

A focus group involves the creation of a setting and agenda calculated to elicit a group response on any issue. Like the individual interview method, the focus group aims at probing community experience and perceptions. Unlike individual interviews, the responses are a function of individual thoughts tempered or catalyzed by group dynamics. Focus groups act like old-fashioned butterchurns, stirring up the most resonant or demo-cratically held values and perceptions curdling in a group.

When does a focus group become the most useful tool available? Typically, the for-mat serves best when:

- Immediate follow-ups on responses would make for a richer study. For example, when a preliminary survey conducted by the Microsoft Library found that users needed more in-depth technical data, a follow-through focus group was organized to "drill down" into the exact kinds of data required. The survey set up the area of pri-ority and the focus group honed down the exact nature of the library's user needs.
- Individual surveys are hard to carry out for logistical or other reasons.
- Statistically larger data is required in a limited time slot.
- Group consensus on issues is as valid as or more valid than individual preferences.
- Existing data is puzzling and requires community interpretation.
- Areas of modification or change are unclear so that a preliminary sense of group priorities is required.
- Community investment is an issue that needs to be jumpstarted or fanned into greater intensity.

Overall, since group interpretation is the purpose of the format, it has been most beneficial when used as an exploratory tool or when an issue needed further clarifica-tion or interpretation. For example, after three SERVQUAL surveys were adminis-tered by the Texas A&M University Libraries, it was clear that there was a gap between user expectations and perceptions; but details remained unclear. A final se-ries of focus groups was held, which the researchers found "useful for identifying ar-eas of improvement" (Ho and Crowley 2003). The librarians at the New Jersey Institute of Technology (NJIT) at Newark conduct a focus group every year to explore different aspects of reference service. A draft of the questions asked in 2005 is posted below (Figure 19-5).

Though a pedestrian format that has been frequently used by many different types of libraries and institutions, focus groups are challenging to organize. As in the inter-view method, the elaboration of questions and their interpretation can be complex. For example, one of the questions at a focus group aimed at assessing "technostress" at the reference desk was "Your job today is to paint the reference desk and everything on it. What colors will you use?" (Rose, Gray, and Stoklosa 1998, 311). How would stippled sage be interpreted? The imagination boggles.

There is also the additional complexity of training facilitators, since the success of a focus group depends very largely on the expertise of the facilitator in both moderating the discussion and recording what transpires. The very creation of a focus group re-quires a high level of preplanning. Random sampling is not conducive to productive discussion, so by definition group members must be selected on the basis of their inter-est or experience in the issues under consideration. The "snowball technique" is fre-quently used to develop further focus groups based on the suggestions of initial participants who may know others in the community who are interested or experienced in the issue area.

Despite these challenges, the focus group format continues to be used by many

---

2005 NJIT Library Focus Group Questions—DRAFT
February 3, 2005

Unless otherwise noted, every question is to be posed to all focus groups (faculty, graduate students, undergraduate students, architecture students).

Web site
1. How frequently do you use the library Web site?
2. How effective are you at finding what you need on the library Web site?
3. What did you use the last time you were on the Web site?
4. What have you looked for on the library's homepage that you have had trouble finding?
5. What are your suggestions for improving the library Web site?
6. What's the best place you go to when looking for a journal article?
7. Where do you go to do your current awareness reading? Do you have trouble finding full text? (fac)
8. Where do you start when you have a research project?
9. What have your experiences been with the following: renewing books online? Placing a hold on a book? Checking your library accounts? Discuss your successes/difficulties in finding a book in the catalog? Finding a journal?
10. Have you used the library Web site at Rutgers? What other library's Web sites do you use?
11. What have your experiences been using databases on-site and remotely?
12. When you use the library Web site, do you feel certain that you've found what you're looking for or not? (excl arch)
13. Have moderator go down the navigation bar and ask for each item: "What do you use this for? What else?" (arch, grad & undergrad) (note for arch moderator: use arch Web site)
14. How often have you used the Image database? Did it suit your research needs? (arch)

Source: Richard Sweency, University Librarian, New Jersey Institute of Technology, 2006.

Figure 19-5 Focus Group Questions Draft

---

different libraries because of the rich dividends it tends to yield. Academic libraries such as Texas A&M have used it to set priorities, and corporate libraries such as the Microsoft Library have used it to add depth to an existing study.

Given its popularity and usage, the ideal dimensions of a focus group have been increasingly identified as:

- Unbiased, unselfconscious, and trained facilitators;
- Six to twelve participants in each group;
- Forty-five-to-ninety-minute sessions;
- Six to ten questions; and
- A minimum of three groups for a preliminary investigation, with the understanding that the larger the number of groups the greater the relevance of the method.

A stellar example of a successful focus group venture is the experience of the Clemson Libraries, which held focus group "summits" that were used as the "basis for . . . strategic and business plans" for the library; details can be found at www.arl .org/arl/pr/libqual_summit.html. The University of Texas adopted the same summit method to develop its own strategic plans. Brown University Library hired a professional firm "for several thousand dollars" to conduct its focus groups and found that the data was well worth the investment, as it "helped the Library build a case with university administrators to fund specific projects for improvement" (Shoaf 2003, 124–132).

Case Studies

Case studies are much like magnifying glasses. They focus on one aspect of librarianship, which is then studied in expanded detail. The case study method has a venerable history that can trace its ancestry to the law schools of 1870 that first introduced case method as a system of learning. What was initially a system of learning has now extended into an accepted tool of assessment in a number of social sciences.

Unlike the other methods outlined so far, the instrumentation used in this method is nonspecific. While surveys use questionnaires and focus groups use mediators, case studies use any or all of the other methods to reach a conclusion. The primary imperative in this method is to posit the case. Once the magnifying glass has settled on a case, it is studied from all angles with whatever means available or possible. The method serves as an excellent organizing tool for in-depth evaluation.

Does nonverbal communication affect patron perceptions of a reference interaction? How well does collaborative digital self-service work? Are student workers effective at reference desk service? Annotated cases can be found in *Evaluating Reference Services* (Whitlach 2000). The methods employed in the above cases included surveys, interviews, direct observation, and diaries. Why then are they case studies? If more than one tool is used to study the same issue, then it becomes a case study. The difference is one of detail and emphasis rather than the adoption of an entirely different evaluation tool.

Since the case study poses the imperative of focus and in-depth evaluation, the method is distinguished by:

*   Multiplicity of assessment instruments;
*   Greater depth of evaluative understanding;
*   Greater reliability; and
*   Relatively limited replicability.

The results following a case study are invariably less "catchy" than those following a quantitative survey. Unlike a pithy percentage or number, the case study relies on triangulating the results of different assessments to best approximate the workings of a reference service or initiative. The results, by definition, are less succinct and far denser.

Case studies are most effective when:

*   A single survey method is unconvincing;
*   A novel service or new collection has been introduced;

- Staff has the time and expertise to expend on multiple assessments and analyses; and
- Advance weighting is attributed to each method in case of discrepancies between two results.

Acting on Assessments

At a first level, assessments allow a reference manager to follow the dictum of "knowing thyself." In that knowledge lies the potential ability to establish priorities, scrape away redundancies, allot proper funding, allow for new initiatives, and provide defensible institutional justification. All of the assessment techniques covered above are important as a means to the end of "knowing thyself." Given that a great deal of time, energy, finances, and effort goes into the completion of an assessment, it is imperative that a reference manager, having gained the necessary knowledge, should act on it. Microsoft Library conducts an annual survey of user needs with the express guideline that "all questions must lead to potentially actionable results."

The New Americans Program at the Queens Borough Public Library did just that by finding direction in both funding and programming through the survey analysis conducted by its Information and Data Analysis Librarian, Wai Sze Chan. Ms. Chan mapped ethnic correlates extracted from the census to create neighborhood profiles that in turn fed into relevant collection development and program initiatives. It is unlikely that something as exotic as a "Toddler Learning Center in Bengali" could have been planned and funded by an external grant without strong survey analysis and presentation.

After a three-step survey of reference services was conducted at the University of Arizona Libraries, a roving reference librarian was introduced to enhance services; signage was improved including name tags on staff; and referrals for technology were organized since that was an area that students had found weak. The coordinator found the results of the assessment study to be "very meaningful" (Norlin 2000, 546–553).

Quantify

If major funding is at stake, a statistical analysis of collected data goes a long way toward exciting external support. However, statistical analyses will invariably involve ancient mathematical beasts such as factor analysis, Likert scales, data reduction tools, chi-squares, and measures of association. Trivial to the average statistician or statistically inclined librarian, data analyses even through the simplifying construct of programs such as SAS and SPSS can be daunting to many a stout-hearted reference manager. At this point, investing in a professional surveyor, or locating a statistically-endowed colleague, or purchasing a preset service such as LibQUAL+™ is money and time well spent. Information about the LibQUAL+™ kit is available at www.libqual.org, and cases about libraries that have used the kit can be found in the 2005 publication, *Libraries Act on Their LibQUAL+ Findings* (Heath, Kyrillidou, and Askew 2005).

Strategize

Absolute clarity in assessment needs also goes a long way toward choosing both the level and type of assessment technique. Some questions to ask are:

- Do you want to launch a new reference initiative? For example, do you want to start 24/7 virtual reference services or live online reference or tiered reference? Survey methods have worked well when broad information on subjective preferences is required.
- Do you merely want to get a "pulse" on user needs and expectations? For example, are patrons satisfied with the answers they have found to their reference questions? Are databases useful? Are reference hours satisfactory? Suggestion boxes and observation methods have succeeded in opinion-based studies such as these.
- Do you want to reprioritize funding allocation? For example, will information assistants suffice for basic reference questions? Should print resources be diverted to electronic purchases? Should a certain area such as local history or small business be given special financial focus? For analytical studies, individual opinions are rarely enough. A focus group that forces deeper interpretations would be far more effective.
- Do you want to attract new funding? For example, will bibliographic instruction in computer technology enhance the reference profile? Will adding lifelong learning commitments to traditional reference add value to overall services? For diagnostic studies that aim to improve services, opinion-based studies alone present relatively feeble input. Case studies that incorporate both subjective opinions and objective quantification are best suited.

Visualize

Scenarios that you may face as a reference manager are:

- The vice president of your graduate college has made several unsubstantiated remarks about faculty having to look elsewhere for their higher research needs. How would you convince her that the reference department is indeed serving the needs of the staff?
- Professional literature claims that 24/7 virtual reference is the library of the future. How would you design a technique to assess whether such services are necessary to your particular library?
- You have just been appointed as the supervising reference librarian of a multibranch county system. Your "feeling" is that annual updates of online general encyclopedias are preferable to purchasing the more expensive print updates. What assessment or data would you use to test your instinct?
- You are the head of reference at a medium sized public library. Your director claims that the following year's budget will be much lower and would like you to reduce reference standing orders by 10 percent. What would you discard and how would you justify your decision?

Assessments: An Imperative

Time consuming though they may be, ongoing assessments of the reference environment are an imperative. Especially given the current diversity and flux in reference services, formats, and information expectations, each reference library will of necessity need to establish as conclusively as possible what makes the current reference environment successful and what to project as long-range reference needs.

Referring to libraries as a whole, the authors of *Future Libraries* state, "The surest path to irrelevance is to allow yourself to be defined by someone else" (Crawford and Gorman 1995). While the statement sounds suspiciously close to something heard on Oprah, it is a valid observation in a world of shifting reference environments. The level of digitized reference material required by a law library may not be anywhere near the level required by a rural public library. The definition of a roving reference librarians could mean anything from moving out from behind the desk; to laptop-toting reference librarians positioned strategically within academic departments, as practiced at Brandeis and Harvard; to mobile outdoor "reference stations" assembled at university campus hot spots, as at the University of Florida (Hisle 2005). The need and extent of reference services requiring virtual-chat software can also range widely among different types of libraries serving different communities.

The evaluation and assessment tools described in this chapter are just that: tools. They are a means to an end. The end to keep in mind at all times is that assessments are well thought out, and thereby convincing measures of performance. The very act of assessing one aspect of reference swivels focus on that aspect. The focus can then lead to a compelling argument for:

- *Evaluating* practices, performance, procedures, and services of the existing reference environment;
- *Foreshadowing* reference services, formats, and practices of the future; and
- *Marketing* the value of reference services to others, such as the community at large, funding agencies, and even the reference staff itself.

As a decision maker who must decide which of multiple alternatives is the best choice; as a manager who must allocate resources to one reference activity over another; and as a spokesperson for a reference room that needs to attract legitimacy and funding from external sources, the pivotal role played by assessments cannot be underestimated.

Recommendations for Further Reading

Cobus, Laura, Valeda Frances Dent, and Anita Ondrusek. 2005. "How Twenty-Eight Users Helped Redesign an Academic Library Web Site: A Usability Study." *Reference & User Services Quarterly* 44, no. 3 (Spring): 232–246. The authors provide compelling evidence that usability testing, with even a small sampling population, was not only instructive, but provided sufficient insight to effect concrete changes. A comprehensive list of similar studies distinguished by their small sampling populations, can be found at www.jkup.net/terms-studies.html.

Dilevko, Juris. 2000. *Unobstrusive Evaluation of Reference Service and Individual Responsibility: The Canadian Experience.* Westport, CT: Ablex Publishing. Based on a government documents reference service in Canada, this somewhat pugnacious title argues that despite the controversy swirling around unobtrusive observation techniques, it can be an assessment tool of great utility.

Heath, Fred M., Martha Kyrillidou, and Consuella A. Askew, eds. 2005. *Libraries Act on Their LibQUAL+ Findings: From Data to Action.* New York: Haworth Press. This title is invaluable for reference departments interested in using LibQUAL+™ to conduct surveys. The experiences of more than two dozen college, university, health sciences, and consortial libraries are presented, so that the survey tool has an immediacy not found in the many structural descriptions of LibQUAL+.

Holt, Glen, and Donald Elliot. 2003. "Measuring Outcomes: Applying Cost-Benefit Analysis to Middle-sized and Smaller Public Libraries." *Library Trends* 51, no. 3 (Winter): 424–440. This article is unique in that it addresses a relatively neglected area of assessment study, namely, the smaller sized public library. The authors describe their efforts to tailor an existing cost-benefit analysis methodology they had earlier devised for the assessment of five large public library systems.

Howley, Sue, and Andrew Stevens. 2003. *WILIP: Summary Report and Next Steps.* London: The Council for Museums, Archives and Libraries. The assessment of reference services can be tightly focused on a single initiative or across a broad spectrum of services. This primary document provides an absorbing account of assessment on a national scale. The Wider Information and Library Issues Project (WILIP), sponsored by a nondepartmental body of the UK government in 2002, essentially mapped all the different types of information resource centers in the nation, conducted in-depth interviews, and provided over 200 suggestions aimed at ensuring the maximum fit between information users and providers.

Hubbertz, Andrew. 2005. "The Design and Interpretation of Unobtrusive Evaluations." *Reference & User Services Quarterly* 44, no. 4 (Summer): 327–335. The author supports this assessment tool by presenting it as a standardized test method. Such a method, he argues, is potentially valuable for establishing relative rankings across libraries. The (mis)use of this tool to assess overall service quality is deemed improper.

Lankes, David, John W. Collins, and Abby S. Kasowitz, eds. 2000. *Digital Reference Service in the New Millennium: Planning, Management, and Evaluation.* New York: Neal-Schuman Publishers. Part IV of this title is committed to the evaluation of emerging digital reference models. The Ask A Question model (currently re-named as Ask A Librarian) at the University of California, Irvine is evaluated. More uniquely, for specialized libraries looking for evaluation models, there is a usage analysis of digital reference at the National Museum of American Art.

Mathews, Joseph R. 2005. *Strategic Planning and Management for Library Managers.* Portsmouth, NH: Libraries Unlimited. While this is a general book on the management of libraries as a whole, Part 3 of this title is a useful exposition on evaluation strategies that can be applied to reference services in particular. A conscious focus on developing a "culture of assessment" amongst all library staff, and most importantly, of being able to parlay the value of services assessed to the world at large, make this a worthy read.

Novotny, Eric. 2002. *Reference Service Statistics and Assessment*. Washington, DC: Association of Research Libraries. Published as part of the SPEC Kit series (#268), the survey of seventy-seven member libraries provides a highly useful compilation on the various methods used by research libraries of all sizes. An interesting general observation by Novotny states that the high level of activity in reference departments juxtaposed against data that shows a decrease in the number of transactions, appears to be fostering a growing opinion that data collection techniques should be revamped.

Ronan, Jana, and Carol Turner. 2002. *Chat Reference*. Washington, DC: Association of Research Libraries. This book has a worthwhile section on evaluating chat reference. Evaluation forms for virtual reference at the University of Guelph, surveys of Ask-A-Librarian at the University of Illinois at Urbana-Champaign, Live Assistance at the Louisiana State University, LibChat at Syracuse University, and online reference at York University (defunct when checked on 2/18/2006) are all covered in separate chapters of the section.

Bibliography of Works Cited in this Chapter

Adams, Mignon, and Jeffrey Beck, compilers. 1995. *User Surveys in College Libraries. CLIP Note #23*. Chicago: ACRL.

Crawford, Walt, and Michael Gorman. 1995. *Future Libraries: Dreams, Madness, and Reality*. Chicago: American Library Association.

Eng, Susanna, and Susan Gardner. 2005. "Conducting Surveys on a Shoestring Budget." *American Libraries* vol. 36, no. 2 (February): 38–39.

Everhart, Nancy. 1998. *Evaluating the School Library Media Center: Analysis Techniques and Research Practices*. Englewood, CO: Libraries Unlimited.

Goetting, Denise. 2004. "Attitudes and Job Satisfaction in Louisiana Library Workplaces." *Louisiana Libraries* 67, no. 1 (Summer): 12–17.

Hernon, Peter, and Robert E. Dugan. 2001. *An Action Plan for Outcomes Assessment in Your Library*. Chicago: American Library Association.

Hernon, P., and C. R. McClure. 1986. "Unobtrusive Reference Testing: The 55 Percent Rule." *Library Journal* 111, no. 7 (April 15): 37–41.

Hisle, Lee W. 2005. "Reference Questions in the Library of the Future." *Chronicle of Higher Education* (September 30), B6–B8.

Ho, Jeannette, and Gwyneth H. Crowley. 2003. "User Perception of the 'Reliability' of Library Services at Texas A&M University: A Focus Group Study." *Journal of Academic Librarianship* 29, no. 2 (March): 82–87.

Listservs such as *PUBLIB*, Dig_Ref, and LIBREF_L are generous with sharing information on personal experiences with assessment methods used. Copious articles can also be found in the *Library Literature* database.

Lubans, John, Jr. 2001. " 'Where are the Snows of Yesteryear?' Reflections on a Suggestion 'Box' That Worked." *Library Administration and Management* 15, 4: 240–245.

Norlin, Elaina. 2000. "Reference Evaluation: A Three-step Approach—Surveys, Unobtrusive Observations, and Focus Groups." *College & Research Libraries* 61, no. 6 (November): 546–553.

Novotny, Eric. 2004. "I Don't Think I Click: A Protocol Analysis Study of Use of a Library Online Catalog in the Internet Age." *College & Research Libraries* 65, no. 6 (November): 523–537.

Oder, Norman. 2005. "FL, SC Studies Tout Return on Public Library Investment." *Library Journal* 130, no. 4 (March 1): 16–18.

Richardson, John V. 2002. "Reference Is Better Than We Thought." *Library Journal* 127, no. 7 (April 15): 41–42.

Rose, Pamela, Sharon A. Gray, and Kristin Stoklosa. 1998. "A Focus Group Approach to Assessing Techno-stress at the Reference Desk." *Reference & User Services Quarterly* 37, no. 4 (Summer): 311–317.

Shoaf, Eric C. 2003. "Using a Professional Moderator in Library Focus Group Research." *College & Research Libraries* 64, no. 2 (March): 124–132.

"Sources of Information on Performance and Outcome Assessment" 1997, gives an annotated bibliography of forty-five books and articles on the subject, available at www.ala.org/ala/acrl/acrlpubs/whitepapers/sourcesinformation.htm.

Stacy-Bates, Kristine. 2003. "E-mail Reference Responses from Academic ARL Libraries: An Unobtrusive Study." *Reference & User Services Quarterly* 43, 1: 59–70.

Staff. 2004. "Better Service Through Data Numbers—Wai Sze (Lacey) Chan." *Library Journal* 129, no. 5 (March 15): 34.

Ward, David. 1999. *Getting the Most Out of Web-Based Surveys*. LITA Guide #6. Chicago: American Library Association.

Whitlach, Jo Bell. 2000. *Evaluating Reference Services: A Practical Guide*. Chicago and London: American Library Association.

20

The Future of Information Service

In general, there are few worse predictors of what the day after tomorrow will look like than the claims of those whose job it is to imagine the future. Science fiction writers, trend spotters, and their ilk often do a masterful job of imagining possibilities, but few have even the most modest success when striving for certainties. The near impossibility of accurate anticipation presents a problem for the information professional, as the settings in which we work are forever changing. Librarianship in the twenty-first century is evolving at a rate that would have been unimaginable to Samuel Green when he first proposed the notion of a reference department well over a century ago. Should we fail to take the mutations of our environment into account we will relegate our libraries to obsolescence. Even so, living according to injudicious and overreaching hypotheses of future forms leads only to maladaptation. While we cannot do without some specific guesswork, it is more important that we learn to recognize the direction in which we are traveling, anticipating not just particular changes, but also the fact of change itself. If we hope to stay vital, we are called upon to change with our discipline, growing as it does.

Change does not, however, entail an outright rejection of all that has come before. In Darwinian theory one finds the notion of evolutionarily conserved traits, elements of a species' genetic makeup that are so effective and powerful as to remain unchanged for millions of years, even as everything else about the organism and its environment are transformed. Libraries in general and reference departments in particular have more than their share of conserved traits, important functions that are likely to remain as they are for generations to come. In spite of this, or perhaps because of it, we have an obligation to understand the mutative chaos that has swept up much of our discipline. In this chapter, we will attempt to map the winds of change even as we recognize some of the rocks that stand firmly amidst them.

As one standard definition has it, reference is "the facilitation of the connection between researchers and the information they desire or need" (Summerhill 1993). Although this description remains accurate, reference services have changed dramatically in the past few decades. As in other fields, the development of computing technology and the rise of the Internet have led to irrevocable paradigm shifts in the work of library and information science professionals. Crucially, such developments are not static, and the growth of the technological sphere is ongoing. Librarians must, by consequence, now focus on what technology their users have adopted and how they can use that same technology in the library to better support patron needs. The ease of using Google and question-answering systems such as Answers.com has made it hard for users to understand that all information is not the same and that search engines and question-answering systems do not always supply accurate or complete information. This is an ongoing challenge to librarians who have turned to a more active role in information literacy to try to help users understand how to evaluate and handle the information they find. Technology and easy access to information are all part of the challenge facing librarians as they reassess their role in reference service. Librarians now realize that they must make their resources and services as easy to use as these simplified online portals.

Many have sought to provide us with a view of the future of reference. David Tyckoson identified features of libraries that will remain constant and those that will change. He said that the constants were the service the libraries provide to their community—the four basic functions outlined by Samuel Green in 1876 (instruction, answering questions, reader's advisory service, and promotion)—and the personal service that librarians provide. The changes Tyckoson foresaw were newer and better tools as a result of technology, an increase in demand for instruction, a decrease in demand for ready reference, and a role for librarians in the creation of information as well as in its conservation (Tyckoson 2003, 15–16).

In another study, Joseph Janes suggested that librarians should continue to work in areas where their strengths lie. These, he suggested, are "concerns about evaluation and quality of information sources, sophisticated tools and techniques for searching, understanding the nature of users, their communities, their needs and situations, compiling and organizing and packaging information resources for their use, helping them to understand how to help themselves and how to use and evaluate information." Janes also envisioned a future that focuses "less on the answers to specific questions and more on providing assistance and support to people with more detailed, more demanding, more comprehensive information needs of all kinds." (Janes 2003, 24).

Lastly, James Rettig suggested that "reference will remain place-based, but will no longer be place-bound. The place at which it is based will not be a reference desk staffed by a reference librarian. Instead it will be an information consultation room in which a librarian can work face-to-face with a user and from which a librarian can work screen-to-screen with remote users" (Rettig 2003, 19).

Models of Reference Service

Just as new ways of watching television programs and listening to music have changed the formats in which they are delivered, so too have the models of reference service grown with reference service itself. In 1988 Barbara Ford called for a reexamination of the reference desk model. She stated, "As long as the reference desk model is uncritically accepted, librarians are not challenged to respond creatively to changes in materials, formats, and research opportunities for our users, and users are not challenged to use any of a variety of printed or computerized sources or aids" (Ford 1988). Ford's words still ring true as in the twenty-first century libraries search for new models of reference service.

Librarians have long known that not everyone needing help approaches the reference desk. Thus the need for new models is evident. The "reference consultation

---

INTERVIEW WITH DAVE LANKES, ASSOCIATE PROFESSOR, SYRACUSE
UNIVERSITY SCHOOL OF INFORMATION STUDIES

What do you think reference librarians will be doing in the future?

I think reference librarians will be tool builders—building pathfinders and Web pages to provide guidance to their users and developing survey instruments to evaluate how well they are meeting user needs. Librarians will be authors developing new finding tools on the Web for their users. They will, through their survey tools, continue to find out how to meet their users' need for information and how they can make library materials more accessible. Librarians must try to figure out the needs of the users even before the requests are made—a kind of SDI service.

Will personal one-to-one skills remain important in library work?

When I ask administrators what skills staff should have, they say that customer service is the most important. Reference is about personal touch and so no matter whether the interaction is in person, on the telephone, or virtually, librarians must continue to relate to their users. They are the intermediary between the users and the library's collection. They work in an island of complexity, unraveling the users' queries and making order out of what often looks like chaos.

Can you say more about how you see reference service developing in the future?

I think the most important thing for the future is for librarians to know their users and adapt their service to how the users want to get their information and other library materials. The librarian must develop a service that will meet the user's needs—it may mean providing service late at night for students or for others answering questions by e-mail.

---

model" was developed by Virginia Massey-Burzio at Brandeis University. In this model the first level of reference service was staffed by graduate students who answered general and directional questions. More complex questions were referred to librarians who worked with users in a more private space, such as an office or cubicle away from the reference desk. Massey-Burzio later moved to Johns Hopkins University Library, where she established a similar service. Although this model was not considered successful, its legacy is apparent in other reference models. Tiered reference service was developed in some libraries. In this model a library might have three levels of service—an information desk at the entrance to the library, a desk staffed by paraprofessionals to answer general, ready reference, and directional questions, and a consultation service for more complicated questions. Libraries have continued to develop variations on this model as a way to better help users in need of in-depth service and to better utilize the skills of librarians.

The positive side of the tiered service is using the librarians for the more complex questions. The negative side is that sometimes the staff at the reference desk do not ask enough questions to find out exactly what the user wants, or the user must wait to get access to a librarian, thus slowing down their ability to get assistance (Tyckoson 1999, 59–60).

Table 1 Models of Reference Service

Type	Definition	Pros	Cons
Traditional reference desk	Librarian serves user at the reference desk	Easy to staff—one service point	Only serve users who come to the desk
Reference consultation model	Complex questions are referred to a consultation service	Uses librarians for complex questions	Limits the number of users who can be served
Tiered reference service	Three levels of service—information desk, general reference desk, and consultation service	Uses librarians for complex questions	Must train staff to do appropriate referrals and limits the number of users who can be served
Team staffing	Librarian and paraprofessional work together at reference desk	Librarian available to answer more difficult questions	Paraprofessional must make appropriate referrals to the librarian
Integrated service point concept	Integration of reference and circulation desks	Only one point of service for users	Requires ongoing training of staff
Roving	Librarians circulate throughout the reference area	Reaches users who have not approached the reference desk	Requires additional staffing
Virtual reference	Librarians answer questions by e-mail and chat	Users assisted who cannot visit the library	Technology slow and harder to communicate with users
Outreach model	Librarians go out to departments, groups, and organizations	Can reach new audiences	Requires additional staffing

Another model, "team staffing," pairs librarians and paraprofessionals or students at the same desk. This works well, since if the user needs the services of a librarian, the staff member can easily refer the user seamlessly to the librarian. By having a librarian at the desk, there is more opportunity to assure that the quality of the service is maintained. However, the success of this model depends on the staff member and the librarian working well together and understanding their roles. If the staff member does not make appropriate referrals or if the librarian interferes with the work of the staff member unnecessarily, this model will not work well (Tyckoson 1999, 60).

Pat Flanagan and Lisa R. Horowitz wrote about the experiment at one of the Massachusetts Institute of Technology (MIT)'s libraries, which they called the "integrated service point concept." Because the in-house activity at the reference desk had been declining, a decision was made to combine the reference and circulation desks and to call it the "Library Services Desk." The users would therefore have only one point of service no matter what their question or need. All staff received training in the systems and products available in the library. The article describes an evolving service that requires ongoing training of staff and rethinking of the roles of circulation and reference staff. This model has possibilities for both academic and public libraries (Flanagan and Horowitz 2000, 329–338).

Roving is another reference service model. Jackson describes roving reference in the following way: "Many times in libraries, patrons are afraid to leave their workstations to go to the reference librarian, or they may just not realize there is an easier, more efficient way of doing their searching. Roving librarians . . . circulate through the workstation areas, asking if patrons are finding what they want" (Jackson 2002, 217). The roving model has been a successful way to reach more users who might not easily approach the reference desk but can benefit from the services of a librarian.

The virtual reference model allows for communication with users who cannot come to the physical library. By either e-mail or chat the librarian is able to provide information in response to the user's query. This model has the disadvantage of not allowing an in-person interview with the user, thus making it harder to ascertain whether the user's question has been fully answered.

Libraries are also reaching new users through an outreach model. Academic librarians go out to subject departments in universities to introduce library services and to provide information about library resources. They sit in on faculty meetings and make presentations about new resources in that department's area of interest. Public libraries go out to community groups and organizations to introduce new resources and services. They can take their PowerPoint presentation with them or a laptop for a live demonstration. School libraries reach out to teachers and administrators to encourage them to integrate information literacy into the classroom. Even special libraries find that without outreach their users do not utilize the electronic resources the library has made available to them.

New Ways of Doing Business

As the Internet has become part of our daily existence, libraries have chosen to compete by adding first e-mail reference, then chat reference, and now reference using IM (Instant Messaging). E-mail reference was a simple addition. Even using basic e-mail software, libraries began to communicate with their users. Though it is harder to conduct the reference interview using e-mail, libraries developed a form for the user to fill out to assist in ascertaining the exact question. Though it can be an uneven service, as some e-mails are answered quickly and others take several days, it can be quite satisfactory especially insofar as it gives the librarian a chance to think about the question and provide a more thorough answer.

Chat reference was patterned after some of the commercial enterprises already using this technology, such as L. L. Bean. The software has improved and has been made more usable for libraries, although the best of it is expensive. The advantage of the chat reference is that it is done in real time, is interactive and immediate, and enables the librarian to do a better reference interview. Chat reference can be done through a consortium or regionally to spread the expense and allow the libraries involved to offer more hours of service. Some consortia offer chat reference 24/7. One of the early services was a pilot project set up by the Library of Congress, the Collaborative Digital Reference Service (CDRS). Their software, QuestionPoint, was then adopted by Online Computer Library Center. Many libraries have chosen to use the QuestionPoint software.

Instant messaging (IM) has been adopted by academic libraries, since they find this appeals to their user population. It is immediate and interactive and can be done from any location. Libraries staff it during the same hours as the library or can additional hours if needed. A successful IM pilot at the University of North Carolina was reported at a 2005 RUSA preconference (Mohanty 2005).

None of these new services can be called wildly successful if one looks at the statistics. Yet there are audiences for these new ways of communication. In some libraries the service has grown, while in others it has decreased. Much of its success or failure may simply revolve around the marketing issue and whether the marketing is continuous. Nevertheless, it is an important effort to reach a mobile and diverse library user population. One way to continue to support this service is to make it a service of a consortium such as CleveNet's KnowItNow in the Cleveland, Ohio, area or of a service such as Maryland's AskUsNow or New Jersey's QandANJ, so the cost and workload can be shared.

Providing New Materials and Formats

Though books will always remain part of the reference picture, digital versions of print titles and new materials in digital format only have flooded the market. Slowly, reference titles available only in print are receding and digital titles are multiplying. Although this seems like a wonderful world for the library user, it is actually a complex world that is not easy to maneuver. In fact, the user often turns to Google or Yahoo, assuming equal quality rather than to the library's databases because they are more user friendly. Libraries have taken many approaches to encouraging the use of their online bibliographic and full-text databases from online tutorials and pathfinders to bibliographic instruction and marketing. They have added new software to aid users. The article linker software, for example, makes it possible for a user to find the full text of article in another database owned by the library when there is only a bibliographic citation. The aggregators make it possible for users to search across several databases on a topic rather than having to identify which database should be used.

More access to online databases is available beyond the library. Thus the library's users can access the databases at home, in their office, or elsewhere. This improved access results in making it easier for the user who finds it inconvenient to visit the library during its hours of service. The library's Web site provides access not only to the databases leased or owned by the library but to other information gathered by the library such as guides to how to research a term paper or a list of reliable Internet sites.

Providing New Services

Face-to-face reference service has declined in the last few years as the Internet has become a more prominent part of users' lives. Coffman and Arret reported on recent ARL statistics that show a decrease of 40 percent in reference transactions between 1997 and 2003 (2004). Libraries have also noted the decline in the number of ready reference questions and an increase in more complicated questions. Users only consult the reference librarian after trying unsuccessfully to find the information on the Internet. Libraries have reached out to new user groups in an effort to compensate for this decline in face-to-face reference. They also have to provide access through the Web to the library and its resources in order to reach users wherever they are. This calls for continual upgrades to the library's technological infrastructure and designing systems that are user friendly. We must find ways to present quality information to our users. It is important to tailor the information to the user's needs.

Librarians have begun to spend more time on information literacy. The complexity of the library's resources, especially the online databases, have made it imperative that the users receive assistance in using them. The information literacy instruction may be one-to-one at the reference desk or in an e-mail or chat session; or it may be a class—either a one-shot class to get users started or part of a collaboration with a teacher or professor to help students get started on a particular assignment.

Librarians have surveyed their users through paper and online surveys and through focus groups to get a better idea of their community's needs and wants. Many of the changes in reference service are the result of this feedback.

INTERVIEW WITH JOSEPH JANES, ASSOCIATE PROFESSOR, UNIVERSITY OF WASHINGTON INFORMATION SCHOOL

What do you think reference librarians will be doing in the future?

I don't have all the answers, but this I know. The information environment has radically changed and will continue to change. The future will be research based rather than reference based. Librarians will spend more time doing online searching, but knowledge of resources will still be important as will evaluation skills. Librarians will still do reader's advisory and will compile pathfinders.

How about the human aspects of reference service? Will the reference interview be the same?

I think the reference interview will be the same. The personal touch will continue to be important, and the librarian will need to inject the personal touch into e-mail, instant messaging, and chat as well as into the face-to-face interview. People skills will remain an important part of reference service. I tell students that the standard phrase I use during a reference interview is "Are you look for something specific?"

What else do you see in the future of reference librarians?

I think the future will be always changing, that reference work will move away from the stable resources that were once the core of reference work and that librarians must be prepared to be flexible and to move ahead with the changes.

What Will Librarians Do?

This newly defined reference service means that the role of the librarian must change. Of course, librarians will continue to answer reference questions, although there may be less of ready reference and more of complex. Many of these requests will be made online rather than in person though users will continue to come to the library. Librarians may want to take on more of the consultation role in order to better help users with complicated questions that require more time and perhaps follow-up. Whitlatch suggests that "answering questions requires more focus on instruction in search strategies and other elements related to the basic information competencies of identifying the type of information needed, and finding, evaluating, and communicating the information successfully" (Whitlatch 2003, 30).

Librarians will continue to do collection development. With less print to order, librarians will concentrate their attention on the evaluation and selection of electronic resources. Each new resource added must then be fitted into the aggregator to make it easier for the user. The new resources must also be introduced to the users for whom it is intended and marketed to an even broader audience.

Librarians will do more information literacy instruction—both one-to-one and in groups. Users need to learn to use electronic resources, the online catalog, and other databases that are available. Librarians will need to incorporate these new electronic resources into presentations that will show how to use them in a particular research situation rather than just introducing them in a general one-shot presentation.

Librarians will develop their reader's advisory skills to provide more personalized service to their users. They will also spend time creating finding tools to guide their users in the ever-more-complex world of information resources. And finally they will continue to develop Web pages to organize and present information to their users in a form that is easy to use and understand, such as pages on how to do research in general or how to research a particular subject area.

Librarians will learn more about marketing. "As part of their marketing competencies, library professionals must have the skill to systematically assess the information-seeking needs and habits of their primary clientele" (Whitlatch 2003, 29). These skills will be learned in library school or in a continuing education course.

Assessment and evaluation will be practiced on a much more regular basis by librarians. Decision making will be based on the results of surveys, questionnaires, and focus groups. Programs and projects will be based on both quantitative and qualitative information.

Reference librarians' role will change as reference continues to evolve. Their new role will be multifaceted and more proactive than in the past. They will work to design better systems that meet their users more personalized needs.

Does Reference Have a Future?

Questions about the ongoing relevance of all aspects of our profession have likely been going concerns since the library of Alexandria burned to the ground. While libraries are certainly subject to change, we need not fear their dissolution. Comparatively speaking, reference service is a new dimension of our institutions, but as we grow both more complex and more open it increasingly seems certain that this service is here to stay. Far more productive, then, may be to ask how that future should be approached. James Rettig has suggested that libraries must respond to their users' values, which are "immediacy, interactivity, personalization, and mobility" (Rettig 2003, 19). As to immediacy, the library's attempts to use chat reference and instant messaging speak to the attempt to meet this user need as well as the attempt to provide reference 24/7. Interactivity has been responded to by chat and IM. Personalization is embedded in the library's attempt to provide a way for the user to personalize the library's Web site to their own needs—by choosing the version of the home page they want or by developing a MyLibrary site with only the information that user needs. The need for mobility has been responded to by making the library Web site and its resources available wherever the user is and at any hour. Rettig has also challenged librarians to become "expert anthropologists of our user communities" in order to serve them well (Rettig 2003, 20).

Marketing is another important component of the library's future. Just as any profit-making or nonprofit organization, libraries must make their present and potential users aware of their products and services. Marketing need not be terribly expensive, but it must be effective. Libraries offer a wide range of materials and services that are often not obvious to the users unless they are highlighted. Especially since so many of the resources and services are online and often remote, libraries must use a variety of media to market themselves—flyers and brochures, the Library's home page, newspapers, radio and television, and Web sites.

The future of reference is best summed up as "high tech and high touch." Libraries will continue to upgrade their technology in an effort to better serve their users. They will also continue to develop personalized services for every user whether that user asks for service face-to-face at the reference desk, by telephone, by e-mail, or by chat. The complexity of the available information services must be matched by support for the individual users (Ferguson 2000, 303). The reference service will be integrated and seamless such that reference service will be provided to match the user's needs no matter where he or she enters the library's sphere. The personal aspect of the library's service will continue to distinguish it from other institutions and will separate it from its competition and fill the needs of its users.

Recommendations for Further Reading

Auster, Ethel, and Donna C. Chan. 2004. "Reference Librarians and Keeping Up-to-Date; A Question of Priorities." *Reference & User Services Quarterly* 44, no. 1 (Fall): 59–68. A study of the competencies required for reference librarians in a changing environment and how librarians were using professional development to upgrade their skills.

Bradford, Jane T., Barbara Costello, and Robert Lenholt. 2005. "Reference Service in the Digital Age: An Analysis of Sources Used to Answer Reference Questions." *The Journal of Academic Librarianship* 31, no. 3 (May): 263–272. A study of whether librarians used print or online sources to answer questions. Print sources were only used 9.38 percent of the time.

Cardina, Christen, and Donald Wicks. 2004. "The Changing Roles of Academic Reference Librarians Over a Ten-Year Period." *Reference & User Services Quarterly*

44, no. 2 (Winter): 133–142. This survey documents the changes in the jobs of academic librarians over a ten year period.

Smith, Michael M., and Barbara A. Pietraszewski. 2004. "Enabling the Roving Reference Librarian: Wireless Access with Tablet PCs." *Reference Services Review* 32, 3: 249–255. Description of a roving reference strategy at Texas A&M University Libraries where the librarians roved the student study areas using tablet PCs to access electronic resources.

Bibliography of Works Cited in this Chapter

Coffman, Steve, and Linda Arret. 2004. "To Chat or Not to Chat—Taking Another Look at Virtual Reference, Part I." *Searcher* (July–August), 38–46.

Ferguson, Chris. 2000. " 'Shaking the Conceptual Foundations,' Too, Integrating Research and Technology Support for the Next Generation of Information Service." *College and Research Libraries* (July), 300–311.

Flanagan, Pat, and Lisa R. Horowitz. 2000. "Exploring New Service Models: Can Consolidating Public Service Points Improve Response to Customer Needs?" *Journal of Academic Librarianship* 26, no. 5 (September): 329–338.

Ford, Barbara J. 1988. "Reference Service: Past, Present, and Future." *College and Research Libraries News* 49, no. 9 (October): 578–582.

Frank, Donald G., Katharine L. Calhoun, W. Bruce Henson, M. Leslie Madden, and Gregory K. Raschke. 1999. "The Changing Nature of Reference and Information Service: Predictions and Realities." *Reference and User Services Quarterly* 39, no. 2 (Winter): 151–157.

Jackson, Rebecca. 2002. "Revolution or Evolution: Reference Planning in ARL Libraries." *Reference Services Review* 30, 3: 212–228.

Janes, Joseph. 2003. "What is Reference For?" *Reference Services Review* 31, 1: 22–25.

Mohanty, Suchi. 2005. *IM Your Librarian: The Success of Instant Messaging at the R. B. House Undergraduate Library.* RUSA MARS/RSS Preconference, June 2005, Chicago.

Rettig, James. 2003. "Technology, Cluelessness, Anthropology, and the Memex: The Future of Academic Reference Service." *Reference Services Review* 31, 1: 17–21.

Summerhill, K. S. 1993. "The High Cost of Reference: The Need to Reassess Services and Service Delivery." *Reference Librarian* 43, 71–85.

Tenopir, Carol, and Lisa A. Ennis. 2001. "Reference Services in the New Millennium." *Online* (July–August), 41–45.

Tyckoson, David A. 1999. "What's Right with Reference?" *American Libraries* (May), 57–63.

———. 2003. "On the Desirableness of Personal Relations between Librarians and Readers: The Past and Future of Reference Service." *Reference Services Review* 31, 1: 12–16.

Whitlatch, Jo Bell. 2003. "Reference Futures: Outsourcing, the Web or Knowledge Counseling." *Reference Services Review* 31, 1: 26–30.

Wilson, Myoung C. 2000. "Evolution or Entropy? Changing Reference/User Culture and the Future of Reference." *Reference and User Services Quarterly* 28 (Summer): 387–390.

Subject Index

24/7 access, 307

A

AACR2 (Anglo American Cataloging
    Rules), 63
Abbreviations, 117
ABC-CLIO, 82
Abridged dictionaries, 113–14
Academic libraries
    changes, 345–46
    information literacy, 275, 276
    reference collections, 289
    style manuals, 121
    time spent with questions, 6
Accessibility of encyclopedias, 71
Accuracy
    bibliographic resources, 64
    biographical resources, 207
    dictionaries, 126
    evaluating, 293–94
    guidelines, 25
    indexes, 148–49
    Internet, 237, 246
    maps, 193
    ready reference, 105, 109
Acronyms, 117
Actors, 206
African Americans, 206
Aggregators, 136, 342
ALA (American Library Association), 9–10,
    11, 274, 305
Almanacs, 95–97
Alternative presses, 139
American Library Association (ALA), 9–10,
    11, 274, 305
Analytical bibliographies, 55
Analytical phrases, 73

Analyzing encyclopedias, 74–78
Anglo American Cataloging Rules
    (AACR2), 63
Answers
    categorizing, 32–35
    from dictionaries, 127–28
    elementary, 39–40
    from indexes, 136
    medical, legal, and business topics, 175
    mistakes, 40–42
    nature, 31–32
    responses to, 36–37
    types, 37
    value-added, 37–38
    visualizing, 35
    See also Questions; Reference interviews
Appeal factors, 259
Approachability, 9, 17, 25, 26
Art indexes, 143–44, 145–46
Artists, 205, 206
Asian Americans, 206
"Ask A" services, 308
Assessments
    acting on, 330
    aspects, 316–17
    books and articles about, 332–34
    case studies, 329–30
    collection, 296
    focus groups, 326–29
    importance, 332
    information literacy programs, 281–82, 283
    observations, 321–26, 333
    purpose, 315–16
    quantifying, 330–31
    reference transaction notebooks, 323–26
    strategies, 331
    suggestion boxes, 317–18

Assignments, 265, 267–71
Atlases, 186–90, 194
Audience
    biographical resources, 207
    encyclopedias, 69–70, 74, 83, 86
    marketing, 310–11
    reference works, 293–94
    web sites, 248
Audiovisual information, 235
Authority
    bibliographic resources, 64
    biographical resources, 207
    dictionaries, 113–14, 125–26
    encyclopedias, 85
    evaluating, 245, 293–94
    geographic sources, 193
    Internet sources, 245–46
    ready reference, 105
    reference materials, 293–94
Authority headings, 42
Authors, 204–5
Author searches, 47
Auto-recommendation lists, 258
Avoidance, 41, 257–58

B
Behavior
    guidelines, 9–10, 25
    information-seeking, 266–67
    observing, 321–26
    problem, 267
    in readers advisory interviews, 257–58
    in reference interviews, 17–18, 22–23
Bennett Library, 307
Berkshire Publishing Group, 82
Biblical concordances, 119–20
Bibliographic control, 62–63, 68
Bibliographic instruction, 136, 273–74
Bibliographic Retrieval Service, 135
Bibliographic utilities, 63
Bibliographic verification, 6
Bibliographies
    articles about, 68
    bibliographies of, 61–62
    collection development, 63–64
    history, 53–54
    national, 57–58

    questions answered, 54–55
    retrospective, 60–61
    scope, 64
    searching, 64–65
    subject, 56–57
    trade, 56
    types, 55–56
    use, 54
Bilingual dictionaries, 122–23
Bills, Congressional, 217–18
Biographical resources
    articles about, 211
    collection development, 206–8
    contemporary people, 200–201
    dictionaries, 204
    encyclopedias, 73–74
    ethnic sources, 205, 206
    indexes, 200
    obituaries, 204
    questions for, 200
    ready reference, 99
    retrospective, 202–4
    searching, 208
    subject-based tools, 204–5
    Supreme Court, 220–21
    use, 199
Biology, 141
Bishop, W. W., 3
Blinklisting, 39
Book groups, 255
Booklists, 261
Bookmarking, 39
Boolean operators, 44, 240, 243, 245
Brandeis Model, 323
British Library Document Supply Center, 150
Brown University Library, 329
Browsing, 36
Budgets, 295–96, 299
Business indexes, 145
Business topics
    characteristics, 156–58
    collecting materials, 173–75
    Department of Commerce, 219–20
    indexes, 145, 172–73
    publishing, 173–74
    questions regarding, 155, 158
    referrals, 157, 176

remote reference, 176
resources, 168–73, 180–81

C
Calendars, 102
Canada
    atlases, 189, 190
    biographical resources, 201, 203
    business resources, 169
    dictionaries, 115
    government publications, 224
    legal resources, 167, 168
    national bibliography, 58
Case studies, 329–30
Cassel Publishing, 122–23
Cataloging, 63
Catalogs, library, 42–43, 57, 136, 174, 257–58
Catalogs, union, 57–58, 63
Category mistakes, 16, 18–19
CDRS (Collaborative Digital Reference
    Service), 342
Census, 104, 330
Central Intelligence Agency (CIA), 220
Chain of command, 304
Chan, Wai Sze, 330
Change
    management of, 305, 311
    in reference service, 12, 337–38, 344–46
    technological, 80
Chat reference, 307, 334
Children's services
    atlases, 188
    dictionaries, 121–22
    encyclopedias, 70, 83–84
    evaluating web sites, 245
    government guides, 223
    indexes, 147
    information literacy, 266–67, 276–77
    medical resources, 160–61
    questions, 265
    reader's advisory, 253
    search engines, 239, 241
Chronologies, 102
Citation guidance, 120–21
Citation indexes, 145–46
Cities, 103
Classification, government publications, 215

Clemson Libraries, 329
Closed-ended questions, 18–19
Closing reference interviews, 21, 23
Collaboration, 39–40
Collaborative Digital Reference Service
    (CDRS), 342
Collection development
    articles about, 299–300
    assessment, 296
    bibliographies, 63–64
    biographical resources, 206–8
    dictionaries, 125–26
    encyclopedias, 81, 84–88
    future, 344
    geographic sources, 192–94
    government publications, 225–26
    indexes, 147–49
    knowledge of users, 290
    medical, legal, and business topics, 173–75
    policies, 297–99
    reader's advisory, 262
    ready reference, 5, 105–6
    scope, 7, 297–98
    selecting reference materials, 7
    tasks, 290–91
    weeding, 296–97
Colleges, 101
Communication, 17–18, 22, 25
Complexity of answers, 33
Concordances, 119–20
Confidentiality, 11, 157
Congress, 205, 217–18, 235; 229, 320
Consortia, 295–96
Consumer guides, 99–100
Control, bibliographic, 62–63
Controversial topics, 268
Convenience, 72, 236
Copyright, 11, 114, 220
Copyright Office, 57, 220
Cornell University Library, 46
Cost
    encyclopedias, 86
    evaluating, 8, 295
    full text, 230
    government publications, 223
    indexes, 149
    marketing, 310–11

Creative browsing, 36
Crisscross directory, 98
Criteria for evaluating materials, 74–75, 207, 292–95
Critical bibliographies, 55
Cross-disciplinary answers, 34
Cultural differences, 26
Currency
    answers, 33–34, 38
    bibliographic resources, 64
    bibliographies, 63–64
    dictionaries, 113
    evaluating, 193–94
    indexes, 149
    Internet, 235, 247
    maps, 193
    medical, legal, and business resources, 174–75
    medical, legal, and business topics, 157, 157–58, 166, 173–74
    need for, 33
    ready reference sources, 105–6
Current issues, 73
Curriculum, information literacy, 279
Curriculum, library school, 235
Cyberguide ratings, 248–49
Cyberplagiarism, 284

D
Databases. *See* Indexes
Demographics, 104, 224
Departments, government, 219–20
Depository libraries, 215, 224, 229
Descriptive bibliographies, 55
Desk atlases, 188
Developmental barriers to information literacy, 266–67
Dialog, 135
Diaries, reference activity, 323–26
Dictionaries
    bilingual, 122–23
    biographical, 204
    business, 168–70
    children's, 121–22
    collection development, 125–26
    for disabled, 123–24
    further reading, 132

general, 113
legal, 165
medical, 159
questions answered, 112
specialized, 115–18
subject, 124
use, 111–12
Dictionary Society of North America, 125
Direct observations, 321–23
Directories, 161–62, 166, 216
Disabled people, dictionaries for, 123–24
Disclaimers, 175–76
Displays, 255
Dissertations, 146
Document delivery, 150
Drug information, 164

E
EBSCO, 138
Education, 101, 141–42, 219
E-government, 214–15, 219, 225–26, 229–30
E-Government Act of 2002, 214
Elections, 222
Electronic sources
    articles about, 299–300
    choosing, 295
    evaluating, 293, 294
    infrastructure, 80
    management, 309
    marketing, 299
    online databases, 342.
    See also Indexes; Internet; *specific topics or sources*
Elementary answers, 39–40
E-mail surveys, 319
Employment, 100
Encyclopedias
    books about, 90–91
    collection development, 81, 84–88
    electronic, 79–81
    general, 74–78
    legal, 165
    medical, 160–62
    scope, 70–71, 80, 81, 87
    specialized subjects, 81–83
    structure, 69–74
Entertainment, 253–54

Entrepreneurship aids, 171
Enumerative bibliographies, 55
Esquivalience, 114
Ethics, 10–11, 157, 277–78, 323
Ethnic indexes, 145
Etiquette, 104
EURALEX, 125
Evaluating
    bibliographies, 64
    biographical resources, 207–8
    dictionaries, 125–26
    encyclopedias, 84–87
    geographic sources, 193
    government publications, 225–26
    indexes, 148–49
    information, 20–21
    information literacy programs, 281–82
    Internet sites, 237, 248–49
    materials, 7–8, 74–75, 207, 291–95
    medical, legal, and business resources,
        174–75
    reader's advisory tools, 259
    ready reference, 105
    search results, 38–39, 245–49
    services, 317
    skills, 26
    staff and services, 9–10
    See also Assessments
Exact phrases, 47
Exchange arrangements, 296
Executive branch publications, 218–19
Ex Libris, 136

F
Facts, searching for
    general, 95–97
    how, 103–5
    local, 97
    what, 99–101
    when, 102
    where, 103
    which, 101–2
    who, 97–99
Facts on File, 82
Factual information, 34
Fair use, 11
Farber, Evan, 274

Federated searching, 48–49
Fiction. *See* Reader's advisory
Finding tools, creating, 8–9
Fish, 219
Flying Spaghetti Monster, 237
Focus groups, 326–29
Follow up
    evaluating, 9, 21, 26
    lack of, 42, 258
    with parents, 270
foreclosing, 257–58
Foreign languages, dictionaries, 122–23
Format of reference materials, 294, 298
Form subdivisions, 43
Franchises, 171
Franciscan monks, 54
Full text, 148–50, 238
Future
    information literacy, 282, 344
    librarians, 339, 343
    reference services, 12–13, 26–27, 337
    technology, 80

G
Gale Group, 98
Gallaudet University Press, 124
Garland Publishing, 82
Gated word dictionaries, 116–17
Gazetteers, 185–86
General facts, 95–97
General Motors, 303
Genres, 261
Geographic sources
    articles about, 197–98
    atlases, 186–90, 194
    collection development, 192–94
    dictionaries, 185–86
    GIS sources, 192
    maps, 184, 186–91, 193, 222
    quick facts, 103
    travel guides, 192
    types, 184–85
    U.S. government publications, 191
    use, 183–84, 194
Ginsparg, Paul, 235–36
GIS sources, 192
Gordonator Precision Search Function, 260

Government assistance, 100
Government Performance and Results Act, 316
Government Printing Office, 214–15
Government publications
    Canada, 224
    collection development, 225–26
    directories, 216
    e-government, 214–15, 219, 225–25, 229–30
    elections, 222
    executive branch, 218–19
    government departments, 219–20
    guides to U.S. government, 215–16
    historical data, 222–23
    international resources, 223
    judicial branch, 220–21
    legislative branch, 217–18
    maps, 222
    materials about, 229–30
    periodicals, 216–17
    printing, 214–15
    questions, 214
    statistical resources, 221–22
    United Kingdom, 224
    use, 213
Grammar guides, 120–21
Grants, 100–101
Green, Samuel, 3–4
Greenwood Publishing Group, 82
Greetings, 257
Grouping terms, 47

H
H. W. Wilson, 138–39
Handbooks, business, 169–70
Handicapped people, dictionaries for, 123–24
HarperCollins, 122
Harvard University, 39, 306–7
Hearing impaired people, dictionaries for, 123–24
Hidden observation, 323
Hierarchy of needs, 156
Hispanic Americans, 206
History
    atlases, 188–89
    government data, 222–23

indexes, 135–36, 142–43
Internet material, 238
of reference service, 3–4
Homework, 265, 267–71
How facts, 103–5
Humanities indexes, 143, 145–46
Hunter Library, 43
Hyphenated terms, 47

I
IAC (Information Access Company), 135
Imposed queries, 21–22, 34–35, 265
Inappropriate answers, 40
Incidental information, 254
Indexes
    aggregators, 136, 342
    articles about, 154
    biographical resources, 200
    business, 145, 172–73
    for children, 147
    companies, 138–39
    history, 135–36
    legal, 166–67
    medical, 145, 163
    newspapers, 58–60, 140
    nonprint materials, 61
    obituaries, 204
    online, 342
    periodicals, 58–60, 138–40
    purpose, 135
    questions answered, 136–37
    reader's advisory, 6, 255, 259–61
    searching, 43–49
    special types of materials, 146–47
    subject-based, 140–45
    use, 136
    See also Electronic sources
Information Access Company (IAC), 135
Information commons model, 306
Information literacy
    children, 266–67
    classroom setting, 279–80
    definition, 273–74
    ethics, 277–78
    future, 282, 344
    impact of Internet, 280–81
    instruction, 6–7, 275–76, 343

materials about, 282–84
standards, 274–75
Information-seeking behavior, 266–67
Ingenta Document Delivery, 150
In-house surveys, 318–19
Instant messaging, 236
Instruction
approaches, 275–76
bibliographic, 136, 273–74
children and information literacy, 266–67
electronic encyclopedias, 81
impact of Internet, 280–81
on indexes, 136
information literacy, 344
materials about, 282–84
one-on-one, 278–79
overview, 6–7
purpose, 273
Integrated service point concept, 341
Intellectual freedom, 11
Intellectual property rights, 11
Interactive information, 236
Intercultural communication, 16
Interlibrary loan, 150
International resources, 223
International Standard Bibliographic Description (ISBD), 63
International Standard Book Number (ISBN), 56
Internet
history, 233
information literacy, 280–81
librarians and, 233–34
material about, 249–50
strengths, 234–37
weaknesses, 237–39
web site management, 309
Interviews, reference. See Reference interviews
Interviews with professors, 339, 343
Investment guides, 170–71
ISBD (International Standard Bibliographic Description), 63
ISBN (International Standard Book Number), 56
ISI Document Solution, 150

J
J. Paul Leonard Library, 44, 45
Janes, Joseph, 343
Jobs, 100
Journals. See Periodicals
Journals of reference activities, 323–26
Judicial branch publications, 220–21
Judicial Council of the California County Law Librarians, 164

K
Katz, William, 4
Keywords, 48, 237–38, 244
Kinesic analysis, 17
Knapp, Patricia, 274
Knowledge of sources, 41–42
Knowledge of users, 290

L
Lankes, Dave, 339
Large print dictionaries, 123–24
Larsgaard, Mary Lynette, 194
Lawyers, 166
Learners dictionaries, 115–16
Learning at the point of need, 278–79
Learning styles, 79, 303
Leavey Library, 318
Legal topics
collection development, 173–75
ethics, 157
guide to web sites, 180
questions, 155, 158
referrals, 157, 176
remote reference, 146, 176
resources, 164–68
use, 156–58
Legislative branch, 205, 217–18, 229, 235
Lexicographers, 125
LexisNexis, 135, 139
LibQUAL+, 330, 333
Librarians
behavior, 17–18, 21–23
future, 339, 343
and Internet, 233–34
mistakes, 40–42, 257–58
performance guidelines, 9–10, 25, 27
Libraries, directories, 62

Library catalog, 42–43, 57, 136, 257–58
Library of Congress, 54, 57, 220, 342
Library of Congress Subject Headings, 42–43
Library science indexes, 144
Limiters, 44, 47–48
Lincoln, Mary Todd, 266
Listening, 9, 23, 25
Listservs, 49, 261
Literature, 101–2, 143, 146, 204–5
Local facts, 97
Local government, 229–30
Los Alamos National Laboratory, 235–36
LURES analysis method, 74–75

M
Machine Readable Cataloging (MARC), 63
Mailed questionnaires, 319
Mall mentality, 72
Management, 304–5, 308–11, 312, 320
Manners, 104
Maps, 184, 186–91, 193, 222
MARC (Machine Readable Cataloging), 63
Marketing, 10, 299, 310–11, 344
Market shares, 171
Maslow's hierarchy of needs, 156
Massachusetts Institute of Technology (MIT), 341
Mass assignments, 268–69
Mass convenience, 236
Mathematicians, 205
McGraw Hill, 123
Mead Data Central, 135
Medical topics
    collection development, 173–75
    ethics, 157
    health statistics, 222
    remote reference, 164, 176
    resources, 145, 159–64, 180–81
    use, 156–58, 175
    web site, 49
Meta-characters, 44, 47
Meta-dictionaries, 118
Meta-search engines, 242–42
Microsoft Library, 327, 328, 330
Mission of reference service, 4, 49
Mistakes, 40–42, 257–58
Misunderstandings, 22

MIT (Massachusetts Institute of Technology), 341
Mobile services, 306–7
Models of reference service, 306, 324, 338–41
Mood and reader's advisory, 256
Movies, 61
Moving, 103
Multimedia in encyclopedias, 79
Multimedia information, 235
Muse Global, 136
Mutual engagement, 5–6

N
National catalogs, 57–58
National Center for Health, 164
National libraries, 57
National parks, 219
Natural language queries, 241
Negative closure, 23
Negotiating the question, 18–20
Neutral questioning model, 16, 18–19
New Americans Program, 330
New Jersey Institute of Technology, 327
News, biographical sources, 201
Newspapers, 58–60, 65, 140
New York Public Library, 106
Nonprint materials, indexes, 61. *See also* Electronic sources; *specific topics or sources*
Nonverbal communication, 16
Northwest Missouri State University, 306
Notebooks, reference activity, 323–26
NTC, 122

O
Obituaries, 204
Observations, 321–26, 333
Occupations, 100
OCLC (Online Computer Library Center), 63
Office of Management and Budget (OMB), 214
Office of the President, 218–19
Omnigraphics, 98
Online Public Access Catalogs (OPAC), 42–43, 57–58, 136, 257–58
Online surveys, 319

OPACs (Online Public Access Catalogs), 42–43, 57–58, 136, 257–58
Open-ended questions, 18–19
Open URL link resolvers, 48–49
Operators, 44, 240, 243, 245
Oregon State University, 304
Organizing reference service, 304–6
Outcome measures, 281
Outreach model, 341
Overviews in reference interview, 36–37
Oxford University Press, 82, 122–23

P
Panic, 41
Parents, 270
Parliamentary procedures, 105
Pastafarians, 237
Pathfinders, 8–9, 41, 278–79, 339
Pennsylvania State University Libraries, 321–22
People. *See* Biographical resources
Perennial Survey, 319
Performance guidelines, 9–10, 25, 27
Periodicals
    government publications, 216–17
    indexes, 58–60, 138–40
    questions about, 54–55
    searching for, 65
Perpetual calendars, 102
Philosophers, 205
Photographs, in biographical resources, 207–8
Pitfalls in answering, 40–42, 257–58
Plagiarism, 277–78, 284
Plays, 146
Poetry, 147
Political maps, 184
Post office, 98
Practicing reference skills, 26, 32
Precision, 38
President, Office of the, 218–19
Printing Act of 1895, 215
Privacy, 11
Private interests, 11
Problem patrons, 267
Professional development, 11
Promotion of reference services, 10

ProQuest, 138
Protocol analysis study, 322
Proximity, 17
Psychology indexes, 144–45
Public libraries
    indexes for, 138
    information literacy, 276–77
    outreach, 341
    pathfinders, 8
    reference collections, 289–92
    return on investment, 316
    time spent with questions, 6
    youth service, 265, 268
Public relations, 310–11
Publishers
    book group guides, 255
    directories, 62, 99
    encyclopedias, 82–83, 85
    government as, 214
    indexes, 138–39, 148
    medical, legal, and business topics, 173–74
Punctuation, 120–21

Q
Quality control of Internet, 237
Quantifying assessment data, 330–31
Queens Borough Public Library, 330
Questionnaires, 318–21
QuestionPoint, 342
Questions
    ambiguity, 15–16
    for biographical resources, 200
    decline, 343
    for dictionaries, 127–28
    for encyclopedias, 71–74
    examples, 32
    for geographic resources, 184
    imposed queries, 21–22, 34–35, 265
    for indexes, 136–37
    instruction, 278
    in library school curriculum, 235
    medical, legal, and business, 155, 158
    natural language, 241
    negotiating, 18–20
    reader's advisory, 254–55
    in reference interviews, 18–20

Questions (*continued*)
    types, 4–6, 32
    See also Answers; Reference interview
Quick reference. *See* Ready reference
Quotations, 119

R
Radiendocrinator, 176–77
Random House, 122
Rapport, 17–18
Reader's advisory
    children, 271
    common mistakes, 257–58
    future, 344
    interview, 255–58
    overview, 6
    purpose, 253–54
    reference tools, 259–62
Ready reference
    books and articles about, 109
    collecting for, 105–6
    definition, 4–5
    encyclopedias, 71
    general facts, 95–97
    recognizing, 34
    sample questions, 94
    types, 94–95
Recall, 38
Reference activity notebooks, 323–26
Reference consultations, 306, 338–39
Reference departments, organizing, 304–6
Reference interviews
    articles on, 12–13, 27–28
    behaviors to avoid, 22–23
    closing, 21, 23
    conducting, 17–21
    ethics, 157
    instruction, 278–79
    poor, 40
    problems, 21–23
    reader's advisory, 255–58
    reasons, 15–16
    studies, 16
    telephone reference, 24
    virtual reference, 24–25
Reference materials, 7–8, 291–95. *See also*
    specific materials

Reference services
    changes, 12, 337–38, 344–46
    evaluating, 9–10, 25–26
    future, 344–45
    marketing, 10, 310–11
    mission, 4, 49
    mobile services, 306–7
    models, 306, 324, 338–41
    types of, 4–6
    See also specific services
Referrals
    dictionaries, 127–28
    encyclopedias, 72
    medical, legal, and business topics, 157,
      176
    systems for, 39, 41
Relevance of sources, 37–38
Reliability
    encyclopedias, 81, 85–86
    Internet sources, 246–47
    ready reference, 105
    value add-ons, 37–38
Religion indexes, 143
Relocation, 103
Research projects, 279
Research questions, 5–6
Respect, 26
Response to answers, 36–37
Results of search, 38–39, 48, 245–49
Retrospective bibliography, 60–61
Retrospective biography, 202–4
Return on investment, 316
Reviews
    indexes to, 146
    medical, legal, and business resources, 173
    for reader's advisory, 260
    sources, 8, 125, 291–92
Rhyming dictionaries, 118
RLG (Research Library Group), 63
Road atlases, 189
Route maps, 184, 189
Roving reference, 17–18, 306–7, 341, 346
Royal National Institute for the Blind, 123

S
San Francisco State University, 44, 45
Scholars, 205

School libraries, 101, 253, 268, 276, 290
Science indexes, 141, 145–46
Scientists, 205
Scope
    bibliographies, 64
    biographical resources, 207
    collections, 7, 297–98
    encyclopedias, 70, 70–71, 80, 81, 87
    evaluating, 148, 293–94
    Internet, 236–37
    reference collection, 298
    reference materials, 293
Scope of encyclopedias, 71
Scribners, 82
Search engines, 239–42, 244–45
Searching
    aggregators, 136, 342
    behaviors to avoid, 22–23
    bibliographies, 64–65
    biographical resources, 208
    choosing terms, 241–42, 244–45
    databases, 43–49
    developing a strategy, 20
    in encyclopedias, 80
    evaluating results, 38–39, 245–49
    handbooks, 249
    indexes, 136, 138, 150
    keywords, 48, 237–38, 244
    librarians guiding, 234
    library catalog, 42–43, 257–58
    natural language queries, 241
    reader's advisory tools, 255, 257–60
    web sites on, 38–39
    worksheets, 45–46
Selecting
    bibliographies, 63–64
    biographical resources, 206
    dictionaries, 125
    encyclopedias, 84
    geographic sources, 192–93
    government publications, 225
    indexes, 147–48
    Internet search tools, 239
    medical, legal, and business resources, 173
    reader's advisory tools, 262
    ready reference, 105–6
    reference materials, 7–8, 281–95

Self-directed management, 304–5
Self-imposed observations, 323–26
Sense-making, 18
Series, 261
Shakespeare, William, 119–20
Short stories, 146
Sign language dictionaries, 124
Simon Fraser University, 307
Simplicity of answers, 33
Slang, 116, 128
Social bookmarking, 39
Social science indexes, 142–43, 145–46
Sociology and encyclopedia entries, 72
Sound, 235
Sources
    categorizing, 33–34
    deducing, 41
    form, 43
    poor knowledge of, 41–42
    ranking, 38–39
    visualizing, 35
    See also specific sources
Special libraries, 37, 277, 290
Staff, organizing, 305–6
State governments, 223, 229–30
Statistics
    analysis, 330–31
    as assessment tool, 10
    circulation, 315
    on education, 219
    general sources, 103–4
    from government publications, 221–22
    on health, 164
    on index use, 149
    international, 224
    from Internet sources, 236
Stemming, 47
Strategies for assessment, 331
Strategizing answers, 40
Structure of encyclopedias, 69–74
Student atlases, 188
"Stump the Librarian" game, 106
Style guidance, 120–21
Subcategorizing, 36
Subdivisions, 43
Subject-based biographical tools, 204–5
Subject-based encyclopedias, 81–83

Subject-based indexes, 140–45
Subject bibliographies, 56–57
Subject classes, 48
Subject dictionaries, 124
Subject directories, 241, 243
Subject headings, 42–43
Suggestion boxes, 317–18
Superintendent of Publications (SuDoc)
    classification numbers, 215
Supreme Court, 220–21
Surveys, 318–21
Synopses, 36–37
Synoptic pictures, 72

T
Taft Group, 98
Teachable moments, 5, 276, 278
Teachers, 268–70, 276, 279
Team-based management, 304–5
Team staffing, 340
Teenagers, 267
Telephone directories, 97–98
Telephone reference, 18, 24, 176
Telephone surveys, 319
Texas A&M University Libraries, 327, 328
Textual bibliographies, 55
Thematic maps, 184, 189–90
Thesauri, 118–19
Theses, 146
Thomson Gale, 83, 138
Tiered reference, 339
Time for answering questions, 32–33
Timelines, 102
Topographic maps, 184
Trade bibliographies, 56
Transaction diaries, 323–26
Travel guides, 192
Trial balloons, 36
Truncation, 47

U
U.S. Government Printing Office, 214–15
U.S. Postal Service, 98
Unabridged dictionaries, 113
Union catalogs, 57, 63
United Kingdom
    biographical resources, 201, 203

business resources, 169
dictionaries, 114–15
government publications, 224
legal resources, 166, 167, 168
medical news, 164
national bibliography, 58
United Nations, 223, 224
University Library at University of Albany,
    304
University of Albany, 304
University of Arizona, 323, 330
University of Louisiana-Lafayette, 319
University of Southern California, 319
University of Texas, 329
User instruction. *See* Instruction

V
Valley Library at Oregon State University,
    304
Value add-ons, 73
Videos, 61, 235
Virtual reference
    articles on, 27–28, 334
    changing, 12
    chat, 341–42
    establishing rapport, 18
    examples, 307–8
    instant messaging, 236
    legal, 164
    medical, legal, and business topics,
        176
    models, 341
    reference interview, 24–25
    training guide, 312
    value-added answers, 38
Visual dictionaries, 116
Visualizing an answer, 35
Visually impaired people, dictionaries for,
    123–24

W
Webfeat, 136
Webliographies, 8–9
Web sites, 8–9, 309. *See also* Internet
Weeding, 296–97, 299
Western Carolina University, 43
What facts, 99–101

When facts, 102
Where facts, 103
Which facts, 101–2
Who facts, 97–99
Wildcard truncation, 47
Wildlife, 219
Williamson, Charles, 3
Winona State University Library, 305
Worksheets, searching, 45–46
Writers, 204–5
Wrong answers, 40

WWW Cyberguide ratings, 248–49
Wyer, James I., 4

Y
Yearbooks, biographical, 201
Yearbooks, legal, 165
Year searches, 48
York College, 306
Young adults, 267
Youth. *See* Children's service
Yuba County Library, 319, 320

Index of Reference Resources Described

100 Ready-To-Use Pathfinders for the Web, 109

20,125 Questionable Doctors: Disciplined by State and Federal Governments, National Edition, 162

2005 Commercial Atlas and Marketing Guide, 195

"2005 Reference Review," 90

"25 High Performance Subdivisions," 43

A

Abbreviations Dictionary, 117

ABC for Book Collectors, 127

ABELL (Annual Bibliography of English Language and Literature), 137

ABI/INFORM, 139, 172

ABI/INFORM Global, 145

Abingdon's Strong's Exhaustive Concordance of the Bible, 119

ABMS Medical Specialists PLUS, 162

"Academic Original Sin," 284

Academic Search Elite, 138, 150

Academic Search Premier, 138, 145

Access: The Supplementary Index to Periodicals, 139

"An Accessibility Study of State Legislative Web Sites," 229

Acronyms, Initialisms, and Abbreviations Dictionary, 117

The ACS Style Guide, 121

Adamson, Lynda G., 271

Advanced Dictionary, 122

The Advanced Internet Searcher's Handbook, 249

African American Lives, 206

Albanian-English/English-Albanian Practical Dictionary, 123

Allee, Nancy J., 180–81

AllReaders.com, 260

Almanac, 95

Alternative Press Index, 139, 150

Ambrogi, Robert J., 180

America: History and Life, 142, 148

America's Newspapers, 140

America's Obituaries and Death Notices, 204

America's Top Doctors, 162

Americana, 71

American Association of School Libraries, 274–75

American Bibliography: A Chronological Dictionary of All Books, Pamphlets and Periodical Publications Printed in the United States from the Genesis of Printing in 1639 Down to and Including the Year 1800, 60

American Bibliography: A Preliminary Checklist for 1801-1819, 60

American Book Publishing Record Cumulative 1876-1949, 60–61

American Book Publishing Record Cumulative 1950-1977, 60–61

American Book Trade Directory, 62

The American Catalogue of Books . . . January 1861 to January 1871, 60

American Catalogue of Books 1976-1910, 61

American Decades, 102

An American Dictionary of the English Language, 113

American English Learner's Dictionary, 112

American Eras, 102

American Fact Finder, 190, 195, 221
American Heritage Dictionary, 112, 113–14, 127, 128
The American Heritage Dictionary for Learners of English, 116
American Historical Fiction, 271
American Law Yearbook, 166
American Libraries, 292
American Library Association, 180, 271, 274
American Library Directory, 55, 62, 65
American Medical Association Manual of Style, 121
American Memory Collection, 188, 220
American Men and Women of Science, 199, 205
American National Biography, 200, 202, 208
American Reference Books Annual, 63, 90, 206, 292
The American Sign Language Dictionary Unabridged, 124
The American Sign Language Handshape Dictionary, 124
American State Papers, 218, 223
American Statistical Index (ASI), 221
American Theological Library Association, 143
American Trade Schools Directory, 101
America Votes, 222
Anderson, P. F., 180–81
Annual Bibliography of English Language and Literature (ABELL), 137
Annual Guide to Graduate Programs, 101
AOL, 239
APA, 120
APA Style Helper 5.0, 120
Applied Science and Technology Full Text, 141
Applied Science and Technology Index, 141
Applied Science and Technology Retrospective 1913-1983, 141
"A Progress Report," 274
ARBA Guide to Biographical Resources 1986-1997, 206
ARBA Guide to Subject Encyclopedias and Dictionaries, 90
Armstrong, Neil, 132
Arp, Lori, 278, 282
Arret, Linda, 307, 343
ARTbibliographies Modern, 144

Art Full Text, 143
Arthur, Gwen, 311
ArticleFirst, 139
Art Index Retrospective: 1929-1984, 144
Arts and Humanities Citation Index, 145
arXiv, 236
ASI (American Statistical Index), 221
Asian American Biographies, 206
Ask, 239
ASKaLibrarian, 236
Askew, Consuella A., 333
Ask for Kids, 241
Ask Jeeves, 239
AskNow, 236
"Assessing the True Nature of Information Transactions at a Suburban Library," 249
Associated Press Stylebook, 121
Association of College and Research Libraries, 281
Association of College and Research Libraries (ACRL), 275
Association of Educational Communications and Technology (AECT), 274–75
ATLA Religion Database, 143
Atlas of Canada, 190
Atlas of World History, 189
AudioFile Magazine, 261
audiofilemagazine.com/audiofileplus.html, 261
Auster, Ethel, 345
Aycock, Anthony, 211

B
Background Notes, 191
Balay, Robert, 63, 65
Ballantine's Law Dictionary, 165
Ballantine's Law Dictionary and Thesaurus, 165
Barancik, Sue, 271
Barker, Joe, 245
Barnes, Susan B., 250
Barnhart, Charles Lewis, 122
Barnhouse, Rebecca, 271
Barr, Linda R., 250
The Barrington Atlas of the Greek and Roman World, 189–90

Barron, Pamela Petrick, 299
Barron's Educational Series, 169
bartleby.com, 95, 113–14, 119
Bartlett, John, 119
Bartlett's Familiar Quotations, 119, 128
Beck, Susan E., 278
Being Fluent with Information Technology, 274
Bell, David A., 249
Ben's Guide to U.S. Government for Kids, 223
Bernstein, Paula, 197
Berkowitz, R. E., 275
Best Books for Academic Libraries, 296
Besterman, Theodore, 61
Best of the Web, 9
Best Reference Books, 296
BIALL Handbook of Legal Information Management, 181
Bibliography of the English Printed Drama to the Restoration, 55
Bibliography of the History of Art, 144
Bibliotheca Americana: 1820-1861, 60
Bibliotheca Universalis, 54
Biographical Dictionary of Hispanic Americans, 206
Biographical Directory of the United States Congress, 1774 to Present, 205
Biography.com, 202
Biography and Genealogy Master Index, 200, 208
Biography Index, 200, 202, 208
Biography Reference Bank, 202
Biography Resource Center, 200, 202, 208
"Biography Resources," 211
Biological & Agricultural Index Plus, 141
Biological Abstracts, 141
Biological Abstracts/Reports, Reviews and Meetings, 141
Biology Digest, 141
Biosis Previews, 141
BIR (Book Index to Reviews), 259, 260
Black, Henry Campbell, 165
Black's Law Dictionary, 124, 158, 165, 177
Blinklist, 39
Bloomsbury English Dictionary, 114
Bodart, Joni, 271
Bond, Mary, 64

Bond's Franchise Guide, 171
Bonds and Money Markets, Mutual Funds, Brokerage Firms, Stock Mutual Funds, Banks and Thrifts, HMOs and Health Insurance, Life, Health, and Annuity Insurers, 171
"The Book Stops Here," 91
Book Index to Reviews (BIR), 259, 260
"The Bookless Future," 249
Booklist, 8, 206, 291
The Book of the States, 223
Book Review Digest, 146
Book Review Digest Plus, 146
Book Review Index Online, 146
BooksandPeriodicals.com, 59
Books and Periodicals.com, 148
Books in Print, 54, 55, 56, 65
BooksInPrint.com Professional, 56
Books in Print Supplement, 56
Books Out Loud: Bowker's Guide to Audiobooks, 61
BooksOutofPrint.com, 56
BookSpot.com, 260, 262
Boorkman, Jo Anne, 181
Boudreau, Signe O., 154
Bouvier's Law Dictionary, 165
Bowker Annual Library and Book Trade Almanac, 62
Bowker's Complete Video Directory, 61
Boyd, Rhonda S., 249
Bradford, Jane T., 299, 345
Bradley, Phil, 249
Brainboost, 241
Brands and Their Companies, 170
Breakstone, Elizabeth, 234
Bridge, Noeline, 211
Brier, David J., 282
Britannica Ultimate Reference Suite, 78
British National Bibliography, 58
Brown, Cecilia, 282
Bucknall, Tim, 153
Buff, Hirko, 312
Bureau of the Census, 191, 221, 226
Bureau of Economic Analysis, 221
Bureau of Labor Statistics, 219, 222
Bury, Sophie, 282
Buschman, John, 282

Business and Company Profile ASAP, 172
Business Index ASAP, 172
Business Information, 157
Business Source Elite, 145, 172
Butcher, Karyle, 306
Butterworth's, 167

C
Calendar of Events, 102
Cambridge Advanced Learner's Dictionary, 115
The Cambridge Biographical Dictionary, 204
Canada Gazette, 224
Canadia, 58
Canadian Books in Print, 56
The Canadian Encyclopedia, 82
Canadian Global Almanac, 96
Canadian Oxford Dictionary, 115
Canadian Reference Source, 63–64
Canadian Who's Who, 201
Canadian World Almanac and Book of Facts, 96
Cardina, Christen, 345
Caron, Martine, 64
Cartographica Extraordinaire, 188
Cassell's Italian Dictionary, 123, 126
Cassell's Latin Dictionary, 123
Catalog of Federal Domestic Assistance, 100
Catalog of U.S. Government Publications, 225
Catalogue of Books and Manuscripts Pt. I, 55
CATNYP, 57
cdc.gov/nchs, 164
Central Intelligence Agency (CIA), 103, 220
Centre for Topographic Information of Natural Resources Canada, 191
Chambers Biographical Dictionary, 204
Chambers Dictionary, 114
Chan, Donna C., 345
"The Changing Roles of Academic Reference Librarians Over a Ten-Year Period," 345
Characteristics of Programs of Information Literacy that Illustrate Best Practices, 281
Chase's Calendar of Events, 102, 106
Chat Reference, 334
A Checklist of American Imprints for 1820-1829, 60

A Checklist of American Imprints for 1830-1846, 60
Chelton, Mary, 256
Chemical Abstracts, 141
Chen, Xiaotian, 154
Chicago Manual of Legal Citation, 165
Chicago Manual of Style, 120
Choice, 8, 206, 291–92
Choice's Outstanding Academic Titles 1998-2002, 296
Chronicle of Higher Education, 233–34
CIA World Factbook, 191, 195, 220
CINAHL, 163
CIS/Index to Publications of the United States Congress, 217
"Citizen Interaction with E-government," 229
City and County Data Book, 223
City Profiles USA, 94, 103
Clendenning, Lynda Fuller, 299
Clinical Pharmacology, 164
cluelass.com, 262
Clusty, 241, 242
CNA (Customer Name and Address), 98
Cobus, Laura, 332
The Code of Federal Regulations, 218
Coffman, Steve, 307, 343
"Collaboration for Point-Of-Need Library Instruction," 283
"Collection Development for New Librarians," 300
College Board, 101
College Handbook, 101
Collier's Encyclopedia, 79
Collins, John W., 333
Collins English Dictionary, 115
Colorado Alliance of Research Libraries, 59
Columbia Gazetteer of the World, 185
Columbia Gazetteer of the World Online, 184, 185, 195
Columbia Granger's Index to Poetry in Collected and Selected Works, 147
Columbia Lippincott Gazetteer, 186
Command Papers, 224
Commercial Atlas and Marketing Guide, 195

"The Communications Studies Researcher and the Communications Studies Indexes," 154
Compact OED, 118
A Complete and Systematic Concordance to the Works of Shakespeare, 119
The Complete Guide to Citing Government Information Resources, 121
Compton's by Britannica, 83, 88
Compton's Encyclopedia, 83
Concise Dictionary of Business, 169
Congressional Directory, 216, 235
Congressional Record, 217, 226
Congressional Record Index, 217
"Congressional Research Service Reports Revealed," 229
Congressional Staff Directory, 216
Connecting Young Adults and Libraries, 268
Consumer Price Index, 219
Consumer Reports, 99, 106
Consumer Reports Buying Guide, 99
Contemporary Authors, 204–5
Contemporary Literary Criticism Select, 205
The Continuum Encyclopedia of Animal Symbolism in Art, 82
Core Documents of U.S. Democracy, 216
Corporate Affiliations, 170
CorporateAffiliations Plus, 170
Corporate Giving Directory, 98
Corpus Juris Secundum, 165
Costello, Barbara, 283, 345
CQ Congress Collection, 218
CQ Encyclopedia of American Government, 216
CQ Guide to the Supreme Court, 221
CQ Researcher, 218
CQ Researcher en espanol, 218
CQ State Fact Finder, 223
CQ Weekly, 218
Cross+Search Plus, 98
Culp, F. Bartow, 284
Cumulative Book Index, 61
Cunningham, Thomas H., 275
Current Biography, 201, 208, 297
Current Biography Illustrated, 201
Current Biography International Yearbook, 201

Current Chemical Reactions, 145
Current Index to Journals in Education, 142
"Cyberplagarism and the Library," 284

D
D'Angleo, Barbara J., 280
D&B's Million Dollar Directory Plus, 172
Dalby, Andrew, 132
Davis-Kahl, Stephanie, 282
Deadly Pleasures, 262
del.icio.us, 39
Demers, Nora Egan, 283
Demographic Yearbook, 224
Dent, Valeda Frances, 332
Departmental Papers, 224
Department of Commerce, 219, 222, 236
Department of Education, 214, 219
Department of Health and Human Services Web site, 219
Department of Housing and Urban Development (HUD), 192
Department of Labor Web site, 219
Department of the Interior Web site, 219
De Proprietatibus Rerum, 84–85
Derry, Sebastian, 300
Dervin, Brenda, 16, 18
"The Design and Interpretation of Unobtrusive Evaluations," 333
"The Development and Evolution of a University-Based Online Library Instruction Course," 283
Dewdney, Patricia, 16, 18, 21, 22, 23
Dewdroppers, Waldos and Slackers, 116
Diagnostic and Statistical Manual of Mental Disorders (DSM-IV-TR), 161
Dialog, 139
DialogClassic, 139, 150
Dictionary of American Biography, 202–3
Dictionary of American Regional English, 112
Dictionary of American Regional English (DARE), 117, 128
The Dictionary of Aquarium Terms, 124
Dictionary of Art, 82, 88
A Dictionary of Books Relating to America from Its Discovery to the Present Time, 60
Dictionary of Business, 169
Dictionary of Business Terms, 169

Dictionary of Canadian Biography, 203
Dictionary of Canadian Biography Online, 203
Dictionary of Dictionaries and Eminent Encyclopedias, 132
Dictionary of Finance and Investment Terms, 169
Dictionary of Insurance, 169
Dictionary of International Business Terms, 169
Dictionary of Literary Biography Online, 205
Dictionary of Marketing Terms, 169
Dictionary of National Biography (DNB), 203
"Dictionaries," 132
Digital Reference Service in the New Millennium, 333
Dilevko, Juris, 333
Directgov, 224
The Directory of American Scholars, 205
Directory of Physicians in the United States, 162
Directory of Special Libraries and Information Centers, 62
DIRLINE, 162
DNB (Dictionary of National Biography), 203
Dogpile, 241, 242
Doll, Carol A., 299
Dorland's Illustrated Medical Dictionary 30th Edition, 159
drugdigest.org/DD/Home, 164
DSM-IV-TR (Diagnostic and Statistical Manual of Mental Disorders), 161

E
Early American Imprints, 60
EarthLink, 239
Earth Resources Observation Systems Data Center, 191
EBSCO Academic Search, 137
EBSCO A-Z, 150
Edmunds guides, 100
Educational Resources Information Center, 137, 219
Education Full Text, 139, 141
Education Index, 141
Education Index Retrospective, 142
Eggleston, Holly, 300
"E-Government," 229

Eisenberg, M. B., 275
Electronic Collections Online, 139
Electronic Data Gathering Analysis and Retrieval, 172
Electronic Journal Miner, 59, 65
"Electronic Maps," 198
Elliot, Donald, 333
Ellis, Lisa A., 278
Emily Post's Etiquette, 94, 104, 107
"Enabling the Roving Reference Librarian," 346
Encarta, 71, 79
Encarta Webster's Dictionary of the English Language, 114
Encyclopaedia Britannica, 71, 72, 74, 77–78, 88, 186
Encyclopaedia Britannica 2005, 87
Encyclopaedia Britannica Online, 87
Encyclopedia Americana, 74, 76–77, 88
Encyclopedia Judaica, 82
Encyclopedia of Applied Physics, 88
Encyclopedia of Business Information Sources, 2006, 181
Encyclopedia of Homelessness, 74
Encyclopedia of Leadership, 74
Encyclopedia of Modern Physics, 88
Encyclopedia of Protestantism, 74
Encyclopedia of Religion, 81, 88
Encyclopedia of Television, 82
Encyclopedia of the American Presidency, 218
Encyclopedia of the Orient, 73
Encyclopedia of the World's Zoos, 82
Encyclopedia of World Biography, 204
Encyclopedia Sherlockianna, 82
EnviroMapper, 191
Environmental Health Perspective, 216
Environmental Protection Agency (EPA), 191, 214
Environmental Sciences, 137
EPA (Environmental Protection Agency), 191, 214
ERIC, 142, 219
EROS (Earth Resources Observation Systems) Data Center, 191
ESRI, 192
Essay and General Literature Index, 146

The Essential Guide to the Best (and Worst) Legal Sites on the Web, 180
EthnicNewsWatch, 145
Eureka, 63
Eurodesk, 49
Evans, Charles, 60
Evans, Donna, 229
"The Exchange," 49
Excite, 241
Expanded Academic ASAP, 138
Expanded Academic Text ASAP, 151
"An Exploratory Study," 17
Export America, 216
ez2find, 241

F
Factiva, 145, 172–73
FACTS.com, 96
Fagan, Bryan, 229
Fagan, Jody Condit, 229
Fallis, Don, 109
Farrow, James, 120
Fasolina, Jennifer, 59
Fast Answers to Common Questions, 109
FaxUSA, 98
FC Search, 101
FDA Consumer, 216
Federal Citizen Information Center, 225
Federal Election Commission Media Guide, 222
Federal Emergency Management Agency, 191
Federal Interagency Council on Statistical Policy, 221
Federal Register, 218, 226
Federal Register Index, 218
Federal Staff Directory, 216
FEDSTATS, 221
Fiction_L, 261
FictionDB.com, 261
"Finding Without Seeking," 254
findlaw.com, 168
"The Firefly," 31
The Firefly Five Language Visual Dictionary, 116
The Firefly Visual Dictionary, 116
FirstGov.gov, 222, 223, 226
First Search, 139, 151

Fitch, Megan, 229
Flanagan, Pat, 341
Flaspohler, Molly R., 279, 281
Fletcher, Lara, 59
Ford, Barbara, 338
Forthcoming Books, 56
Foundation Directory, 101
Foundation Directory Online, 101
Four-Year Colleges, 101
Franchise Annual Directory, 171
Francis, 143
Franklin, 225, 226
Frassle, 39
French Sixteenth Century Books, 55
Fricke, Martin, 109
Fulltext Sources Online, 59, 65, 148
Fundamental Reference Sources, 132
Fundamentals of Collection Development and Management, 300
Furl, 39
Future Libraries, 332

G
Gage Canadian Dictionary, 115
Gail, Susan B., 206
Gale's Literature Resource Center, 205
Gale Database of Publications and Broadcast Media, 65
Gale Directory of Databases, 59, 65
Gale Directory of Publications and Broadcast Media, 59
Gale Encyclopedia of Alternative Medicine, 160
Gale Encyclopedia of Children's Health, 160–61
Gale Encyclopedia of Medicine, 160
Gale Encyclopedia of Mental Disorders, 161
Gale Encyclopedia of Multicultural America, 72, 82, 88
Gale Encyclopedia of Surgery, 161
Galvin, Jeanne, 278
Gandhi, Smita, 312
Garland Encyclopedia of World Music, 81
Gates Jr., Henry Louis, 206
General Business File, 145
General Catalogue of Printed Books to 1975, 58
General Science Full Text, 139, 141
General Science Index, 141

Genovese, Michael, 218
Genreflecting, 255, 260–61, 262
Geobase, 137
Geographic Information Systems and Libraries, 198
Geographic Names Information System (GNIS), 186
Geography and Map Division of the Library of Congress, 191
GEOnet Names Server, 186
Gers, Ralph, 21
Gesner, Conrad, 54
Get Them Talking, 311
"Getting More from Your Electronic Collections Through Studies of User Behavior," 153
Getty Museum, 206
Getty Research Institute, 185
Getty Thesaurus of Geographic Names Online, 185
Gigablast, 239, 245
Ginsparg, Paul, 235
GlobalBooksinPrint.com, 56
Glose, Mary B., 59
Gluck, Myke, 198
GNIS (Geographic Names Information System), 186
GODORT (Government Documents Round Table), 225
Goode's World Atlas, 188
Goodin, Dan, 90
Google, 239, 240
Google Maps, 184, 190
Google Power, 250
Google Uncle Sam, 216
Government Assistance Almanac, 100
Government Documents Round Table (GODORT), 225
"Government Information in the Digital Age," 229
Government Online Bookstore, 225
Government Periodicals Index, 216
Government Printing Office, 225, 226
Government Publications Unmasked, 229
GPO Access, 225, 226
GPO Online Public Access Catalog, 226
Granville, Bartholomew de Granville, 84

The Great EB, 91
Grokker, 241
Grolier Multimedia Encyclopedia Deluxe iMac Edition, 83
Grolier Online, 71, 80
Gross, Melissa, 21
Grzinek's Animal Life Encyclopedia, 82, 89
Guide, 99
"Guidelines for Behavioral Performance of Reference and Information Service Providers," 9–10, 25
Guidelines for Medical, Legal, and Business Responses, 180
Guide to American Law, 165
Guide to Collective Biographies for Children and Young Adults, 271
The Guide to Cooking Schools, 101
Guide to Reference Books, 63, 65, 292
A Guide to World Language Dictionaries, 132

H
H. W. Wilson, 61
Hacker, Diana, 250
Hammon Citation World Atlas, 188
Hammond World Atlas, 187, 195
Handbook of American Business, 170
Handbook of Emerging Companies, 170
Handbook of Private Companies, 170
Handbook of Private Schools, 101
Handbook of World Business, 170
HAPI (Hispanic American Periodicals Index) Online, 137
HarperCollins New World Atlas, 187
Harris, Frances Jacobsen, 266
Harris, John, 70
Harvard College Library, 55
The Harvard Concordance to Shakespeare, 119
Harvard Dictionary of Music, 124
He, Joy, 229
Health and Wellness Resource Center, 163
Health Reference Center, 145
Health Reference Center Academic, 163
Health Source, 163
Health Source Plus, 145
Heath, Fred M., 333
Henniger, Maureen, 250
Hensley, Randy Burke, 274

Hernon, Peter, 215, 318
The Hidden Web, 250
Hieros Gantos, 168
Higgingotham, Evelyn Brooks, 206
Hill-Donnelly Cross Reference Directory, 98
Hispanic American Periodicals Index Online, 145
Historical Abstracts, 142–43
Historical Atlas of Canada, 189
Historical Atlas of the U.S., 189
Historical Statistics of the United States, 222
History Abstracts, 148
History of Cartography Gateway, 188
History Resource Center, 148
History Resource Center: U.S., 143
History Resource Center: World, 143
Hoffman, Paul S., 283
Holt, Glen, 333
Hoover's Handbook of Private Companies 2005, 158
Hoover Handbooks, 170, 177
HopStop.com, 185
Horowitz, Lisa, 341
Hotbot, 241
House of Commons Papers, 224
Howley, Sue, 333
"How Twenty-Eight Users Helped Redesign an Academic Library Web Site," 332
Hubbertz, Andrew, 333
HUD (U.S. Department of Housing and Urban Development), 192
Humanities and Social Science Index Retrospective 1907-1983, 143
Humanities Full Text, 139, 143
Humanities Index, 143
Hutchins, Margaret, 4

I
"I Don't Think I Click," 322
"If You Build It with Them, They Will Come," 284
IIS (Index to International Statistics), 221
"Illinois Libraries/OCLC Tackle Government Information Online," 230
Illustrated World Atlas, 187

Index Chemicus, 145
Index to International Statistics (IIS), 221
Index to Legal Periodicals, 167
Index to Publications of the United States Congress, 217
"Indicators of Accuracy for Answers to Ready Reference Questions on the Internet," 109
InfoMine, 190–91, 243
Information Gateway, 9
"Information Literacy and High Education," 283
Information Literacy Competency Standards for Higher Education, 275
"Information Literacy Standards for Student Learning," 274–75, 277
Information Please, 96
Information Power, 274–75
Information Science Full Text, 144
InfoTrac, 135
InfoTrac Custom Newspapers, 137, 140
InfoTrac Expanded Academic, 137
InfoTrac Junior Edition, 147
InfoTrac OneFile, 137, 138
InfoTrac Student Edition, 147
Innovative Interfaces Web Bridge, 48
interactive-law.co.uk, 168
International Dictionary of Finance, 169
International Directory of Little Magazines and Small Presses, 59
International Index, 143
International Index to Black Periodicals Full Text, 145
International Literary Market Place, 99
International Repertory of the Literature of Art, 144
International Subject Guide Series, 117
International Who's Who, 201, 209
International Who's Who in Classical Music, 201
International Who's Who in International Affairs, 201
The Internet Archive, 237
Internet Movie Database, 61, 206
The Internet Public Library, 9
Introduction to Reference Sources in the Digital Age, 250

Introduction to Reference Sources in the Health Sciences, 181
ipl.org, 95
Irregular Serials and Annuals, 58–59
Italian Sixteenth Century Books, 55
ITP Nelson, 115
iWon, 239
Ixquick, 241

J
Jackson, Rebecca, 341
Jacobs, A. J., 90
Jacobs, James A., 229
Jacobs, James R., 229
Jacso, Peter, 292
jake, 148
Janes, Joseph, 91, 250, 338
Jennerich, Edward J., 16
Jennerich, Elaine Z., 16
Johnson, Anna Marie, 283
Johnson, Peggy, 300
Johnson, Roberta, 261
Journal of the American Medical Association, 173
Judicial Staff Directory, 216
Julien, Heidi, 267
Junior Dictionary, 122
JuniorQuest, 147

K
Kabdebo, Thomas, 132
KartOO, 241
Kasowitz, Abby S., 333
Katz, William, 4
Katzer, Jeffrey, 16
Kazlauskas, Edward, 17
Kearley, Jamie, 283
Kelley Blue Book, 100
Kelly, James, 60
Kem, Kathleen, 16, 27
Kennedy, Scott E., 292
Kenney, Ann Jason, 188
Kent, Jack, 31
Kent District Library, 261
Kids Search, 48
King, Donald W., 154
Kister, Kenneth F., 91, 132

Kister's Best Dictionaries for Adults and Young People, 132
Kister's Best Encyclopedias, 91
Kluegel, Kathleen, 38
The Know-It-All, 90
"Knowledge Management and Reference Services," 312
Knowledge Quest, 282
Kogan, Herman, 91
Kuhlthau, Carol Collier, 254, 276
Kyrillidou, Martha, 333

L
Lam, R. Errol, 16
Lampert, Lynn D., 277–78
Lands and Peoples, 71, 83
Lankes, David, 333
Lanning, Scott, 275
Larousse, 123
Law and Legal Information Directory, 166
The Law and Politics Book Review, 173
Law Library Journal, 173
Law School Admission Council, 101
LAWCHEK, 166, 167
Lawrence, John R. M., 292
"Lawrence Looks at Books," 292
Lawyer Locator, 166
Leach, Susan M., 154
League of Women Voters Democracy Net, 222
Lebbin, Vickery Kaye, 282
Legal Research for Beginners, 157
Legal Research In a Nutshell, 157
Lenholt, Robert, 283, 345
"Lessons Learned About Developing and Coordinating an Instruction Program with Freshman Composition," 283
Lewis, Linda K., 300
Lexicon Technicum, 70
Lexis, 166–67
LexisNexis, 135, 139, 217, 221
LexisNexis Academic, 139, 151
LexisNexis Butterworth's, 167
LexisNexis Company Analysis, 139
LexisNexis Congressional, 218
LexisNexis Country Analysis, 139
LexisNexis Current Issues, 139

LexisNexis Government Periodicals, 139
LexisNexis Statistical, 139, 221
Librarian's Internet Index, 9, 106, 107, 243
Libraries Act on Their LibQUAL+ Findings, 330, 333
Library, Information Science and Technology Abstracts, 144
"Library Instruction and Information Literacy," 283
Library Journal, 8, 206, 291–92
Library Literature, 137, 144
Library of Congress, 57, 226
Library of Congress American Memory Collection, 188, 220
"Life Among the Lexicographers," 132
lii.org, 95
Lindauer, Bonnie Gratch, 283
Liptak, Deborah A., 229
Literary Market Place (LMP), 52, 62, 65, 94, 99
Literature Resource Center, 209
LitFinder, 146
LMP (Literary Market Place), 55, 62, 65, 94, 99
Local and Regional Government Information, 229
"Location, Location, Location," 197
Locus, 262
Loertscher, David, 292
Lubans, John, 317
Lycos, 241

M
Macmillan Dictionary for Children, 121, 128
Macmillan English Dictionary, 116
Magazines for Libraries, 58–59, 148
Magill On Literature Plus, 94
Maid, Barry M., 280
Major Modern and Contemporary Visual Artists, 205
Malenfant, Chuck, 283
Managing and Analyzing Your Collection, 299
Managing the Twenty-First Century Reference Department, 312
Mann, Thomas, 237
Mann, Wendy, 229
mapquest.com, 184, 190, 195

Market Share Reporter, 171
Marquis Who's Who on the Web, 201
Martin, J. Kay, 299
Martin, Mary, 229
Martindale-Hubbell Law Directory, 166, 177
Massey-Burzio, Virginia, 339
MasterFILE Elite, 138
MasterFILE Premier, 136, 138
MasterFILE Select, 138
Masterplots, 101
Masterplots Complete, 102
Masterplots II, Drama Series, 102
Masterplots II, Short Story Series, 102
Mathews, Joseph R., 333
Maughan, Laurel S., 283
MBA Programs, 101
McClure, C. R., 318
McDermott, I., 197
McDevitt, Theresa R., 229
McGraw-Hill Encyclopedia of Science and Technology, 82, 89
McGraw Hill School Dictionary, 122
McKenzie, Gail, 299
McLachlan, Karen, 249
McMillen, Paula S., 283
"Measuring Outcomes," 333
Medical and Health Care Books and Serials in Print, 181
Medical Dictionary (Stedman), 124
The Medical Library Association Encyclopedic Guide to Searching and Finding Health Information on the Web, 180–81
Medical Reference Services Quarterly, 173
Medline, 145, 163
MedlinePlus, 163
Merck Manual of Diagnosis and Therapy, 160
Merck Manual of Medical Information—Home Edition, 160, 177
Mergent Online, 172
Mergent's Bond Records, 158
Merriam-Webster's Biographical Dictionary, 204
Merriam-Webster's Collegiate Dictionary, 112, 114, 118, 128
Merriam-Webster's Dictionary of Law, 165
Merriam-Webster's Geographical Dictionary, 185

Merriam-Webster's Third New International Dictionary, 126
Metafind, 48
Meyer, Nicholas E., 206
Michell, Gillian, 22
Middle Ages in Literature for Youth, 271
Middle Search Plus, 147
Mirwis, Allan N., 91
Mitchell, Susan, 197
Miyagishima, Bryan, 283
MLA Handbook for Writers of Research Papers, 120, 128
MLA International Bibliography, 137, 139, 143, 149
Modern Language Association (MLA), 143
Molnar, John Edgar, 60–61
Mood, Terry Ann, 16
"More Than Just Maps," 188
Moss, Ria W., 181
Moving and Relocation Directory, 103
Moyer, Jessica, 254
MSN Search, 239
Mudrock, Theresa, 109
Murphy, Teri J., 282
Muse Global Muse Search, 48
My First Britannica, 84
MyWay, 239

N
N.A.D.A. Appraisal Guides, 100
Nanny, Mark, 282
National Archives and Records Administration, 218
National Atlas of the United States, 190
National Center for Education Statistics, 219
National Center for Health, 163, 164
National Center for Health Statistics, 222
National Cyclopedia of American Biography, 203–4
National Directory of Nonprofit Organizations, 98
National Economics Accounts, 236
National Five-Digit Zip Code and Post Office Directory, 98
National Geographic Atlas of the World, 187, 195

National Geographic Concise Atlas of the World, 188
National Geographic Society, 190
National Geographic World Atlas for Young Explorers, 188
National Health Service (NHS), 49
National Imagery and Mapping Agency, 192–93
National Library of Medicine, 163
National Newspaper Index, 140
National Oceanic and Atmospheric Administration (NOAA), 192
National Parks System Web site, 214
National Research Council, 274
National Union Catalog, 54, 55, 57–58
National Union Catalog: Pre-1956 Imprints, 57
Neal, James, 305, 312
Nelson Canadian Dictionary of the English Language, 115
"Networked Resources, Assessment and Collection Development", 300
"Neutral Questioning," 16
"The Never-ending Search for People," 211
Newbery and Caldecott Awards, 271
New Book of Knowledge, 72, 83, 89
New Book of Knowledge on the Web, 83
New Cars and Trucks Buyers Guide, 100
A New Dictionary of Irish History from 1800, 126
"New Economic Models for the Federal Depository System," 230
New England Journal of Medicine, 173
New Fowler's Modern English Usage, 121
The New International World Atlas, 186, 195
New Oxford American Dictionary, 112, 114, 123, 129
Newsbank, 137, 140
Newsbank Public Library Collection, 140
Newsmakers, 202
Newspaper Source (EBSCO), 140
New This Week, 106
New to Parsippany, 97
The New Walford Guide to Reference Resources, 63, 65
New York Public Library, 9, 57
New York Public Library Guide to Reading Groups, 255

New York Times Obituaries Index, 1885-1968, 204
New York Times Obituaries Index, 1969-1978, 204
New York Times Updating, 106
NHS (National Health Service), 49
NICEM Film and Video FinderOnline, 61
Nilsen, Kristi, 16
NOAA (National Oceanic and Atmospheric Administration), 192
NOAD, 114
Nolan, Christopher, 21
Norlin, Elaina, 324
Notess, Greg, 245
NoveList, 255, 259, 262
Novotny, Eric, 322, 334
NTC's American English Learner's Dictionary, 116
Nursing Programs, 101

O
O'Sullivan, Carmel, 277
Occupational Outlook Handbook 2006-2007, 100, 107
Occupational Outlook Quarterly, 216
Odden's Bookmarks, 190–91
"ODLIS: Online Dictionary for Library and Information Science," 132
OED News, 125
Office of the Public Sector Information, 224
Official ABMS Directory of Board Certified Medical Specialists, 158, 162, 177
Official Guide to ABA-Approved Law Schools, 101
"Ohio5 Government Documents," 229
Ojala, Marydee, 211
OLDMEDLINE, 163
Ondrusek, Anita, 332
onelook.com, 95
Online Public Access Catalog (OPAC) for GPO's Integrated Library System, 226
On the Properties of Things, 91
Opposing Viewpoints, 268
"Oranges and Peaches," 22
Oud, Joanne, 282
Overy, Richard, 189
Owen, Tim, 35

Owusu-Ansah, Edward K., 283
The Oxford American Writer's Thesaurus, 118
Oxford Atlas of the World, 187
Oxford Dictionary of English 2003, 114–15
Oxford Dictionary of Modern Quotations, 119
Oxford Dictionary of National Biography, 200, 203, 209
Oxford Dictionary of Phrase Sayings and Quotation, 119
Oxford-Duden Pictorial, 123
Oxford English Dictionary, 112, 113, 125, 129
Oxford-Hachette, 123
Oxford Large Print Dictionary, 123
Oxford New Concise World Atlas, 188
Oxford New Historical Atlas of Religion in America, 189
Oxford-Paravia, 123
The Oxford Rhyming Dictionary, 118
The Oxford Starter, 123

P
Pack, Thomas, 91
PAIS Archive 1915-1976, 142
PAIS International, 136, 137, 139, 142, 217
Parsippany-Troy Hills Public Library, 97
PatronBooksInPrint.com, 56
Payne, Lisa, 282
"Pedias, Familiar and Otherwise," 91
Peker, Lana, 104
People's Network Enquire, 307
Periodical Titles, 117
Perry-Castenada Library, 190
Persson, Dorothy, 154
"Peter's Digital Reference Shelf," 292
Peterson's, 101
Phillips, Lori, 283
Physicians Desk Reference, 158, 161
Pietraszewski, Barbara A., 346
Pink, Daniel H., 91
Planning for Results series, 305
Play Index, 146
Pollard, A. W., 55
Pollution Management, 137
Poole's Index to Periodical Literature, 135
Poor Richard's Almanac, 95
Power Search, 48
Practice Profile, 166

Primary Search Plus, 147
"Print Encyclopedias Making a
    Comeback," 91
Profiles of American Colleges, 101
Project Vote Smart, 222
Project Wombat, 49
The Properties of Things, 84–85
Prophet, Mary, 229
ProQuest Dissertations and Theses, 146
ProQuest Newstand, 140, 151
ProQuest Research Library, 137, 138, 151
PsyArticles, 144
Psychology and Behavioral Science Collection,
    145
PsycInfo, 137, 144, 149
"PsycInfo Tutorial," 154
*Publication Manual of the American
    Psychological Association*, 120
Public Libraries, 262
Public Libraries Briefcase, 173
*Publishers, Distributors and Wholesalers of the
    United States*, 62, 66
Publishers Weekly, 262
PubMed, 145, 163
Punt, Edith M., 188

Q
Q&A NJ, 236
Queryserver, 241
"Question Negotiation and Information
    Seeking in Libraries," 16
Quicklaw, 167

R
Radford, Marie L., 16, 17, 250
"Raised by Wolves," 312
*Rand McNally Commercial Atlas and
    Marketing Guide*, 190, 195
Rand McNally Road Atlas, 189, 195
*Random House Historical Dictionary of
    American Slang*, 116
The Random House Webster's Quotationary, 119
*Random House Webster's Unabridged
    Dictionary*, 113
*Reader's Advisory Services in the Public
    Library*, 256

Reader's Digest Children's Atlas of the World,
    188
Reader's Guide Abstracts, 139
Reader's Guide Full Text, 138, 139
Reader's Guide Retrospective, 139
Reader's Guide to Genre Fiction, 261–62
Reader's Guide to Periodical Literature, 137,
    138, 147
"Reading Behaviour and Electronic
    Journals," 154
readinggroupchoices.com, 255
ReadingGroupGuides.com, 255
*Recommended Reference Books for Small and
    Medium-sized Libraries and Media
    Centers*, 292, 296
Reddick, Christopher G., 229
Reference & User Services Quarterly, 282, 291
Reference Center, 122
"Reference Classics Ahead of Their Time,"
    300
"Reference eBooks," 300
"Reference Evaluation," 324
"Reference for Students," 292
"Reference Librarians and Keeping Up-to-
    Date," 345
"Reference Reviews Archive," 292
"Reference Service for Maps," 198
"Reference Service in the Digital Age,"
    345
Reference Services Review, 282
Reference Service Statistics and Assessment,
    334
*Reference Sources for Small and Medium-sized
    Libraries*, 292, 296
Registrum librorum Angliciae, 54
Reitz, Joan, 132
Repertoire d'Art et d'Archeologie, 144
Reports, 99
*Research and Documentation in the Electronic
    Age*, 250
"Researching and Shaping Information
    Literacy Initiative in Relation to the
    Web," 282
Research Library, 145
Resource Discovery Network, 243, 247
Rettig, James, 338, 345

"Revising Ready Reference Sites," 109
Richey, Deborah, 230
The Riverside Shakespeare, 120
Robert's Rules of Order Newly Revised, 105
Robinson, Judith Schiek, 215
Rogers, Michael, 230
Roget, Peter, 118
Roget's International Thesaurus, 118, 129
Roget's New Millennium Thesaurus, 112, 119
Rohweder, Roger, 259
Romantic Times Book Club, 262
Romero, Joseph, 132
Ronan, Jana, 334
Roorbach, Orville, 60
Roper, Fred W., 181
Ross, Catherine Sheldrick, 16, 21, 23, 254, 256
Ross, Mary Bucher, 312
Routledge Encyclopedia of Philosophy, 81
Rumsey, David, 188
RUSA Quarterly, 262
Rutgers University, 278

S
Sabin, Joseph, 60
Samson, Sue, 300
Saricks, Joyce, 256, 259, 261–62
Sarkodie-Mensah, Kwasi, 312
School Library Journal, 282, 291–92
Schreiner, Susan A., 211
Science and Technology in Canadian History: A Bibliographic Database, 64
Science and Technology Review, 216
Science Citation Index, 145
Science Full Text Select, 141
"Science Journal: Wikipedia Pretty Accurate," 90
Science Resource Center, 141
SciFinder Scholar, 141
Scopus, 141
The Scout Report, 250
Scribner Encyclopedia of American Lives, 204
Seamans, Nancy H., 284
"Secrets for Managing Materials Budget Allocations," 299
Serials Directory, 59

Serials Solutions, 150
Serials Solutions Article Linker, 48
Serward, Lillie J., 21
Shakespeare Folios and Quartos, 55
Sharkey, Jennifer K., 284
Shaw, Ralph R., 60
Shepherd's Historical Atlas, 184, 188
Sherman, Chris, 250
Shoemaker, Richard H., 60
Short Story Index, 146
Shuler, John A., 230
Singer, Carol A., 230
SIRS Researcher, 142, 151
Smellie, William, 74
Smith, Duncan, 259
Smith, Linda C., 198
Smith, Michael M., 346
Social Sciences Citation Index, 145
Social Sciences Full Text, 139, 142
Social Sciences Index, 142, 143
Social Sciences Index Retrospective 1907-1982, 142
Sociological Abstracts, 137
Somers, Michael A., 211
Somerville, Mary M., 284
Source Book of Franchise Opportunities, 171
Southeastern Oklahoma State University, 280
Sowards, Steven W., 109
"Specialized Encyclopedias for In-Depth Information," 91
Spurl, 39
SRI (Statistical Reference Index), 221
"Staffing for Results," 305
Standard & Poor's Register of Corporations, Directors and Executives, 169–70
The Standard Periodical Directory, 59
"State and Local Documents Roundup," 230
State and Local Government on the Net, 223
State Department, 214, 220
The Stateman's Yearbook, 103, 107
Statistical Abstract of the United States, 103, 107, 221, 226
Statistical Abstract of the United States, 2006, 94

Statistical Abstracts, 223
Statistical Reference Index (SRI), 221
Statistical Yearbook of the United Nations, 224
STAT-USA, 221–22
Stedman's Medical Dictionary, 159, 177
Stevens, Andrew, 333
Strategic Planning and Management for Library Managers, 333
Strauss's Handbook of Business Information, 181
Straw, Joseph E., 16, 25
Strong, James, 119
"Structure and Choices for Ready Reference Websites," 109
Stryker, Judson, 283
A Student's Dictionary, 121
Student Dictionary, 122
"Student Perceptions of Information Literacy," 284
Stumpers-L, 49
Style Manual for Political Science, 121
Subject Books in Print, 56
Subject Encyclopedias, 91
Subject Guide Series, 117
Sullivan, Danny, 245
SuperPages, 97
Survey of Current Business, 219–20
Sweeney, Richard, 328
Sweetland, James H., 132
Swope, Mary Jane, 16

T
Tapping the Government Grapevine, 215
Taylor, Robert S., 16
"Teaching Information Literacy Using the Short Story," 282
"Teaching, Learning and Research," 282
Tennant, Roy, 38
Tenner, Elka, 198
Tenopir, Carol, 154
Teoma, 240
Terraserver, 190
THOMAS, 168, 217, 226
Thomas Global Register (R) Europe, 169
Thomas Register of American Manufacturers, 169, 177
Thomsen, Elizabeth, 211

Thorndike, Edward Lee, 122
Thorndike-Barnhart Children's Dictionary, 122
"The Three Arenas of Information Literacy Assessment," 283
TIGER mapping service, 191, 192
Time Almanac with Information Please, 96, 107
TIME for Kids Almanac, 96
The Times Atlas of the World, 186, 195
Times History of the World, 189
Times of London Concise Atlas of the World, 187
"TIP: Tutorial for Information Power and Campus-Wide Information Literacy," 283
Toll-Free Phone Book USA, 98
Topozone, 190
Torence, Matt, 300
"The Transition of U.S. Government Publications from Paper to the Internet," 230
Trevisa, De John, 91
Triheim, Johann, 54
Tronier, Suzanne, 306
Tucker, James Cory, 300
Turner, Carol, 334
Turner, Nancy B., 278
"Turning Techno-Savvy into Info-Savvy," 282
Twait, Michelle, 300
Two-Year Colleges, 101
Tyckoson, David, 300, 338
Tyler, David C., 154

U
U.S. Bureau of the Census, 191
U.S. Catalog, 61
U.S. Congressional Set, 222
U.S. Department of Defense's National Imagery and Mapping Agency, 192–93
U.S. Department of Housing and Urban Development (HUD), 192
U.S. Election Atlas, 222
U.S. Gazetteer, 186
U.S. Geological Survey, 190–91, 192
U.S. Government Manual, 216, 226
U.S. Government on the Web, 215

U.S. News and World Report's Ultimate College Directories, 101
U.S. Serial Set, 218
Ulrich's International Periodicals Directory, 54, 58, 59, 65, 66, 148
Ulrichsweb.com, 59
Ultimate Guided Tour of Stock Investing, 171
Ultimate Visual Dictionary, 112, 116
"Undergraduate Students," 300
Union List of Artist Names, 206
United Nations, 190, 223
United States Code, 217
University of Minnesota, 205
University of Texas, 280
University of Washington Libraries, 97
University of California at Berkeley, 281
University of Texas, 190
University of Washington, 9
Unobtrusive Evaluation of Reference Service and Individual Responsibility, 333
"Usability Testing of an Online Information Literacy Tutorial," 282
Used Cars and Trucks Buyers Guide, 100
"Utilizing Blackboard to Provide Library Instruction," 283
UXL American Decades, 102

V
Value Line Investment Survey, 157, 170, 177
"Verifying Personal Names on the Web," 211
Video Source Book, 61
Virotto, Frank, 284
Virtual Reference Canada, 307
Virtual Reference Training, 312
Virtual Training Suite, 247
"Visibility as a Factor in Library Selection of Ready Reference Web Resources," 109
Visual and Performing Arts, 101
Vivisimo, 242
Voices from the Gaps: Women Artists and Writers of Color, 205
Vox/NTC, 123

W
Wallraff, Barbara, 132
Walter, Greg, 55

Warner, Dorothy A., 282
Washington-Hoagland, Carlette, 154
Washington Information Directory, 216
WBIS Online, 203
Web of Science, 145–46
Web Research, 250
Web Site Source Book, 98
Webster's Geographical Dictionary, 186
Webster's New Explorer Large Print Dictionary, 123–24
Webster's Third New International Dictionary, 113, 129
Weessies, Kathleen, 198
Weimer, Katherine H., 198
Weiss Ratings' Guides, 158, 171
West's Encyclopedia of American Law, 158, 165, 177
Westlaw, 165, 166, 167, 221
"What's Coming Off the Shelves?", 299
What's Next?, 261
What Do I Read Next?, 255, 260
What to Read, 255
"When You Need to Know Who's Who," 211
"Where's Waldo?", 211
"Where in the World?", 197
"Where Was I?", 197
Whitaker's Almanack, 96
Whitaker's Books in Print, 56
Who's Who, 201, 209
Who's Who among African Americans, 206
Who's Who in America, 99, 199, 200, 205, 209
Who's Who in American Education, 201
Who's Who in American Politics, 201
Who's Who in the East, 201
Who's Who in the Midwest, 201
Who's Who in the West, 201
Who's Who in the World, 99
Who's Who of American Women, 201
Who Was Who, A Cumulated Index 1897-2000, 203
"Why Print and Electronic Resources Are Essential to the Academic Law Library," 300
Whyte, Susan Barnes, 276
Wicks, Donald, 345
Wikipedia, 79

WILIP: Summary Report and Next Steps, 333
Wilkinson, Frances C., 300
Wilson, Paula, 109
Wilson, Yvonne, 230
Wilson Biographies Plus Illustrated, 202
Wilson Business Full Text, 139
Wilson OmniFile Full Text, 139, 151
WiseNut, 239, 245
Wood, Gail, 284
Woodward, Beth, 278, 282
Woolls, Blanche, 292
Words on Cassette, 61
Words to Rhyme With, 118
World's Best Thin Books, 271
World Almanac, 94
World Almanac and Book of Facts, 95, 107
World Almanac Reference Database, 96
A World Bibliography of Bibliographies, 61
World Biographical Information System (WBIS Online), 203
The World Book Dictionary, 122
World Book Encyclopedia, 71, 74, 75–76, 89, 122

The World Book Student Discovery Encyclopedia, 84
WorldCat, 63, 66, 139, 225
The World Factbook, 103
World Guide to Libraries, 62
Worldmark Encyclopedia of the Nations, 186
World Market Share Reporter, 171
World of Poetry Online, 147
World Wide Words, 132
Worley, Loyita, 181
Wu, Michelle M., 300
Wyer, James I., 4
xrefer.com, 95

Y

Yahoo! Search, 239, 240
Yahooligans!, 241
Yen, David C., 229
Yeo, Shinjoung, 229

Z

Zia, Helen, 206
ZLB (Zentral und Landesbibliothek), 307

About the Authors

Kay Ann Cassell received her BA from Carnegie Mellon University, her MLS from Rutgers University, and her PhD from the International University for Graduate Studies. She has worked in academic libraries and public libraries as a reference librarian and as a library director. Ms. Cassell is a past president of the Reference & User Services Association of ALA and is active on ALA and RUSA committees. She is the editor of the journal, *Collection Building*, and is the author of numerous articles and books on collection development and reference service. Formerly the Associate Director for Collections and Services for the Branch Libraries of the New York Public Library where she was in charge of collection development and age level services for the Branch Libraries. She is now Assistant Professor in the School of Communication, Information and Library Studies at Rutgers, the State University of New Jersey.

Uma Hiremath is Principal Librarian and Head of Reference at the West Orange Public Library, New Jersey. She was Supervising Librarian at the New York Public Library where she worked for five years. She received her MLS from Pratt Institute, New York and her PhD in political science at the University of Pittsburgh.